THE OPEN CHURCH

By the same author:

THE TIBER WAS SILVER

A NEW GENERATION: AMERICAN AND
CATHOLIC

MICHAEL NOVAK

THE
OPEN
CHURCH

VATICAN II, ACT II

THE MACMILLAN COMPANY, NEW YORK

The author wishes to thank *The New Republic* for permission to use in somewhat different form the articles "Act One of the Vatican Council," January 12, 1963 and "The Coming Vatican Council," August 27, 1962, as well as permission to use material from "Winds of Change in Rome," November 16, 1963, and "Intrigue in the Council," January 11, 1964; *Commonweal* for permission to quote from an article by Robert McAfee Brown, December 27, 1963; *The Catholic Reporter*, Kansas City, Missouri, for permission to use material from various news stories appearing in the October-December, 1963, issues; *The Catholic Herald*, London, for permission to quote from an interview with Cardinal Ottaviani, December 27, 1963, which appeared originally in French in *La France Catholique*; Vallecchi Editore for permission to quote from pages 103 and 64 in *Concilio aperto* by Mario Gozzini, 4th edition, © 1963 by Vallecchi Editore, Firenze. "Who Is the Church?" by John Cogley is reprinted with permission from *America*, The National Catholic Weekly, 920 Broadway, New York, N.Y.

First Printing

The Macmillan Company, New York
Collier-Macmillan Canada, Ltd., Toronto, Ontario

Library of Congress catalog card number: 64–18270

Printed in the United States of America

for my younger brother Dick,

age 28
a priest of Holy Cross,
who on the day this book was completed,
January 16, 1964,
many thousands of miles away,
in the village of Narayanganj, East Pakistan,
was killed in rioting between Moslems and Hindus,
whom he loved

ACKNOWLEDGMENTS

In reporting the speeches of the Council Fathers, I have had access to the daily official communiqués and the daily summaries prepared by the American bishops, and in a few cases to a copy of the original discourse. Quotation marks, therefore, usually indicate a direct quotation from one of the summaries, rather than from the original text. On certain occasions, corrections of the official communiqué were made orally in the English-language press conferences, especially through the vigilance of the Reverend Robert Trisco of the Catholic University of America; where necessary, I have corrected the communiqué accordingly. Since the summaries were necessarily prepared in great haste, in quoting them I have occasionally made required grammatical emendations.

CONTENTS

INTRODUCTION

ROME IS AT ANY TIME a city of sudden beauty. At any turn of the street a pillar, an arch, a fountain is apt to startle one's memory with recollections of forgotten times. All day long, one is aware of fountains where water is running or of walls of narrow brick or heavy dirty stones, which have seen generations of men come and go. Rome sheds the generations of men like so many skins. The silver water continues to flow from the jester's mouth; the ancient cypresses and olives stand calm and untroubled. A man comes, shares their life for a moment, and disappears.

Into Rome in the autumn of 1963 came a new generation of such men, twenty-three hundred prelates, old and young, from around the world. They came to write the second chapter of one of the great stories of history. Some were aware of the greatness of the story, some were not. Some seemed to grasp the essential drama, some did not. But the Holy Spirit, Who does not need that men should understand, dwelt within these men. Through the meals that they would share together, through the men they would be seated near in St. Peter's, through the discussions and arguments they would chance to hear, through the state of their stomachs in adjusting to an Italian diet and of their psyches in adjusting to the uncertain Roman weather, through the troubles that reached them by air mail from their dioceses at home, the Holy Spirit would be instructing them. Their every organized action, their every mood, their every new insight and new or reinforced conviction would add a phrase, a sentence, a paragraph to the story that would be written through them.

What is the story that is being written through these men? We are too close to the text to read it well. We are as apt to be mistaken in our understanding of it as to be even partially correct. In the dialogue between God and history, men who are living very rarely understand the significance of what God has said. They may be loyal to Him or disloyal, in this way or in that. They rarely see where their actions end or what were the real effects of the movements they espoused. As the Council Fathers gathered in Rome in the last week of September, 1963, it was difficult to understand the exact meaning and direction of the work that had been begun in the first session the year before. As the weeks of October passed and then of November, it became even more difficult to understand. It will take a century perhaps, or two centuries, before the event is put in sufficient focus for men to grasp it simply. From our position, while the Council is still going on, we grope more in darkness than in light. It is not that we lack for theories about what is going on; it is rather that our theories are inevitably partial, and probably partisan. The facts which seem important to observers caught up in the events may prove in the perspective of time to have been insignificant; small things which occur unobserved may one day prove to have had a great effect upon subsequent history.

The historian who ventures out upon these waters before time has given him perspective runs the danger of bringing back a map no more accurate than Amerigo Vespucci's chart of America. The historian who writes contemporaneously with the event hopes at best to present a tentative, useful map. Where he is uncertain, inaccurate, or even misleading, later historians who correct his deficiencies should find that they had to go where he went and see as he saw in order to prepare their own accounts.

The historian of the present moment stands somewhere between the daily chronicler and the philosopher of history. His theory must serve as his perspective. Because he writes close to the events as they happen he risks misapprehending and even distorting them. But, because he writes while those events are still in the making, he also shares, even if only remotely, in their making; for he offers men who shape that moment a way of understanding what they are about. They may not agree with his interpretation; yet even in reacting against it they are affected by it; they make of him, in spite of himself, a doer. The obligation on his conscience, not to be more partisan than he can help being, and to be faithful rather to the fullness of the moment than to his wishful interpretations of the moment, weighs upon him keenly. In writing a history of the present moment, a man is engaged in struggling against himself.

This then is the story of the second session of the Second Vatican Council, and how it passed. It is a work at once of history and of interpretation. It attempts to record, from one man's point of view, the events of that second session. It attempts to provide some tools for estimating where the Vatican Council is going, and what it means. The major tool it uses in interpreting the Council is a philosophical one: an inquiry into the method and the language by which the Council continues to express itself.

For centuries the Church has not *appeared* to be developing a Godlike race. It has not appeared to be forming men to integrity, to courage, to humble charity. It has seemed to many to call men to lead an unreal life, an irrelevant life; "ecclesiastical" is now a narrow and petty term. Many men hate the Church. Many are indifferent to her. In our age, the Church has hardly been threatened by schism, but the young and the intelligent drift steadily away from her. The Church has seemed to be both immobile and unhistorical. No matter how one might try to explain away these appearances with the rhetoric of transcendence and eternity, those with critical minds came to suspect that what one meant was "irrelevance." The transcendence seemed all too self-interested; the eternality seemed all too committed to certain temporal forms. The Church seemed hypocritical.

This story, then, is the story of an apparently immobile and irrelevant Church finding its way back into the sources of concrete history. The search has not been smooth, or unopposed; nor is it yet complete. Other councils have faced the same fundamental problem of renewal and reform, and not succeeded. The effort sometimes calls to mind the myth of Sisyphus: pushing the boulder to the summit, but never quite lodging it. Perhaps, when all is said and done, we shall only have to begin once more rolling the stone up the hill.

Three things make the interpretation of the second session of the Vatican Council especially difficult. The first of these is that it is difficult even to be clear about the interpretation of the first session, held in the fall of 1962. The second difficulty is that "the good Pope," John XXIII, fell asleep in the Lord in June of 1963 and was no longer present in September to "confirm the brethren." They missed his strength. The third difficulty is that as the second session opened, and to some extent even as it closed, the character of the new Pope, Paul VI, was not yet clear. Such is the close relationship between the College of Bishops and the one among them who is their center of unity that when the character of the one is unclear the character of the other is obscured as well. In the first part of our history, it will be worth our while to dwell on each of these difficulties in turn.

In the fifth chapter, we shall pause to do some harder, more taxing work: to get at the heart of what is variously known as "conservative," "triumphal," "immobile" theology—that theology which once dominated in the Roman Catholic Church, and which in the Second Vatican Council began at last to be complemented by other theologies. If we are to understand what it is to live in an "open Church," we must try hard to come to grips with what exactly it is like to live in a "closed Church." The non-historical orthodoxy of the last few generations has produced its saints; but it has also presented a withered, wrinkled face to the world. To many, and not only enemies, it has seemed a nightmare Church, a sophisticated version of paganism in which untruth was not immoral if one was loyal to the Church's interests, and in which law and legalistic forms were served more faithfully than the living God. It seemed to some as though men formed in a system like that which fashioned Dostoevsky's Grand Inquisitor held influence in the Church—men who fundamentally feared freedom, and replaced Christian authority with juridical obedience; who knew what was good for their people better than their people did; who treated their people (and their fellow bishops outside of Rome) like children. For universality, such men seemed to substitute conformity to Rome; for the new law of charity, Roman law; for the morality of the Gospels, the mores of the Vatican; for Catholic sensibility, Latin sensibility.

Yet it is not on the level of sensibility, or law, or even morality that the closed Church can best be understood. On these levels, passion waxes too hot, and the argument is useless. The stronghold of the closed Church is its theology, complacent in its possession of the absolute truth, full of fears about other ways of pursuing understanding. The men who love the splendor of papal Rome, the clarity of Roman law, the absoluteness of non-historical theology, are not despicable, mean, or uncouth men. They are men who have tried to live outside of history. They are good men, victims of the system they faithfully and loyally serve. It is not that they are bad—"they are only out of touch." If the opening of the Church means anything, it means displacing their system from the center of the Church.

Those who love such a system will continue to take shelter in the Church; but they can no longer dominate within the Church. Yet long habit and the accustomed taste of power are not quickly discouraged. Those who serve the system of the last few generations are buoyed up by a sense of their own absolute correctness. The conviction that they alone represent the true Church endows them with the strength of threatened tigers. They win the respect of those who admire courage; they no longer convince the believing intelligence. It requires some close methodological discussion to describe their position and to offer a way out of it.

In the chapters of Part II, we must come to grips with the history of the second session, its debates, its events, its personalities. This history is not clear, but ambiguous; not all the nobility or intelligence is on one side. Nor are "the sides" very clear. Our aim will be to concentrate on the contrasting conceptions of theology and of theological method, which were regularly at war in the conciliar discussions. In Part III, we describe the emergence of the bishops of the United States as the coming leaders of the Catholic world. In Part IV, we consider some of the problems of the Church in the modern world which will come before the Council in the third session, or possibly the fourth, and show how an open theology might attempt to tackle them. In that way, having shown how "non-historical orthodoxy" is unable to come to grips with history, we take up the challenge of trying another way: through an open Church. For the open society, which the moral sense of the world increasingly compels men to try to create, finds resources of energy and insight in an open Church. It is the same human hunger to understand, that same root of his dignity and freedom, which propels the open society and drives forward the life of the Church: it is that hunger, to embrace one's destiny intelligently, which Christ came to fulfill. In opening the Church, the Second Vatican Council automatically speaks to the world, just as Pope John, by opening his lips, found the world was his audience. Men listen; the Church has only to speak. If she still has the accents of Christ, she will be understood.

"SOMETHING OF THE PROPHETIC IS ABROAD IN OUR TIME."
Cardinal Montini, *to the people of Milan*

"POPES DIE; COUNCILS PASS; THE CURIA REMAINS."
Cardinal Siri, *of Genoa*

"THESE, HOWEVER, ARE DIFFICULTIES IN THE WAY OF IM-
PROVEMENT, WHICH EMINENT MEN ARE ABLE TO OVERCOME;
AND IT IS WELL THAT THEY SHOULD CONFRONT THE OBSTA-
CLES WHICH THEY ALONE CAN ULTIMATELY REMOVE."
Lord Acton

"CERTAINLY, IF I AM OBLIGED TO BRING RELIGION INTO AFTER-
DINNER TOASTS . . . I SHALL DRINK,—TO THE POPE, IF YOU
PLEASE,—STILL, TO CONSCIENCE FIRST, AND TO THE POPE
AFTERWARDS."
Cardinal Newman, *in reply to Gladstone*

"ALL HUMAN THINGS, GIVEN ENOUGH TIME, GO BADLY."
Father Gustave Weigel, S.J.

I

JOHN AND PAUL

1

POPE JOHN'S SESSION, 1962

I

POPE JOHN'S SESSION, and his encyclicals, brought about a change in principle and mood. At the highest position of the Church, down through the majority of the Council of Bishops, the idea of reform had taken hold. The chief point for reform was in the area of liberty: liberty to study, liberty to discuss, liberty to differ, liberty to converse with all other men. How could the Church of Christ ever have lost liberty? But it had. The wave of enthusiasm and relief that swept the Church and the world were because of the return of liberty, and at the return of Catholics into the midst of the human race, out of their defensive isolation.

Those who live in the forefront of modern civilization at first felt pessimism concerning the Second Vatican Council, to be convened in Rome on October 11, 1962. In Rome, in the summer heat, the work of the preparatory commissions had come to an end—in summary form, the proposals from sources all over the world made a book of 2,060 pages, and the reports filled 15 projected volumes. The 103-member central commission, unquestionably the most powerful institutional force to spring into being for the Council, had sifted and coordinated this vast accumulation of material.

No council in the Roman Catholic Church's history—there had been twenty previous ones—had been so well prepared. Unlike past councils, no secular powers bid to interfere with it, and no princes or kings or heads of state were to be in attendance; the wall between Church and State worked both ways now. Unlike past councils, this one was not called to meet any one crucial decision or immediate social-religious upheavals. The degree of psychological freedom, therefore, and the hope of constructive gain had never been so great. Why then the pessimism?

In the first place, several misunderstandings engendered impossible hopes. "Ecumenical" is an old word, whose traditional reference is not to the union of Protestant, Orthodox, and Catholic Christians, but rather to the gathering of all the Catholic bishops of the world. The contemporary Council was not, therefore, "ecumenical" in the usual sense. Indeed, as the months went by (and despite the herculean efforts of men like Cardinal Bea, president of the Secretariat for Christian Unity), the theme of union with Protestants and Orthodox seemed to have taken an increasingly remote place in preparatory discussions. No doubt Pope John himself, in a fallible moment, so to speak, gave rise to these false hopes by his initial ambiguous use of "ecumenical"; and no doubt he was among those who wished the hopes were not false ones.

A second impossible hope was that renewal of the Church might come by some dramatic action, some whisk of a wand, or sweeping legislative fiat. The life of the spirit has its own laws: if the Church is to be renewed, it cannot be merely by better organization, by modernizing its techniques. No means of mass-producing saints is conceivable. Nor is there any simple solution to a thousand modern dilemmas, like corporate responsibility, nuclear diplomacy, or the tendency of the mass media to degenerate to the lowest moral and aesthetic denominator. No group of men, whether prelates or ministers of state, is going to resolve contemporary dilemmas by meeting to discuss them.

But an additional problem was that some members of the Roman Curia—that civil service of the Church—had been at least suspicious of, if not hostile to, the Council from its inception. Pope John startled Rome by his impromptu announcement of the Council in January, 1959; it seems fortunate that the bolt came from the blue, or it might have been stayed. It is difficult to get this matter clear because of traditional Latin secrecy. But secrecy breeds gossip—no city in the world breeds as much as Rome—and many take revenge upon secrecy by broad jests and parables. In a number of Roman stories in the summer of 1962, one heard the accent of truth.

One of these said that Pope John, walking in the Vatican, told a worker: "Here, I'm in command; but I do what others want." Another (almost certainly not authentic as to fact) told that each time a curial cardinal asked for a delay in convening the Council—if Pope John died before its start, it might well never be held—the good Pope moved the date up another month. A third story capped the sequence by turning a proverb into fact: the Curia saw it couldn't defeat the Council and so decided to join it. Nearly every preparatory commission was headed by a curial cardinal, and the stamp of the Curia was strong on the matter prepared for discussion. Most of the preparatory schemata, in fact, were later rejected by the Council as unsuitable even as bases for discussion.

But it is clear that Pope John knew how to work with the Curia and maintain its good will—an effort Pius XII in his later years did not deign to make. Pope John consulted the Curia; he saw its members regularly; he filled its vacancies immediately. (He said from the beginning he would be a peaceful Pope, working by benevolence, not force.) Furthermore, the Curia itself is not a monolith. Many of its members, especially those who have had opportunities to work abroad, are far from the stereotype which some others fill so well. Cardinal Agagianian has spoken warmly of the perspective visits to America have given him; Cardinals Bea and Cicognani and others are thoughtful and open men. Pope John significantly reserved to himself all final powers of decision concerning the agenda. He presided over the Central Commission, and when he was not present appointed various cardinals—no single one—to take his place.

The Curia, although it makes the administrative wheels of the Church go round, is not the Church. It is a career service, organizational, jealous of its tasks and its traditions. The introduction of non-career men into high posts demoralizes those in the ranks. Granted sincere devotion to the Church, ambition makes the Curia run; ambition is the ecclesiastical lust. Moreover, for many priests from poverty-stricken areas of Italy, the Curia is a place where money is available; every papal bull, every favor, that passes through the hands of a clerk has its price—in the Italian fashion. In the United States, for example (prices vary), the office that forwards the papal bull which creates a monsignor receives $280.

The great weakness of the Curia is its limited intellectual horizon. Italy—and Spain—have not participated in the intellectual and cultural revolutions of the North. Industrialization, pluralism, self-critical individual conscience, democracy, and above all the idea of law for the sake of (not against) freedom—these are not yet part of the Italian experience. The Italian cleric refuses to concede that progress rests with the Northern countries; in his view, the Church remains the glory of civilization, all else is a step backward or apart. One reads frequently in *L'Osservatore Romano* of recognition "by all the world" of the splendors of the Church. (*L'Osservatore* is a highly rhetorical paper; in this, it reminds one of *Pravda*; its triumphalism is extraordinary.) The Italian cleric refuses to concede that his own flock is largely ignorant, with a childish, immature faith. "We have not failed to preach the Gospel," Cardinal Valerio Valeri once retorted, bristling, in response to such a suggestion. The Italian cleric uses the rhetoric of "progress," "bring up to date," "adaptation," but he does not share the experience of what Americans, for example, mean by these words.

A Vatican official to whom I spoke in 1962 expressed the complacent optimism of the *L'Osservatore*; but as I left his office and walked in the hot, clear Italian sun, I began to see that "optimism" depends on what you're hoping for. "Revolution, swift change, no," he said, waving a finger. "But changes in an organization so that, who knows? in a hundred years . . ." (By "changes in organization" his tone suggested "slight adjustments.") "No thanks, Monsignore," I thought in the sun, "that's very pessimistic."

Besides the figure of Pope John himself, however, there were resources in the Church to prevent the trivialization of the Council. Countless more non-Italians than ever before had been flying in and out of Rome for three years. Whereas in 1870 seven hundred bishops took part in Vatican Council I, between three and four times that number descended on Rome in 1962. In St. Peter's, the microphone gave them equal voice, no matter where they sat. Cardinal Alfrink of Utrecht had already suggested before the first session, that the Central Commission be continued as a permanent international body of the Church. The Curia had a good reason to be afraid.

One could expect the French, German, and Lowlands bishops to speak as vigorously as is their wont. Cardinal Feltin of Paris had, that summer, abolished the cassock as the street wear of his priests, and ordered black or gray suits worn in its place. The indefatigable Cardinal Bea had given thousands of talks and interviews and written countless letters the three previous years in the cause of Christian unity. Cardinal Léger of Montreal had appointed a conference of laymen to prepare free and critical suggestions for the Council. Some among the German hierarchy had long championed liturgical reform, the vernacular, and the admission of converted Protestant ministers, who are married, to priestly orders.

Many American bishops were handicapped by comparative lack of facility in Latin, but some, like Archbishop Cody of New Orleans (Archbishop Rummel's aggressive new coadjutor), were masters of the tongue. In the past, American bishops had been exceedingly tender with the Curia, even subservient, much to the distress of the hard-pressed French and Germans. The closest in number to the Italian hierarchy (240 to 440), their decisions in this Council were going to be exceedingly weighty. It was, in fact, the hundreds of bishops who listened to the give-and-take of argument, and then voted as seemed best to them, who later controlled the Council.

There was a great deal of room, then, for—as Catholics put it—the Holy Spirit to direct the Second Vatican Council. Who would speak first? Which arguments would find the most impressive champions? At what moments and to what effect would Pope John speak up to give a new turn to the discussions? What unknown bishop, vigorous of mind and speech, would reverse a prevailing mood? Councils have always been dramatic in the past, for the weight of their decisions is felt for centuries. But because this was the first truly universal Council, with members in large numbers from many continents other than Europe, the drama was unsurpassed: a critical point had been reached.

Men had "increased and multiplied, and possessed the earth"; the Gospels had been "preached to all nations." What is at stake in the Second Vatican Council is the universalization of the Church. It is not what the press was to report from day to day—the cryptic press releases that non-professional priests in the press office prepared during the first session: the Latinized phrases—that are to be significant at the end of this century. What will endure are the fissures in the prevailing self-conception of the Church—rooted in Roman law, tied to Latin traditions, limited publicly to Italian-Spanish intellectual experience.

Pierre Teilhard de Chardin, Jesuit author of *The Phenomenon of Man*, against whose works the (curial) Holy Office issued a mild but firm warning in August, 1962, called this process the breakthrough into the "noosphere"—men thinking not as Italians, or Americans, or French, but as men. Pope John's sudden proclamation of a world-wide Council lifted the Roman Catholic Church closer to that break-through in fact (that which it has always claimed in theory) than would have seemed possible for generations.

From the blue the proclamation came—while he was at prayer, Pope John thought of it, and turned in his subsequent sermon to announce it. What the Christian world waited to see was how deeply, even if very quietly, the lightning was going to shake the existing walls, so that a newer Jerusalem might be begun again—that endless beginning again which is the task of the Church in history.

II

Cracks did appear in the centuries-old walls of curial power at the first session. Though the dismantling is still to be done, the old edifice was condemned. The Council opened on October 11 under hardly promising skies; but winds of liberation and optimism were blowing when it closed on December 8. Three years before, Pope John had said the Council was called "to let fresh air into the Church," and many sniffed the sharp scent of change. But no one expected the success of the Council to be so complete. Theologians like Hans Küng and Karl Rahner, who before the Council bore the odor of heresy (to curial nostrils at least), became the lights of Rome, lecturing to the Council Fathers of one national delegation after another. The party of reform, fearful and pessimistic as it assembled in the Curia's own city, came, saw, and conquered. Who indeed could have imagined the extent of their great success, even three months before?

The Curia, civil service of the Church and executive arm of the Pope, quickly learned to respect the Council. It had taken charge of the preparations and confidently set its own stamp on them. That stamp was largely Latin in character; not deeply rooted in the study of the history of the People of God: not scriptural, not patristic. That stamp represented, rather, a peculiarly ahistorical, categorizing analysis which marked Scholasticism in its decadence, whose contemporary analogue seems to be linguistic analysis in philosophy. Such methods produce some good: clear notions, for example; but much of the sweep of life has to be ignored to make them work.

Even to those who hoped a great deal from Pope John, the outlook was not good. Pope John was not the free man a Pope might seem to be in theory; he could get no more results than men by their free obedience would yield him; he was forced time and again to yield to the recalcitrance of those around him. In his famous opening address on October 11, he called them "prophets of doom." He seemed at the start of the Council unwilling to buck the Curia directly but his splendid address made his sentiments clear enough: he called for a pastoral, not a polemical or an academic, Council and he voiced every large theme dear to the reformers. Then he retired to his chambers and left the Council in the hands of the twenty-seven hundred Fathers, his few early interventions seeming to favor first the reforming, then the Latin party. It was as though he were not sure which way power would incline—which way, therefore, he would later have to live with.

Three dramatic turning points determined the outcome. The first took only twenty minutes of the first general meeting. When a list of committee chairmen, prepared by the Curia, was presented for automatic approval, first Cardinal Liénart of France, seconded by Cardinal Frings of Cologne, who was speaking for Cardinals Doepfner of Munich and Koenig of Vienna (hence for all the Germans), asked for a recess in order to discuss the candidates. After their first surprise, the assembled twenty-seven hundred Fathers broke into slowly thunderous applause. No vote was needed. They adjourned for *aggiornamento*: to draw up their own lists. Suddenly, dramatically, effective institutional power in Roman Catholicism had swung from the Curia to the Council of Bishops. For the first time in their episcopal lives (the last Council was in 1869), many of the bishops felt in their fingertips, so to speak, a surge of the power they were ordained to exercise. They began to be conscious of themselves as a Council: as a college succeeding the College of Apostles. In a stroke, Roman Catholicism was put on all twelves again, after having inclined for centuries in a single direction: curial Rome.

It is difficult to discuss the next two turning points without a warning. It is somehow necessary to talk about "parties" at the Council, and the American press regularly used the descriptions "liberal" and "conservative" to designate these parties—as if good Democrats should sympathize with the reforming churchmen, and Goldwater Republicans find natural alliances with the party of Ottaviani. The *National Review* was doctrinaire enough, in fact, to carry an article by Evelyn Waugh called "The Same Again Please: A Layman's Hopes of the Vatican Council." Waugh urged the preservation of the customary level of mediocrity, on the grounds that it reduced meddling and favored individualism. (The essay ought to be a required reference for insight into the spiritual malaise of Waugh's protagonists.) Moreover, the right-wing press of Italy—*Il Tempo, Il Borghese*—regularly and cynically exploited the news of the Council, to support the positions of the Curia, that "last bastion of freedom in Italy and in the world," as they called it. The financial and political interests of the Italian right wing depend upon an intransigent Church—it is not the *Church* they care about.

There is, then, a carryover—human nature—between politics and religion. But the differences between politics and religion prohibit the simple transference of the language of one to the realities of the other. A Council Father did not register as a member of a party; the political structure of his homeland often had no relation to his theological convictions; the confrontation between the two parties was not programmatic. The issue was one of *ésprit*, of habit of mind, of purpose; we shall try to clarify it more exactly in Chapter 5. For now it suffices to say that the issue was whether to continue in the trajectory of the late Middle Ages and the Council of Trent, or to set contemporary sights.

The second turning point occurred on November 21 in the discussions on the sources of Revelation. After a badly worded question was put to the floor, the reforming party fell short of a two-thirds vote to send back to committee the schema presented by Cardinal Ottaviani's preparatory commission. Not many days earlier, the reformers had wisely established a precedent for this vote by a seemingly unnecessary vote on the schema on the liturgy; but now they seemed to have failed. On the next day, however, on the grounds that a schema displeasing to the majority was not worthy of the Council, Pope John took the side of the reformers and ordered the schema to committee. The good Pope went further: he named Cardinal Bea, leader of the reformers, as co-chairman with Cardinal Ottaviani in what had previously been the latter's committee. The Church had rounded another turn.

The turn was crucial because two different approaches to theology, and therefore to human life, were at stake. The theology of clear and distinct ideas—curial theology one might say—has tended to specify

Scripture and Tradition as two clearly separate sources: "What has God revealed about the human situation? Whatever is found *either* in Scripture *or* in Tradition." This distinction put the guardians of Tradition, the Holy Office finally, in a position of equal normative weight with Scripture itself; then, too, they interpreted Scripture. The position is intolerable to Protestants, and not pleasing to many Catholics, for it offers too limited and too unhistorical a view of the faith.

The vote of November 21 and the Pope's intervention made clear that the Council of Bishops was taking a different tack from the previously prevailing curial theology on the relation of Scripture and Tradition. Theologians like Austria's Rahner and America's Tavard had been insisting that whatever God has revealed to us (it isn't much, finally, and it sets us the arduous task of trying to understand it) is found in Scripture, and that the New Testament itself is largely a product of a Tradition—a written record of what preachers were saying to the early Christian communities. There is one source of God's Word: Scripture, as interpreted by Tradition, by the living Church. The teaching of the Church must ever be fecundated by reflection on Scripture and studies of a long, but especially the early, Tradition. Curial theology tends to be cut loose from history, different in tone and impact from the Bible. Contemporary theology is strong by reason of its historical sense, its recovery of the concrete, its technical gains in stating the historico-literary meanings of Scripture, its proximity to prayer and life. The reform party at the Vatican Council is far from turning its back on intelligence in favor of some evangelical enthusiasm. On the contrary, it draws its strength from the vigorous archeological, anthropological, and textual advances of the last seventy-five years—advances which have turned it to a sense of time and history. Christ spoke in the concrete, we work out our lives in the concrete, it is in the complexities of the concrete that the science of theology begins and ends: God's condescension to human history. The present Council is "pastoral" because it is attending to the world in which it takes place, not because it is less scientific than is desirable. On November 21, contemporary theology came abreast of curial theology and by so doing changed the vectors of the future.

The third turning point came at the close of the first session of the Council. Pope John announced the norms that would guide the interim commissions whose task it would be to prepare the schemata for final ratification in the Council's second session the following autumn. Pope John placed Cardinal Cicognani, former Apostolic Delegate to the United States and now Vatican Secretary of State, at the head of the commission, to be composed of "several cardinals and bishops." It was clear that the preparatory schemata which Cardinal Ottaviani brought to the first session were to be set aside, and new ones worked out. In spite of harassments from pre-Council Rome, contemporary theology is so rounded and rich that, given an equal chance, it cannot fail to embarrass its predecessor. Hopes for the interim commission were high. "It cannot fail," said Cardinal Ritter of St. Louis. "The tide is irreversible," a Protestant observer said.

III

The first session was groping its way toward new institutional forms. There were strong demands that the College of Bishops retain some kind of permanent international commission—an annual meeting of representatives in Rome, for example. The world view of the Curia is too small for an international Church. But the de-Latinization of the Curia promised to be a long, difficult task; career services do not lend themselves to swift reorganization. Dr. Hans Küng, whose *The Council, Reform and Reunion* was internationally admired, though banned in Italy, repeated several times that the United Nations in New York is more catholic than the Church. The first session of the Council broke the Church out of its narrow channel, but *it did not secure the breakthrough in an effective institutional way*. Nevertheless, talk was rife of "the new Church." Theologians who were pessimistic before the Council—like Küng himself—were amazed at the dimensions of the victory won by the reformers (and did not fail to point out that many of these reforms were those sought by the Protestant reformers). The bishops returned to their homelands re-educated in their theology, aware of their role in an international not a parochial Church, astonished (some of them) to have heard cardinals and bishops sharply arguing positions which they once might have thought faintly heretical or "offensive to pious ears." The Protestant observers at the Council sympathized with the liberty and range of opinion among the Council Fathers, though no one, of course, dreamed of sudden reunion among Christian churches.

In America, laymen and junior clerics seemed to go at their contemporary studies with more vigor, speak more openly, be less defensive. Throughout that spring, diocesan newspapers reported more and more interfaith meetings between Catholic and Protestant clergymen. Interfaith cooperation in the cause of racial justice increased. On the other hand, Bishop McVinney of Providence cast aspersions on those who spoke of change in the Church. "The Church has been thriving for two thousand years," he said. "Why break up a winning team?" Many American bishops—even during the second session—were reluctant to admit, or to face, all that was going on at the Council.

For there has been in America, ever since the condemnation of the non-existent heresy "Americanism" at the turn of the century, little of the audacity and directness of French or German Catholicism. Even in reporting the Council, the American press, both secular and Catholic, failed, at first, to be as tart and as informative as the European press. One reason was that many European prelates took the rule of secrecy about Council proceedings far less seriously than their English-speaking confreres. Father Raymond Bosler, editor of the Indianapolis *Criterion,* published a November 12 story from *Le Monde* to illustrate the difference. But the news of cardinal arguing with cardinal and the success of the spokesmen of contemporary theology did not fail to get around.

The pseudonymous Xavier Rynne published his first "Letter from Vatican City" in *The New Yorker* not long after the first session had opened. That letter, a report on the theological conflicts and jealous maneuverings among Roman universities and congregations, lit up the Council like a lightning flash. Bishops fortunate enough to receive copies from friends had to protect them almost with their lives. Dozens of photostatic copies were made. Other hundreds were mimeographed. The letter dramatized for countless of the English-speaking prelates the cultural-theological conflict that the Council had been called to resolve. They began to see—what many had looked at without noticing before—why windows in the Church needed opening.

Then Mr. Robert Kaiser's stories began to appear regularly in *Time.* Perhaps he was played false by the lightness and flippancy of *Time's* style; many Catholic readers in the States did not quite trust his stories. No reporter knew more about the Council; had talked with more of its personalities, prominent or minor; had more sources of information to tap. Sunday-evening dinners at his apartment became a rendezvous of stimulating and well-informed persons. In the English-speaking world, at least, perhaps no source was to have quite the catalytic effect as *Time* on opinion outside the Council and even to an extent within it. It is perhaps symptomatic of America's coming of age in the Church, then, that after the first session of the Council America was to produce the sharp, informative books that in earlier times one had to await from Europe. Probably every American bishop, and many of the clergy, read both Rynne's subsequent book and Kaiser's before the second session. Often bishops did not like these books; ironically, non-American prelates received them more warmly than American. They were banned by the Holy Office from being "put on display" in Rome, just as the second session opened. The English-speaking press had become through them a potent force in the Church.

The procedures deriving from the Inquisition and the Italian Renaissance on which Rynne and Kaiser threw such light—with, no doubt, the ardor and partisanship of pioneers—do not thrive well in the day; the free Anglo-Saxon press may do more to reform the Curia than foreseeable administrative changes. But many American bishops, for example, found it hard to believe that the Curia could be "all that bad." "That would imply," one bishop said, "the Church has been run by a pack of scoundrels. I know some of the men being written about. They're devoted men." The reluctance to believe the worst has been deftly expressed in one of the hundreds of limericks that became current at the second session. It deserves to be quoted:

> There was a New Yorker named Rynne
> Whose reports when in doubt he kept thin.
> But Bob Kaiser of Time
> Thought conjecture no crime
> And every doubt Rynne left out he put in.

Many protest the picture drawn by these books—some protest the books more than they protest the sometimes ugly facts.

Meanwhile, after the first session, Hans Küng, chairman of the theological faculty of Tübingen, came to the United States to lecture in many major cities. Philadelphia, San Diego, and St. Paul quietly refused to let him speak. Los Angeles tried to keep him out, but even there a large-scale tea was given him. But in other cities, four, six, and eight thousand people came to hear him. The tension in the halls was electric. In his clear, forceful voice, his blond hair shining in the lights, Father Küng brought the careful, strong theology of Europe to American audiences caught up in the enthusiasm of Pope John's *aggiornamento*. He created an impact no American could, for Catholic America somehow still depends upon Europe for its imaginative life. We receive, John Updike says, "our supernatural mail on foreign soil"—or from foreign lecturers. Dr. Küng (he does not like to be called "Father") spoke about freedom and lack of freedom— coining a new word "unfreedom" which Bishop Ahr of Trenton confessed publicly he couldn't understand at all—in accents which American Catholics, caught up in a highly juridical, authoritarian, smoothly run Church were thrilled to hear.

Father Küng's reputation, of course, was only enhanced by the fact that he, together with Fathers Gustave Weigel, S.J., John Courtney Murray, S.J., and Godfrey Diekmann, O.S.B., were prohibited by the administration of the Catholic University of America in Washington from lecturing there. It was widely assumed that the president of the university acted in the spirit of, or under the orders of, the university's powerful neighbor, Archbishop Egidio Vagnozzi, the Apostolic Delegate to the United States, who has not been known to favor the *aggiornamento* of Pope John and the Council. Another limerick commemorates this "C.U. affair":

> Of Murray, Weigel, Diekmann and Küng
> The praises were everywhere süng.
> The delegate then
> Seemed out-of-date when
> He gave orders to have them all hüng.

In April, Cardinal Bea visited the United States, giving three lectures in Harvard's Sanders Theater which, again, were tense and electric in their impact. Catholic and non-Catholic theologians spent three days in discussion, breaking the academically virginal interfaith silence of Cambridge.

Thus Pope John's first session of Ecumenical Council Vatican II unleashed great moral and spiritual forces in America and elsewhere. Undoubtedly, many higher ecclesiastics in Rome and some in America found this new power uncomfortable; it was not theirs. "Something prophetic is abroad in our time," Cardinal Montini had said in Milan. On the other hand, as John Cogley has remarked, some people are religiously tone-deaf; they just don't understand religion. Many people who are professionally religious are like that; they do their duty and fulfill their tasks—but the Holy Spirit! They would rather have the good order of a well-run organization, where everyone does as he's told and no more. Charisms, insights, spirits belong to a bygone age; now we have only the juridical machinery.

But Pope John stood as an image before the eyes of all. His image touched a tender point in the hearts of countless bishops, that tip of their aspirations where they wished to be as much like Christ as he, as pastoral and warm as he. His appeal was almost irresistible. Even against their long-ingrained habits, many in the Church began to be drawn toward the simple, the direct, and—as it seems to us in our time, for all its ordinariness—the prophetic faith of the Gospels.

To understand the Vatican Council, we have to dwell for a little on the character of Pope John.

2

THE PRESENCE OF POPE JOHN

POPE JOHN XXIII lived out in his life what the Second Vatican Council is trying to condense into words. In a pontificate of five brief years, Pope John made Christian unity seem one day possible. He spoke to those who believe in God and those who do not believe in God and they all understood. Pope John was the focal point of the Roman Catholic Church, and through him, as through a prism, God's pursuit of man touched and burnt millions of hearts around the world. In a moment, in a twinkling of an eye, Pope John was what the Church wishes to be. He showed other bishops what their office might be like. He showed priests how they might speak and be heard by those whom they gave their lives to serve. He showed people how close they might be to their shepherds. Pope John lived the Gospels. It is much harder to write a series of decrees which will guide other bishops, priests, and people in trying to live those Gospels. For many, Pope John will always speak louder than the Council.

The presence of Pope John was felt among the Council Fathers throughout the second session. On November 21, for example, the first speaker to take the floor, Bishop Jaime Flores Martín, of Barbastro, Spain, began his favorable comment on the schema for the unity of Christians by saying, "This schema leads us into the path of ecumenism which was so dear to Pope John XXIII." On October 28, one of the most important days of the Council, on one of the rare occasions in which Pope Paul entered into the Council chamber, Cardinal Suenens was called upon to invoke the memory of Pope John in a way so explicit and at such great length that he can only

17

have wished to make the presence of Pope John unforgettably active in the Council. We shall have to defer until later a description of the dramatic circumstances in which Cardinal Suenens gave his discourse, and its effect upon the Council. But here we can report some of Cardinal Suenens' words in order to understand how, in one way at least, the figure of Pope John was ever present to the Council Fathers.

Climbing into the pulpit of St. Peter's, in the presence of Pope Paul VI, the patriarchs, cardinals, archbishops, and bishops of the world, together with a few hundred laymen, the Cardinal preached the following sermon:

When he was elected, John XXIII might have seemed to be a "transitional pope." He was indeed transitional, but not in the way expected nor in the ordinary sense of the word. History will surely judge that he opened a new era for the Church and that he laid the foundations for the transition from the twentieth to the twenty-first century.

But it is not our purpose to assess the full significance of the pontificate that has just ended; that would be rash and premature. What we should like to do in this solemn gathering, called at the wish of Pope Paul VI now gloriously reigning, is simply to try to represent before us for a few moments the figure of John XXIII, in a collective act of filial piety and deeply-felt gratitude.

Each one of the Council Fathers keeps in his heart the vivid remembrance of our last meeting with him, here in this very place, close to the tomb of Peter. Each one, as he listened, asked himself: "Is this a final good-bye? Will the father, talking to us now, ever see his children again?" We realized that we were listening to a kind of Discourse at the Last Supper. . . .

The television, the radio, and the press brought his death so close to us that it was like a death in the family. Never has the whole world taken part at such close quarters in the poignant stages of a mortal sickness. Never has it shown such unanimity of feeling. "The death of the saints," says Holy Scripture, "is precious in the sight of God." The death of John XXIII was precious also in the sight of the world. The Pope transformed it into a final proclamation of faith and hope; he made it something like the celebration of an Easter liturgy.

A few weeks before his great leave-taking, the Supreme Pontiff had said in the course of an audience: "Every day is a good day to be born, and every day is a good day to die. I know in whom I have believed." He went to meet his end with the serenity of a child going home, knowing that its father is waiting there with open arms. What could be simpler?

When he heard the members of his household sobbing round his bed, he protested: "Don't cry, this is a time of joy." When the end drew near, he asked to be "left alone with the Lord" to recollect himself. But some echoes of his prayer could be heard when he recovered consciousness. He could be heard repeating the words of the Master: "I am the Resurrection and the Life," words which in such a moment took on their fullest meaning. And then his lips formed this last, barely audible, heartfelt cry, full of filial love for the Blessed Virgin: "My Mother, my hope." And it was the end. . . .

John XXIII has left us.

Yet we dare to believe that he is more than ever present in our midst. The dead do not cease to live, but live more fully. In the mystic reality of the Communion of Saints they act more penetratingly and intimately and with greater power. . . .

John XXIII is present in our midst in a twofold way.

First of all, he is present in his well-beloved successor, Pope Paul VI, the august continuer of his work, who gave expression on the morrow of the Pope's death to the unanimous hope of the Church and the world: "The tomb of John XXIII," he proclaimed, "will not be able to confine his heritage. . . ."

And more recently still, have we not ourselves heard the solemn witness to this continuity, expressed in the never-to-be-forgotten discourse which opened the second session of the Council? On each line and between the lines, the same breath of Pentecost was perceptible. We heard the same invitation to openness and dialogue, to doctrinal and pastoral charity, the same insistence on constructive, positive work, the same solicitude to translate the Gospel's eternal message into a language modern people understand. It is clear that Providence has given Pope Paul VI to the Church to give form and substance to the prophetic intuitions of his predecessor.

John XXIII is present in our midst in another way, mysterious and profound. He is with us by reason of the sacrifice of his life, which he offered up for the happy outcome of the Council's labors.

On this point there comes to mind an incident at Castel Gandolfo in July of last year. John XXIII had spent the day, pen in hand, studying the preparatory schemata. In the course of an audience he read aloud some of the notes he had written in the margin. Then, suddenly, he stopped and said: "Oh, I know what my personal part in the preparation of the Council will be. . . ." And after a pause, he concluded: "It will be suffering."

He did not specify what the suffering would be, but it was easy to
see that he was thinking of his coming death. Not in vain had he read
in the Gospel that the grain of wheat must die in the earth for the
sake of the harvest. With all his heart he believed in the spiritual
value of total sacrifice fully accepted. He knew that, once again, death
would be the source of life. In accepting it with his truly noble spirit,
he has given to God and to all of us the supreme gift: he has loved us
unto the end, as his Master did.

In finem dilexit eos.

We must now try to describe the figure of the Pope, whose memory is forever fixed in the heart of every one of us. His winning personality was too rich to be reduced to a few characteristics: all we can
do is to sketch some dominant traits which brought him so close to us
and to the men of our time.

If one had to express it all in one word, it seems to me that one
could say that John XXIII was a man surprisingly natural and at the
same time supernatural. Nature and grace produced in him a living
unity filled with charm and surprises.

Everything about him sprang from a single source. In a completely
natural way he was supernatural. He was natural with such a supernatural spirit that no one detected a distinction between the two.

Filling his lungs, as it were, he breathed the faith just as he breathed
physical and moral health.

"He lived in the presence of God," one wrote, "with the simplicity
of one who takes a walk through the streets of his native town."

He lived with both feet on the ground, and with vibrant sympathy
he was interested in the everyday concerns of people. He knew how
to stop at the side of a road to talk with ordinary people, to listen to
a child, to console an invalid. He was concerned with the construction
of an airport and he prayed for the astronauts.

But he also lived completely in the world of the supernatural, in
the familiar company of the angels and saints. He loved to share his
preferences with others, and here also he showed the courage that characterized his friendships. He surprised St. Joseph by introducing him
into the Canon of the Mass, and some saints from the region of Venice
and Lombardy by raising them to the altars . . .

This successful alliance between grace and nature explains another
harmony, so striking in John XXIII, that existed between his life and
his teaching. In him there was no dualism. After the example of the
Lord, of whom St. John said that "His life was light," the deceased
Pope enlightened men by the very course of his existence. . . .

John's spontaneous, forthright, ever-alert goodness was like a ray of sunshine which dispels the fog, which melts the ice, which filters its way through without even being noticed, as though it were its right. Such a ray of sunshine creates optimism along its path, spreads happiness with its unexpected appearance, and makes light of all obstacles.

It is thus that John XXIII appeared to the world, not as the sun of the tropics, which blinds one with the intensity of its brilliance, but rather as the humble, familiar, everyday sun which is simply there in its place, always true to itself even though it may be momentarily veiled by a cloud, a sun which one hardly notices, so certain is its presence.

John XXIII was not so naïve as to believe that goodness would solve all problems, but he knew that it would open hearts to dialogue, to understanding, and to mutual respect. He had confidence in the power of the charity of Christ burning in a human heart.

He knew also that truth penetrates more easily into the hearts of men when it appears to them as a revelation of love. Did not the Master say: "My words are spirit and life"? And does not Scripture teach that "he who does not love does not know God, for God is love"? And, in the unspeakable oneness of His nature, is not God Himself love and truth, truth and love?

John XXIII could reveal God to men, perhaps better than others more brilliant or more scholarly, because for so many years he was the faithful witness of the living God, of the God Who loves men.

On the day after his entrance into the Church, a certain convert justified his choice by these words: "I believe that the greatest truth exists where there is the greatest love."

John XXIII had made these words his own. They were strikingly illustrated in his life, the memory of which will endure through the course of centuries.

But there is a secret to loving others to this extent: a man must forget himself. Charity, it has been said, is "pure concentration on the existence of others" (Lavelle).

To be completely dedicated to others, one must banish all self-interest. Forgetfulness of oneself conditions the gift of oneself.

John XXIII leaves us the memory of someone who, in his own eyes, did not exist. He put himself beyond all earthly vanity: self-denial was a constant value for his soul. This fundamental humility allowed him to speak of himself with detachment and with humor, as if he were speaking of somebody else.

Let us listen to him as he introduces himself to his newly acquired subjects, the faithful of the Patriarchate of Venice:

"I wish," he told them, "to speak to you with the utmost frankness. You have waited impatiently for me; people have told you about me and written you accounts that far surpass my merits. I introduce myself as I really am. Like every other person who lives here on earth, I come from a definite family and place. Thank God, I enjoy bodily health and a little good sense which allows me to see matters quickly and clearly. Ever ready to love people, I stand by the law of the Gospel, a respecter of my own rights and of those of others, a fact that prevents me from doing harm to anybody and which encourages me to do good to all.

"I come of humble stock. I was raised in the kind of poverty which is confining but beneficial, which demands little, but which guarantees the development of the noblest and greatest virtues and which prepares one for the steep ascent of the mountain of life. Providence drew me out of my native village and made me traverse the roads of the world in the East and in the West. The same Providence made me embrace men who were different both by religion and by ideology. God made me face acute and threatening social problems, in the presence of which I kept a calm and balanced judgment and imagination in order to evaluate matters accurately, ever preoccupied, out of my respect for Catholic doctrinal and moral principles, not with what separates people and provokes conflicts, but rather with what unites men."

The same authentic accents are heard again a few weeks before his death on the occasion of the bestowal of the Balzan Peace Prize: "The humble Pope who speaks to you," he said, "is fully conscious of being personally a very small thing in the sight of God. He can only humble himself. . . . In all simplicity, We speak to you just as We think: no circumstance, no event, no matter what honor it may bestow on Our poor person, can puff Us up or do harm to the tranquillity of Our soul."

No one was surprised to read in his personal diary reflections such as the following:

"This year's celebrations for my priestly jubilee have come to an end. I have allowed them to be held here at Sofia and at Sotto il Monte. What an embarrassment for me! Countless priests already dead or still living after twenty-five years of priesthood have accomplished wonders in the apostolate and in the sanctification of souls. And I, what have I done? My Jesus, mercy! But, while I humble myself for the little or nothing that I have achieved up to now, I raise my eyes toward the future. There still remains light in front of me; there still remains the hope of doing some good. Therefore, I take up again my staff, which from now on will be the staff of old age, and I go forward to meet whatever the Lord wishes for me" (Sofia, October 30, 1929).

"My recollections are delighted with all the graces received from the Lord, but at the same time I feel humiliated for having been so niggardly in the use of my talents, for having rendered a return without any proportion to the gifts I have received. I find here a mystery which makes me shudder and at the same time stirs me to action" (August 10, 1961).

"The Vicar of Christ? Ah! I am not worthy of this title, I, the poor son of Baptist and Mary Ann Roncalli, two good Christians, to be sure, but so modest and so humble" (August 15, 1961).

If we shift our gaze from the man to the work he accomplished, his life appears as a threefold grace: a grace for the faithful of the Catholic Church; a grace for all Christians; a grace for all men of good will.

His life was a grace for the faithful, above all because of the Council he convoked; this was the culmination of his pastoral activity.

John XXIII wanted this Council: he rightly said this desire was an answer to an inspiration of the Holy Spirit, inviting him to assemble in Rome all the bishops of the world.

At the opening of the Council he made a calm declaration of "his complete disagreement with those prophets of doom who are always forecasting disaster." "We have no reason to be afraid," he added; "fear comes only from a lack of faith."

He obeyed God's call, peacefully and without knowing exactly how all of this was to be worked out. "When it comes to a council," he once said smilingly, "we are all novices. The Holy Spirit will be present when the bishops assemble; we'll see."

Indeed, for him, the Council was not first of all a meeting of the bishops with the Pope, a horizontal coming together. It was first and above all a collective gathering of the whole Episcopal College with the Holy Spirit, a vertical coming together, an entire openness to an immense outpouring of the Holy Spirit, a kind of new Pentecost. . . .

Thanks to John XXIII, God has once again visited His people: Christ the Saviour sends His Spirit to His own, to teach them, in His name, all truth and to explain to them what before they could not bear nor fully grasp.

The Council is the light of the Holy Spirit which will penetrate deeper into the Church, and through the Church, into the world; it is a gift of God's magnanimity to our age.

The Pope followed the various phases of the Council with that superior wisdom which was his and which appears in these lines which date from his mission to Paris:

"By the grace of God, my affairs are going well. I go about them calmly and watch over them all. And I see them fall into their proper place one after the other. I bless the Lord for the help He gives me, thus preventing me from complicating simple matters, and assisting me rather to simplify the more complicated."

May John XXIII receive, from the heights of heaven, the expression of the Council Fathers' deepest gratitude for the singular grace of the Council, for his confidence in the Episcopate, which is more than ever unshakably united to the successor of Peter, to Peter who yesterday was called John and who today is named Paul, and to whom we pledge the same love and the same indefectible loyalty.

His life was a grace for all Christians.

For to him we owe a new atmosphere, a new climate, which enables us together, as brothers, to meet the obstacles which remain to be overcome on the path to a full and visible unity. This climate we owe to his charity and to his sincerity.

To his charity, which opened the hearts of men to dialogue, to a predisposition to judge favorably, to understanding. Better than anyone else, John XXIII knew that the search for Christian unity does not proceed along the path of diplomatic negotiations, but looks rather to the very depths of men's spiritual lives.

We grow in closeness, one with another, in his judgment, according to the very measure each one allows himself to be taken over by the life and charity of Christ. As we become more and more one with Him, we cannot but grow in closeness to our brothers. Every effort for union, by the very fact that it is an act of charity, has in itself unitive value.

This climate of rapprochement we owe also to his sincerity, which was so manifest. No one, contemplating his life, could charge him with authoritarianism or ambition.

One day as he was showing a visitor his private library, he stopped before the edition of writings and speeches dating back to his years as Patriarch of Venice. He took down one of the volumes and said: "Do you know what I feel when I look at these volumes?" He hesitated a moment, and then said, "I feel sincere."

This confession gives us the secret of his influence. Is it not this moving sincerity which struck the observers during the audience he had with them the day after the Council opened?

"As for you," he told them, "read my heart: you will perhaps learn more there than from my words. How will I forget the ten years spent in Sofia and the other ten in Istanbul and Athens? . . . I often met Christians belonging to various denominations. . . . We did not debate; we spoke; and though we did not discuss, we loved each other.

Your presence here, which we cherish, and the emotion which fills my priestly heart . . . urge me to confide to you how my heart burns with a desire to work and to suffer for the coming of that hour when Jesus' prayer at the Last Supper will be realized for all men."

His life was a grace for the world.

John XXIII was the Pope of dialogue, and this has special reference to the men of our times.

It is not easy to make the world of today hear the voice of the Church. It is drowned by too much noise; there is too much static and interference in the air for the message to get through.

In spite of these obstacles, John XXIII managed to make himself heard: he broke through the sound barrier.

The words of John awakened a response.

Men recognized his voice, a voice speaking to them of God, but also of human brotherhood, of the re-establishment of social justice, of a peace to be established throughout the whole world.

They heard a challenge addressed to their better selves, and they raised their eyes toward this man whose goodness made them think of God. For men, whether they know or not, are always in search of God, and it is the reflection of God that they sought in the countenance of this old man who loved them with the very love of Christ.

And this is why they wept for him as children for their father, pressing around him to receive his blessing.

And the poor wept for him; they knew he was one of them and that he was dying poor like them, thanking God for the poverty that for him had been such a grace.

And the prisoners wept for him: he had visited them and encouraged them with his presence. Who does not remember that visit to the prison of Rome? Among the prisoners were two murderers. After having heard the Holy Father, one of them approached and said: "These words of hope that you have just spoken, do they also apply to me, such a great sinner?" The Pope's only answer was to open his arms and clasp him to his heart.

This prisoner is surely a sort of symbol of the whole of mankind, so close to the heart of John XXIII.

Now that his pontificate has come to an end, how can we without deep emotion reread the words he spoke in 1934 as he was leaving Bulgaria. We recognize John XXIII in this farewell message, a message that has prophetic value.

"Oh my brothers," he said, "do not forget me, who, come what may, will remain always the fervent friend of Bulgaria.

"According to an old tradition of Catholic Ireland, on Christmas

Eve each home puts a lighted candle in the window to show Saint Joseph and the Blessed Mother, searching for a place to stay, that inside there is a family waiting to receive them. Wherever I may be, even at the ends of the earth, any Bulgarian away from his native land passing by my house will find in the window the lighted candle. If he knocks, the door will be opened, whether he be Catholic or Orthodox. A brother from Bulgaria, this will be title enough. He will be welcome and will find in my house the warmest and the most affectionate hospitality."

This invitation has gone far beyond the borders of Bulgaria; John XXIII addressed it to all men of good will, irrespective of national frontiers.

He will be for history the Pope of Welcome and of Hope. This is the reason his gentle and holy memory will remain in benediction in the centuries to come.

At his departure, he left men closer to God, and the world a better place for men to live.

II

Pope John was present to the Council Fathers not only in Cardinal Suenens' speech. He was also present in the memories and hearts and inspirations of many of the Council Fathers and many of the *periti* (theological experts) who accompanied them. He showed that a man, a priest, a Pope, could live in the twentieth century and still, after all the ambiguities and trappings of history, speak to men of Christ in the accents of Christ, in ways which men could take to be the ways of Christ. Simple, humble, good, for many years dismissed as "a clown," temporizing, uncourageous; and then suddenly courageous and active,[1] Pope John did not start the modern Christian renaissance; he was not the originator of leading ideas or leading movements; he had not, before he became Pope, distinguished himself for his contributions to those movements. But Pope John did something more important than any movement or any formulations of an idea or any support for a program. Pope John lived his special life.

Of course, there are as many ways of being oneself as there are men. Pope John was not always, in the eyes of men, what he appeared to be in the end. He understood very well the wisdom of compromise. "There are some souls," he wrote in *Pacem in Terris*, "particularly endowed with generosity, who, in finding situations where the requirements of justice are not satisfied in full, feel enkindled with the desire to change the state of things, as if they wished to have recourse to something like a revolution. It must be borne in mind that to proceed gradually is the law of life in all its expressions. Therefore, in human institutions, too, it is not possible to renovate them for the better, except by working from within them, gradually." His own path, previous to his becoming Pope, was strewn with gradual measures. The Synod of Rome, over which he presided in 1959, did not to any hopeful degree "open the windows" which the Council was to open. He allowed the woefully anachronistic and impracticable constitution *Veterum Sapientiae*, ordering that classes be taught in Latin in all seminaries, to appear over his name. He allowed the Holy Office to issue a *monitum*—though a mild one— against the works of Teilhard de Chardin. When the Council Fathers elected very few members of the Curia to the conciliar commissions, he salved the pride of the Curia by naming many of their members among the nine appointments for each commission he reserved to himself, and by naming a curial cardinal to head every commission. He allowed a curial man to be Secretary General of the Council. Overcoming countless obstacles, Pope John managed to get his Council together; he managed to open the Church as Christ was open—not asking the world to conform first, but entering the world as it is. He kept his eyes fixed on the essentials, and understood how to realize his dreams by gradual methods. On the other hand, he did not sell his soul in a thousand minor compromises.

There are many manners of expressing truth. When God wished to reveal to men the secret of their own lives and the nature of His Own life, He spoke a Word; but that Word was not a book or a school of thought but a life, the life of His Own Son. Thus Pope John, like the Word he served, told us about the mystery of our times and our own destiny, not with a book or with a school of thought, but with a life. Life comes before lessons; lessons are only for life.

Pope John's slow, lingering death burnt his memory into the minds of nearly all men now living. For the first time in the history of humankind, the whole race was caught up in the death agony of one of their number, and were conscious of him as a great religious man, a follower of Christ, who was offering his suffering for them: for the sake of the Council and for peace. "Any day is a good day to die," he had said. "My bags are packed." Every quarter hour, in the United States, the news bulletins followed this man's progress toward death. The world was united in sorrow, sympathy, and love. Men were learning how it is good to die, and to share a good man's death together. Cardinal Montini in Milan exclaimed at the phenomenon. L'Unità, the Communist daily, put out a special issue on Pope John. Mario Gozzini, in Concilio Aperto (The Open Council), noted that Pope John became the first "Teilhardian" man: the man uniting all men as one.

"There is no longer an atheistic world," the Italian priest-poet Davide Turroldo said after Pope John's death. "Now we see it is enough for a man of God to appear."

NOTE

1. The fascinating study by Robert Rouquette, S.J., "The Roncalli Enigma," *The Catholic Mind*, LXI (November, 1963), pp. 33–42, shows what a poor impression Pope John had made in Paris as Nuncio, and in how little esteem he was held by those who had contact with him.

3

THE CHURCH AFTER JOHN: POPE PAUL VI

"THERE IS NO DOUBT," commented *Le Monde* after the papal election of June, 1963, "that Paul VI is, of all those who might have succeeded Pope John, the one who is closest to his thinking." [1] Pope John is known to have revealed in his diary the conviction that Cardinal Montini would be his successor. There is no doubt that Pope Paul desires above all things else to imitate John and to continue John's work. But between desire and reality may fall a shadow. That is why the great drama of the second session of Vatican II was in large measure concerned with how well the new Pope would live up to the pontificate of the old. There were many, not only in Italy, who were hoping that the new Pope would reverse the dangerous tendencies of Pope John. There were many who were hoping that Pope Paul would implement these tendencies in practical courses of action. The pressures upon him were, from the beginning, immense.

What kind of a man is Pope Paul VI? He is a slight man with a prominent nose and balding head. He has large, clear gray-blue eyes, under black bushy brows. His look is intense, reflective, sensitive. His mind seems to be working constantly, criticizing its own reflections. He moves swiftly, like a man of action, but with a guarded gentleness. He is not a man of sun and wind; when he offers his ring to be kissed, his hand is very white and very thin. He projects emotional intensity, but he does not communicate easily and spontaneously the warmth and affection of Pope John. It is not that Paul's heart burns less warmly; it is only that his style, abilities, and habits have made him a very different man from John. At first Pope Paul seemed to be groaning inwardly with the desire to manifest his heart as Pope John manifested his. He now seems reconciled to the fact that he cannot always do as John did. He is his own kind of man.

The village in which John-Baptist Montini was born, on September 26, 1897, lies at the foot of the Italian Alps in northern Italy. The mountains of his birthplace, the mountains echoed in his name, are useful symbols of his firmness and his intelligence. His father was the editor of the Catholic daily *Il Cittadino*, and served three terms in parliament as a member of Italy's Popular party—the predecessor of the Christian Democratic party. The young Montini escaped the Italian seminary system, for even when he began his studies he was not obliged, on account of his ill health, to reside at the seminary. He lived with his family at home. He was pensive and spent much time alone, reading and writing.

As a young priest in Rome, John-Baptist Montini worked especially with young men at the university. He did a brief stint in Warsaw in 1923, as secretary to the Nuncio, but his health drove him south within a few months. In Rome again, he helped organize various programs of Catholic action. He steadfastly resisted the inroads of Mussolini's Fascists among the youth, even when Mussolini took to violence and the use of police. When direct resistance would not work, he turned to passive non-collaboration. He said, when the going got tough in 1926, "If we can't march with banners flying, let us work in silence." He helped to found and contributed to a small magazine, *Studium*, one of whose purposes was to prepare a hard core of intellectual Catholics to replace the order of Mussolini. In March of 1933, young Montini, by now a monsignor, was called to work exclusively in the Vatican Secretariat of State.

Archbishop Pizzardo, later to emerge as one of the arch-conservatives in the Council, was the man who wrote to the young Montini, informing him of his new appointment to the Secretariat of State. Thus began Montini's association of almost thirty years with the Curia. At first, under Pius XI and then under Pius XII, the young secretary at the Vatican came under the influence of two severe and strong-minded men. Pius XII, particularly, was one who wished to be informed, not advised. Monsignor Montini was expected to produce ideas and have a command of the facts. He was not expected to pretend to have authority over policies of action. Under Pius XII, Montini was one of two Undersecretaries of State. He worked long hours and was very lonely. He made enemies. He translated two volumes of Maritain into Italian, and for his efforts was accused of bringing "Maritainism" into Italy. In 1944, the Cardinal Secretary of State, Cardinal Maglione, died; Pius XII decided to be his own Secretary of State, with the help of the young Monsignors, Montini and Tardini.

In the early 1950's, Montini helped Pius XII draft new legislation, never enacted, for reforming the Curia. In the same years, he also began to favor the de Gasperi forces in the Christian Democratic party; Pius XII was beginning to think de Gasperi was a little far to the left. A whispering campaign was begun against Montini in the Curia, and, apparently, was made to reach Madre Pasqualina, the Pope's housekeeper and nurse. A consistory for the naming of new cardinals was to be held in 1953. Pius XII, it is said, did not want to name Montini a cardinal, and so could not name Tardini one; another story says Tardini refused, so Montini had to. In any case, on January 12, 1953, at a secret consistory of certain cardinals in the Vatican, Pius XII revealed his intention of naming some new cardinals in the future. The Pope added: "There is one further matter which we cannot pass over in silence. It was Our intention to raise to the Sacred College the two distinguished prelates who preside, each in his own section, over the Secretariat of State, and their names were the first entered on the list of cardinals-elect . . . however, these two prelates, giving palpable evidence of their virtue, have so insistently requested that they be dispensed from accepting so high a dignity that we have considered it opportune to accept their repeated petitions and desires in this matter."

In an apostolic brief a short time later, the Pope made Tardini and Montini Pro-Secretaries of State with special privileges. But many in Rome saw in their failure to be named cardinals more than mere humility. When by December 12 of that same year John-Baptist Montini lay face down on the pavement of St. Peter's in the ceremony of consecration as a bishop, before leaving Rome to take up his new duties as Archbishop of Milan, the trend of events seemed still clearer. Pius XII was seventy-eight and already ill. Four years later he would be dead, and Archbishop Montini, not even a cardinal, was away in Milan.

It was surprising that Montini should have built up a reputation for being "left" or "revolutionary"; perhaps it was only that his job in the Vatican was to deal with the political left, while Tardini took the right. Much more than Americans would tolerate in an American bishop, he was later inclined, as Archbishop, to meddle in politics. Moreover, as he lived out his nine gray years in Milan, he seemed to men who knew him there rather "right" than "left." They saw little that was revolutionary in his social doctrine or practice. He was, of course, the first archbishop of Milan since St. Charles Borromeo not to come as a cardinal. He dissuaded a friend from a minor project that ran counter to curial predilections: "Now is not the time; prudence is not enough; astuteness is required." No one can deny that he threw himself, with all his rich emotions, into the task: the story of his falling to kiss the cold, wet pavement as he arrived in the city on January 6, 1955, is already legend. He made himself tour the factories of Milan, carrying his Mass kit in a black attaché case. Two policemen generally motorcycled in front of his black Mercedes. He began a program of building new churches in the sprawling suburbs, at the rate of better than a dozen a year. Milan, his bride, was a city of 3,750,000 souls, and the slightly more than 1,000 churches were not always where the people were. He came to know the problems of an industrial society better than any other Italian prelate. Unlettered immigrants from the south poured into his city. Morality learned in an agricultural society was breaking under the strain of the choices, "temptations," and pressures placed upon it in a modern city.

The new Archbishop always had at his command words of insight and feeling. He spoke at the Second World Congress of the Lay Apostolate in Rome in 1957, giving fundamentally a very conservative talk, and yet with an unmistakable longing for better things. (I was in the audience that day, a student in Rome, and remember being both touched and disappointed; I also remember believing at the time that Montini was a favorite of Pius XII, and sure one day to be a Pope.) He said, among other things: "The Christian mission is very original. It is very demanding. It is, however, easier to live it than to define it." His peroration was the following: "We shall love our time, our civilization, our technical science, our art, our sport, our world. We shall love striving to understand, to have compassion, to esteem, to serve, to suffer. We shall love with Christ's heart."

The theme of suffering and persecution was always close to his lips.

"Montini has suffered extremely in his life," an associate says. He was always a loner, in his youth, in his labors in the Curia, in Milan. His hours have been habitually grueling: the last one to put out his lights, the first to be up. An image remembered in the Vatican is of the frail Sub-Secretary walking down the gloomy hallways alone, turning out lights, before retiring for the night. He hated the intrigue of the ambitious in the Curia. In a letter from Milan to Pius XII he wrote, it seems ironically, of the "calm spiritual air" one breathes within the walls of the Vatican.

In Milan, he was frequently indecisive. Having expressed a solid, perceptive observation, he was likely to add: "Other bishops look at it differently; maybe I'm wrong." He seemed to be still afraid, and when he did move it was as likely as not to be in fits and starts, at random. Beautiful plans were laid, but accomplishments were not great. Little by little, his paper, *L'Italia* moved from right to left. But as late as June, 1960, he addressed a letter to his priests warning them that the new "opening to the left" in Italian politics was unsafe, dangerous, and offered with "insufficient guarantees." Moreover, he tried to justify this advice with the marshaling of general theological and practical principles, in almost professorial fashion. *Corriere della Sera*, unfortunately, obtained and printed the letter.

In February of 1961, the Archbishop also blasted ACLI, an association of Italian Catholic laborers dedicated to the education of workers in social and economic matters. One of the things that especially displeased him in ACLI was the belief that ideologies were becoming neutralized by concrete realities, and that now was a time for greater efforts at "mutual understanding." On the other hand, *L'Italia* had by now moved far enough left to invite stinging letters from more than two-score parish priests in the archdiocese, who therewith canceled their subscriptions to their own diocesan newspaper.

Perhaps pressure from Rome dictated much that Montini did. Without having seen *La Dolce Vita* himself, he tried to prevent certain groups in Milan from writing about it and taking it seriously as a highly moral film; groups in Rome felt exposed by it. In 1962, on the other hand, the Cardinal was not afraid to buck *Confindustria*, the Italian NAM. Asked by them to protest against certain actions by labor unions, he told them, in effect, to see to the beams in their own eye. He also wrote an article in *La Famiglia Christiana*, opposing Cardinal Ottaviani's public statement that Italians, in conscience, were obliged to vote the Christian Democratic ticket. Cardinal Montini said their obligation was to vote according to their conscience.

He did have some success in Milan. Monsignor Clancy notes that Montini was credited with surprising victories over the Communists in the local elections of January, 1957.[2] Pietro Secchia, director of the recruitment drive which had swollen the party membership from 400,000 to 2,000,000, was dispatched from Rome to Milan in 1955, the same year the Vatican sent Montini to Milan. "Charity can give birth to a modern world," Montini preached. "If it has not yet appeared it is because we have not yet applied the eternal law of the Gospel. . . ." "One of the greatest evils of our time is precisely this: that Christians are not Christian." Monsignor Clancy reports that the non-Communists gained control in the following plants: Fiat, Officine Mecchaniche, Falck (steel), Pirelli (rubber); 60,000 workers were involved. In 92 other factories, the non-Communist vote rose from 8,701 to 13,803; the Communist shrank from 21,463 to 17,893.[3] *The New York Times* headed the story: "Pope's Ex-Aide Defeats Milan Red Chief."

"If the pastor begins to move, if he goes out and seeks, if he calls, if he suggests—then he has a chance of succeeding," the Archbishop had written. "It is the priest who must make the first move, not the people."[4] He was able to move on all social levels, something as extraordinary among Italian priests as it is ordinary among American. "The workers were not the first to abandon religion," he said, "but the industrialists and economists of the last century who dreamed of founding programs, civilization, and peace without God and without Christ."[5] He described the sarcasm which modern Europeans have for priests: "The heir of the long-dead Middle Ages, the ally of selfish conservatism, the high priest of a silenced litany, the stranger in life: this is the priest." He added that "the clergy [has] started its self-examinataion."[6] His own diocese was fruitful in vocations, but Italy itself, which in 1875 had 150,000 priests for 26 million people, in 1963 had 83,000 for 60 million.[7] His famous mission in Milan, prepared for five years in advance and aimed at "a rebirth of the sense of religion in the consciences of the people," put Milan under a three-week bombardment by several bishops, 600 priests, and 65 seminarians,[8] preaching to every class of person, in every locality, in stores, in banks, in factories. How much good was actually done is unknown, but all Milan felt the excitement at the time.

II

When Pope John announced the convening of an Ecumenical Council, Cardinal Montini was the first major prelate to come to the support of the idea. When the bishops from all over the world gathered in Rome, Montini, alone of all the Council Fathers, was the guest of Pope John in the Vatican. In the Council he was comparatively quiet. At the Italian bishops' meeting of October 14, 1962, the first time in history that the full complement of Italian bishops had ever met together, Cardinal Montini countered proposals of Cardinal Siri of Genoa and Cardinal Urbani of Venice concerning how to draw up a list of 160 candidates for the various conciliar commissions. Cardinal Montini urged the Italians not to make up a list based only on geography but to choose according to the culture, experience, and piety of the men concerned.

In the early weeks of the Council, Cardinal Montini wrote a letter to his people in Milan in which he expressed his fears for the progress of the Council. "What kind of theological plan can there be for this immense and formidable discussion? There doesn't seem to be any established plan. Will it be possible to establish one now?" Just before the debate on Scripture and Revelation, he wrote again to Milan. "Only those who are acquainted with the development of theology, of the progress in biblical studies, and the heat of the controversies on these questions, inside and outside Catholicism, can appreciate the apprehensions, the hopes, the fears which this argument brings to the conciliar assembly." About the liturgy he also wrote to his people in Milan: "The unity and the spiritual communion of diverse tongues and manners of expression seemed to result in such a variety, not less marvelous and powerful than that resulting from a rigorous uniformity of rites, in which everyone can participate with profit. Catholicity, which is multi-form, ought to be a rich argument for the unity of the Church."

Cardinal Montini hardly spoke at the first session of the Council. There were those who said that Pope John himself had ordered Montini not to make himself a controversial figure. Whatever the reason for his silence, Cardinal Montini broke it in the first week of December (he had spoken earlier only once, on the liturgy), joining a long list of others who attacked the schema "De Ecclesia" presented by Cardinal Ottaviani's theological commission. In that speech, Cardinal Montini recalled the goals which had been set by John XXIII and noted how the schema failed to fulfill those goals. He added that the schema on the Church should concentrate on the Episcopal College, on the power of the bishops, and on the sacramentality of the episcopate. These last themes were favorites of Montini's. In his pastoral letter of 1962 he had written: "The treatise on the nature and function of the episcopacy, in harmony with the Roman papacy, is one which could result in a new and harmonious affirmation of the unity, not only juridical but living, of the Church around the chair of St. Peter, and give a start, without any vindictive intention, to a greater and a more organic internationalization of the central government of the Church." John-Baptist Montini was to make these themes central at the second session.

On the death of Pope John in the beginning of June, 1963, Montini said of the universal response: "Why do they mourn his death everywhere in the world? What marvel of spiritual convergence produces this thing without precedent in history? Everyone of us has felt the attraction of that personality, has grasped that the sympathy that enveloped him was not a delusion or a fashionable whim; it was a secret revealing itself—a mystery which absorbed us, a mystery of two words, which, united in magic power, dazzled our eyes—the words *truth* and *charity*." On Friday, June 7, Montini preached in his cathedral: "John has shown us some paths which it will be wise to follow. Can we turn away from these paths so masterfully traced? It seems to me we cannot."

Before coming to the conclave for the election of a new Pope, Montini did not try to rush his work in Milan to a conclusion. He left his work hanging as though it were a normal trip. Two days before leaving for Rome, he said to a group of priests at the Milan seminary, "Perhaps the time is ripe for a non-Italian pope."

Meanwhile, the world waited. The issue of renewal and reform in the Church was at stake. To keep watch over the situation, non-curial cardinals came to Rome quite early: Cardinals Liénart, Ritter, Meyer, Léger came ten days or more before the conclave.

Speculation ran very high. More than ten of the progressive cardinals met with Bea on Tuesday evening, June 18. Their first ballot, it is said, went for Cardinal Suenens of Belgium; realistically, they were hoping for Montini or Lercaro. It was said that the conservative cardinals would oppose the election of Cardinal Bea "to the death."

As the cardinals were ready to begin the conclave on Wednesday, June 19, a peculiar sermon was preached to them by Monsignor Tondini, a curial official whose title was "Secretary of Briefs to Princes," a position given to one whose pre-eminent accomplishment is elegant Latin. He spoke in pessimistic, fearful tones of the contemporary world, damning Pope John with patronizing praise. Monsignor Tondini tried to warn the cardinals against electing another man like John. Someone—Pope John?—must have been stressing the warm, natural, ordinary virtues too much, for the new Pope, he insisted, should set himself "with total effort, to re-establish the supernatural virtues in the lives of Christians." In today's world Monsignor Tondini saw no moral order, only "the politique of suspicion and fear." Modern governments abuse man "because they consider him a machine from which to draw temporal advantages for himself and principally for the State." [9]

The elegant Latinist did not try to block the Council, directly. "The Catholics of every continent pray that the great undertaking will be carried through to fulfillment. But it will be for the Pope, whom you, eminent Fathers, will choose from your midst, to establish the suitable time for its renewal." The new Pope would "determine and judge if the questions, studies, and particularly spiritual dispositions have yet attained that maturity which will bring about the results awaited by the soundest part of humanity." Monsignor Tondini feared "the dominant confusion of ideas," and the "mutual distrust and the antagonisms of people" which he found in our time. There is no provision in Roman Catholic services for walking out on a preacher. The cardinals suffered in silence. Monsignor Tondini was allowed unimpeded to sketch for them the physiognomy of one of the "prophets of doom" among whom the new Pope, like Pope John before him, was going to have to spend his days.

That afternoon, at five o'clock, after the stately procession of the cardinals from the Pauline chapel, the conclave was sealed off from the world. On Thursday morning the balloting began, two ballots in the morning, two in the afternoon.

In forty-two hours, one of the shortest conclaves in history, on the sixth ballot (many reports say the fifth), John-Baptist Montini was elected to succeed Peter—and John. The Dean of the College of Cardinals, Cardinal Tisserant, flanked by Cardinals Gonçalves Cerejeira and Ottaviani, representing the cardinal priests and the cardinal deacons, respectively, walked slowly through the Sistine Chapel to the green-covered table at which John-Baptist Montini sat without moving. The voice of Cardinal Tisserant broke the silence: "Do you accept your election as Supreme Pontiff which has been canonically carried out?"

There was a brief silence as Cardinal Montini stood before the chasm between his status as cardinal and what his status would be if he accepted. He said: "I accept—*in nomine Domini*. In the name of the Lord."

Another question remained to be asked. Cardinal Tisserant asked him: "By what name do you wish to be known?"

Montini's voice was now firm. "I will be Paul."

The Cardinal Deacon led Montini away to the sacristy where he was to vest himself in the robes of a Pope.

III

Outside in the keyhole piazza, the "lock of the world," the huge crowd, growing rapidly, buzzed with suspense. Cardinal Ottaviani, who stepped out on the distant balcony to announce the news to those in the blazing square, did not have to get further than *"John-Baptist"*—before the crowd broke in *"Montini!"* Cheers and jubilation! (Some newspapers, gambling on the outcome, were already packed on trucks, ready to roll.) Cardinal Ottaviani beamed; Cardinal Bea beamed. In the Vatican hallways, Cardinal Spellman turned with unsuppressed pleasure to Cardinal Micara and said, "You saw, Your Eminence, you saw! We did as you ordered us to do." [10] Everybody's man was in.

When the new Pope, tall but thin, appeared at the balcony, many in the crowd murmured: "Pacelli! Pius XII!" Gone was the heavy, rotund, jocund John. Here was the pensive, reflective, careful Paul.

At the luncheon after the conclave, the new Pope resumed his former place at the table. After lunch, he closeted himself with Cardinal Koenig of Vienna—a fact which many took to be a sure sign of his interest in maintaining Pope John's opening to the east. He next saw Cardinal Bea, who carried thence messages to the Gregorian University and the Biblicum that there would be "no more suppressions." He opened the seals on the deceased Pope's study and was seated at the great desk without the usual delay "for decency." He worked that night until 1:30 A.M., preparing his first radio message to the world. The next night he worked until 2 A.M., and the next night late again.

On Saturday, in his first radio message to the world, the new Pope promised: "The pre-eminent part of our pontificate will be occupied with the continuation of the Second Vatican Ecumenical Council. All men of good will look to it. This will be our principal work and in it we intend to spend all the energies which the Lord has given us."

On Sunday, Pope Paul met Cardinals Spellman and Cushing, and Archbishop Martin J. O'Connor, Rector of the North American College. He next saw Cardinal Ruffini of Palermo, and then Cardinal Suenens. At noon, for the traditional appearance at the window, he chose a floor lower than the one on which Pope John regularly appeared, and at his side was Cardinal Suenens. Pope John had had Cardinal Wyszynski of Poland beside him. Those alert to symbolism began to keep their eyes on Cardinal Suenens' future.

For the date of his coronation, again symbolically, Pope Paul surprised many papalists by not choosing June 29, the feast of St. Peter, and great feast in Rome. Instead, he chose the next day, June 30, feast of St. Paul. The day of the coronation—held outside in the piazza, after the blazing sun had begun to send evening shadows across the stones—was a glorious one. On Pope Paul's head was set Pope John's crown, the triple-tiered tiara of the Popes, this one a gift from the people of Milan.

But becoming a Pope is not so easy as receiving the tiara of the Popes. Following the path opened up by John is not so easy as resolving to follow it. The months ahead became a great trial for Montini. The fate of the Council depended in great measure on how he weathered that trial.

NOTES

1. Quoted in *Apostle for Our Time: Pope Paul VI*, by John G. Clancy (New York, P. J. Kenedy & Sons: 1963), p. 196.
2. *Ibid.*, pp. 96 ff.
3. *Ibid.*, p. 98, note.
4. *Ibid.*, p. 94.
5. *Ibid.*, pp. 103–104.
6. *Ibid.*, p. 119.
7. *Ibid.*, note.
8. *Ibid.*, p. 116.
9. I owe these quotes to Monsignor Clancy's account, *ibid.*, pp. 169–71.
10. *Ibid.*, p. 193, note; quoted from *La Stampa*, Turin, June 23.

4

THE TALK TO THE CURIA

MID-SEPTEMBER was an exciting time in Rome. Almost every day Pope Paul took another step toward solidifying the prospects of the second session of the Council. Though the preparatory work for this session had been nearly three months behind schedule when he took office, the new Pope had rescheduled the second session to be only three weeks later than Pope John had planned—exactly the time that had elapsed between Pope John's death and his own election. Pope Paul was not heeding the advice given his electors by Monsignor Tondini—nor heeding the immense pressures brought to bear on him by political and religious groups strong in the Vatican.

On September 16, the Pope made a symbolic gesture in support of his long-standing convictions about the power of the bishops; he announced that at the Council the bishops might wear their *mozzettas,* or short violet silk capes, a sign of their jurisdiction in their own dioceses. (Many bishops, already at sea, now regretted having left theirs at home.) He also announced that the first item of business at the Council would be the document "on the Church."

The day before, on September 15, the Pope had announced that laymen would be invited to the Council. This news excited the press of the world: the Church was taking cognizance of laymen again, and if now only as auditors, perhaps one day as speakers too.

The Pope also announced a new source of power in the Council: a board of four moderators to direct the proceedings on the floor. The composition of this board was startling: Julius Cardinal Doepfner,

Archbishop of Munich, Leo Jozef Suenens, Archbishop of Brussels, Gregory Peter Cardinal Agagianian, Armenian Prefect of the Congregation for the Propagation of the Faith, and Giacomo Cardinal Lercaro, Archbishop of Bologna. Cardinal Lercaro was the Italian prelate second only to Montini in the estimation of his peers; Cardinal Agagianian was, of all the curial cardinals, the one most acceptable to the majority—and an Eastern prelate to boot; Cardinals Doepfner and Suenens were leaders of the progressive majority. At the first session of the Council, the presidential council of ten cardinals had directed the meetings of the assembly; each of the ten had presided in rotation. Now the Pope addressed his letter to Cardinal Tisserant, in which these announcements were made, not to the "President of the Ecumenical Council," but to the "Chief of the College of Presidents of the Council." It appeared that the more conservative college of presidents named by Pope John (one had died, and three new ones were appointed by Pope Paul during the summer [1]) was being replaced by the highly progressive moderators.

True, the exact line of authority was not clear. The twelve presidents were charged with seeing that the rules of the Council were kept; the moderators were charged with executing the rules in the daily prosecution of business. But in case of conflict, who had preeminent authority? Could the moderators devise means of expediting the procedures? Had the presidents become mere figureheads? One of the most dramatic conflicts of the second session arose out of this lack of clarity. It seemed even in mid-September that Pope Paul had gone only halfway with a progressive measure.

On September 26, just before the second session was to begin, several changes in the Council rules were also announced. In brief, the new rules emphasized greater freedom. *Item:* A group of fifty bishops could sign a new document to present to the Council, to replace the one under discussion, and submit it to the moderators for transmission to the coordinating commission. *Item:* In each commission, if five members desire a secret vote, the president must allow it. *Item:* To close discussion on a point, only an absolute majority is required; to approve a document or a part of a document, a two-thirds majority is required. *Item:* A bishop who wished to speak on a given chapter after cloture was invoked could gather five signatures to his intervention, and thus acquire the right to speak before the Council could move on.

It is clear why these changes were greeted with general approval—a free, open Council was guaranteed. But the changes later came back to haunt the Council Fathers. A parliament of twenty-three hundred men is, to begin with, quite unwieldy. (Four hundred less attended than the year before; many, bored by the long hours of speculative Latin discussion, sought reasons of health or business for not returning.) Not all have a businesslike sense of procedure. Some of the Spaniards and Italians, especially (it turned out), loved to sermonize and recreate the pages of textbooks they recalled from seminary days. Or a given Council Father would suddenly receive an insight never experienced before, and feel compelled to narrate it to the others—who, often, had got the point long ago. Many of the Council Fathers simply did not seem to understand that repetition is an annoyance; their idea of an argument seemed to be constant insistence on an accepted position, without any attention to the flow of the debate. A few were there to teach, not to learn.

Moreover, the flow of debate was made as artificial as possible. The procedure for getting on the floor was to prepare one's speech at least three days in advance and submit it as soon as possible to the secretaries of the Council.[2] There, supposedly according to the order in which the speeches were received, a list of speakers for each day was arranged. (There was ample reason to believe that this order was tampered with rather freely; some bishops found themselves far down on the list—the debate, then, already cut off—when they were sure they had put their name on the secretary's list at the earliest possible moment.) There was very little direct confrontation on the floor. Most of the bishops do not speak Latin fluently enough to alter their speeches much, once written. The requirement of handing them in three or four days before they are given makes it impossible to foresee the trend and tension of the debate. Only the cardinals had the privilege of speaking on any day they chose, submitting their names on the morning of their discourse. Important exchanges, therefore, usually had to come through them. "Today they're wheeling out the big guns," a young American auxiliary bishop used to say, on glancing over the morning's list.

But the greatest artificiality thrown in the way of real discussion was the firm insistence on the use of Latin. Cardinal Cushing of Boston more than once offered to pay the costs of installing a system of simultaneous translation, as commonly used by every international gathering in the contemporary world. Severe resistance developed to his idea. "The time is not yet ripe," one American bishop later wrote home, implying that not too many shocks can be given at any one time to the Roman way of doing things. Even though the Phillips company was making experiments near the end of October, nothing came of their elaborate preparations. There were technical difficulties with feedback from the public address system, and the sound was impossible to contain within St. Peter's; persons with transistor radios could pick up the discussions outside. But the main difficulty seemed to be reluctance to make the system work. Most of the Council Fathers go along with the resistant ones, as though not to snuff the smoldering flax or crush the bending reed. Thus, they were even willing to swallow the requirement that, if there *were* a simultaneous translation system, they would have to write their speeches in Latin and turn them in two days *earlier* than before, so that they could be translated in time.

On the other hand, the Protestant observers already had simultaneous translation, done by priests like Father Gustave Weigel, S.J., and Monsignor Francis Davis—at great labor, to be sure—on the spur of the moment. Rome is full of young priests and candidates for the priesthood who could easily, with a half hour's head start, render any Latin talk into their own language with accuracy. But the issue is obviously not one to be settled rationally; the opposition is not arguing from reason. The "open Church" can open itself only gradually from the odd logic in which it is still partially enclosed. The Council Fathers who do not spontaneously share this odd logic go many extra miles to try to understand it, sympathize with it, and find some merit in it; they are the most tolerant men in the world.

Occasionally, however, their efforts break down. Thus the bishops of the United States were determined to give the English-language press the best access they could to Council news. The International Council Press Board, on which they had representation, devised some strange rules for reporting the speeches on the Council floor. Pope Paul had decided to lift the rule of secrecy which covered the debates within St. Peter's, and to maintain it only for the discussions in the commissions, which prepare the documents for the Council floor. The press office was charged with preparing summaries of the speeches given on the floor—but *speeches were not to be attributed to their speakers*. Apparently, some cautious fathers had the idea that if their words proved open to public criticism, they could always deny that they had spoken them. Bishop Albert R. Zuroweste of Belleville, Illinois, substitute chairman of the United States bishops' press committee (Archbishop Joseph T. McGucken of San Francisco was delayed by illness from arriving at the opening of the Council), shrugged his shoulders to the pressmen and said, "I don't pretend to understand it. We'll just have to live with it."

Meanwhile, Father Edward L. Heston, C.S.C., the dynamic, well-liked English-language press officer who prepared the daily summaries, solved the problem nicely. He simply numbered the speakers and numbered the summaries correspondingly. A straightforward matter was handled deviously to obtain a straightforward end: the regular merry-go-round of moral life in Italy. (Meanwhile, Father Heston also engineered another breakthrough. At first, the press officers listened to the speeches in relays, took notes on them in Latin, and carried them to a central desk, where then the official communiqué was made up and translated into the major languages. After one day of that, Father Heston decided he would write his own summaries; he asked Bishop Zuroweste to back him up—and he did. Step by step the Americans carved out an intelligent press policy.)

II

As the Council prepared to get under way, wags in Rome devised several rules to help newcomers learn the Roman way of doing things:

Rule I: When an issue is complicated, make a bow to each party in the debate, do nothing to resolve it; let everyone privately pursue his own policy.

Rule II: When an issue is simple, find a devious way of solving it.

Rule III: When in doubt, delay.

Rule IV: If delay threatens to injure ambitions close to your heart, don't delay even if you doubt; but be ready with profuse apologies.

Rule V: If questioned about your actions, be indignant, deny having acted, and insist on the doubts and issues until you find an explanation that will content your antagonist. Then admit that yes, in *that* sense, you did act, but after all . . .

Rule VI: In any action, act so ambiguously but forcefully that your action is taken in its strongest sense by those who do not have the nerve to question you, but is susceptible of the mildest possible interpretation if someone with nerve does question you.

Rule VII: Learn the moral sensibilities of others, so that you can always insist on allegiance to them in your preamble; but do not be bound by them. *Shorter version:* Suffer a thousand modifications of detail, but never a change of principle.

Rule VIII: Please everybody, without ceasing to pursue your own interests.

Rule IX: Assume that Anglo-Saxons think in terms of the same intrigue as you do; they've only mastered Rule VII better than you have, and so *seem* to be more honest.

Rule X: Work harder at Rule VII.

There are other things to learn about Rome. Efficiency is not a Roman virtue. It usually takes three visits to an office to accomplish the business of one visit. A sense of humor is indispensable. The incongruous is daily fare. Common sense does not thrive in the climate. To criticize, one must first praise. To get at a thorny point, one must raise thirty or forty innocuous ones in the vicinity; the thorny one should then be dropped casually, with the effect, however, of exploding a land mine in the living room.

III

On Saturday, September 21, Pope Paul VI summoned all the members of the Roman Curia and the workers of the Vatican to a special audience in the Hall of Benedictions, the enormous room over the huge porch of St. Peter's. Lay clerks jostled with monsignors, cardinals smiled greetings to guards and functionaries. It was eight days before the Council was to open; the convocation was unusual. Secretly, everybody wondered what was up. They expected the usual triumphal rhetoric; but they were not sure. At exactly 10 A.M.—with a precision not Roman—Pope Paul entered the room, before everyone was seated or even assembled. A hush came over the hall as he walked down the aisle through their midst on foot. He had no script in his hand. At his place in front, he began to tell them in a quiet voice that what he had to say might prove long; therefore, he was granting the rest of the day as a holiday. Smiles, scraping of feet, and loud applause. As the din subsided, he smiled and added that, in view of the ever-mounting cost of living in Rome (rents had gone up 30 percent during the summer), he was also granting each of them a raise. The applause was now louder and the mood warmer.

Pope Paul's prepared discourse, which he then drew out to read, was a jewel of Italian rhetoric, subtle, civilized, telling. When he concluded, the applause swelled ever louder until he finally broke in on it to intone the "*Sit nomen Domini Benedictum*" and impart the papal blessing. His words left his hearers visibly heartened, and members of the Curia were still saying for some days afterward: "What a talk! It needed saying. At last!" But the talk was a two-edged sword; in which direction it cut most it was then too early to tell. On the one hand, the Pope came to the defense of the Curia and praised them with much feeling. On the other, he spoke frankly and incisively of the changes to come. It was this latter thrust that appeared most significant to many observers, who headlined their reports as "HISTORIC TALK!" That Pope Paul could also win the warm gratitude of the vast majority of his auditors seemed to them only a tribute to his increasingly evident ability.

Those around the world who had been waiting for Pope Paul to declare himself now seemed satisfied. "The Pope," he described himself in the middle of his talk, "who has today made his own the legacy of John XXIII, of happy memory, and makes of it a program for the entire Church." He voiced every theme dear to the progressive speakers at the first session of the Council. There seemed to be no question as to what style Pope Paul wished to give the Church, of which, borrowing Pope John's usage, he called himself "in time and in merit the last of the servants of the servants of God." Moreover, the skill with which the new Pope expressed himself surpassed the expectations of his supporters. Just three months before, to the day, he had stood at the window of this same Hall of Benedictions to receive the recognition of the people as their new Pope; now he was already proving himself a master. Those who wished for a Pope of strong intelligence and will, to make the intuitions and dreams of Pope John into institutional reality, seemed in Pope Paul to have received their wish.

For most of his talk, the Pope praised the Curia. "I speak to you," he said, "with a triple intention: to praise you, to bring you peace, to exhort you." He recalled his own thirty years of working in the Curia, his friendships, his mentors, his memories of both trying and joyous days. He spoke in a soft Italian, under whose affection and intimacy was the grip of intelligence and will. Pope Paul insisted again and again that, as regards the Roman Curia, he himself is the absolute authority. Describing the essential relation between Pope and Curia, he regularly used expressions like "conformity of spirit," "immediate adherence," "absolute obedience," "identity of view." He reviewed the purposes and role of the Curia: to be the administrative, consultative, executive arm of the Pope. In subtle order, he said that "the justification, or rather the glory" of the Curia is its relation to him. He said that "its necessity, its utility, its dignity, its authority" derived from its being "the instrument of which the Pope has need and of which the Pope . . . makes use in carrying out his divine mandate."

The Pope's insistence on his own authority was interpreted in two ways. On the one hand, in the context of his praise for the Curia and his insistence that the Curia itself would "formulate and promulgate" its own reform, he seemed to be reserving to himself the project of reorganizing this ancient institution. He gave the Curia credit for desiring "earlier even and more ardently than your critics to meet with specific skills the ever new and growing demands of the office you hold." Projects for the reform of curial operations had been in preparation since the time of Pius XII—Montini had helped formulate them—and much that was called "new reform" had been under study for a decade or more.

On the other hand, the Pope seemed to be clearing away doubts and obstructions concerning who, exactly, holds the authority in Rome. His discourse had the effect, intended or not, of making perfectly clear that when he sets the style and the direction in the Curia, no one therein has any justification for opposing him. Each of his purposes—"to praise you, to bring you peace, to exhort you"—seemed a phase in his presentations of the reforms to be expected. He spoke as if everyone knew that reforms were needed; he recalled that the present order of things dated from 1588 under Sixtus V, and has not been revised since 1908 under Pius X and 1917 under the new code of canon law. "It is understandable," he said, "how such an order can be burdened under the weight of its own venerable age." Even his severest phrases here seemed palatable to his audience, for he explained that these reforms will be formulated and promulgated by the Curia itself.

The core of the Pope's thought lay in the next few sentences. He mentioned these specific lines of reform: (1) The Curia would need a "larger supranational vision." (2) It would need to be "educated with a more accurate ecumenical preparation." Pope Paul here quoted from St. Bernard, the eleventh-century reformer: "Why not choose from all over the world those who one day will have to judge the whole world?" (This choice of St. Bernard was subtly done; only a few paragraphs before the Pope had congratulated the Curia for its piety and devotion in these terms: "Today . . . St. Bernard would not write his burning pages on the Roman ecclesiastical world, nor would the reformers of the sixteenth century.") (3) The Curia "will not be jealous of the temporal prerogatives of other times, nor of external forms no longer suitable for expressing and teaching truths of profound religious meaning." (4) The Curia will not be "miserly with its powers, which today, without injuring universal ecclesiastical order, bishops themselves can exercise better locally." (5) "Questions of economic advantage will never have weight in suggesting a certain reserve and a certain centralization of organs of the Holy See, unless necessary for the good of ecclesiastical order and the salvation of souls." This last point was often overlooked by the press. The economic issues did not become apparent, at first.

Pope Paul then elaborated on the fourth of these points, though cautiously. He observed that even now the various branches of the Curia rely on bishops around the world for advice and help. "We will go further: If the Ecumenical Council should manifest a desire to see associated in a certain manner and for certain questions, in conformity with the doctrine of the Church and canon law, some representatives of the bishops, particularly those who direct dioceses, with the supreme Head of the Church, in the care and the responsibility of ecclesiastical government, surely the Roman Curia will not be in opposition." This hint to the Council was not overlooked; very often Council Fathers were to refer to it in the coming weeks.

Taken together, these five points, and especially the fourth, included every needed line of reform. If the Curia is international in outlook, many objections against it fall. If the bishops regain the use of the powers that by right belong to them, to decide the status of certain marriage cases and liturgical usages, for example, and so regain the sense of creativity and responsibility which these powers encourage, the Church will doubtless become much more sensitive to local conditioning and needs. If an international "cabinet" of representative bishops is formed to meet regularly in Rome, a new check and balance will be inserted into the institutional structure of the Church, more in conformity with the ancient collegial character of the episcopacy.

"We were about through with travel by this time," Bishop Robert E. Tracy wrote back to his people in Baton Rouge, Louisiana, in his biweekly *Rome Letters*, "and were anxious to get to work. We had been grabbing every newspaper and magazine article on the council as we went through France, Germany, and Italy; and we had read of the new council rules, the new observers, and the Pope's address to the curia. Now we wanted to talk to our friends at Rome and hear the reactions and explanations that all this must have provoked."

Rome was indeed buzzing over the "bombshell" the Pope had exploded in his talk to the Curia. *L'Osservatore Romano* had carried the talk the following day, under the following headline: "PRECIOUS NORMS AND INDICATIONS FOR THE PRESENT SOLEMN HOUR OF THE CHURCH TO THOSE WHO HAVE HIGH RESPONSIBILITIES AND WORK IN THE ROMAN CURIA." The long subtitle quoted these lines from the Pope: "*It has seemed to Us, since the beginning of Our apostolic mission, a duty to give a sign of Our paternal benevolence to the persons who direct and who compose the Roman Curia, and to make them feel how much it pleases Us, how much it presses Us to know that We are in communion with them . . . for the good of and the example of the whole Church and of its mission in the world, and to the glory of Him Who is Our all, Our Lord Jesus Christ.*"—"*Most studious and most expert must the Roman Curia be to live up to its role; as you know, as you also desire, as you yourselves are longing . . . to meet with specific virtues the always new and growing exigencies of the office which is demanded of you.*"—"*From all over the world men look to Catholic Rome, to the Roman Pontiff, to the Roman Curia. The duty of being authentic Christians is here its weightiest.*"

But a feeling was abroad in Rome that September that Rome *is* the center of the most authentic Christianity. The Curia had taken the talk in stride. No hard steps had been taken by the Pope. Basically, their interests appeared to have been defended. Hadn't the Pope noted that many criticisms of the Curia were unfair? Hadn't he said of the Holy Office, focal point for much of the criticism, "Function most delicate, to be custodian or echo of divine truths and to fashion a language and enter dialogue with the human spirit"? While the partisans of reform read this statement as a subtle lesson to the Holy Office that languages change and need fashioning anew, and that doctrine is revealed not in Latin-scholastic isolation but in dialogue with men who live in history, members of the Holy

Office found the words innocuous enough—if, perhaps, a little imprecise, coming from one who was not a professional in the work.
("The Holy Office *is* already updated," Cardinal Ottaviani was
to say in an interview with a newsman.)

No matter how good the Curia might be, the Pope suggested, it
could never be good enough to measure up to the standards of the
Gospels; it is always fair game for critics. But the Roman mind
already has a rule for this kind of warning: "Memorize the words of
the law, but realize that men are men. The law is perfect and men
are not. No serious reform need be made." The Pope urged the
Curia to accept criticisms as a stimulus, to receive them with humility,
with reflection, even with gratitude. "Rome has no need to defend
herself by becoming deaf to suggestions which come from upright
voices, and all the less when these are voices of friends and brothers."
Moreover, the Pope spoke of "perennial reform," new conceptions
and institutions, and revised structures. These words did not suggest
the *"semper eadem"* of the Roman tradition. Finally, his emphasis on
the international scope of the problems of the Church and on the
need for the internationalization of the Curia, struck reformers one
way, but men of the Curia another. Are not apostolic delegates and
nuncios constantly keeping Rome in touch with the recalcitrant
problems of the world-wide variety among men? And are not men from
all nations even now serving in every branch of the Curia? "Yes,"
the answer could come back, "but after a very short time the non-
Romans become more Roman than the Romans—they learn to do
consciously what the Romans have imbibed from birth." *Romanità*
is not necessarily acquired by birth; it is taught; newcomers require a
period of "formation." Moreover, it is a disease. To get action in
Rome, one must become like the Romans; one must weave one's own
spider web, according to the Roman rules.

In short, as a piece of rhetoric and perhaps of courage, Pope Paul's
talk to the Curia was a masterpiece. It aroused the hopes of the reformers, and for many weeks they were to quote his invitation to form
a new "senate" or a new "cabinet" of bishops, displacing the Curia
as the institutional body closest to the Pope. But the Curia is not
alarmed by words or suggestions. It was legislated into being, and only
legislation will reanimate it. Meanwhile, those concerned were determined to see to it that this coming Council legislated nothing that
would be of irrevocable harm to the Church as they understood it,

i.e., to the curial structure which with their own ears they had just heard Pope Paul praise. To understand their mentaility, or more exactly their theology, will require some hard work; but it is impossible to grasp the meaning of the Second Vatican Council without coming to grips with that theology. As we remember that in this last week of September chartered planes full of bishops were flying in from Tokyo, from Africa, from South America, from New York, let us halt for a moment to do that work. And recall as we do so that Pope John, Cardinal Bea, Pope Paul himself—and many others— found their way out of the system we are about to analyze.

NOTES

1. The presidents named by Pope John were: Cardinals Liénart of France, Tappouni (Syrian Patriarch of Antioch), Gilroy of Australia, Frings of Germany, Pla y Deniel of Spain, Spellman of the United States, Ruffini of Italy, Caggiano of Argentina, Alfrink of the Netherlands, and one curial cardinal, Tisserant, who is Dean of the Sacred College of Cardinals.
2. The Secretary General was round-faced, white-haired, handsome Archbishop Pericle Felici, affable and pleasant; the Subsecretaries were five in number: Bishops Morcillo of Spain, Villot of France, Krol of the United States, Kempf of Germany, and Nabaa of Lebanon.

5

THE SCHOOL OF FEAR

THE CHIEF STORY of the second session is the story of the erosion of a school of theology, the theology of the "prophets of doom." It is the story of the growing ascendancy of other theologies, more contemporary and more ancient, over the immobile and abstract theology which since the Reformation has predominated in the Church. The secondary story concerns a procedural struggle. In that struggle, the representatives of the contemporary and ancient theologies, who were in the majority at the Council, tried to make the central organs of the Council, and of the Church, more responsive to their views. The majority struggled against a minority, but the minority held the key parliamentary positions. Partisans of the minority chaired most of the commissions, and held higher representation on the commissions than they did in the Council. They had more than their share of members among the twelve council presidents. The Secretary General of the Council, Archbishop Felici, was one of their leaders. Two of the moderators, on the other hand, Cardinals Suenens and Doepfner, were leaders of the majority; a third, Cardinal Lercaro, was highly thought of by the majority; and the fourth, Cardinal Agagianian, was among the most respected of the minority.

The maneuvering and struggling for parliamentary power makes a more engrossing story than the development of theology; actions arrest attention more easily than ideas. But in the long run, when actions are forgotten, ideas are still being studied, meditated on, and giving rise to new actions. For that reason, although we cannot slight the record of events, let us pause to try to understand the move-

ments of thought which are still at stake in the Council. Here lies
the essential meaning of the Council. Unless the theology is grasped,
nothing of importance is grasped. It is, in fact, the difference in
theology which even the common mind of the peoples has already
sensed, under the metaphors of "winds of change," "fresh air," "open
doors," and even the word "renewal." The difference in theology—in
attitude of mind—is so fundamental that even the outward history of
the Council recorded in the public press has been a parable about it.
Those who have read the press dispatches and the articles have
grasped the parable. Many of them are struggling to analyze it in
more precise and clearer terms.

When Pope John, and Pope Paul after him, called for an *aggiornamento* in the Church, by that very fact they shook the justification on
which the unrenewed, unreformed institutions within the Church
rested. The resistance was vigorous, sometimes direct, sometimes
subtle. The resistance to renewal and reform is not very widespread;
but it runs very deep, for the theology on which it rests runs deep.

We need a name for this entrenched theology of the last four
hundred years. One might call it "Roman theology," but its supporters
are found in many cities, in many lands; moreover, by no means all
of the theologians of Rome support it. One might call it "curial
theology," but many of its adherents do not belong to the Roman
Curia. One might call it "the theology of the Holy Office," for it is
that most noble of offices which has been chiefly charged with pre-
serving it; but the name would then call too much attention to too
small a group, and leave untouched the many more proponents spread
throughout the world. One might call it the "theology of the Counter-
Reformation," but that title embraces far too much and, besides,
awakens old polemics which do not accurately describe what is at
stake. Interpreters of the first session were fond of using the terms
"liberals" and "conservatives," "progressives" and "traditionalists,"
"reactionaries" and "innovators"; but these terms, besides borrowing
too much from political life, are not faithful to Christian history:
all Catholic theologians wish to conserve the Word given to the
Church, and to preach it anew to progressing ages. The debate at
issue is how best to conceptualize and to formulate the tradition for
our time, once having recovered it.

Another proposal for naming the entrenched theology of the last
four hundred years is to call it by its leading characteristics: "immobile

theology," or "abstract theology," or "triumphal theology." This proposal seems to strike more nearly at the heart of the matter. It emphasizes that the fundamental point at issue is a question of methodology: Is there more than one Catholic theology? If so, what methods do these theologies use? By what means is "the mind" of the Church discovered? The root issue, then, is not: which among alternative *propositions* shall we choose as best representing the faith given to the Church by God. The root issue is: by what *method* shall we decide which of two alternative propositions best represents that faith.

Debate on the floor of the Council can succeed in covering up this root issue. The debate can seem to concern the meaning of contrasting propositions. It can seem to concern the attitudes, or points of view, or schools of thought, of the contesting Council Fathers. It can seem to concern the limited aims, local problems, or abiding personal interests of the individual disputants. Because the Council Fathers pit themselves against each other on all these various levels, the root question is often obscured. Moreover, Pope John declared in his opening address that the Council was to be a "pastoral" Council. But what is a pastoral theology? How does one decide which of two contrasting propositions is best suited for the needs of men? What are the principles for making a good pastoral decision in questions of theology?

A friend once told me a story which helps shed light, and humor, on the issue. He was talking to an Italian priest who had just spent many months in a certain area of South America, and several more months in North America. The priest exclaimed that he admired the Church in this region of South America much more than the Catholicism he had seen in North America. My friend, aware that the region of South America in question lacked clergy, and even faithful, asked the priest, "But you said that the churches there were empty, that the people were going Communist, and that the country lacked vocations; and here you have seen nothing but full churches, many vocations, thousands going to the sacraments." "Ah, yes," the priest answered, "but there the doctrine is so pure!"

When is doctrine pure? Faced with two propositions, each with the same number of words, each in the same language, each trying to express the same point, by what method does one decide which of the two is more faithful to the Gospels? Sometimes, for example, the key word in the proposition cannot be found in the Scriptures, either because the formulation is not in a scriptural language, or because the precise point did not explicitly arise in biblical history. *Homoousion,* "of one substance with," the key phrase of the Council of Nicaea in 325, was such a word.[1] "Papal infallibility," from the First Vatican Council, in 1870, is another. (Latin, the language of that Council, is not a scriptural language.)

The problem of theological method is a ticklish one, and we will do well to leave it to theologians; one of the greatest of them has long been at work on it.[2] But, for our present purposes, we must also have a rough idea of what is involved. In his opening address and in *Pacem in Terris,* Pope John XXIII saw to it that the Council was founded on two principles: the principle of historical development and the principle of concrete reality. Both of these principles insist upon attention to concrete history: to the men, movements, and events of history. Both principles insist that the man who uses them must enter the stream of history and work from within it, conscious that his words and his concepts are conditioned by it (the principle of development), and that his theories must meet the test of concrete facts, movements, and events (principle of concrete reality). The first principle is aimed against the idea that words have meaning outside of their historical context, or are unconditioned by their origins. The second is directed against the idea that ideology is "pure" and should be judged only in the light of logic; it insists on judgment of institutions, men, and events as they appear in fact as well as in theory. Both principles deny the man who uses them the right to claim that he or his ideas are uninfluenced by history, or that he need not undertake the work of bringing his ideas and methods to the bar of concrete reality. Words are not enough; abstract definitions are not enough; his views must meet the test of facts, from both the present and the past.

However, many thinkers at the Council seemed to be afraid of these two principles. For these principles seem to deny them the safety of their stand on the ground of unshakable, unchangeable, and unconditioned propositions, and their claim that these propositions are correct, complete, efficacious, and triumphant, *whatever* the historical realities around them. Many at the Council seemed to be afraid of history. They preferred the bright, clear world of their truths. They saw danger in admitting that the formulation of these truths was conditioned by historical events, and that their efficacy (not their truth) was to be judged by their success in the actual world, not by their coherence in a book or a system. Pope John's twin principles, in short, called for a shift in theological method which many found frightening. *"Fratres, caveamus!"* a certain cardinal pleaded with his brother bishops on one occasion at the second session: "Brothers, let us beware!"

II

The theology which has been entrenched for the last four hundred years, then, might fairly be described as "non-historical" or even "anti-historical." It favors speculation which is not called to the bar of historical fact, past or present; moreover, it often seems to fear principles which would make it face such a bar. It sometimes discourages speculation altogether, and confines itself to making commentaries on a theoretical structure once built up, in the late Middle Ages, in the past. It would be fair to name this theology "anti-historical orthodoxy," because it defends a system of propositions as orthodox, while refusing to commit itself to the work of investigating that system's historical justification, or making it relevant to the historical realities of the present. It would be fair to call it "anti-historical orthodoxy," but a more neutral designation is simply "non-historical." For it defends an orthodoxy suspended, as it were, outside of history, in midair.

How did such a non-historical orthodoxy come to get its grips on the Roman Catholic Church? That question we must leave to historians of an earlier time, since our province is the history of our own. But we would be remiss in our efforts to untangle the meaning of the Second Vatican Council if we did not attempt, at least, to describe the complex of attitudes which have made, and make, non-historical orthodoxy attractive to many minds of the present. The force of its viewpoint is very strong; once stand on its ground and accept its perspective, and ways to escape it are very few indeed. Its inner coherence and power encourage its proponents in the view that they are right and all others are wrong; they can *see* the connection of every small part within their system, and any novelty sets off alarms that speedily catch their attention. What those outside the system say seems, by comparison, fragmentary, unsystematic, unrelated to central propositions, and even noxious; they must regard it as trivial and futile, or divergent and alarming. What is not harmonious to their system jars their ears; "offensive to pious ears," they say. Since they believe their system to be established on central, irreversible principles, they do not scruple to make disharmonies on the periphery, if they become too loud, to cease. They believe their system to be valid without any need for historical justification; like Leibniz and Spinoza, they begin outside of history. Within their system, they are imperturbable and triumphant. No one outside it can, in their eyes, render the Church half the insight, coherence, and faithfulness their system can. Those who do not recognize the value of their system must lack logic, the taste for clarity, or good will. The system, to initiates, is overpoweringly self-evident.

What are the ingredients of this system? Lord Acton, describing the intellectual situation as he knew it almost a hundred years ago, is of immense help in the search for historical perspective. The students of the men he describes, after all, were teaching in Rome when many of those who are now Council Fathers studied there. Several of his essays are indispensable for understanding non-historical orthodoxy, particularly the essays "Ultramontanism," "The First Vatican Council," "The Munich Congress," "The Political System of the Popes," "The Catholic Press," "The Roman Inquisition." [3] Acton is not always impartial; neither is he always delicate. But he is unfailingly incisive, perceptive, and broad of vision. Cardinal Newman was equally depressed by the intellectual climate he found in Rome just after his conversion. In later times, Newman wrote of Roman theology with more gentleness than Acton; but then Acton was a man of action and a layman, not so given to the caution of clerical speech. As a consequence, his effect on his time may not have been so great as Newman's; but his descriptions of the situation now seem all the more accurate. Indeed, to read Acton's essays on the theological currents of his day is to read, in prophecy and figure, the problems of our own. At times, one could believe him to be writing at the Second, rather than the First Vatican Council.

Lord Acton was exceedingly hard on the entrenched non-historical orthodoxy. He constantly described that school as afraid; as, in the end, intellectually lazy; as isolated from contact with unbelievers; as jealous of its authority; as unscrupulous in its treatment of other schools; as fearful of sources of evidence outside its own system. He did not think that that orthodoxy, historically, represented the full belief of the Church. He described a different kind of loyalty to the Church, which is based on scrupulous adherence to fact, a kind of loyalty in which religion and love for fact are one. He espoused that admirable ultramontanism which "signifies a habit of intellect carrying forward the inquiries and supplementing the work of authority."[4] He distinguished between the mere present interests of the Church and the truth which the Church serves: "The Catholic is subject to the correction of the Church when he is in contradiction with her truth, not when he stands in the way of her interests."[5]

"From the beginning of the Church," he wrote, "it has been the law of her nature that the truths which prove themselves the legitimate fruits of her doctrine have had to make their slow way upwards through a phalanx of hostile habits and traditions, and to be rescued not only from open enemies but also from friendly hands that are not worthy to defend them."[6]

In "Ultramontanism," he described a situation not unlike that which obtained in our own day, before Pope John's Council: "With scarcely one exception, all those who were most eminent in religious science have been denounced, by men not less zealous and devout than themselves, as the corrupters of doctrine and enemies of the Church; and the distance between the two parties was such as to justify a doubt as to their agreement in the same faith or in the same morality." He went on to name names: "This persecution of those who really advanced religious knowledge is, on the one hand, a natural and direct consequence of that common spirit which manifests itself in different ways in the philosophy of Kleutgen and Clemens, the politics of Donoso Cortés, the polemics of Veuillot, the educational theories of Gaume, and the historical method of Rohrbacher and Guéranger, and, on the other, the most characteristic symptom of the present condition of the Church."[7] At this period of his life, though he later became much more discouraged, he wrote: "These, however, are difficulties in the way of improvement, which eminent men are able to overcome; and it is well that they should confront the obstacles which they alone can overcome."[8]

Again and again, Lord Acton protested that the thinkers he was opposing were afraid, and afraid because isolated from rational intercourse with those who did not share their beliefs. He describes the habit of Catholic polemicists, who, from some unjust attacks, had come to find it difficult to believe that statements against the Church can be sincere. "It is scarcely possible for Catholics to avoid feeling aversion and contempt for men whom they conceive to be wilfully distorting truth; and therefore, instead of confining themselves to the refutation of falsehood, which they are persuaded their opponent does not desire, they endeavor to expose his iniquity. This temper of mind was gradually transferred from controversy with aliens to discussions among Catholics, where there was the new element of insubordination, to which the origin of errors might be attributed." [9] A moment later, he analyzes some of the sources of this habit of mind: "In some places, the want of that forbearance which public assemblies often engender between men subject in common to a local special disciplinary system; in others, the terror which anticipated or the temper which followed great social convulsions; in others, the extreme fierceness or perfidy of an infidel press." [10]

Lord Acton saw two erring parties in the Church of his day: one which was willing to sacrifice truth on behalf of religion, and one which was willing to make of some scientific opinion the arbiter of doctrine.[11] The one violated basic morality, the other dogma. He showed that the true antithesis to "the unscrupulous school," [12] the first erring party, was not a preference for the latest established scientific opinion. There is no need to choose between being "loyal" and being a modernist. There is no need to subject doctrine to scientific opinion, in order to be faithful to scientific conscience. He insisted that "the highest intellectual development" of the Catholic mind demanded a union of strict scientific integrity with a deep religious spirit. He deplored the tactic of defending the Church against every uncomfortable fact, by any device, according to the theory that "there is but one thing needful; and all facts and all opinions are worthless except to minister to the salvation of men and the promotion of religion." [13] Of men who held such a theory, he said: "Those defenders were not conscious traitors, and honestly thought their own cause that of the Church." [14] Even the best-informed Catholics seemed habitually afraid of giving scandal, and too circumspect to question the limits of authority; [15] thus they, too, were drawn into complicity with the school of fear.

The rise of this school, Acton judges, "depended, first, on the low ebb of scientific knowledge, and on its open hostility to religion, and, secondly, on the absence of any literary co-operation of Catholics with Protestants. Among its leaders there were men of great virtues and talents, and at least one man of genius; but there is not one to whom secular learning is really indebted." [16] The men of this school renounced modern scientific studies, in favor of commentaries upon their own, as they thought, completed system. "The want of contact with men who believed in other religions left them in ignorance of real difficulties and of their true solution. To the opposite circumstance of familiarity with non-Catholic science we trace . . . the highest intellectual development of the Catholic system." [17] The school of fear overlooked the discipline required by science; it insisted, instead, on the discipline of docility to its authorities.[18] "A particular suspicion rested on history because, as the study of facts, it was less amenable to authority and less controllable by interest than philosophical speculation. In consequence, partly of the denial of historical certainty, and partly of the fear of it, the historical study of Dogma in its original sources was abandoned, and the dialectical systematic treatment preferred." He continues: "Theology became almost entirely scholastic. It was regarded as complete, not susceptible of development, looking backwards and not forwards, more interested in the vindication of authoritative names than in the cultivation of those original studies which are needed for its advance." [19] "The defense of a thesis is easier than the discovery of truth." [20]

The fundamental moving force of this movement, "which for a time had its centre at Rome," is the "dread of an outward independent criterion." [21] The school was convinced of "the weakness of human reason and the malice of the outer world." [22] In its effort, then, to escape the discipline of science and the need for hard, risky work, it thrashed about to find a safe, easy criterion of truth. "Divines of this school, after preferring the Church to the Bible, preferred the modern Church to the ancient, and ended by sacrificing both to the Pope." [23] But it was not exactly the Pope they trusted; Acton, no doubt too bitterly, accused this school of coming closer and closer to disregarding history and making its own present convictions the measure of the faith: "According to Petavius, the general belief of Catholics at a given time is the true work of God, and of higher authority than all antiquity and all the Fathers. Scripture may be silent, and tradition contradictory, but the Church is independent of both. Any doctrine which Catholic divines commonly assert, without proof, to be revealed, must be taken as revealed. The testimony of Rome, as the only remaining apostolic Church, is equivalent to an unbroken chain of tradition. [Acton here cites Bellarmine in a footnote.] In this way, after Scripture had been subjugated, tradition itself was deposed; and the constant belief of the past yielded to the general conviction of the present." [24]

Moreover, in Acton's time, this school did not stop at controlling doctrine, but used its system of convictions even in the suppression or the disregarding of facts.[25] In another place, Acton cites several egregious instances of the mishandling of facts by Schütz, Rohrbacher, Audin, Nicolas, de Maistre, Balmez, Guéranger, Perrone.[26] Cardinal Newman, in his famous letter to the Duke of Norfolk in answer to Gladstone's attack on the Vatican decrees, shows how a scientific historian answers the charge that Pope Honorius, who was condemned by the Sixth Ecumenical Council, had not spoken heresy as a Pope, but in his capacity as a private bishop; but Acton relates how Cardinal Bona advised, in Rome, suppressing the historical text which showed that Popes themselves had for centuries condemned Pope Honorius in their professions of faith.[27] Acton describes the type of loyalty required: "It is the duty of the son to cover the shame of his father; and the Catholic owes it to the Church to defend her against every adverse fact as he would defend the honor of his mother." [28] "Assured that nothing injurious to the Church can be true," [29] he will appeal, against plain fact, to "a higher order of truth." [30] "First, it was held, the interests of religion, which are opposed to the study of history, require that precautions should be taken to make it innocuous where it cannot be quite suppressed. If it is lawful to conceal facts or statements, it is equally right to take out their sting when they must be brought forward." [31] Yet it is well, again and again, to recall that this system makes good men its victims: "Those defenders were not conscious traitors, and honestly thought their own cause that of the Church." [32]

But what, then, did they imagine the Church to be? As we have already quoted, the Church had been shrunken up, in their own eyes, from Scripture and the ancient Church to an ever narrower circle of truth: their own system of non-historical orthodoxy, their own present convictions. At the fulcrum point of this system, they said, was the Pope. "*Ego, ut ingenue fatear, plus uni summo pontifici crederem, in his, quae fidei mysterium tangunt, quam mille Augustinis, Hieronymis, Gregoriis,*" announced Bishop Cornelius Massus at the Council of Trent. "I confess, in all simplicity, that I would rather believe what a single pope has to say on those things which touch the mystery of faith than a thousand Augustines, Jeromes, or Gregories." [33] And an Italian theologian wrote in a textbook about the time of the First Vatican Council: "Catholics don't have to be concerned about the critical study of the Bible or hermeneutics. . . . They already have, I insist, a building absolute and perfect, in whose possession they may stand safely and securely." [34] It was seriously believed that the late medieval scholastics had said all there was to say about the content of Revelation; it remained only to preserve intact and to comment upon what they had done. Lord Acton quotes the comment of a Professor Kuhn: "If we believe the modern restorers of Scholasticism, the older divines taught with one voice exactly the same doctrine on all the chief points of science which they now proclaim as perfect wisdom and genuine Catholic science." With this "wholly unhistorical view," Professor Kuhn continues, they "make their own intellectual work much too easy, and that of others unnecessarily difficult." [35]

Afraid of modern society, seeing the pillars on which centuries of speculation had rested (the spurious "donation of Constantine," for example, and the fictitious "Pseudo-Areopagite") knocked by historical research from under them, many Catholics sought for some absolute on which to rest their faith, in religion as in politics. [36] Society was becoming more complex; the professions of law, medicine, philosophy, art, and politics were moving out from the easier relationships of simpler times. Instead of embracing the new world with optimism or even calm confidence, many Catholics tried to fix the Church in the relationships of the medieval world, or even the sixteenth century. [37] They withdrew their hopes from the laymen living in the world and devoted with professional integrity to their secular disciplines, and even from the priests who until this time had been closer to the people, even, than to their bishops. They drew in their hopes even from the bishops, and founded them upon one rock and it almost solely: the Pope. "The laity had been gradually compelled to give up its rights to the priesthood," Acton writes in describing the criticisms leveled against the nineteenth century system by the Catholic Congress of Hungary, meeting on October 17, 1869, "the priests to the bishops, and the bishops to the popes. Hungary undertook to redress this process, and to correct centralized absolutism by self-government." [38]

With their back turned against historical studies, and their loyalty fixed in one focal point, the proponents of the school of fear had to justify the great weight of hope they were resting on this fulcrum. They were led to insist that the Inquisition was consistent with Catholicism.[39] They came, increasingly, to be defending an abstraction: it was not this or that historical Pope they trusted in, but the papacy; it was not this or that Pope whose authority they accepted, but the papacy's. But what is the papacy? The Holy See. And who is the permanent Holy See, while Popes come and go? The Roman Curia.

"The Council of Trent," Acton wrote in one of his acerbic moments, having hoped that the First Vatican Council would rectify the pessimism of three hundred years, "impressed on the Church the stamp of an intolerant age, and perpetuated by its decrees the spirit of an austere immorality. The ideas embodied in the Roman Inquisition became characteristic of a system which obeyed expediency by submitting to indefinite modification, but underwent no change of principle. Three centuries have so changed the world that the maxims with which the Church arrested her decline now arrest her progress. To break effectually with that tradition and eradicate its influence, nothing less is required than an authority equal to that by which it is opposed." [40]

III

The First Vatican Council, under Providence, did not succeed in modifying the Roman system. But, as if offering a rock in the storms the next ninety years were to bring, it succeeded in focusing the attention of the Catholic world upon a line of extraordinary Popes. Before marching soldiers closed that Council in 1870, seven hundred Council Fathers had approved the decree stating that the Roman Pontiff, of himself and without the consent of the bishops, could in matters of faith and morals, when speaking formally to the universal Church, speak infallibly. At the time, the decision seemed to non-Catholics preposterous, the last boasting gasp of a decaying Church. To many Catholics, the decree at first seemed untimely; but by far the largest number received it in peace. Gradually, though some renounced the faith, and others were afraid that the narrowest minds would seize on this decree and pervert it, even acute critics like Acton came to see that the decree was susceptible of a moderate and strictly limiting interpretation. The Pope might witness to the faith of the Church infallibly, but only under stringent conditions. The Pope became, then, a clear focal point for the authentic voice of Catholic faith; and the conditions under which he could express the formal belief of the Church were very narrowly marked.

In the years that followed, the Roman Pontiffs, together with a growing band of intellectuals in Germany, France, the Lowlands, Italy, England, and America, formed, as it were, an unspoken alliance. They generated a renaissance of Catholic intellectual and social life. Pope Leo XIII, in 1891, issued his famous encyclical letter *Rerum Novarum* on "The Condition of the Working Class." He also encouraged a renewal in Catholic theology and philosophy, through a consideration of the historical sources of Catholic thought.

Pope Pius X gave an impetus to liturgical reform; however, the extreme severity of his condemnation of "modernism" in 1908, though some statement was necessary, seemed to uproot many healthy plants together with the tares. It kept Catholic theology from significant creative growth for more than a generation. Thus, on the one hand, non-historical orthodoxy remained supreme within the central organs of the Church, both in Rome and in most local dioceses.

On the other hand, artists, novelists, philosophers, theologians, historians, politicians—men in all walks of life—were creating new forms of Catholicism in the world. From time to time, subsequent Popes gave an impetus to their work: in 1931, Pope Pius XI recalled Leo XIII's *Rerum Novarum* with a sequel, *Quadragesimo Anno* on "The Reconstruction of the Social Order." He wrote another encyclical on Catholic Action, and another on marriage. He concluded negotiations with Mussolini on the papal states and the status of the Vatican. Pius XII at times continued the movement of Catholic participation in the history of our time—in his famous Christmas letters on peace, the social order, and democracy, and in his charter for modern biblical studies, *Divino Afflante Spiritu*—and at times was almost as severe on intellectual matters, e. g., in *Humani Generis*, as Pius X had been.

It was thus an uneasy Church which Pope John XXIII inherited, a Church powerful in the world and yet widely held to be irrelevant to humanity's main concerns. For almost a hundred years, the Popes had been good Popes, without scandal. They showed extraordinary energy for creative measures. They were often far in advance of local bishops, and often far in advance of the Roman Curia. The Church had new energies, and indeed new continents of thoughtful and industrious peoples. But the structures of the Church still seemed geared to the world of the western Mediterranean basin, the social situation of preceding centuries, and the non-historical orthodoxy of the schools. To many inside the Church, these structures seemed like massive walls inhibiting creative growth, and falsifying the position of the Church in the world. They were prepared for many generations of quiet labor, before their cause of renewal and reform could gradually emerge as successful.

When Pope John XXIII announced that he would call a Council, many of these struggling ones were pessimistic. They were afraid that their strength was insufficient, while the walls around them seemed to be too massive. They were afraid that the forces of non-historical orthodoxy would, once again, as under Pius X and Pius XII, mow new growths of weeds and wheat together, with great severity. Creative intellectual growth needs elbow room; the speedy condemnation of "error" and the heaping of suspicion on men whose methodology is different from that of non-historical orthodoxy kept too high a proportion of Catholic studies thin, timid, and repetitive. Often those who seemed to be doing most for Catholic scholarship seemed the most harassed. If one did not stay within the system of non-historical orthodoxy, one was vulnerable at any moment.

How would the bishops react when they came to Rome? There were almost four times as many of them in 1962 as in 1869, some twenty-seven hundred against seven hundred, from dioceses in America, Africa, and Asia which did not exist in 1869. But, before 1962, there was little to suggest that these swollen numbers of bishops, from all the great continents, were anything but proponents of that non-historical orthodoxy which almost everywhere seemed to dominate the seminaries and the colleges. If many members of the Roman Curia seemed nervous at the prospect of two thousand bishops descending on Rome with their theologians, others outside the Curia were afraid that the Council would only succeed in fixing the minds of the Council Fathers even more firmly in the non-historical orthodoxy, Latin social views, and centralized structures long entrenched in the Church.

It is a mistake, of course, to describe the Second Vatican Council as a struggle between the bishops of the world and the Curia. Some from within the Curia do not share the non-historical views largely represented there. Many bishops from other lands learned non-historical orthodoxy in the seminary, and still support it. Moreover, as events in the second session showed, other bishops fundamentally retained the views of non-historical orthodoxy even when their great practical sense led them to vote for measures of renewal and reform. Many, full of good will, learned the catch phrases and jargon of other theologies than they had learned in the seminary, but had not the time to think through all of their theology anew. As a consequence, curious self-contradictions and misuses of newly acquired terms occurred. Some great intellectual conversions were recorded. Some bishops, particularly among the Americans, insisted that there were not two "parties" at the Council and that many bishops were voting now "yes," now "no," as each issue recommended itself to them on its merits. Perhaps, then, for most of the bishops it was not the fundamental theological struggle but less speculative considerations which weighed most in their thinking. Still, the fact that so many men, of mature age and high station, were willing to change their views was inspiring in the extreme.

IV

For the Second Vatican Council is characterized by the depth of the theological conflict in its ranks. The issue is not exactly one of Curia versus the world, or Latin bishops versus Northern bishops, or traditionalists versus innovators; though cultural and temperamental factors have played their part in the great theological differences. The fundamental struggle at the Second Vatican Council is between non-historical orthodoxy and other theologies. These latter theologies claim, each in its way, to throw a new light on the meaning of the Word given the Church. None is, or pretends to be, exclusive of other theologies. None denies the good services provided the Church by non-historical orthodoxy. But each demands of non-historical orthodoxy the right to exist; and it is precisely that right which non-historical orthodoxy, in fact and perhaps in theory, is constantly threatening.

Non-historical orthodoxy tolerates no equals; is jealous of its own authority; is tigerish in attacking every possible obstacle to its own freedom and autocracy. It pretends to stand, not only as one theology among many, but as the *"aedificium absolutum sane ac perfectum,"* the wholly perfect and absolute expression of faith, in which it suffices to rest firmly and securely. In non-historical theology, original research is vain; the preparation of a more elaborate commentary is scholarship; the fluent comparison of accepted texts is erudition; the discovery of exact synonyms for what one has been taught is originality; the proposal of a resolution for a textual contradiction is speculation. The orders of speculation and practice are so far distinguished that one is not directly responsible to the other. What is said in the "thesis" need not be realized in the "hypothesis"; the "principle" may have as many "exceptions" as "applications"; the "essence" may not be available in any "instance." For non-historical orthodoxy, one needs to be able to operate in two worlds: that of logic, words, principles, and abstractions; and that of practicality, realities, facts, and concrete instances. Besides, one needs to build a bridge between the two. One needs to formulate "rules of thumb" and "directories" for applying the ideas of one world to the realities of the other.

Non-historical orthodoxy is, therefore, a cumbersome way of thinking. It seems to encourage intellectual duality: one has to think twice, once for theory and once for practice. Sometimes facts do not fit theory; what, then, shall one say? When the order of practice contradicts the order of theory, on which level should one speak?

Moreover, non-historical orthodoxy encourages, or rather insists upon, the view that "truth is unchanging." But it does not seem to notice that languages change, that intellectual viewpoints and methods change, that new facts (even about ancient happenings) are discovered, that men's manner of understanding even the same sentences change. What, then, about truth remains unchanging? The answer differs with each "truth" that is in question. "The sun moves around the earth" once seemed to be a fixed truth, as fixed as the earth it described. "Mary was immaculately conceived" once seemed a matter of theological uncertainty. "The donation of Constantine" once seemed a fundamental historical fact. "Christ is consubstantial with the Father" once seemed a verbal innovation. "The bishops share in the universal pastorship with the Pope by divine right" even now seems to some false and to others a matter that is and always has been true. The sentence "Truth is unchanging," in other words, is a fog which tells us nothing of the hard objects, the "truths," it is meant to describe. It is a misleading expression. "Truth" may be unchanging, whatever it is when thus considered in the abstract. But, in the concrete, men's struggle to understand is not static and unchanging. Men's point of view, experience, conceptions, and language change. Men's grasp of "truths" therefore changes, too.

Finally, non-historical orthodoxy likes the world of principles, ideals, theories, platitudes, perfections. So long as a matter is understood juridically—in the purity of its logic and its connection with principles—you may, then, in practice, use casuistry to meet hard facts. A certain unscrupulousness in the concrete may thus be combined with the most delicate sense of principles. Non-historical orthodoxy encourages the moralizer, the preacher, the rhetorician in us. It does not encourage getting down to cases and getting on with concrete proposals. Non-historical orthodoxy encourages lovely images and elevated sentiments; it finds the actual world bewitching, dangerous, and "dirty." It thus combines triumphalism about the glories of the Church with pessimism about the contemporary world. Non-historical orthodoxy, therefore, encourages loyalty to the ideal Church, without worrying about how to make the actual Church efficacious in the present world. It visualizes the Church as an anvil on which the ill-willed world rains its unavailing blows; the Church is always triumphant, without moving. The order of fact, history, concrete reality is the enemy; the Church must try to remain in the pure world—the pure world of irrelevance. Men are to blame, real, concrete, historical men, for not lifting their minds to the loftier realm where non-historical orthodoxy lies.

The bewitching feature of non-historical orthodoxy is that it apes the Catholic doctrine of the supernatural and the natural. It aligns the supernatural with the world of logic, juridical clarity, order, perfection. It aligns the natural with the world of history, individuality, difference, change. When it urges men, "Lift up your minds," it means that they should shift their mental focus from the real world they know to the ideal world where all is serenity, triumph, beauty, and holy sentiment. It does not mean that they should reflect that just as they are, in their individuality, in their particular circumstances, in the uncertainties and risks of their personal situation, they are sons of God. It encourages them to retreat from the real world, instead of to be more faithful to it. It encourages them to treat it as a temptation or a defilement or a punishment, rather than as a moment-by-moment conversation with Providence, in which His will and His love are steadily revealed. It encourages a conscience formed around abstractions or general laws, rather than a conscience formed around personal and concrete decisions. As a consequence, it makes the supernatural world appear to be an artificial, abstract, distant world, instead of the world of sun, moon, stars, and wind into which Christ was born, and which He redeemed. It complicates and falsifies man's approach to God, by introducing the confusing, dualistic philosophy of two worlds, one supposedly ideal and the other supposedly ugly, into our reflections on our faith. There is only one world, fallen and redeemed. Each object, event, and person that touches our life is a grace. "Everything," as Bernanos said, "is grace." It is possible to be very simple in one's belief, and very direct, as Pope John XXIII understood.

Perhaps we have said enough to show what is at stake in the Second Vatican Council. Theologies alive to history, formed by history, loving, respecting, and criticizing history, are struggling to find a right to exist within Roman Catholicism. Each of them offers its light for the illumination of a faith greater than they, a faith as great as the Word Himself. One theology, long entrenched in the Church, pretends to exclusive rights over the faith. The men who serve it are convinced that if they are defeated the faith is defeated with them. Men who support the other theologies believe that Catholic faith is greater than the one theology thinks.

Those who like safety ask, where will the multiplication of theologies lead? Try to box the Holy Spirit, or measure His boundaries. The school of fear has taken on itself an impossible task, which with all the suppression in the world it could not achieve.

The opposing theologies, however, have not pretended to have an exclusive right to truth and so, perhaps, are not overburdened by the impossible. The task they undertake is difficult, but asks no more of men than dedication and hard work. As we began with Acton's description of the entrenched theology, perhaps we can end with his description of the theology to come:

". . . Catholics can no longer shut themselves out from contact with the world, nor shelter themselves in ignorance. When all opinions are perpetually canvassed in a literature over which no authority and no consideration for others has any control, Catholics cannot help attempting to solve the problems which all the world is discussing. The point is, that while they solve them religiously, they should likewise solve them scientifically. . . ." [41] Having defined this "double task," Acton then describes his "Catholic in the highest sense of Catholicism": he is "one who makes no parade of his religion; who meets his adversaries on grounds which they understand and acknowledge; who appeals to no extrinsic considerations—benevolence, or force, or interest, or artifice—in order to establish his point; who discusses each topic on its intrinsic merits—answering the critic by a severer criticism, the metaphysician by a closer reasoning, the historian by a deeper learning, the politician by sounder politics and indifference itself by a purer impartiality. In all these subjects . . . [he] discovers a point pre-eminently Catholic, but also pre-eminently intellectual and true. . . ."

Lord Acton, of course, does not envision an *"aedificium absolutum sane ac perfectum"* for his Catholic. He writes: "Not that his labor is an easy one, or one being capable of being brought to a close. Each generation has to carry it forward. None can complete it; for there will always be some progress to be made, some new discoveries to adopt and assimilate, some discord to harmonize, some half-truth which has become an error to lop away. It is a process never to be terminated, till God has finished the work of educating the human race to know Him and to love Him."

This is a work, he adds, "which no Catholic can deem either impracticable or unnecessary. It is not an idle enterprise: if we seek, we shall find. Religion can be made intelligible if we take the pains to make it so. . . . Authority may put itself in opposition to its own code; but the code [will then be] vindicated by the defeat of authority. . . ."

The Second Vatican Council is trying to come to grips with the world in which the Church of the twentieth century finds itself. It is trying to insert the Church back into the center of historical life, with respect for the moment of history in which it acts. There are those who are afraid of this venture; and the story of the second session of the Vatican Council is largely a story of the struggle of these well-placed, powerful few against the majority. It is a story all the more dramatic because each side believes that it is right.

NOTES

1. Cf. "Newman on Nicaea," *Theological Studies*, XXI (1960), pp. 444–53.
2. Bernard J. F. Lonergan, S.J., who has already laid the empirical groundwork and tackled the philosophical questions involved, in *Insight: A Study of Human Understanding* (New York, Longmans, Green, 1957; 1958).
3. Cf. *Essays on Church and State*, ed. by Douglas Woodruff (London, Hollis and Carter, 1952), and *History of Freedom and Other Essays*, ed. by Figgis and Laurence (London, Macmillan, 1922).

4. "Ultramontanism," *Essays on Church and State, ibid.,* p. 66.
5. *Ibid.,* p. 82.
6. Quoted by Douglas Woodruff in his introduction, *ibid.,* p. 33.
7. "Ultramontanism," *ibid.,* p. 64.
8. *Ibid.,* p. 65.
9. *Ibid.,* p. 63.
10. *Ibid.,* p. 64.
11. *Ibid.,* p. 65.
12. *Ibid.,* p. 60
13. *Ibid.,* p. 53.
14. *Ibid.,* p. 54.
15. *Ibid.,* p. 83.
16. *Ibid.,* p. 66.
17. *Ibid.*
18. *Ibid.* Cf. pp. 79, 50.
19. *Ibid.,* p. 50.
20. *Ibid.,* p. 42.
21. *Ibid.,* p. 50.
22. *Ibid.*
23. *History of Freedom and Other Essays, op. cit.,* p. 514.
24. *Ibid.*
25. *Ibid.,* p. 515 f.
26. *Essays on Church and State, op. cit.,* pp. 54–61.
27. *Newman and Gladstone,* ed. by Alvan Ryan (University of Notre Dame Press, 1962), p. 179; *History of Freedom and Other Essays, op. cit.,* p. 516.
28. *Essays on Church and State, op. cit.,* p. 53.
29. *Ibid.*
30. *Ibid.,* p. 51.
31. *Ibid.*
32. *Ibid.,* p. 54.
33. Quoted in *History of Freedom and Other Essays, op. cit.,* p. 515.
34. *Ibid.,* 514.
35. *Essays on Church and State, op. cit.,* p. 76. From *Katholische Dogmatik,* i, 916.
36. Acton consistently notes the uneasy correlation between attitudes in religion and in politics. Cf., e.g., *Essays on Church and State, op. cit.,* p. 50 and *passim.*
37. *Ibid.,* p. 77, where Acton quotes Bishop Ketteler, and p. 78, Eckstein.
38. *History of Freedom and Other Essays, op. cit.,* p. 510.
39. *Ibid.,* p. 520.
40. *Ibid.,* pp. 493–4.
41. *Essays on Church and State, op. cit.,* pp. 83–85, is the source for this and the remaining quotes from Acton in this chapter.

II

A PLACE FOR PROPHECY

6

THE POPE'S OPENING ADDRESS

I

THE EVENING BEFORE THE COUNCIL was one of Rome's most fragile, perfect ones. St. Peter's lay in the light of a silent three-quarter moon; water rose and fell in the twin fountains embraced by the colonnades. At eleven o'clock, the windows of the Pope's apartment blinked into yellow light. Those walking in the square wondered how late the Pope would be working on his speech for the morrow, and what he would say.

Early the next morning, Sunday, September 29, members of the press fought their way through the shoving, elbowing people at the doorway far around to the rear of St. Peter's. It did not help matters that they had press cards and special tickets. Many of those pushing and twisting toward the door, particularly the Italian nuns, had no tickets at all. One American girl took a vicious elbow in the ribs from a nun: her baptism by fire in Italy. The journalists were squeezed through the funnel of a narrow two-person doorway by a crowd twelve persons thick.

At length, they sat on the reserved, green felt-covered benches only six or seven rows from the Bernini altar at which the Pope would sit. Standing, they could see down the long nave where the tiers of seats for the Council Fathers rose. The chairs of the bishops were in green; red curtains dropped from the arches overhead, cutting off the side aisles. The Council Fathers were gradually assembling in their white surplices and red mozzettas: black faces and yellow, old and young. The Protestant observers sat in the circle nearest to the papal throne.

Pope Paul had decided there would be no formal procession for the opening. When he entered the basilica, to the applause of the bishops and the visitors, he entered on foot, raising his arms in warm greeting. He did not enter with the usual papal pomp, nor did he bless the bishops; he came as a brother. The Mass, however, celebrated by the dean of the cardinals, Cardinal Tisserant, seemed more of a public spectacle than a religious observance. Only at rare moments—for the recitation of the creed, for example—were all invited to participate; and in those moments, emotions pent up, they did so lustily. Nor was there permission for laymen to complete the sacrifice by going to communion. The Mass was a courtly ceremony, suitable for kings.

After the Mass, through which he prayed from his kneeler, the Pope recited the oath against modernism, a juridical, polemical oath that seemed to unwind the clock by fifty years; not in its doctrinal substance, but in its tone. That done, the Pope sat again on his throne clad in white. While an aide held the microphone near his lips, and another took from his hands each page of his discourse as he read it, he began to read with high emotion. The Pope spoke with such intensity that one knew he had struggled with the talk; one knew he had wanted it to count. It was a talk worthy of Pope John. It was to dominate the first part of the second session, as Pope John's opening discourse of October 11, 1962, dominated the first session.

"Greetings to you, brothers!" was the refrain of the first part of his talk. And already in the second paragraph the Pope was revealing his own sentiments about the major problem of the second session. "Here, around him who is last in time and merit, but identified with the first Apostle in authority and mission, the Successor of Peter, you are gathered, venerable brothers, you too apostles, descended from the apostolic college and its authentic successor. . . ." A moment later he was saying: "The Lord is Our Witness when, at this first moment of the second session of the great Synod, We declare to you that in Our mind there is no intention of human predominance, no jealousy of exclusive power, but only desire and the will to carry out the divine mandate which makes Us, of you and among you, brothers, the Supreme Shepherd . . ."

"We are indeed now in the pontifical office," he said, recalling his election just three months previously; and that recollection led him to:

Our most beloved John XXIII. To all of us who had the good fortune to see him seated in this same place, his name brings memories of his lovable and priestly presence as he opened the first session of this Second Vatican Council on October 11 of last year, with that speech which to the Church and the world seemed like a prophetic voice for our century. The speech still echoes in our minds, pointing out to the Council the path it has to take, thereby freeing us from all doubt and weariness which we may encounter along the difficult road we have undertaken. O dear and venerated Pope John, may gratitude and praise be rendered to you for having resolved—doubtless under divine inspiration—to convoke this Council in order to open to the Church new horizons, and to tap the fresh spring water of the doctrine and grace of Christ Our Lord and let it flow over the earth. As if by divining heavenly counsels and penetrating into the dark and tormented needs of the modern age, you have gathered the broken thread of the First Vatican Council, and by that very fact you have banished the fear wrongly deducted from that Council, that the supreme powers conferred by Christ on the Roman Pontiff to govern and vivify the Church, were sufficient, without the assistance of the Ecumenical Councils. You have summoned your brothers in the episcopate, the successors of the Apostles . . . to feel united with the Pope in a single body . . . that the sacred deposit of Christian doctrine be guarded and taught more effectively.

Pope Paul then recalled Pope John's additional aim, "more urgent and at this time more salutary—the pastoral aim." He quoted John: "nor is the primary purpose of our work to discuss one article or another of the fundamental doctrine of the Church . . . [but] to consider how to expound Church teaching in a manner determined by the times." Pope Paul elaborated:

> You have awakened in the conscience of the magisterium of the Church the conviction that Christian doctrine is not merely truth to be investigated by reason illuminated by faith, but teaching that can generate life and action; and that the authority of the Church is not merely limited to condemning contrary errors, but extends to the communication of positive and vital doctrine, the source of its fecundity. The teaching office of the Church, which is neither wholly theoretical nor wholly negative, must in the Council manifest ever more the life-giving power of the message of Christ Who said: "The words I have been speaking to you are spirit and life."

The Pope's cry was: "Let us, therefore, brothers, go forward!" He asked them what was their starting place, their way, and their goal, and to all three he answered: Christ.

> Oh! Let this Council have the full awareness of this relationship be-
> tween ourselves and the blessed Jesus—a relationship which is at once
> multiple and unique, fixed and stimulating, mysterious and crystal-
> clear, binding and beatifying—between this holy Church which we
> constitute and Christ from Whom we come, by Whom we live and
> toward Whom we tend. . . .

The Pope called Christ by the name dear to the East, *Pantocrator*,
"the maker and ruler of the world," for in Eastern theology Christ is
seen as a cosmic figure, the pattern in which worldly history was
conceived; the West has preferred the equally biblical but legal image
of Redeemer.

> We recognize Ourselves in the figure of Our Predecessor, Honorius III,
> who is represented in the splendid mosaic in the apse of the Basilica
> of St. Paul's as a humble worshiper, tiny and prostrate, kissing the feet
> of a Christ of gigantic dimensions, who as a kingly teacher dominates
> and blesses the people gathered in the Basilica, which symbolizes the
> Church.

The Pope, his voice taut and intense, then urged that the Council
start with this vision of Christ in thinking of the Church which
Christ "is forming by means of faith and the sacraments, as generations of mankind succeed one another—a Church which is spiritual
and visible, fraternal and hierarchical, temporal today and eternal
tomorrow." He added: "If we keep our attention on Christ, then we
shall better be able to understand the main objectives of this Council."
Of these, he listed four: "the self-knowledge, or if you like, the self-
awareness of the Church; the reform of the Church; Christian unity; the
dialogue of the Church with the contemporary world." He then listed
some of the images by which Holy Scripture describes the Church:

> the building raised up by Christ, the house of God, the temple and
> tabernacle of God, His people, His flock, His vine, His field, His city,
> the pillar of truth and, finally, the Bride of Christ, His Mystical
> Body . . . the Church has come to see herself as a historic, visible
> and hierarchically organized society, animated by a mysterious prin-
> ciple of life.

II

Quietly, Pope Paul made a break with non-historical orthodoxy.
Far from taking past statements of the Church about herself as frozen

footprints, he took them as historically conditioned and partial insights, which always need to be penetrated more deeply and understood more fully. In the past, he said, the Church has said about herself only "part" of what must be said.

> The celebrated encyclical of Pius XII, Mystici Corporis, has in part answered the Church's longing to express her nature in a full doctrinal form, but has also served to spur her to give herself a more exhaustive definition. The First Vatican Council treated of the subject, and many external influences have caused it to receive attention from students, both within the Church and without. Among these influences are the intensification of social life in temporal matters, the development of communications, and the need to judge the various Christian denominations according to the true and univocal conception found in divine revelation.

The Pope went on to reinforce his conception of doctrinal development. He did not conceive the Church as a timeless, unchanging, juridical "perfect society"; he insisted on a living, historical conception.

> It should not come as a surprise that, after twenty centuries in which both the Catholic Church and the other Christian bodies distinguished by the name of church have seen great geographical and historical development, there should still be the need to enunciate a more precise definition of the true, profound and complete nature of the Church which Christ founded and the Apostles began to build. The Church is a mystery; she is a reality imbued with the divine presence, and, for that reason, she is ever susceptible of new and deeper investigation. Human thought moves forward. Man advances from empirically observed fact to scientific truth, from one truth he derives another by logical deduction, and, confronted by the complexity and permanence of reality, he bends his mind now to one of its aspects, now to another. It is thus that thought evolves. The course of its evolution can be traced in history.

Pope Paul's insistence on the development of doctrine is, of course, crucial for understanding the Second Vatican Council. At Vatican I, the great students of history did not prevail; non-historical orthodoxy prevailed. In the designs of Providence, much good may have been brought the Church by her rigidity in the intervening period. But now it is historical orthodoxy, not non-historical, which is in the ascendancy; the Church is becoming conscious once again of what she was for most of the centuries of her life: the people of God, in dialogue with God in time.

> The time has now come, We believe, when the truth regarding the Church of Christ should be examined, coordinated and expressed. The expression should not, perhaps, take the form of a solemn dogmatic definition, but of declarations making known by means of the Church's magisterium, in a more explicit and authoritative form, what the Church considers herself to be. This self-awareness of the Church is clarified by faithful adherence to the words and thoughts of Christ, by respectful attention to the teaching of ecclesiastical tradition and by docility to the interior illumination of the Holy Spirit, who seems to be requiring of the Church today that she should do all she can to make known what she really is.

Accepting another sheet of his discourse, the Pope went on:

> For this reason, the principal concern of this session of the Council will be to examine the intimate nature of the Church and to express in human language, so far as that is possible, a definition which will best reveal the Church's real, fundamental constitution and manifest its manifold mission of salvation. The theological doctrine has the possibility of magnificent developments which merit the attentive consideration of our separated brethren also, and which, as We ardently hope, may make the path toward common agreement easier.

The Pope then made explicit the major theme of the session, alluding to the suggestions which he had sown into his talk to the Curia on September 21.

> First among the various questions that this consideration will raise, venerable brothers, is one which affects all of you as bishops of the Church of God. We have no hesitation in saying that We look forward with great expectations and confidence to this discussion, which, taking for granted the dogmatic declarations of the First Vatican Council regarding the Roman Pontiff, will go on to develop the doctrine regarding the Episcopate, its function and its relationship with Peter. For Us personally it will provide doctrinal and practical standards by which Our apostolic office, endowed though it is by Christ with the fullness and sufficiency of power, may receive more help and support, in ways to be determined, from a more effective and responsible collaboration with Our beloved and venerable brothers in the Episcopate.
>
> Next it will be necessary to elucidate the teaching regarding the different components of the visible and mystical Body, the pilgrim,

militant Church on earth, that is, priests, religious, the faithful, and the separated brethren who are also called to adhere to it more fully and completely.

III

Next the Pope embraced the program of reform. The Bride of Christ must look on Christ to "discern in Him her true likeness."

> . . . if in doing so she were to discover some shadow, some defect, some stain upon her wedding garment, what should be her instinctive, courageous reaction? There can be no doubt that her primary duty would be to reform, correct and set herself to rights in conformity with her divine model.

The "essential attitude" of the Second Vatican Council, he said, is such self-sanctification that the Church might say: "Who sees me, sees Christ."

> . . . in this sense the Council is to be a new Spring, a reawakening of the mighty spiritual and moral energies which at present lie dormant. The Council is evidence of a determination to bring about a rejuvenation both of the interior forces of the Church and of the regulations by which her canonical structure and liturgical forms are governed.

"Yes, the Council aims at renewal." However, he said:

> We do not imply that the Catholic Church of today can be accused of substantial infidelity to the mind of her divine Founder. The Church will need courage to correct those imperfections which are proper to human weaknesses. The reform at which the Council aims is not, therefore, a turning upside down of the Church's present way of life or a breaking with what is essential and worthy of veneration in her tradition, but rather it is an honoring of tradition by stripping it of what is unworthy or defective so that it may be rendered firm and fruitful. Did not Jesus say to His disciples: "I am the true vine and it is my Father who tends it. The branch that yields no fruit in me, he cuts away; the branch that does yield fruit, he trims clean that it may yield more fruit"?

Pope Paul made biblical studies the heart of this renewal. "The first requirement of this reform will certainly be a more diligent study and a more intensive proclamation of the Word of God." He hoped that the document on Catholic worship, so long discussed in the first session, would "be brought to a happy conclusion in the second."

"The Council has a third object," the Pope continued. At this point his voice began to become more tremulous and he was leaning forward in his chair, making inhibited chopping gestures with his free hand, reminiscent of the early gestures of President Kennedy. This object:

> may be called its spiritual drama. This too was put before us by Pope John XXIII. It is that which concerns other Christians, those who believe in Christ but whom we have not the happiness of numbering amongst ourselves in the perfect unity of Christ, which only the Catholic Church can offer them. This unity, objectively speaking, should be theirs by baptism and it is something which, virtually at least, they already desire. For recent movements, at present in full development in bodies of Christians separated from us, reveal two things. The first is that the Church of Christ is one alone and therefore must be unique. The second is that this mystic and visible union cannot be attained save in identity of faith and by participation in the same sacraments and in the organic harmony of a single ecclesiastical direction, even though this allows for a great variety of verbal expressions, movements, lawful institutions, and preferences with regards to modes of acting.

This paragraph caused much consternation among Protestant groups and many Catholics. The word "direction" was at first rendered "control" in the English translation given the press. The original Italian text had *direzione*; the official Latin text used *regimen* or "order." The Pope, thought Father Gregory Baum, a member of the Secretariat for Christian Unity, was alluding to the formula of the World Council of Churches, in New Delhi, and thus his meaning was quite different in connotation from "control." The next sentence supported Father Baum's interpretation: "There can be no doubt about the attitude of the Council with regard to the great numbers of the separated brethren and of the possibility of multiplicity in the unity of the Church." On the other hand, the Pope still spoke about non-Catholics in terms of Catholic "expectation" for those "many sheep of Christ who are not at present within the unique fold." The Second Vatican Council is one "of invitation, of expectation, of confidence, looking forward toward a more widespread, more fraternal participation in its authentic ecumenicity."

The Pope's emotions were nearing the breaking point as he addressed the Protestant observers who sat nearer to him than his own brother bishops. "Our voice trembles," he said as his text

matched the fact, "and Our heart beats the faster both because of
the inexpressible consolation and fair hope that their presence stirs
up within Us, as well as because of the deep sadness We feel at their
prolonged separation."

The next lines made history, and the Pope's voice, as he said them,
cracked. He seemed to know full well that, for the first time in many
generations of Catholic history, the Roman Pontiff was admitting to
the guilt of his people—or, at least, to their possible guilt, for the
Pope spoke not in the indicative but in the conditional:

> If we are in any way to blame for that separation, we humbly beg
> God's forgiveness and ask pardon too of our brethren who feel them-
> selves to have been injured by us. For our part, we willingly forgive
> the injuries which the Catholic Church has suffered, and forget the
> grief endured during the long series of dissensions and separations. May
> the heavenly Father deign to hear our prayers and grant us true
> brotherly peace.

The Pope then sat back and, at a lower pitch, addressed himself
again to the observers, and, then, to those groups among the Eastern
Orthodox which did not accept the invitation to send observers:

> Our manner of speaking toward them is friendly, completely sincere
> and loyal. We lay no snares; we are not motivated by temporal inter-
> ests. We owe our Faith, which we believe to be divine, the most can-
> did and firm attachment. But at the same time we are convinced that
> this does not constitute an obstacle to the desired understanding with
> our separated brethren, precisely because it is the truth of the Lord
> and therefore the principle of union and not of distinction or separa-
> tion. At any rate we do not wish to make of our Faith an occasion
> for polemics.
>
> Secondly, we look with reverence upon the true religious patrimony
> we share in common, which has been preserved and in part even well
> developed among our separated brethren. We are pleased to note the
> study made by those who seek sincerely to make known and to honor
> the treasures of truth and of genuine spirituality, in order to improve
> our relations with them. We hope that just as they are desirous to
> know more about our history and our religious life, so also, they would
> wish to make a closer study of our doctrine and its logical derivation
> from the deposit of divine revelation.
>
> Finally we wish to say that, aware of the enormous difficulties still
> in the way of the desired union, we humbly put our trust in God. We
> shall continue to pray. We shall try to give better proof of our efforts

of leading genuine Christian lives and practicing fraternal charity. And should historical reality tend to weaken our hopes, we shall try to recall the comforting words of Christ: "What is impossible to man's powers is possible to God."

IV

"Finally," the Pope added, turning to the fourth aim of the Council, "the Church will build a bridge to the contemporary world." He noted that, as the Church seeks to renew herself within, she automatically becomes the object of attention by the whole world. "You yourselves, venerable brothers," he lifted his eyes to look down the long nave of white-clad figures,

> have experienced this remarkable phenomenon. Indeed, you yourselves, when you were undertaking the labors of the first session aglow with the opening words of Pope John XXIII, instantly felt the need of opening, as it were, the doors of this assembly, and of suddenly shouting to the world a message of greeting, of brotherhood, and of hope.

Had this in fact happened, he noted, "it would be said that the prophetic gift of Holy Church had suddenly burst into expression," and that you had unexpectedly determined "to treat no longer of your own limited affairs but rather those of the world, no longer to conduct a dialogue among yourselves but rather to open one with the world."

Looking at the contemporary world, the Pope felt tempted "to be frightened rather than comforted; saddened rather than gladdened; anxious for defense and condemnation rather than for trust and friendship." The first sorrow he felt was for those behind the Iron Curtain; and here he seemed to be departing from the peaceful, optimistic ways of Pope John.

> We ought to be realists, not hiding the savagery that from many areas reaches even into this universal Synod. Can we be blind and not notice that many seats in this assembly are vacant? Where are our brethren from nations in which the Church is opposed, and in what conditions does religion exist in these territories? At such a reminder our thoughts are grieved because of what we know and even more because of what we cannot know about our sacred Hierarchy, our religious men and women, our countless children subjected to fear, to persecutions, to privations, to oppression because of their loyalty to Christ and to the Church. What sadness we feel in the face of such sufferings, and what displeasure to see that in certain countries reli-

gious liberty, like other fundamental rights of man, is being crushed by principles and methods of political, racial, or anti-religious intolerance! The heart grieves to have to observe that in the world there are still so many acts of injustice against goodness and the free profession of one's religious faith. But, rather than in bitter words, our lament must be expressed in a frank and human exhortation to all who may be responsible for these evils to put aside with a noble heart their unjustified hostility toward the Catholic religion, whose followers ought to be considered neither as enemies nor as disloyal citizens, but rather as upright and hard-working members of the civil society to which they belong. Finally, to the Catholics who are suffering for their faith we send, also on this occasion, our affectionate greetings, and for them invoke special divine assistance.

Nor does our sorrow end here. The view of the world fills us with crushing sadness because of so many evils; atheism is pervading part of the human race and is bringing in its wake the derangement of the intellectul, moral, and social order, the true notion of which the world is losing. While the light of the science of nature is increasing, darkness is spreading over the science of God and in consequence over man's true science. While progress is perfecting in a wondrous way every kind of instrument that man uses, his heart is declining toward emptiness, sadness, and despair.

We would have a hundred things to say on these complicated and, for many reasons, sad conditions of modern man, but not now. Now, as We were saying, love is filling Our heart and the heart of the Church assembled in Council. We look upon our times and upon their varied and contrasting manifestations with immense tenderness and with immense desire to offer to men of today the message of friendship, of salvation and of hope which Christ has brought into the world. For "when God sent His Son into the world, it was not to reject the world, but so that the world might find salvation through Him."

Let the world know this: the Church looks at the world with profound understanding, with sincere admiration and with the sincere intention not of conquering it, but of serving it; not of despising it, but of appreciating it; not of condemning it, but of strengthening and saving it.

We will do well to quote the conclusion of his discourse in full, for its image of the open Church.

From the window of the Council, opened wide on the world, the Church looks toward some categories of persons with particular solicitude: it looks toward the poor, the needy, the afflicted, the hungry, the suffering and sorrowing. Humanity belongs to the Church, by the right which the Gospel gives her; and she likes to repeat to all who make up the human race: "Come to me, all of you!"

She looks toward men of culture and learning, scientists, artists; and also for these she has great esteem and a great desire to receive the fruit of their experience, to strengthen their intellectual life, to defend their liberty, to provide a space in which their troubled spirits can expand joyously within the luminous sphere of the divine word and divine grace.

She looks toward the workers, toward the dignity of their person and their labors, toward the legitimacy of their hopes, toward the need, which still afflicts them so greatly, of social improvement and of interior elevation, to the mission which may be recognized as theirs, if it is good, if it is Christian, to create a new world, of free men and brothers. The Church, Mother and Teacher, is close to them!

She looks to the leaders of nations, and in the place of the grave words of warning which the Church must often address to them, she substitutes today a word of encouragement and confidence; take courage, rulers of nations, today you can give to your peoples many good things necessary for their life: bread, education, work, order, the dignity of free and peaceful citizens, provided only you truly know who man is, and only Christian wisdom can show you this in its true light; working together in justice and love, you can create peace, that greatest good which is so longed for and which the Church defends and promotes so greatly, and you can make of humanity a single city. God be with you!

And then the Catholic Church looks further still, beyond the confines of the Christian horizon, for how can she put limits to her love if she would make her own the love of God the Father, "Who rains down His grace on all men alike," and "Who so loved the world as to give for it His only-begotten Son"! She looks, then, beyond her own sphere and sees these other religions which preserve the sense and notion of the one supreme, transcendent God, creator and sustainer, and which worship Him with acts of sincere piety and base their moral and social life on their beliefs and religious practices. It is true that the Catholic Church sees in such religions omissions, insufficiences, and errors which cause her sadness, yet she cannot exclude them from her thoughts and would have them know that she esteems what they contain of truth and goodness and humanity. For the Catholic Church is in the forefront of those who, as a necessary duty of true civilization, strive to preserve religion and the worship of God in modern society. She is the most vigorous upholder of God's rights and mankind.

Other vast fields of humanity fall under her gaze: the new generation of youth desirous of living and expressing themselves, the new peoples now coming to self-awareness, independence, and civil organization, the innumerable men and women who feel isolated in a troubled society that has no message for their spirit; and to all without exception she proclaims the good news of salvation and hope, to all she offers the light of truth and life and salvation, for God "wills that all men be saved and come to the knowledge of the truth."

Venerable brethren. Our mission as ministers of salvation is vast and onerous. We are joined here in this solemn assembly so as to fulfill it better. May the deep, fraternal union of our spirits be to us a source of vigor and guidance. May our union with the Church in heaven bring us support. . . . May Mary, whom we invoke from our hearts, assist us with her powerful motherly aid. May Christ preside over us, and may all be to the glory of God in the Holy Trinity, whose blessing We now presume to bestow upon you all, in the name of the Father and of the Son and of the Holy Ghost.

When he had finished, the Pope tried to read greetings in various languages. His voice was hoarse. He was emotionally drained. He read a few lines in Greek. Then he said with a tired gesture to his master of ceremonies, Archbishop Enrico Dante, *Basta!* "Enough." He waved aside the other pages and rose to leave. The ovation was thunderous. The second session had gotten off to a powerful start. It seemed to all—with hesitations over a phrase here or there—that the new Pope was another Pope John; an even more articulate and more intellectually penetrating Pope John. The second session began with euphoria.

7

THE PEOPLE OF GOD

I

THE HISTORY OF THE SECOND SESSION can be told in terms of a few outstanding dates. From September 30 to October 15, the Council moved surprisingly well; the work was hard, the discussions thorough, the tone of the debate very high. Non-historical orthodoxy was taking a beating on the floor; and the document under discussion marked a great advance beyond the non-historical document rejected the year before. On October 15, however, the moderators, who until that time appeared to be running the Council, proposed a fourfold vote which soon became the object of a bitter struggle behind the scenes. October 15, thus, marked the end of the Council as an open debate between non-historical orthodoxy and the other streams of theological reflection in the Church. From then on, the important history of the Council happened behind the scenes. In front of the scenes, on the elaborate stage erected inside St. Peter's basilica, the Council Fathers brought forward ever more telling intellectual arguments against non-historical orthodoxy, while those who took the part of non-historical orthodoxy rehearsed again and again the lines that had once secured applause, juridical order, and power.

On October 16, the subject of the layman was brought up on the floor—the first time in the history of the Church that a solemn conciliar discussion was devoted specifically to the role of the layman in the Church. On October 22, Cardinal Leo Jozef Suenens of Malines, Belgium, discoursed on the place of prophecy in the Church, in the outstanding intervention of the session, a pivotal point in the reflections of many of the Council Fathers. On October 28, an unusual ceremony was held in St. Peter's to commemorate the anniversary of Pope John's election to the papacy five years before; Pope Paul presided and Cardinal Suenens preached the moving sermon from which we have already quoted. On the next day, the Council Fathers voted by the narrowest of margins—forty votes—to include the treatment on the Blessed Virgin Mary in the document on the Church rather than separately. They thus changed the future direction of Catholic piety by incalculable proportions, of the highest cultural significance. On October 30, the Council manifested its mind in an overwhelming endorsement of the doctrine on the co-responsibility of the world's bishops for the universal Church—the central issue in the entire Second Vatican Council.

On November 8, Cardinal Joseph Frings of Cologne, after three days of sharp attacks on the Roman Curia, dared to call the procedures of the Holy Office "a scandal"; and Cardinal Alfredo Ottaviani, Secretary of the Holy Office, highly emotional and indignant, declared that the Cardinal from Germany must be "speaking from ignorance, not to use a harsher word." On November 11, the subcommission studying the chapter on religious liberty surprised the plenary session of Cardinal Ottaviani's theological commission by recommending a *nihil obstat* for the chapter, and won a resounding vote of approval from the commission. On November 21, the first three chapters of the document on the unity of Christians were enthusiastically accepted by 90 percent of the Council Fathers, and a chance to vote on the last two chapters, on the Jews and on religious liberty, was promised "in the next few days." On the second-last day of debate, November 29, Bishop Charles H. Helmsing of Kansas City, Missouri, reminded the Council of these two chapters and asked the Council Fathers, "Why not now?" On December 4, at the last ceremony of the session, the Council voted almost unanimously to accept the constitution on Catholic worship argued over so strenuously the year before. They also accepted, over the reluctance of some, the decree on the media of social communication. And on that day Pope Paul announced his surprise trip to Palestine—the first Pope to revisit the Holy Land since Peter left it.

These are the dates which leap to mind as one thinks of the second session. It was not, exteriorly, a dramatic session. Its own legislative fruit was little, though it reaped the harvest of the preceding year.

Its central concern—the co-responsibility of the bishops—was over-clouded by the partisans of non-historical orthodoxy, despite the manifest will of the Council Fathers. Its eagerly awaited decisions on the chapter on the Jews and on religious liberty were, under the most distressing circumstances, indefinitely postponed. The Council had opened on September 29 with mute but bursting hopes; was nurtured by the high, original tone of the first two weeks; and then gradually descended ever deeper into discouragement. Its hopes were momentarily and dramatically lifted by the great events of the "three days of October," October 28–30, and by the courage and integrity of the criticisms of the Roman system in the first week of November. But, although the majority at the Council appeared to grow from day to day, and although some partisans of non-historical orthodoxy were reached, convinced, and converted as each new issue of the Council arose, the power in the second session appeared to be ever more tightly concentrated in the hands of a few—the champions of a system identifying Catholic truth with their own contingent, personal ideas. It was they who openly affirmed that they would not feel bound by the will of the Council expressed in the famous five votes of October 30—and they who had power so to threaten, since they were charged with writing the text. It was they who prevailed upon Pope Paul to delay the consideration of the chapter on the Jews and on religious liberty. It was they who desired a speedy end to the Council.

Unfortunately, a long history cannot be so dramatic as a brief summary. Many good and noteworthy events happened on the Council floor or in the city; many excellent talks were given. From the point of view of the present study, these talks were of the highest significance. For the documents presented by the preparatory commissions took their starting place in non-historical orthodoxy. All the talks had to begin with this system as a reference point. As the closed bud must give place to the flower, so was the Church of the dying Middle Ages developing into the Church of the centuries to come. The new Church was continuous with non-historical orthodoxy and consistent with it; but it was much greater, moved on a deeper plane, grasped many more distinctions, drew more fully on the roots which had fed it, and reactivated roots that had not been drawn upon for centuries. But men, though they know eternal life is better, are afraid to die; and infants, could they choose, might never leave the womb. So were there groans and fears at the second session of the Council.

II

The first few days of debate in the Council came as a surprise. The document under discussion, on the nature of the Church, was a much better document than the one that had been dramatically rejected the year before. It was more or less biblical in tone, open, ecumenical. "It is an imperfect text," the Jesuit, Karl Rahner, said, "but we are entitled to be hopeful for the future: if offers a doctrine whereby the Church says to herself that she is *sent to serve not to reign.*" How did such a promising text come from Cardinal Ottaviani's theological commission? That commission is not so conservative as reports have pictured it, as several events in the second session were to indicate. Secondly, the "old guard" on the commission found nothing heterodox in the new text; they found it vague, poetical, loose, but they let it pass. The text was thus the result of a compromise. It satisfied the guardians of non-historical orthodoxy, and it pleased the Council Fathers by being rather fresh and alive; but it was not deep and penetrating. In the Council, it took only a day and a half of debate to win for it an overwhelming vote of approval as a good starting point for discussion: 2,231 to 43. (Twenty-seven votes were null. Many Fathers persisted in failing to use the special magnetic pencils required by the counting machine, or in using them incorrectly.)

The document was composed of four chapters: The Mystery of the Church, The Hierarchy, The People of God, The Call of Everyone to Holiness. These four chapters were printed up in two gray fasicicles, two chapters in each, totaling twenty-eight pages of text, notes, and brief commentary. The preceding July, much longer versions of these documents had gone out, numbering forty-seven and thirty-one pages each. The new document, therefore, had been greatly shortened. Its aim was not thoroughness but relevance: to stress the fundamental questions before the Church at mid-century. Its emphasis was on the ways in which the Church belongs to the world. "The schema on the Church," Cardinal Doepfner of Munich had written, "has not the slightest intention of formulating revolutionary principles. Like every other Council, the Second Vatican Council is pursuing its task deeply intent on remaining faithful to the divine constitution of the Church in the light of tradition. Nevertheless, we cherish the hope that this text will succeed in setting forth the fundamental principles which are to direct and guide subsequent Council discussion on the duties of bishops, the apostolate of the laity, the ecumenical movement, and numerous other problems and tasks of the Church in our time."

The very first day of debate indicated what was going to happen in the session. Cardinal Joseph Frings of Cologne, in the name of sixty-six German and Scandinavian bishops, opened the second session by praising the text. He applauded its pastoral and ecumenical spirit, its avoidance of a juridical and apologetic tone unworthy of the Council, its return to Scripture and many theological traditions, and its treatment of non-Christians. The document, in short, represented a break with non-historical orthodoxy. But not entirely. It contained, he noted, more on the infallibility of the pope than on the teaching office of the bishops. Cardinal Giuseppe Siri of Genoa immediately presented the fears of non-historical orthodoxy, though he was willing to accept the schema in general. The schema "is not precise enough . . . theological progress is not achieved by saying things less clearly than they were previously said. Silence concerning points might give rise to incorrect deductions."

Some other speeches of the morning are worth noting. Archbishop Casimir Morcillo, of Zaragoza, Spain, served warning that the Spaniards at the Council were less and less to be found in one camp; he, too, complained about the text's juridical tone and needless repetition concerning papal primacy; he requested that special mention be given to the patriarchs—whose title in the Church is older than that of cardinals. Bishop Ferrero di Cavallerleone of Italy treated the Fathers to a pious sermon on the Blessed Virgin Mary, of whom he wanted more mentioned in the document. Bishop Giuseppe Gargitter of Bressanone, Italy, on the other hand, represented the progressive Italian voices at the Council with a request that the notion of "the people of God" be treated *before* the chapter on the hierarchy; in the Church, the people come first. The dignity of the people, he said, can be developed without detriment to the place of the hierarchy.

"The human and the Christian," Father Yves Congar, O.P., said at a press conference on October 4, "are coinciding more and more. It is no longer possible to separate anything from anything—which accounts for the favor found in ideas encountered in the works of Teilhard de Chardin, who affirms that creation is one thing only, and that from the smallest mineral to Jesus Christ there is a chain of reality, a solidarity." Theology is taking advantage of the ever increasing interrogation put to it by the world; "the world is much more present than the Council may imagine, for it is merely hidden by the ecclesiastical vocabulary." The Church is "coming back from rather far," he said. All kinds of ideas long forgotten are being "recovered to consciousness in these last sixty years—a recovery in which lay people have played a decisive part. . . . In the middle of the nineteenth century, numerous theologians denied to lay people the right to defend the Church." How did this come about? Gregory VII tried to free the Church from temporal power by building up a juridical system based upon the rights of the hierarchy; the laity was made to become more and more passive in the Church. "But a new era has arrived." The term "people of God," becoming so popular in this session, is "as old as Abraham." But Father Congar could remember hearing it first in modern times when he was released from a concentration camp after the Second World War.

Even as Father Congar spoke, the argument between non-historical orthodoxy and the other Catholic theologies was only becoming more evident in the Council. Cardinals Siri, Ruffini, Bacci, with the regular help of Bishop Carli and Archbishop Florit, of Florence; Archbishop Marcel Lefèbvre, the Superior General of the Congregation of the Holy Spirit; Cardinal Arriba y Castro, and several others spoke for non-historical orthodoxy. Most of the other speakers of the Council, in varying degrees, appealed to other theologies. There was a great unanimity among the Council Fathers; even the split between non-historical orthodoxy and the majority did not approach the violent disagreement of many previous councils. Moreover, the split was in general between men who could see both sides of a question and those who could see only one side. It was rare that the partisans of non-historical orthodoxy conversed; ordinarily, they merely raised objections that arose in the context of their own tradition.

The men of the other schools of theology, on the contrary, had almost all attended seminaries in which non-historical orthodoxy reigned supreme: "As we all learned in the seminary," Cardinal Spellman of New York once appealed to them. The majority adopted the tactics of patience and calm. They almost always prefaced their interventions with words of assurance, or words meant to dispel fear. They diagnosed, very accurately, that the opposition was largely unself-critical and too narrow in its intellectual base to feel secure in its position. The opposition could neither justify its own historical origins, nor feel confident in its relevance to the contemporary world; they saw themselves as holding out faithfully against an uncomprehending and evil world, a world racked with confusions and danger. Not that the leaders of the opposition lacked intelligence or erudition: far from it. But intellect is as much a habit of mind as it is a store of propositions and skill in argument; and non-historical orthodoxy by its very nature deprives itself of the requirements of a realistic habit of mind, in preference for the world of its own ideas. It does not reflect on its own development in human history, nor test itself against the realities of the world in which it lives. Thus there was not very much of a dialogue at the second session of the Council. One group was trying very hard to make it easy for the other to stay in communion with the rest; the partisans of non-historical orthodoxy, for their part, looked on the others with suspicion, fear, and the deeply felt impulse to halt them before "they go too far." One side tried to calm the other; in return, the others repeated their preachments of warning and alarm.

Between the two most articulate groups stood the vast majority of the Council Fathers, not speculatively inclined enough to articulate all that was going on, but intelligent and sensible in their grasp of the practical problems of the Church in the modern world. Most of them had long taken Rome "with a grain of salt," and had as little to do as they could with the involved and tortured directives that emanated steadily from the Curia. They tried to be faithful and loyal, sometimes the more so in proportion as they were distant from Rome; the Irish and the Americans must surely be the most loyal sons the papacy has ever had, more faithful to the letter of the law than even those in the Curia who write the law. The spokesmen of renewal and reform thus found ears that heard, hearts that responded, when they spoke in the great basilica. Many bishops had long believed in their hearts that serious reform was needed, even when the non-historical orthodoxy that had been pounded into their heads in the seminary offered them no language for expressing such convictions. To these, the Council came as a release. To others, practical, hard-headed argument, day after day, did what their seminary education had not done, perhaps could not have done. They came to grips with the problems of the universal Church; they began to realize that, as bishops, they were not just minor executives in a great corporation, but responsible pastors of the entire world. They could not avoid responsibility for the choices which the Church continually must make in history. They could not merely leave everything to Rome; if they did, that, too, was a choice they would have to answer for to God, in the scorching light of the Gospels.

An expert on Latin America estimated that, though 85 percent of the speeches given on the floor by Latin American bishops or in the name of Latin American bishops were in favor of the principles of renewal and reform, nevertheless, probably less than 30 percent of the Latin Americans were deeply convinced by these principles; most were simply following the trend, hesitantly. Perhaps the same was true of the bishops of the United States and some other nations. With the exception of Cardinals Spellman and McIntyre, the leading American prelates were articulate spokesmen of reform. Moreover, at least half of the Americans, solidly if not spectacularly, and most of the others at least hesitantly, supported the momentum bequeathed the Church by Pope John.

Two visions of the Church, then, were being proposed to the Council Fathers as they were trying to decide what the Church had to say of herself to the world. In one view, the basic terms to describe the Church are power and authority; the main connecting bond in the Church is taken to be jurisdiction and legal membership. The image that serves this view best is that of the pyramid or the military chain-of-command; absolute monarchy is its closest political correlative (though all political images limp when used of the Church). The word "society" can be defined, and so can "perfect society"; and with these two definitions and a small number of postulates one can deduce the most astounding number of "truths" about the rights, duties, and inner constitution of the Church—with the utmost clarity, rigor, and precision. The Church, then, is a pyramid at whose monarchical apex is the Pope, who holds supreme and universal jurisdiction; his right arm is his Curia; then come the bishops, to whom he grants jurisdiction to care for their given dioceses; then come priests, who share in the jurisdiction of their bishops; then religious, whose way of life is established and guided by the Church; and then, as it reaches the mass of laymen who make its base, the pyramid disappears from canonical sight, for there is nothing to say about laymen except that they have no jurisdiction and are not professed religious. This vision of the Church is inevitably clerical. It is something relatively new in the Church, for its origin depended on the rising influence of canon law after the early Middle Ages, and on the deceptively easy—but devastatingly erroneous—transition back and forth between the late scholastic theology of essences and the concepts of canon law. Indeed, in many seminaries of the world, canon law and scholastic theology are treated so interchangeably that canon lawyers often teach theology, and even write the texts. Few notice the difference, as if the matter of theology and philosophy were amenable to the methods of canon law.

The other view competing for the attention of the bishops is best expressed by the metaphor of concentric circles. Its basic terms are service, rather than power; community of purposes and motives, rather than jurisdiction; a covenant of a people with their God, rather than a structure of clerical authority imposed upon a nation. This conception begins first with the people who are called by God, "His people." In the metaphor, the widest circle represents this people. They love God by loving their neighbors; serve Him by serving them. Within this people, God gives special power to certain ones, in order that they may minister to the needs of their people; these are the priests called from among men, and chiefly the bishops. Within the circle of bishops, God singled out one of them, Peter and his successors, to "confirm" the others, as "the servant of the servants" of God. Within the Church, within the gathering of bishops, the Pope has special power and prerogatives—the papal primacy—for his special tasks and services. Service, not power; spirit, not letter; fatherliness and brotherliness, not arbitrary will.

In Rome during the Council, seminarians in certain colleges were getting lectures insisting that such a view of the Church is "mystical," or "poetic"; that the first view is the hard view, the real view, the indispensable view. Certain professors in Rome felt that their whole profession was under attack in the Council; they were sullen, moody, often angry in class—and ideas which they voiced were sometimes subsequently voiced in the Council. Some, particularly (but not exclusively) Italians and Spaniards, seemed to find it difficult to see how anything moral could be meaningful without an "obligation"; and how anything could be an "obligation" without an explicit, often-repeated law. They do not seem to have as much respect for law as for its sanctions. They seem to respect power rather than law. Consequently, through their view, deviousness easily becomes part of the game of life.

Moreover, the view which favors juridical power seems more prone to magic than the view which favors service. For jurisdiction can seem to be a "magic fluid," a mystical gift passed on from hand to hand. Where it is lacking—say, in a priest without explicit faculties who hears the confession of a dying man—the theory is forced to posit an auxiliary leap, an *"Ecclesia supplet"* (the Church supplies what is in this case lacking), a bit of prestidigious make-believe on the part of God. The theory attempts to confine God's grace within petty human laws and an imperfect juridical system, and then to allow enough escape gaps for God's "universal salvific will" and His "mercy" to find their way outside the system, after all. The theory invites the pseudo-problems of the world of fantasy—what would happen if a priest, with faculties, drunkenly consecrated all the bread in a bakery?—because it is not a theory based on the real world, but on abstract definitions. Ultimately, it finds answers even to its pseudo-questions (which it loves to contrive), for its escape-gap postulates enable it to cover all contingencies. The system is a marvel of internal coherence, and even of verisimilitude; it is easy to see how it wins so many admirers and adherents.

On the pastoral level, the shift from the vision of the Church as a legal power structure, to the view of the Church as a service—from pyramid to concentric circles—focuses more attention on the people in the Church and their real, daily problems. It favors the decentralization of the Church, not into isolated fragments, but into local churches in communion with one another and gathered around the Bishop of Rome, each mindful that all together make one people. It leads naturally to the decentralization of the Roman Curia proposed by Pope Paul, for it suggests that the right order at the heart of the Church is Pope-Bishops-Curia, rather than Pope-Curia-Bishops. And its vision receives support from "the principle of subsidiarity" often proposed by recent Popes; *viz.*, that what a lower order of power can do and is doing, a higher power should not try to do. Perhaps we hardly need to mention that the Gospels also seem to favor the view of the Church as a service.

The first and most important debate in which the second session of the Vatican Council became involved was characterized by these different conceptions. Let us follow that debate for a while, since its repercussions on the Church in our own neighborhood—wherever that may be—are profound.

III

The dominant impression which the Catholic Church in the United States has made upon the secular public is that of a power bloc, Victorian in its conceptions and ruthless in the pursuit of its own interests. Few outside the Church, howsoever good-willed and unprejudiced, see in her the communion of the faithful grouped around the eucharist and manifesting the life of the Gospels. There has been confusion, it appears, even in the minds of Catholics, even in the minds of priests. The Church in her daily life seems to be a power organization, officially involved in money-making campaigns and in public attacks on those external moral developments that threaten her life. Publicly, she sometimes reacts as if she were insecure, unloved, and obsessed with two or three points of her moral code.

Chapter 1 of the document on the Church tried to give the children of the Church a new conception of her life. It focused not on outward power or juridical cohesion. It tried to move away from the concepts of bureaucracy and law, to the concept of inner life. The Church is the communion of those who share the life of God. For reasons not clear to men, God wished to share His life with others, whom He created, with whom He speaks in history. Every man is invited and pursued; each is free to receive this life in himself. If his answer is yes, he is drawn into this life of insight and love. The Church is this common inner life. But as God became man, physical and limited in time and space, so the Church is also human, external, limited by the conditions of time and space. It has buildings men can enter: water, wax, bronze, glass, flame they can see or touch; incense they can smell; ministers whose voices they can hear; members who are skilled in every profession and live in the world. The Church is a community of men who talk, pray, act, inquire. The Church is a community in which individuals try to know more and love better. They thus try to make more room in themselves for God's life, which is insight and love. The Gospels say that "God is truth" and "God is love." But participles are best; God is not static. His life is knowing and loving: free insight and creative love. The Church is all the world which responds to Him; it is, in Guardini's phrase, "All creation redeemed and at prayer."

To express these beliefs, the document chose biblical images to describe the Church: a living body, a shepherd and his flock, a vine-yard, the house and temple of God, the heavenly city, the bride of Christ. To express the situation of this people in history—that history which goes back the hundreds of millions of years during which the earth was prepared to be an apt habitation for man—the document chose the image of a pilgrimage: a people stumbling, groping, learn-ing through difficulties and tragedies. Yet that people gathers as one at the thanksgiving, the eucharist, under its ordained leaders, and can be confident that God is with His people whatever the trial. The Church bears witness to its Lord in times of poverty and the cross—more honestly, perhaps, than in times of affluence. Moreover, all belong to this people who follow their honest conscience. All the more so, those non-Catholic Christians belong to it who share with Catholics so many of the realities of the Christian faith. The full life of this people, however, is found in the Roman Catholic Church, which is now renewing and reforming itself. Those who pursue God's will in non-Christian religions have a special bond of communion with Catholics, over and above those shared by non-believers.—As a summary of the chapter, not without justice, John Cogley wrote a little poem, in *America*, which we should quote:

WHO IS THE CHURCH?
Who?
You.

The document was, therefore, a long way from the exclusivism or integralism of non-historical orthodoxy. It was not a cover for indifferentism, but the very opposite; it was an appeal to the honest pursuit of conscience, a recognition of those things of the spirit which already unite men, an invitation to all men of good will to look on the world of men as sharing one spiritual patrimony, one sonship under God.

As a consequence, the document was an attempt to break from the defensive Romanism of the Counter-Reformation; it abandoned a polemic now dead. But some among the Council Fathers still felt besieged, not, perhaps, by living opponents but by the opponents who still preoccupied their textbooks: Renan, Tyrrell, the modernists of fifty years ago. On October 1, Cardinal Ernesto Ruffini, the most loquacious speaker at the first session, objected to the text's use of the word *sacramentum*—mystery, reality veiled in signs—to describe the Church, because that word had been used by George Tyrrell, an apostate priest and a leading modernist. Cardinal Augustin Bea of the Secretariat for Christian Unity, the next day pointed out that, in spite of many good features, the document derived too exclusively from Catholic theology between the Reformation and the end of the nineteenth century. Cardinal Ruffini, it seems, had not noted that before the twelfth century *sacramentum*, used of the Church, meant what the text desired it to mean.

In the introduction to the fourth edition of his useful book, *Concilio Aperto*, Mario Gozzini describes the "residual polemicism" that characterizes certain circles in Italy, and the "tendency in certain Roman circles to maintain Italian Catholics in a state of theological adolescence." He decried the "religious underdevelopment" of the Italian press and culture. "Not by chance was Italy the only country in the world where one could write, in these last months, unheard-of nonsense, about the Pope having become a modernist, or about the Church having been converted to Communism." [1] Pope Paul was to warn journalists not to interpret the Council along nationalistic lines; but one cannot, in fairness to historical judgment, neglect the fact that theology is conditioned by the culture in which it is developed, and that the non-historical orthodoxy of these "certain Roman circles" still harbors fears about its great archenemy, modernism. The defect of modernism was that, in opposing non-historical orthodoxy, it fell prey to relativism. In opposing non-historical orthodoxy at Vatican II however, the Council Fathers were not giving way to "the spirit of the age," and certainly not to relativism; they were trying to do justice to the Gospels and to conscience, within the context of our time. But without listening to the argument, the partisans of non-historical orthodoxy insisted on refighting the battles of 1870 and 1910.

For example, on October 2, Bishop Luigi Carli of Segni, Italy, said to be the *porta-voce* of Cardinal Ottaviani, warned the Fathers that the Church was founded on Peter alone, not on Peter and the College of Apostles. He cited Vatican I, Denziger 1821 (the standard collection of conciliar decrees). He noted that at Vatican I Cardinal Schwarzenberg's argument that the Church is founded "on the foundation of all the apostles" had been rejected, but now this phrase was found in the text. Bishop Carli's own pre-conciliar pastoral letter, defending the collegiality of the bishops, was at this time removed from sale in Vatican bookstores.

On the other side, Cardinal Joseph Ritter of St. Louis called the schema too static; it did not even mention the dynamic elements in the life of the Church: the giving of the sacraments, the preaching of the Word. The Ukrainian Archbishop of Winnipeg, Maximus Hermaniuk, deplored the title borrowed from pagan Rome, "Roman Pontiff," and suggested in its place "Pastor of the universal Church." He disliked the excessive Romanità of the document. Cardinal Gracias of Bombay insisted: "It is important throughout this chapter that the Church should be presented as wishing neither to dominate society nor to constitute a state within a state, but as ministering and serving the world. The Church was founded by One Who came to serve and Who told His followers: 'Whoever wishes to be first among you, shall be the servant of all.' The Church grows in the world only to save the world and enrich it morally and spiritually." Cardinal Lercaro of Bologna noted that the text was more emphatic than Pius XII's Mystici Corporis on the unity of all baptized Christians; it called the Church a "new people," and "new creation," not just a psychological, ethical, or religious grouping. He called on Cardinal Ottaviani's theological commission to rise "to greater heights" and to "rethink the whole chapter," not on minor points but on the general content of the whole. He encouraged the most outspoken Fathers of the majority—Silva Henriquez of Chile, Rugambwa of Africa, Gracias of India, Guano of Italy, Ancel of France—to take advantage of the new Council rules and insist on working directly with the theological commission.

During the week, Bishop Garcia of Spain wanted to extend the definitions of Vatican I about the infallibility of the Church to include "virtually revealed truths, necessarily connected doctrine, and dogmatic facts." Cardinal Ruffini wanted the text to use the concept of the Church as a juridically perfect society, and Bishop Carli wanted more emphasis on the primacy of the Pope. Cardinal Micara asked the Council for a strong condemnation of modern-day errors. He listed four such errors now "passed by in silence and permitted to be spread among the laity and clergy, in books which even have ecclesiastical approval." The errors were: the minimizing of the doctrine of eternal punishment in hell; the mitigation of the doctrine of Trent on original sin; errors condemned in Pius XII's

Humani Generis but "still circulating"; and the neglect of the warning in Pius XII's *Mystici Corporis* that "those who do not pertain to the visible Catholic Church . . . cannot be secure with regard to their eternal salvation."

It was on this note that the first week closed. "The unhistorical," C. S. Lewis once wrote, "are usually, without knowing it, enslaved to a fairly recent past."

NOTE

1. Vallecchi Editore, Florence, 1963; pp. 5, 16.

8

THE CO–RESPONSIBILITY
OF BISHOPS

I

"THE DECISIVE POINT in the document on the Church is the description of the function of the entire Episcopate as a body—the College of Bishops—*as a body*, not as individual bishops, nor even as a sum of individuals." Thus, on October 1, Karl Rahner put his finger on the heart of the second session. The partisans of non-historical orthodoxy grasped the importance of the point, too. To restore the co-responsibility of bishops for the universal Church would be to modify the recent system of government in the Church, whereby the Pope, theoretically alone, but in actual fact through the recommendations of the Roman Curia, has made all decisions for the universal Church. The Curia owes its existence to the Council of Trent, in 1588; since then, the meetings of the Consistory which had long been the Pope's "senate" have been abandoned. Pope Paul VI had given evidence in his writings before and during the first session, and in his address to the Curia on September 21, that Rome desired to restore some such senate.

The actual word "collegiality" seems to have a modern history of less than fifteen years, so thoroughly has the idea been forgotten in the Latin Church. Father Yves Congar suggested in a lecture on October 4 that the Council should go slowly and choose its words well. Even by that date, he could see that "the partisans and adversaries of the concept of collegiality do not understand the same reality under the same word."

What, exactly, is collegiality? Officially, discussion on the point occupied the Council from October 4 until October 15; but even after the long-delayed crucial vote of October 30, the opposition returned to the point again and again during the month of November. Pope Paul VI had said that the document on the Church is the pre-eminent concern of the Council; the doctrine of co-responsibility is the heart of that document. No issue is so important to the Second Vatican Council; episcopal collegiality will characterize Vatican II as papal infallibility characterized Vatican I.

To help reporters sort out some of the many conceptions of collegiality, Father Gustave Weigel, S.J., made several distinctions at the American press conference on October 11. First there is an *ontological* sense of collegiality. Christ had created a real bond of spirit among his bishops, which is renewed through the ages by episcopal consecration; they are "different" once they are drawn into this grace, and divine life becomes operative through their actions. To become a bishop is to be lifted into a special fellowship of service and grace. Second is the *collective* sense: the college is simply the accidental gathering of many bishops, especially at a council. A third is the *juridical* sense: the college must have a legal basis, a legal function, otherwise it isn't a college; especially the Spaniards, with many Italians, seemed unable to understand any other kind of college. A fourth is the *ecclesiastical* sense: the college is simply a practical device developed by the Church in history, and codified in law. In some sense, the bishops form a college. In which sense?

The difficulty here, as in so many arguments among men, did not lie only with the definition given to the word, as if the correctly phrased proposition would unlock the puzzle, while all incorrect definitions would fail. The difficulty did not lie in contrasting definitions; it lay in different *habits of mind*. Some bishops had different criteria of relevance and evidence than others; one argument satisfied one man's criteria, but not another's. It turned out that as the days went on the minds of nearly all the bishops were satisfied, as the vote on October 30 proved. But four hundred or so remained to be convinced. If we can judge by the arguments on the floor, it seems that the difficulty of the minority was that they were not at all self-critical. They were so preoccupied with their own method of deciding questions that they never stopped to ask themselves: "Is this the only method? the best method? where did it come from and why am I adopting it?" They seemed convinced that they had no need to question their own procedures; imprisoned in those procedures, they sought satisfaction which they could never have. Had they been less inclined to believe that others were near heresy, and begun to critcize themselves, they might soon have come to discover their insufficiency. Instead, many erected their insufficiency into a bulwark which argument could not penetrate. Others showed enough good will to try to understand; but they were unable to find their way outside the very categories which prevented them from understanding. To follow the efforts of the minority is perhaps, then, the best way to discover what collegiality is *not*, and to see the necessity of choosing another starting point.

The subject was introduced on the floor by Archbishop Hermaniuk on October 1, in the same talk in which he had deplored the excessive *Romanità* of the entire document on the Church. He made three successive points: (1) the power of the College of Bishops can be exercised either by the Pope alone, as its head, or by the bishops, with the Pope; (2) the power of the college ought to be exercised continually, not only when an ecumenical council is in session; (3) in practice, a smaller, representative body of bishops should exercise this power when a council is not in session. He argued from Scripture, the tradition of the Oriental Church, and Pope Paul's talk to the Curia. Cardinal Ruffini and Bishop Carli countered this talk, as we have seen, by leaping to the defense of the primacy of Peter, to whom alone it was said: "Thou art Peter and on this rock I will build my Church."

Meanwhile, Cardinal Alfrink of Utrecht presented a number of arguments to show that Christ founded the Church on "Peter with all the other apostles," to whom as a group He had said: "Whatever you shall bind on earth shall be bound also in heaven; whatever you shall loose, shall be loosed." One of his arguments, not the best, was the phrase from the Apocalypse about "the twelvefold foundation." Another was the ancient liturgical symbol of placing twelve crosses on the foundation stone of every new church building. Another was based on Ephesians 2:20, about the Church being built on the "foundation of the apostles and the prophets."

On October 4, Cardinal Ruffini was on his feet again, warning against "false doctrine and interpretations." The text from Ephesians, he said, referred not to "the twelve" but to "all preachers of the Gospel." After Christ left the earth, the apostles never once acted as a college except at the Council of Jerusalem. "I have not yet been convinced that Christ formed the apostles as a college."

Bishop de Castro of Granada, Spain, did not think the Council should settle controversies about the consecration of bishops, which were still standing from the Middle Ages. But young, handsome Cardinal Siri of Genoa surprised everyone on the 7th by beginning: "There can be no doubt that all bishops, acting with the Roman Pontiff, constitute a real council." He meant, of course, "in an ecumenical council," in which "the bishops depend on Peter" for their full power. He wanted the schema made "clearer and more coherent with the statements of Vatican I, lest there be restricting consequences for papal primacy."

On October 8, Archbishop Dino Staffa, of the curial Congregation of Seminaries and Universities, said he thought the issue was whether full and supreme power in the Church belongs *either* to the Episcopal College *or* to the Pope. The answer to that has already been given by Vatican I. He used the words of the *relator* who introduced the text at Vatican I, to show that the power of the Pope over the bishops is at all times supreme, immediate, and complete. The *relator* himself had rejected the idea that the supreme power belonged *both* to the bishops *and* to the Pope. "This would replace the monarchial structure of the Church with an aristocracy," Archbishop Staffa argued. He cited Bossuet and Innocent III, and insisted that, whatever discussion the Council gives to the collaboration of Popes and bishops, all decisions on the matter belong to the Pope.

His Beatitude Alberto Gori, the Latin Patriarch of Jerusalem, concentrated on the dangers in the doctrine. "In the past, historical circumstances favored a centralization of power." Now a clearer statement of the teaching of the Gospels is required. But many dangers threaten us: (1) too great a reaction against centralization can foster a spirit of rebellion; (2) the independence of local churches can lead to their over-involvement in local and national affairs, as history shows; (3) reform of local abuses by effective action from above is more difficult, "as witness the reactionary tendencies of some Oriental churches"; (4) if bishops throw off the yoke of the tempering authority of the Pope, then priests and laity in the diocese will be encouraged to do likewise. "We should insist on respect for papal authority and for the legates of the Pope. The schema should provide for the presence of papal legates at episcopal conferences." The collegiality of the bishops needs the "action of its independent and experienced head, the Roman Pontiff," to sustain it.

On October 9, Archbishop Emile Blanchet, rector of the Institut Catholique of Paris, showed how difficult it is to straddle non-historical orthodoxy and other theologies. In non-historical orthodoxy, much importance is attached to a tag describing each dogmatic proposition: "of faith," "of divine faith," "of ecclesiastical faith," "theologically certain," "probable," and the rest. How should the present text be tagged? The Bishop was afraid that "such qualifications would not do justice to the concrete, living realities expressed in biblical images and Church tradition. Abstract ideas do not grasp realities completely. . . ." He finally suggested following Pope Paul's opening address, "so that if special emphasis for a doctrine is desired, the form of the decree would itself indicate this." The Bishop's remarks seemed to indicate that Roman Catholic theology in the future, once so juridically clear, was going to be more representative of Scripture and of reality—and that this was going to create confusion for many theologians.

It remained to hear a thoroughly juridical view of the Church. Archbishop Sigaud of Diamantina, Brazil, said that a bishop has jurisdiction outside his own particular diocese only when he attends one of the rare ecumenical councils of history, and only then because the Pope approves the acts of the Council. National episcopal conferences have juridical effect only when approved by the Pope or by the bishop in his own diocese. A permanent "world parliament" in the Church was unknown to Christ and never heard of for twenty centuries. Bishop Biagio D'Agostino of Vallo di Lucania, Italy, immediately added that "we must remember that the Church always remains especially a juridical society," to rule and to lead; and consequently he deplored the silence of the schema on the subject of clerical obedience and obsequium.

II

October 10 was a glorious Italian summer day. The sky was a rich cobalt; the wind that swept it and the ancient city between the great circle of the Apennines was scented with the cleanliness that follows several days of rain. The gray, weathered stones and pillars of St. Peter's were a glaring white; pennants of Italy's green, white, and red flapped in the wind above Castel Sant'Angelo.

Inside St. Peter's, Auxiliary Bishop Galea of Malta took the juridical distinction between the power of orders and the power of jurisdiction, and tried to find his way to the doctrine of collegiality. He ended by confessing his bewilderment and said the Council would have to allow time for "further study." Auxiliary Bishop Demetrio Mansilla Reyo of Burgos, Spain, could find no text of the early Church Fathers supporting the "strict juridical meaning" of collegiality; but he did not note that concern for strict juridical meaning came into the Church only rather late and locally.

Bishop Casimir Morcillo of Zaragoza, Spain, one of the Under-Secretaries of the Council, claimed that "the juridical form of the Church is a response to the needs of the Church." He did not find the concept of collegiality "quite so clear in Scripture and tradition as has been affirmed." He cherished a "prudent doubt" and said, "Though my heart is drawn to it, my head is opposed." He tried a compromise: "Ecumenical councils show that recognition of the College of Bishops does not weaken the primacy. Even though this matter may not be of divine law, nothing prevents the Church from recognizing it as a matter of ecclesiastical law." Father Aniceto Fernandez, master-general of the Dominicans, came to the defense of the primacy, as he conceived it. The Pope does *not* have supreme power as the head of the Episcopal College, but as the vicar of Christ. Even if a commission of bishops is appointed to advise the Pope, its power derives from the Pope.

The next day, the Archbishop of Santiago de Compostela, Spain, Cardinal Fernando Quiroga y Palacios, explained that he could understand the collegiality of the bishops, in the sense of a stable union of many bishops working for a common end; such a collegiality was clearly instituted by Christ. But could the College of Bishops make laws? They seemed to be able to do that only in ecumenical councils, a creation, he thought, of ecclesiastical law. He was not ready to admit that the legislative power was given by divine law. Then Archbishop Joseph Slipyi, who had recently returned from many years of imprisonment in Siberia, added his great prestige to those who opposed collegiality. He had been greeted by a warm ovation from the Council Fathers as he rose to speak the day before. Overcome, he had put off his talk for a day. Now he exclaimed: "Strictly speaking, the bishops of the Church do not constitute a college because a college must be founded on a juridical and legal basis." Then Bishop Vittorio Costantini of Sessa Aurunca, Italy, a diocese of 60,000 souls, had a comment on every issue under discussion. He declared that papal infallibility "is the work of the Holy Spirit and not dependent on human prudence or the Church." The "consent of the Church" is not required before, but after, papal definitions.

But not all the Spanish or Italian bishops were on one side. In the name of sixteen Spanish bishops, Bishop José Cirarda, auxiliary of Seville, Spain, endorsed the sacramentality of episcopal consecration; the sacrament, he said, not the later granting of jurisdiction, is the source of the bishop's power to sanctify, teach, and rule. Nor were all the Northern Europeans on the side of the majority: Archbishop Marcel Lefèbvre said that a Senate of Bishops was bound to limit the authority of the Pope and of individual bishops as well. His comment brought to light another facet of non-historical orthodoxy; it insists strenuously on the authority of the Pope, and equally strenuously on the individualistic liberty of each bishop under the Pope: each a Pope in his own diocese, as it were. Moments later a young Spanish bishop, José Pont y Gol, criticized the text as "too authoritarian," and too laden with the excessive use of the words "power" and "authority."

The last talk of the second week of the session, however, fell to the young Italian Giuseppe Bettazzi, consecrated only that week. The oils still fresh on him, as it were, the new Bishop arose to defend an overlooked Italian tradition on collegiality. "This doctrine is not, as many wrongly believe, a Gallican invention intended as an attack on the primacy. It has been defended by many Italian theologians and jurists, including some members of the Roman Curia." In a dazzling fashion, whose effect was only heightened by the fact that he is an auxiliary of Cardinal Lercaro of Bologna, moderator for the day, the fledgling Bishop quoted a list of various theologians and Popes, from Torquemada to the present, including Urban VII and Innocent IX, who had supported the theory of collegiality. Speaking with verve and vigor, he argued that episcopal consecration is the source (1) of all episcopal powers, and (2) of incorporation into the Episcopal College. When he had concluded, the assembly—against the rules—broke into warm applause. Italy itself is no longer a monolith, the applause seemed to say. A four-day bishop was telling some of his confrères, in effect, that they didn't know their own tradition.

Bishop Bettazzi could not go unanswered. On Monday morning, Bishop Carli responded that the word "college" is proper neither to the apostles nor to the bishops. It creates historical and theological difficulties. It is based on no valid proofs from Scripture. The rite of consecration of bishops is not a proof. But, of course, there *is* a collegiality of mutual help and good fellowship. The Pope is independent of the College and the Council should say so clearly—Vatican I offered a better statement than the present text. The Council should not rely on the theologians of the past (i.e., not even Italian theologians), but should make up its own mind. It "is the responsibility of this Council to decide whether or not the time is right for the Roman Pontiff to make the collegiality of the bishops an official doctrine of the Church." Even the phrasing of his conclusion contained his theology of the Church: the *Pope* would define the doctrine.

Meanwhile, Archbishop Pietro Parente, assessor of the Holy Office, discoursed as if the Council Fathers did not believe that Peter was the rock on which the Church had been founded (Matthew 16:18). "The pre-eminent position of Peter must be safeguarded." The bishops must act "always in dependence on the Pope."

Bishop Vincenzo Jacono of Italy, tried his best to accept the idea of collegiality as complementary to the primacy. But he kept coming back to the idea that if the Pope were not independent of the consent of others in defining doctrine, then he would not be the foundation rock of the Church. The College of Bishops is infallible in its ordinary and universal teaching, he reasoned, with and under Peter. But if the College takes some part in deciding major issues for the universal Church, it should intervene only on occasions and in ways determined by the Pope. Archbishop Garcia De Sierra, Coadjutor of Oviedo, Spain, tried to find a juridical collegiality established by divine right, and couldn't, concluding that "the whole question is highly controversial and really should not be discussed in the Council." Archibishop Fares of Catanzaro, Italy, asked the Council to refrain from speaking of ministry and service—only moral attitudes, after all—lest detriment be done the power bestowed on the hierarchy.

The partisans of non-historical orthodoxy were knocking on the wrong door, and it would not open. As Cardinal Meyer of Chicago pointed out, to look for a juridical conception of collegiality in the New Testament is to forget that "the New Testament is not a code of law and does not give juridical explanations." Yet "the unity of the new people of God was reflected in the apostles not as individuals but as a group." He pointed out that the early Christians quite understood that Christ had founded an episcopal community of twelve; the eleven immediately elected Matthias to replace Judas; all were together on Pentecost; all together instituted the diaconate.

Several days later, on the 14th, Cardinal Frings admitted that a strictly juridical concept of collegiality cannot be found in the ancient tradition; but neither can a strictly juridical concept of papal primacy. Not all the truths of faith were clear from the beginning: not the assumption of the Blessed Virgin, nor the primacy and the infallibility of the Pope. He then cited many texts from the early Fathers of the Church to show how the College of Bishops existed in the early days, acted even juridically, and was even called the *collegium episcopale* by Optatus Milevitanus and other early writers.

On October 8, Bishop Jean Rupp of Monaco read a long list of texts from the Fathers of the Oriental Church in support of collegiality. Auxiliary Bishop Joseph Heuschen of Liège followed with a still longer list of texts. Bishop André Charue of Namur gave an exceedingly clear account of the four main biblical arguments for the foundation of the Church "on Peter with the other apostles." But the big day in the debate had been October 7; after that day, Cardinal Gracias told the Council Fathers—in English—"arguing for collegiality is like flaying a dead horse." He suggested that Cardinal Newman's *Essay on the Development of Christian Doctrine* ought to be the text whereby the Council should proceed.

For on October 7, after Cardinal Siri had subtly attacked it, a battery of powerful speeches supported the doctrine. One after another, from their different areas of competence and points of view, the spokesmen of the majority tried to assuage the fears of the minority, and then present their arguments. "Let us not fear to set forth traditional doctrine in new words," gray-haired, erect Cardinal Léger of Montreal urged the Council. Let us proceed with "calm" investigation and "avoid fear." Stress on collegiality does not derogate from the primacy of the Pope; it illuminates more clearly the unique ministry of Peter. In the light of ministry and service, moreover, bishops themselves "should endeavor to avoid such manifestations of splendor as may have been appropriate at a time when they enjoyed civil power, but which are out of place today."

Cardinal Koenig of Vienna showed that "the supreme power of the College of Bishops in the Church, together with and under the Pope . . . is not new teaching; it is found in tradition, among Oriental Catholics, in theological manuals, and, applied to an ecumenical council, in Canon 228." In collegiality, there is no derogation of the power of the Pope; moreover, "the teaching of this schema was held at Vatican I even by those Fathers upholding the infallibility of the Pope." The fears expressed at Vatican I concerning the expression "foundation of the Church on Peter and the other apostles" had been neutralized by time—no Catholic now doubted the primacy of the Pope. He cited the opening address of Pope Paul, which asked that the teaching on the episcopacy be "examined more deeply."

Then Cardinal Alfrink of Utrecht arose to rebut Cardinal Ruffini's resistance concerning Ephesians 2:20. But his main thrust was meant to allay fear. Insistence on collegiality "should give rise to no fear that an attempt is being made to lessen the dignity of the Roman Pontiff." Such fear may come from a preoccupation with love and fidelity to the Pope, but "fear is an obstacle to seeking the truth." He cited Pope Paul's encouragement to the bishops to renew the Church according to the Gospels, by clarifying the character of the bishops gathered around the universal pastor. Cardinal Lefèbvre of Bourges then spoke of "the fear which some have that a statement on the Episcopal College may compromise papal primacy or infallibility," and again pointed to the invitation given by Pope Paul to study the matter deeply. Cardinal Laurian Rugambwa, the tall young Negro Cardinal of Bukoba, Tanganyika, asked for a clear statement that a bishop receives a universal mission in the Church by his very consecration as a bishop, and that bishops are "pastors of the whole world," each required to help the other.

Maximos IV Saïgh, venerable Patriarch of Antioch, arose next and spoke, as usual, in French: "The definition of the primacy in Vatican I has frequently been exaggerated and thus has become an obstacle to union. It is not the primacy itself, clear in the Bible and tradition, which is an obstacle, but its exaggeration and misuses of power." He praised the present schema as a great improvement over the one rejected by the Council the year before, and over most theological manuals. "It should be stressed," however ,"that the real head of the Church is Christ and Christ alone, not the Pope." For Orientals it should be made crystal-clear that the power of the

Pope does not detract from the universal office of the bishops. The universal power of the Pope should be understood as a means of service. The appointment of bishops by the Pope is not according to a law of God, but is a contingent fact of the Western Church and should not be made a rule of law for the entire world. The Patriarch added a paradoxical conclusion: "Once freed from exaggerations in doctrine and in practice the Roman primacy will not only cease to be the principal obstacle to union among Christians, but will become the chief force which seeks and maintains this union. The primacy is absolutely indispensable as the center of unity for the Church."

Bishop De Smedt of Bruges, the most eloquent man at the Council, praised the intimate bond of union between Italians and the Holy See, and said that today all Catholics can aspire to the same closeness. Rapid communication is possible in a world united more closely than ever before. Thus, the Pope's task of "confirming the brethren" is made much lighter. "It is now desirable and imperative that the Pope, in matters of graver importance, communicate with the other bishops and with episcopal conferences." A desire for the internationalization of the Curia, moreover, expresses more love, not less, for the Holy See.

Bishop John Van Dodewaard of Haarlem, Holland, speaking for the Conference of Dutch Bishops, argued in terms of canon law, from the *supreme* power of ecumenical councils (canon 288), which is *ordinary* and not delegated. He urged that the final text of the schema express the idea of the ordinary supreme power of the Episcopal College. (It was as though the Dutch bishops had said: "All right, we'll argue juridically, if you want.") Finally, a Yugoslav bishop, Zazinovic, argued for a permanent representation of the bishops at Rome, with more power than the Curia. After October 7, the arguments for collegiality only grew tighter and stronger; and those against it had gradually to relinquish point after point. But, of course, many of the opposition were not convinced.

III

Despite the arguments of the minority, it was the spirit of Cardinal Newman that presided over the Vatican Council—that Newman who, as Pope Paul was to say publicly on October 27, "traced an itinerary, the most toilsome, but also the greatest, the most meaningful, the most conclusive, that human thought ever traveled during the last century, indeed one might say during the modern era. . . ." For it was Newman who justified, in the midst of those who sensed heresy in any intellectual work beyond the narrow confines of non-historical orthodoxy, the way by which the Church might find her way outside of those confines, without falling prey to historical relativism or skepticism. It was Newman who, at first, did not think the declaration of papal infallibility at Vatican I was "opportune." He felt that passions were too high, and that political and philosophical events in Italy were too limited and special to form a matrix for the universal definition that was to come. Newman wholly accepted the doctrine of infallibility; but he would have wished to see it placed in a fuller and more traditional context than that of Vatican I. The task of Vatican II was to begin to supply that context.

Almost every time the document of Vatican II used the phrase "the Episcopal College," however, it added the description "which cannot act independently of the Pope." One archbishop, noting that this description recurs thirty times in the short document, thought the number "excessive." But the partisans of non-historical orthodoxy cannot cease insisting on their conception of papal primacy; it is their chief theological support. As a symbol the papacy had become indistinguishable from their own existence and theological interests.

Maximos IV declared (and the Anglican Bishop Moorman concurred) that stripped of its exaggerations the primacy of Peter is an inevitable and beneficial service to the universal Church. As a focus of unity, as a single, clear voice of the faith of all, the papacy offers incalculable service to the servants of God. But one may note that the institution is fraught with the dangers of blasphemy, idolatory, the lust for power, intellectual laziness, ignorance, imprudence. In practice, the papacy is a difficult vocation for a man to try to live with; his every limitation limits the whole Church. Even conceptually, however, the papacy is difficult to understand correctly. Carried too far in the direction of the absolute monarchies of temporal kings, it is a blasphemy; it would supplant the humble Christ with Moloch, in whom men would find, not the vicar of Christ, but tyranny over the human spirit. That is why it is important, in fidelity to the Gospels, to see the papacy primarily as a ministry united very closely to the whole Church. The primacy of Peter is a gift of the Holy Spirit to the Church and for the Church; it is not to be conceived separately from the other gifts of the same Spirit to the Church. The Church is one temple, one body, one dwelling place of the Spirit.

In this context, Archbishop Joseph Descuffi of Smyrna, on October 11, pointed out an ambiguity in Vatican I's definition of the Pope's infallibility. In the famous formula, Vatican I declares that the Pope *ex sese et non ex consensu ecclesiae,* "of his own right and not because of the consent of the Church," can speak infallibly, under certain stringent conditions, on questions of faith or morals. The Archbishop thought that the phrasing of Vatican I created a pseudo-problem by opposing the two infallibilities, that of the Pope and that of the Church: what would happen if they conflict? For the same Holy Spirit grants both infallibilities: can He be in conflict with Himself? In its life and belief the Church as a whole can never be separated from the Pope. Both are secured by God from teaching heresy. "*Ex sese,*" of his own right, does not mean "from his own personal gifts." It means "in other words, by special assistance from God," and the Archbishop wanted this clarification inserted into the original definition.

An American Archbishop, Lawrence J. Shehan of Baltimore, confessed to the Council the same day that this text of Vatican I is "probably the main source of difficulties with our separated brethren." He asked no attenuation, only a clarification. A papal definition of doctrine "is never to be understood as against the consent of the Church. For since we believe the Pope to be infallible through divine assistance, by that very fact we believe that the assent of the Church will never be lacking to his declaration. It cannot happen that the body of bishops can be separated from its head; it cannot happen that the universal Church can fail." Thus God protects His Church and guarantees her passage through the vicissitudes of history. Pope and Church; Church and Pope—they are inseparable. Vatican II should make clear their inseparability.

These suggestions by the two archbishops do not try to remove the force from the "*ex sese.*" They do not hint that the Pope must first consult the bishops or the Church by some juridical, democratic machinery, before voicing his special witness to the faith of all. They do point out that it is the Holy Spirit who speaks through the Pope —the same Spirit Who vivifies the entire Church. The Church is not a human society, organized around human rules; God lives in it, humbling Himself to act through human voices. The Pope is not a magical figure, a spiritual dictator who can make Catholics believe today what they did not believe yesterday. But when today the Catholic people need a clear, strong voice of the faith they have long shared, the Pope is there, by the grace of God, to minister to their need.

Thus the arguments in St. Peter's in the autumn of 1963 did not attempt to minimize the role of the papacy. Paul Blanshard, author of *American Freedom and Catholic Power*, was surprised: "They're not taking back Vatican I at all, are they?" On the contrary, the majority at the Council tried to give back to the papacy its evangelical glory: that he who is greatest in the Church might appear as the servant of all; that Peter might feed all; that, with all his brother bishops gathered around him, he might confirm their faith. The majority tried to find terms to express this complementarity of the ministry of the bishops with the ministry of the Pope. To do so, they had to lower the secondary, instrumental language of jurisdiction, law, and power to second place, and raise to the first place the language of fraternity, mutual service, and diversity of roles. The partisans of non-historical orthodoxy feared this primary language. It was "too mystical," "merely moral," "dangerous to the primacy." But the majority thought the Church is indeed a mystery, that moral bonds are the strongest of all, and that their own loyalty to the primacy is no less ardent—but perhaps more evangelical—than that of the minority.

9

LATIN OR UNIVERSAL?

I

IN SPITE OF UNDERLYING DIFFERENCES in the attitudes and habits of mind which slowly became apparent in the speeches on the floor, the first two weeks of the second session were very peaceful. Then on October 11, Isaac Ghattas, the Coptic-Catholic Bishop of Thebes in Egypt, gave more evidence than anyone before him of how partial the document on the Church remained. He wished to know why the patriarchates of the East, "a providential institution in the life of the Church," did not have a place in the schema. "Unfortunately, though it is universal in intention, the schema is decidedly Latin in execution. The treatment seems to regard the universal Church as being only the Latin Church." The patriarchate is neither "exotic" nor a special "privilege" granted to minority churches. The Church of the East has not only different vestments and rites, but a different institutional structure. "This identification of the Latin Church with the universal Church is the root of all difficulties with the Orientals. They cannot accept any such mentality."

A week later, Father George Tavard, A.A., expert of the Council and member of the Secretariat for Christian Unity, described for *La Croix* (October 19) the divergent intellectual tendencies on the Council floor. The parting of the ways did not arise because some emphasized the primacy, while others emphasized collgiality—that way of posing the problem misses the point. Still less did it arise from questions concerning how to realize the doctrine of collegiality in practice—a question for later developments in canon law to decide.

117

"The problem is," he wrote, "how, after so many centuries in which the thinking, life and the administration of the Church developed in a legalistic direction, to think about the Church in a way essentially theological." The debate on chapter 2 began "to separate those who make an effort to envisage the structure of the Church outside the structures of canon law, and those who do not." A council is not, in principle, a servant of laws: it makes law. "It opens new avenues for the law because it plunges not only the bishops, but the whole Church into the Word of God, Who through Scripture and through history (which is Tradition) speaks to us."

"Is it as last possible," he asked, "to contemplate the stucture of the Church according to other patterns than those of power, of jurisdiction, of authority? Can our episcopate, formed by scholasticism and canon law and accustomed to the exercise of power, see itself in its *ensemble* with eyes which are not the eyes of jurists?" If it cannot, it will draw still firmer lines of distinction between the powers of Pope, bishops, clergy, and laymen; it will harden the positions which the First Vatican Council left open. The theology of power will evacuate still further than it already has the "great glory of the episcopate." If, on the contrary, the debates on the Church represent the "slow birth of a theology of the Church, both centered on Christ and pastoral, the Council will allow the Church and its hierarchy to be seen in their supernatural reality: the Church as the community of the children of God, listening to His word and participating in the presence of His Christ: the hierarchy, as a service one of another according to justice and love, for the glory of God alone." The issue of the doctrine of Vatican II on the Church is, he concluded, quite plain: "Will it be Catholic or simply Latin?"

On Monday, October 14, as if in answer to Bishop Ghattas and in anticipation of Father Tavard, the Oriental Patriarchs at the Council were called to "go up higher"—to sit, not after the cardinals, among the archbishops, but opposite the cardinals, equal in rank with them. The gesture was small, but gratifying. Moreover, Dr. Emilio Inglessis of Greece was added to the group of lay auditors, to represent the Catholic laity of the Oriental Churches.

The claims of the Eastern Churches against the Latin Church have been almost without number; the depth of feeling can scarcely be exaggerated. Thus it is ironic that the Latin Church should have become increasingly indebted to the Eastern Church in the second session. Day after day, Eastern prelates gave illuminating, vigorous speeches on the floor. They brought back into the center of the Church an ancient witness to the faith long overlooked in the West. Moreover, the direction in which they looked—toward the East—gave immense promise for the future of the world.

Hundreds of millions of fervent, devout, faithful Christians live in those vast areas of the world hardly known to the Westerner and now shut off by a political curtain. One had to think of Dostoevsky meditating on the Gospels, and of Pasternak. Perhaps someday men of East and West will be able to speak to one another; the world is growing toward a Teilhardian whole. From henceforth, merely to ignore one another is impossible.

In the Eastern Churches, the tradition of collegiality has continued uninterrupted since apostolic times. For some Eastern Churches, collegiality without the primacy has meant the loss of clarity and effectiveness in the world; they themselves admit it. On the other hand, the great scandal to the East has been the highhanded, imperialistic, complacent treatment accorded by the Latin Church to those Eastern Churches in communion with Rome. Words hardly suffice to repay the damages or heal the wounds. The Latin Church has forced the Eastern Churches toward Latinization. She has gone to great lengths to install Latin bishops in Eastern cities; she neglects to give even huge flocks of Eastern-rite Catholics in Western cities shepherds of their own. "There are in America approximately 125,000 Maronites and 50,000 Melkites who have not so much as a Vicar General of their own rite but are subject to the Latin ordinaries. 10,000 Italo-Greeks and 5,000 Syrians have no priests or parochial organization." [1] On the other hand, the Latin Patriarchate of Jerusalem was established for 4,000 Latin-rite Catholics. "Latin *archdioceses* in Greece, Iraq, and Turkey listed populations of 3,000; 2,180; 1,930; and 190 in the latest data released by the Vatican. Canon Law permits an Eastern non-Catholic who joins the Church to adopt any rite he wishes, including the more prosperous and prestigious Latin, while requiring Western Christians who join the Church to adopt the Latin rite. Jews cannot be received into the Church by clergy of the native Melkite church, but only by Latin-rite authorities. Eastern clergy may not engage in any missionary activity outside their dioceses without special permission, which means that the Catholic Church's missionary effort is virtually a Latin-rite preserve. . . ." [2]

The rites, customs, and spirituality of the East were formed in the patristic era, while the customs and spirit of the West underwent the great changes of the medieval and scholastic period. The two cultures incarnate Christian faith differently; in each, culture and faith have become like "two in one flesh." To take away Eastern culture from Eastern faith is to kill a living organism. But the Latin tendency toward abstractions, toward uniformity, whatever its good intentions, attempts to forge a pan-Catholicism, absorbing other Churches into the patterns of *Romanità*. "Innumerable statements (and *faits accomplis*) of the several curial Congregations, no less than the greater part of the new code of Eastern Canon Law indicate how little understood the Eastern-rite Churches are, how violently unwanted they have been by some of the highest officials in the Catholic Church. Respect for the rights and traditions of the Eastern Churches, so often proclaimed by the Holy See, has for so long been ignored and violated by Latin Catholics that, as a Melkite prelate recently wrote, 'their action has laid the Pope and his Curia open to a charge either of duplicity or of dangerous weakness.' . . ." [3]

Yet, with great charity and humility, the Eastern Churches in communion with Rome have remained faithful to Rome. They seem to realize that non-historical orthodoxy is only a transitory aberration in the life of the Church; it is, like the new wine skin of the Gospels, too new to contain the old wine of Christianity, and is doomed to split under the strain. The Eastern patriarchs tried to point out to their Western brothers that the document on the Church "does not pay sufficient attention to the long-standing tradition of the Oriental Churches." As Archbishop Elias Zoghby of Egypt told the Council on October 16, "The doctrine of the primacy, which the Oriental Church has never denied, has been so elaborated through the many years of separation that it cannot be recognized by the Orthodox. The unilateral nature of the schema, with its emphasis on Western theology, will prevent a dialogue with our separated brothers. Each time mention is made of the power of bishops, attention is called to its subordination to the Pope, which suggests that papal power is nothing other than some kind of limitation of episcopal power. Instead of its obsession with the primacy, the schema should not neglect more essential points, e.g., the priesthood of Christ. . . . The authority of the Pope, which is not absolute, isolated, and independent, cannot be understood except in relationship to the College of

Bishops. . . . It is a wonder that so many doubt the doctrine of collegiality, for it is manifest in the first centuries of the Church—important questions were always decided in synods—and has remained intact in the Orient."

II

Ironically, the second-most-debated point in the document on the Church was a minor point, the restoration of a permanent diaconate. But the debate disturbed emotional energies connected with the psychology of sex, and the issue of celibacy began to emerge from the shadows. The debate on the diaconate would have seemed like comic relief in the serious argument over collegiality, except that it was sometimes embarrassing to see how much emotion the issue generated. The long experience of the Orientals and the Protestant observers with a married clergy was a steadying influence on some members of the Council; their married life was an ever-present, quiet contrast to Roman celibacy. The Council made no move whatever to do away with the celibacy of priests. Priestly celibacy is by no means essential to the life of the Church; its advantages do not always seem to outweigh the harm it does; but in general the Council seemed satisfied with present discipline.

The reason for restoring the permanent diaconate is to allow married men in mission countries, in the absence of priests, to exercise the functions of ordained ministers. Deacons do not have many powers; they cannot say Mass or hear confessions. But they can preach from the pulpit, lead prayers, and distribute communion. Moreover, the very presence of an ordained man in some remote villages, or in areas of large cities which lack priests, offered the Church a new means of stability and permanence. "In Africa we are living in the first century of Christianity," one bishop told his brothers; "we are living under the conditions of the early Church, and need every means Christ gave the early Church." To many bishops in established lands, however, the restoration of the diaconate seemed at first an exotic gesture, a bit of romantic archaism. Hard, practical men, they at first wanted none of it.

In the early days of the Church, deacons were those who ministered to the poor, read the Gospels at Mass, distributed the eucharist. As the centuries passed, the institution atrophied until, now, a deacon is simply a fourth-year student in theology who is soon to be ordained a priest; and he is, as a deacon, already vowed to celibacy and irrevocably committed to the clerical state. Many thought that the restoration of the ancient diaconate would only create new problems, and serve no good end. Thus, when debate was first opened on chapter 2, Cardinal Spellman of New York bypassed the urgent problem of collegiality to blast the lines about deacons out of consideration, before they were overlooked. He marshaled six arguments against the restoration. (1) The question is disciplinary; this document is dogmatic. (2) It is hard enough to build seminaries for future priests; how will we find houses for future deacons? (3) The permanent diaconate became obsolete because priests could handle its functions; it is still obsolete. (4) Today lay religious and laymen increasingly handle such functions. (5) The proposal for a permanent diaconate proceeds "mostly from liturgists" who wish to restore ancient practices without taking into account present conditions; not everything is good just because it is old. (6) Vocations to the priesthood might fall off if these permanent deacons are not bound by the law of celibacy.

Then Cardinal Ruffini said that the permission for permanent deacons to marry "would inflict a grave wound on ecclesiastical celibacy." Cardinal Antonio Bacci of the Roman Curia next agreed that the proposal of married deacons was "both inopportune and dangerous." Older ideas, he said, are not always better—in these things, the Curia is for new ideas. If the law of celibacy is relaxed, he said, new seminaries will be needed for deacons; vocations to the priesthood would decrease, since youth will choose what is easier. "Open a *fenestrella*," he concluded, "next it will be a *fenestra*." A married diaconate is one window the Council is not to throw open.

So the argument raged on. Nearly every Italian bishop who spoke opposed the "wound to celibacy" that a married diaconate would render. Most of the Yugoslav and Polish bishops were opposed. Thirty-eight Portuguese bishops had a spokesman say: "If a candidate does not have the knowledge and the celibacy of a priest, he is not apt for the diaconate; if he does, he should become a priest. . . . Everyone here agrees that married deacons would harm priestly celibacy." Cardinal Siri opposed the break with celibacy; in a later interview with the press Cardinal Ottaviani called it "dangerous." A Slav bishop warned about possible economic and moral difficulties, scandal, concubinage, the invalid marriages of the deacons' children

—and regaled the Council Fathers with the report of a conversation with an Orthodox priest who told him how lucky he was to be celibate. An Italian missionary bishop used some simple common sense to argue that since those who receive communion usually need to go to confession first, the usefulness of deacons wouldn't amount to much; priestly vocations will decline; and deacons will find it hard to survive financially, since they won't receive the Mass stipends which many priests live on. Bishop Carraro of Verona could see theological, pastoral, and ecumenical reasons for a restored diaconate —but not a married diaconate.

There seemed to be almost absolute block in the minds of some of the bishops against uniting marriage to holy orders under any form. It seemed to outsiders that the celibacy of these bishops had been so precarious, at least unconsciously, that if they had had the choice they would never have accepted it. How else explain the claim that if deacons could marry fewer would wish to be priests? American seminarians in Rome, reflecting on the severe regulations they encountered there, smiled at the debates on the Council floor; they were made to live in an environment of such fearful attitudes day after day. Sophistication in the psychology of the celibate life seems rare in Italy. Young men put in cassocks from the time they are ten or eleven, and rigidly separated from ordinary human contacts with lay people of either sex, do not know very much even about the physiology of sex.

But the missionary bishops of the world, who had desperate need for new forms of help, were not content to let the matter rest because of the squeamishness of some. Several bishops of Thailand and Laos had Bishop Peter Carretto warn the Council "not to miss the point" —more men are needed than a law of celibacy will allow. During World War II, laymen had done the work of deacons in those countries, without any special training; with training and the special sacramental graces of holy orders they could do even better. In the name of the Conference of Bishops of Venezuela, Bishop Henriquez-Jimenez said that the duty of the Council "is not to repeat what we already firmly hold, but to progress"; he supported both collegiality and the married diaconate.

But the "big guns" on this issue were those of Cardinals Doepfner and Suenens; Cardinal Landazuri Ricketts of Peru and Bishop Kémérer of Argentina; and an African, a Bolivian, a Chinese, and a Dutch-Indonesian who spoke together on October 10. Cardinal Doepfner spoke first, on October 7, demolishing point by point the arguments of Cardinal Spellman. The threefold division of the hierarchy into bishops, priests, and deacons is of divine institution and belongs in a chapter on doctrine. The schema accepts the principles of Trent, recognizing varying conditions of place and time. It does not try to solve all the practical issues involved in the restoration of the diaconate, but provides a doctrinal basis. New seminaries will not be required, for no new functions will be instituted; those already doing the work of deacons will simply be allowed to receive the sacrament of deacons. There will be no danger to celibacy, for the diaconate is a special vocation distinct from the priesthood. "Deacons are not second-class priests"; and married men-catechists in mission lands already do the work. The purpose of the schema is "to open the door" to further examination.

On October 8, Cardinal Landazuri spoke for ninety-five Latin Americans in presenting eight arguments for the restoration of the diaconate: Christ instituted the sacrament, so its graces should not go unsued; ministers converted to Catholicism could find a new field of work; the married life of deacons would throw into relief the unique sacrifice of priestly celibacy; seminarians unsuited for the priesthood might find a place in the diaconate, and so forth. Cardinal Suenens completed the power play with theological arguments. The diaconate, he said, is a sacrament and part of the very constitution of the Church. The question should be treated from the point of view of grace, not merely from the point of view of practicality. The operation of grace in the deacons of the early Church was obvious; the Church should always entrust certain tasks only to those with the sacramental grace necessary for establishing a community of grace. The present Church has a right to the graces Christ established for it. The Council is not asked to prescribe anything, but to leave the doors open, especially for small isolated communities, and for immense communities lacking the experience of the Church as a family. He rejected the *a priori* argument that a married diaconate would harm the law of celibacy or bring about a decrease in vocations; it is a gift of grace and will strengthen the Christian community. He then suggested an extraordinary procedure: a vote on this question as soon as discussion on the chapter was closed.

On the 10th, four missionary bishops spoke with great eloquence.

Bishop Yu-Pin of Nanking asked for deacons—married if so desired locally—"on account of the lack of vocations caused by persecution," and because married deacons would build "a bridge" between the clergy and the laity. An African pleaded with great intensity; a Bolivian asked for immediate help. The Indonesian bishops all desired deacons, but were divided on the question of celibacy. But it was Bishop Kémérer on the 14th who clinched the argument most effectively. He spoke just after more than a half dozen talks against a married diaconate; he spoke simply. He said that the requirement of celibacy would frustrate any hope of easing the critical situation in Latin America. Statistics mislead when they show one priest for every six thousand Catholics there; in many localities, there is one for every thirty thousand. Celibacy requires a special grace, "but also certain national conditions, lacking in some times and places." Married deacons "canonically and theologically would belong to the hierarchy, but psychologically and culturally to the people." Deacons would continue in their professions, and assist in the parishes on weekends. "The restoration of the diaconate is our great hope; and it is the wish of many bishops in Latin America that you, Venerable Fathers, do not deprive us of this hope when the matter comes to a vote. The door is already open, and if among you there are some who do not wish to enter, we shall not force you to enter. But we graciously beg you not to close the door on us, because we *do* want to enter. Allow us to do so!" The Council Fathers broke out into spontaneous applause. The case was won.

III

Friday afternoon, October 18, the English-language newsmen gathered again in the basement of the USO building. The smell of fresh American coffee was in the air. The men from the wire services, the great newspapers, the weeklies and monthlies sat smoking and sipping coffee. The room overflowed with visitors; seminarians stood leaning against the walls. Father John B. Sheerin, C.S.P., moderator of the meeting, began tapping a glass on the ping-pong table, behind which sat seven experts.[4] Father Sheerin called on Father Godfrey Diekmann, O.S.B., editor of *Worship* magazine at Collegeville, Minnesota, and one of the most respected theologians at the Council. Father Diekmann, a tall, handsome, broad-shouldered Benedictine, with trim white hair and a rich enunciation of English, read from a few notes he had made about the Christian conception of celibacy. His few words were in answer to a request from several American newsmen, who had been buzzing for days about the heated discussion over what seemed to them a minor matter, the celibacy of deacons. The horror in which some of the Council Fathers seemed to hold the idea of married clerics seemed to them a little strange. A few of them already had the idea that the celibate life was an odd kind of life. The emotional intensity of the arguments against married deacons only seemed to confirm their opinion.

Father Godfrey noted that Christian celibacy is not to be regarded as a state in rivalry to marriage, much less in opposition to it. Scripture begins with a story of God blessing a marriage, and ends with the vision of the Spirit and the Bride. "And we might say: all the story in between expresses God's relation to man in terms of marriage." The book of Genesis says that it is not good for man to be alone. "This is absolutely true. Man is a social being; his personality must be completed by another person or persons. Love of another is essential to human personality." Celibacy is not contrary to marriage; it has meaning in Christian terms only as something parallel to marriage, a species of marriage, a "spiritual marriage. . . . It is not something negative, i.e., a not-getting-married. Of its nature it is positive: a fuller dedication of love and life energies to Christ, and therefore to one's fellow men. If it is merely negative, it is spinsterhood, male or female; the spinsterhood of the selfish, of pinched and warped personalities."

The example of Christ was "thought to be relevant for other ministers, and was gradually applied to bishops, priests, and deacons." Celibacy in its ideal form is "not repressive or restrictive; it is a freeing of the energies of priest, or bishop, or deacon for fuller dedication to his people." Celibacy is not of divine law, but "is a disciplinary Church law which could be changed. There are different customs in East and West. Yet despite painful and even egregious failures in practice, especially from the fifth to the tenth century, the ideal has been insisted upon."

"Celibacy is misnamed as a 'single state,' if by that is meant anything like taking advantage of freedom from the duties of married life in order to be more or less exclusively concerned with self. After all, it is axiomatic that charity, the love of God, is the highest commandment; love of neighbor is identical with it." Unless celibacy is distinguished by greater love and service of one's fellow men, it is not Christian celibacy; it might be called unnatural.

Father Godfrey thought it might be said that many married Catholics are resentful of the celibate clergy who insist on the laws concerning married life. "You have easy talking," they say. Perhaps, if some of those who are in holy orders are married men, deacons, for example, then they could give an example of clerical married life. They would have the experience of marriage in their own lives, and would contribute to a better rapport and mutual understanding between clergy and laity.

IV

The treatment accorded the press was much better in the second session than in the first. There were still many inconveniences: the room set aside for many hundreds of newsmen at the noon briefings had not nearly enough tables and chairs, and for all-day use the toilet facilities were minimal. But the Vatican is slowly learning modern ways; to complain would be premature. The bishops of the United States,[5] moreover, did all they could to make the work of the press easier, more thorough, and more comfortable. Father Edward L. Heston, C.S.C., worked late into the afternoon before he even stopped for lunch, getting out the mimeographed summaries of the speeches of the day. Father Robert Trisco kept minute and voluminous notes on every speech on the floor, in order to answer questions in detail. Father Sheerin of *The Catholic World*, and Elmer von Feldt of the NCWC news department, did all they could to line up special interviews and experts at the hour-long conference each afternoon. Bishop Albert R. Zuroweste of Belleville, Illinois, devised many extra projects and benefits, arguing steadily before the special press commission of the Council for a more sensible program. All in all, there was too much news for journalists to gather; one would have had to be at four different places at once to be at every conference, talk, or event that was worthy of attention. The Council demanded seven-day weeks, fourteen-hour days of the newsmen. Two or three generations of theological advances were being packed into one, in an intense exposure of the world's bishops and theologians to free and open confrontation.

On October 1, at the very opening of the Council, Pope Paul himself graciously agreed to give an audience for the press. The audience might not have been as pleasant as he planned, but it deserves to be recorded; for it indicates some of the human problems of a universal Church.

The day of the audience was a brilliant, hot day; the audience had been scheduled for noon. Of course, noon, Roman time, means 12:20, and those who had hurried through the streets and across the piazza to meet at the bronze doors stood mopping their brows. When the doors were finally opened, the hundreds of pressmen—and many other persons who had no press cards—were made to hurry up flight after flight of stairs, perspiring, and irritated because certain groups were running ahead to get the front places. The Holy Father was no doubt hoping to give the press a generous reception; his aides seriously failed him. There were not one-third enough benches in the small room. The sun beat upon the closed windows; not a breath of air was allowed to enter to relieve the body heat building up in the room. Moreover, nuns, seminarians, and priests pushed and shoved unmercifully. The center aisle between the rows of benches was jammed tight. The courteous and socially conscious in that aisle, until they learned to defend themselves, were elbowed, pushed, and mauled. The editors of *L'Osservatore Romano* themselves did not hesitate to push their way through the aisle and toil their way from bishop to highly placed friends until they had assumed places, complacently, near the doorway through which the Pope was to enter. At the very last moment, just as the Holy Father was entering, young men with floodlights and television equipment, every inch the *paparezzi* of *La Dolce Vita*, pushed their way through the enwedged mass of people, much to the Holy Father's discomfort.

Pope Paul is a kindly, intense man; seated in his white cassock on the dais, a monsignor at either side, he read the speech in French that had been prepared for him. He admitted that reporting a Council is "a difficult task." This imposing assembly "has some similarity with large human gatherings, when in reality it is quite different. In fact, there could be a temptation to search out certain villains: nationalism, conflicting tendencies, parties, historical and geographic differences, as for instance between East and West. If attention is limited to these externals, or if it undertakes to emphasize them, then the reality of things is altered, even falsified. For all the bishops are trying to avoid giving any substance to these divisions, in order on the contrary to be guided by the objective divine truth which they profess and by the fraternal charity which animates them."

After the brief talk, the bishops present advanced to kiss the Pope's ring and exchange a few words. A few eminent laymen—the editors of *L'Osservatore Romano*, for instance—did the same. Then the Pope blessed the assembly. He had hardly concluded when a mad rush developed among those priests and seminarians who had earlier pushed their way to the front. Benches were overturned in a sudden clamor. Clerics rushed up the stairs of the dais clutching for the Pope's hand. The guards and masters of ceremony could not immediately form a protective wall. A look of terror passed momentarily across the Pope's face, and then his guards opened a way to the door and, clenching his teeth, he speedily made his exit. Many of the newsmen, Catholic and non-Catholic, who were seeing the Vatican for the first time, began to feel a certain sympathy for the poor prisoner.

NOTES

1. Thomas E. Bird, "Ecumenics and the East," *The Commonweal*, LXXIX, 8 November 15, 1963), p. 222.
2. *Ibid.*
3. *Ibid.*, p. 221.
4. At various times these were: Fathers Gustave Weigel, S.J.; Francis J. McCool, S.J.; Monsignor George G. Higgins; Fathers Eugene H. Maly; Frederick McManus; Robert Trisco; Francis J. Connell, C.Ss.R.; Bernard Häring, C.Ss.R.; John Long, S.J.; George A. Tavard, A.A.; Gregory Baum, O.S.A.; Thomas Stransky, C.S.P. Godfrey Diekmann, O.S.B., Piet Fransen, S.J.
5. Besides their work for the press, the American bishops also provided another useful service at the Council. Three of them, Archbishops Krol and Hallinan and Bishop Tracy, acting with the mandate of the others, began publishing a "Council Digest" of the speeches given in St. Peter's. A staff of young priests prepared the terse, accurate summaries every day, and the NCWC office in Rome sent them out by messenger to the hotels and residences where the nearly two hundred American bishops in Rome were staying. Other English-language prelates heard of the "Digest" and by October 24 over eight hundred copies were being distributed, *"sub secreto,"* to bishops of nineteen nations: i.e., to more than a third of the Council Fathers. Non-Americans began queuing up for the digest at 4, Via della Conciliazione, every afternoon at 4:30.

10

THE LAYMAN

IN THE THIRD WEEK of October, the Fathers of the Council finally opened debate on chapter Three of the document on the Church, "The People of God and the Laity." It was a chapter—were they to take it seriously—which could change the philosophy to be favored in the Church. For as soon as the Council began to grapple with the problems of the layman, it began to grapple with the world of history in which the layman lives: with the many kinds of democracy in the world, with men of different professions and beliefs, with ennui and conflicting ideals, with the power of armies and the ambiguities of love. When the Council would wrestle with the world of the layman, it would touch ground.

The opening of this debate, moreover, marked the first time in twenty centuries of the Church's history that she was giving explicit solemn attention to laymen in the Church. Even so, it may be doubted if many of the Fathers really grasped how clerical the Church is, how preoccupied it is with ecclesiastical matters, how great a chasm yawns between it and the world of men. Some of the best talks of the session, nevertheless, were given while this subject was on the floor. The Church will never be the same again.

After a brief introduction in which it describes the people of God as a fellowship of love and truth, chapter 3 speaks of the equality of all the members of the Church. The people of God is one: in it all have the same baptism, the same grace, the same call to perfection, the same salvation, the same hopes, the same charity, the same means of salvation. In Christ there is no inequality of nationality, social condition, or sex. All do not follow the same way of life and do not show the same generosity. Yet all are called to holiness. There are different functions in this one, same people: teachers, pastors, the faithful, and superiors. Yet all are tied together, superiors serving the people and the people obeying and cooperating with their superiors. The laity are the faithful who, being assumed by baptism into the people of God, serve God in the ordinary Christian way and fulfill their part of the mission of the Christian people, *but are not members of the hierarchy or the religious state*; the definition is, in other words, largely negative.

The chapter then goes on to speak of the universal priesthood of all believers. There is an essential difference, and not simply one of degree, between the ministerial priesthood of the clergy and the universal priesthood of the faithful. The universal priesthood is exercised in baptism, confirmation, the eucharist, and matrimony. Moreover, laymen participate in Christ's priestly, prophetic, and royal functions. In the "sense of faith" which they have, taught them by God and articulated in response to those commissioned to teach them, they manifest the Church's indefectibility.

Next, the document speaks of the vocation of all laymen to the apostolate. Their common task, it asserts, is to announce the faith and add religious value to the things of the world. Secondly, they are to promote the conditions required for the spread of religion, and to assist in the development of moral values in the world. Thirdly, they are to sanctify themselves and others through the daily secular tasks they perform, in order that the whole world may "shine with the spirit of Christ." Lastly, in their relations with the hierarchy, laymen are encouraged to show a generous, frank, and free mind, in explaining their needs and their desires to their pastors. It notes that they have the right, and sometimes the duty, to give their opinion concerning the good of the Church or the community. It insists, however, that they could best exercise this right through official channels, where such exist; and that they always do well to exercise it with charity, prudence, truthfulness, humility, courage, and due respect. The chapter says, finally, that laymen must obey their superiors, especially those whose authority was instituted by Christ. They should obey them even when these superiors may provoke criticism. They should not forget to pray for their superiors.

Meanwhile, a plan was afoot, championed by Cardinal Suenens and many others, to divide this chapter into two sections, one on the people of God and the other on the laity. The first section, on the people of God, would become chapter 2 of the schema on the Church, and the second section would become chapter 4. Thus, the schema on the Church would begin with a first chapter on the Church as a Mystery; go on to a second chapter on the Church as the people of God; then to a third chapter on the hierarchy within the people of God; and then to a fourth chapter on the laity. The fifth chapter would be the one that had been the fourth chapter, on the calling of all the people of God to holiness.

In its intention, this new chapter on the laity was something exciting and original in the life of the Church. It evoked, in general, a very different spirit from the clerical conception of the Church which had prevailed in the past. The document, nevertheless, was rather negative, clerical, and groping; it barely entered into the real life of laymen. It was like the first bather of the summer cautiously dipping his toe into the sea. The work is painstaking, but it may prove worth our while to follow some of the talks given on this chapter on the laity. For, at this stage of the second session, what happened on the floor was still of major importance. It was only a week, or perhaps two weeks later, that it became apparent that important things were taking place behind the scenes as well; only later still did it turn out that what was taking place behind the scenes was more important than what was taking place out front.

For on October 15, Cardinal Suenens, the moderator of the day, followed up a hint he had dropped earlier, and announced that the moderators would propose four votes to the Council on October 17, to give guidance to the theological commission on the most controverted points of chapter 2. The procedure was a novel one; but it seemed reasonable and sound to most of those who heard it. The debate on chapter 2 had been protracted—even to the point of tedium—and the standing vote to close it was nearly unanimous. The talks on the floor had not followed any order; collegiality was all mixed up with the diaconate, and much that had been said had been repetitous, useless, or confusing. For many of the bishops, a public vote seemed to offer the surest path to clarity. But apparently the moderators had neglected to clear their decision through the council of presidents; through Archbishop Felici, the Secretary General; and

—as became known much later—through Cardinal Ottaviani. The four votes were not proposed before the general assembly on the 17th, nor for many days thereafter.

Late in the morning of October 16, then, after the last receding tide of debate on chapter 2, Cardinal Ernesto Ruffini arose to give the opening talk on the layman in the Church. The schema indicates, Cardinal Ruffini said, that the laity has a mission directly from Christ; in reality, their only mission comes through the hierarchy. Secondly, to speak in terms of rights for the laymen without defining the limits of these rights is to incur the danger of laymen interfering in the proper exercise of the powers of the hierarchy. "Unless the imprecise terminology in the text is corrected, there is a danger that pastors and bishops may encounter difficulties in cases where they must disagree with the laity. If the laity feels it has a juridical right to share in the mission of the Church, this could lead to a weakening of the position of the hierarchy." Thirdly, the schema tends to reduce episcopal offices to a service, and thereby minimizes the proper role of authority. Fourthly, the schema speaks of the *sensus fidei*, the "sense of faith" among the faithful, as infallible; only the teaching Church is actively infallible, any other infallibility is passive. Fifthly, the schema seems to indicate that charisms are common, ordinary facts in the Church today, whereas in fact they are very rare.

Gentle Cardinal Cento of the Curia spoke next. "As president of the commission on the lay apostolate," he said, "I am grateful to those who wrote this schema for providing a foundation for our later one." Cardinal Cento approved of the division suggested by the coordinating commission, which would make the part on the people of God chapter 2 of the whole schema, and the part on the laity chapter 4. The schema, he said, provides much food for meditation, both for priests and for laymen. Cardinal José Maria Bueno y Monreal, Archbishop of Seville, Spain, took the microphone. He thought that the schema said many things that were worthy of praise. But he found the concept of the people of God a new one, lacking in sufficient development to serve as a mature way of explaining the Church. He preferred to have the Council Fathers lean more on the concept of the Mystical Body. Cardinal Antonio Bacci of the Roman Curia followed him, saying that the use of the term "universal priesthood" in relation to the laity is most objectionable. Cardinal Bacci was the Latin expert at the Council and he explained that the phrase "universal priesthood" means priesthood in that perfect, fullest sense which only Christ enjoys. Others only participate in this priesthood; the hierarchical priest, for example, in a twofold power over the mystical body of Christ and over the physical body of Christ. But the laymen shares in the priesthood only in a wider, metaphorical sense. Cardinal Bacci, therefore, wanted the word "universal" removed from the text and something inserted to show that the word "priesthood" is to be taken in the wider, imperfect sense.

Thus ended the first day of debate on the layman in the Church.

II

Every day, Monday through Friday, the Council opened with a solemn Mass at 9 A.M., followed by the enthronement of the book of the Gospels at the head of the assembly, as though to remind the Fathers of what they were about. It was nearly ten, or later, before debate got under way. Two hours of actual debate a day does not seem long: in eleven weeks, the Council met less than eighty-four hours in public debate. On the other hand, two hours of Latin discourses, following each other like clockwork every ten minutes (as one man speaks, the next steps to a microphone, ready to begin as the first concludes), is tiring in the extreme. Twelve, sixteen, eighteen speakers a day delivered themselves of their reflections, in a variety of voices, a variety of accents. It may be instructive to recreate a given day in the debate—or, rather, to combine the best talks of two unusually fruitful ones—in order to suggest the frustrating feeling of a debate without conversation or dialogue, a debate of speeches prepared at least three days in advance; and yet to appreciate how good some of the orations were. For there is something to be said for the formality of the proceedings and the polish of some of the talks.

On Thursday, October 17, Bishop Louis Rastouil of Limoges, France, led off the debate on the layman by noting that in the Old Testament the people of God was essentially a priestly people. He expressed approval of many things in the text but was interrupted by the moderators when his comments took on the aspect of a sermon. Bishop Stanislas Lokuang of Tainan, China, in the name of fifteen Chinese bishops, noted that the idea of a universal priesthood is easily understood in the Confucian tradition, for that tradition has no official ministerial priesthood. Offerings made by heads of the nation or heads of the family are considered as the offering of the

whole nation or the whole family. Bishop Franz Hengsbach of
Essen, Germany, doubted that the concession of more responsibility
to the laity would endanger the hierarchy's authority; there is a
greater danger, he said, in denying the laity more responsibility. "If
we don't grant further responsibility to the laity, the hierarchy will
be unable to fulfill its obligations to the world, and will frustrate the
impulse of the Holy Spirit." He criticized the schema for being too
abstract.

"For four hundred years the faithful have been waiting for a positive conciliar statement on the place, dignity, and vocation of the layman," Bishop John J. Wright of Pittsburgh then announced. Bishop
Wright, one of the best known and respected American prelates
before the Council, was breaking his long public silence to speak for
the first time in the Council hall. He asked that the schema be
accepted as "a good beginning." He wanted it to be accepted as it
is, "unless it can be made stronger." He wanted it remembered that
the whole movement toward a proper appreciation of the lay apostolate had been given impetus by Pius XI and Pius XII, and had
been furthered by the teachings of many theologians and the experiences of many Catholic Action groups under bishops around the
world. Now is the opportunity for the whole Church in council to
give a theological and organic foundation to Catholic Action. The
laity know very well that their priesthood differs from the ministerial priesthood, and they rejoice in the priestly character of the
Church, but they will also rejoice if the hierarchy takes the initiative
in putting an end to the false notion that the Church is only clerical.
The traditional canonical notion of the layman is negative—it defines
him as one who is not a cleric, not a religious—and must be replaced
by a positive and organic concept. Once the Council has defined the
theological nature of the laity, the juridical bones of the Church will
come alive with theological flesh and blood.

A short while later Bishop Arthur Elchinger, the Coadjutor Bishop
of Strasbourg, France, described the conditions of life in which the
modern Church finds itself. The schema speaks well, he said, on the
Mystical Body, the people of God, the family of David, and the universal communion of the sons of God, which are established through
baptism and the other sacraments. "But our pastoral experience
urges us to ask: how can these notions of universality and community,
often understood juridically and abstractly by the faithful, come to

have a personal and vital effect in their lives, unless their deeply rooted individualism is changed—unless they learn a sense of Catholic community, through the concrete, daily experience of brotherly union?" He asked the Council Fathers to remember that many recipients of the sacraments are in effect spiritual gluttons, egotistically seeking in religion their own individual security. Under modern living conditions, men often feel lonely, useless, and anonymous: our parishes are too huge to teach them any sense of community. Moreover, the spirit of institutions from other times offers no help. Every day more of our people turn to religious sects which offer an experience of brotherhood; even secular organizations offer a more vivid experience of community than the Church. The individualism of former times has become a vice; bishops, priests, and people must create the experience of Christian community in renovated parishes, in small groups less dependent on geography than on the various professions of modern life. Faith and charity seek an ecclesial experience.

Bishop Philip Hannan, auxiliary of Washington, D.C., also urged that the schema be more concrete. Laymen, he said, should be invited to bear witness to the faith in every aspect of their lives and to take an active part in those organizations which have great influence on modern living; for example, parents' education associations, workers' unions, professional and political organizations. He also urged that, where the text asks for official channels through which Catholic laymen could make their views known to the clergy, it should be amended to add: "and these channels should be established where they do not already exist." He noted that the National Councils of Catholic Men and Women in the United States lets advice of great value become lost simply because the layman does not want to appear bold before the bishops.

Archbishop Mario Castellano of Siena, Italy, thought that the document was too Latin in style, too much like the scholasticism of the classroom. He wanted the text more positive and more scriptural. Archbishop Louis Mathias of Madras, India, spoke of the shortage of priests in the world and said that, as a result, "we must fall back on the laity. . . . Our hope is in dedicated members of the laity who will be as totally consecrated to spreading the kingdom of Christ as the clergy strictly so called."

Bishop William Philbin of Down and Connor, Ireland, then gave one of the most memorable talks of the entire session. He spoke of a false image of the Church very common in our time. "We should be very careful," he said, "that the schema does not encourage the false idea that the Church is concerned exclusively with the afterlife, and little or not at all with the secular aspects of life. This schema, unless amended, will further strengthen that false image." The chapter "should do better justice to the mind of the Church on the affairs of this world." First, Christian charity toward the poor ought not to be merely remedial, a rescue operation after the fact, but a constructive force before the fact: Christians must strive to reduce poverty and to obviate injustices in the world. Secondly, it is the duty of the Council to point out the way for laymen to supernaturalize their daily work; the Council should give the blessing of the Church not only to traditional occupations but also to the modern technical arts, to science, to international social work, and the rest. The Council ought also to support the demands of social justice, against the unfair distribution of goods. Thirdly, the natural human virtues: industry, temperance, self-discipline, and others must be stressed, if the Council is to have a good name before the world. The example of Mary and Joseph should be invoked and the place of the Christian family extolled. Nor can the Church condemn artificial birth control without helping solve the great problems of the married couple. "As it stands now, the schema treats unrealistically of an ideal world, not of the world in which fallen man struggles and sweats to provide for his own, and to win heaven."

On Friday, October 18, once more not a word was said about the promised four votes, which now came to be known in the press as the "mystery votes." The vote on the whole of chapter 3 of the document on the liturgy was taken—votes on amendments or chapters of the liturgy document were taken almost every day. Sixteen speakers then addressed themselves to the question of the layman. Of these talks one of the most notable was by Cardinal Gracias of India. "We should not forget that we are dealing with laymen in the concrete, with individuals living in the world, subject to all the laws and weaknesses of human nature. Consequently our approach to the apostolate of the laity must be practical and realistic, not theological and mystical. . . . Some members of the hierarchy neither seek nor want the collaboration of the laity. When it is occasionally offered, they give the impression that accepting it is something of a privilege. The laity have not only a call and an invitation, but also a right, to share in the mission of the Church." This does not mean a share in the mission of the hierarchy; the hierarchy has a special part in achieving the mission of the universal Church. Laymen "must engage in secular activities and through these activities bring the sacred into the profane, and ennoble and sanctify their daily lives." As he did each time he spoke in the Council, the Cardinal broke into English—thus startling many of the English-speaking prelates with his sudden intelligibility—saying that escapism can never be the Christian's philosophy of life; the Christian belongs in the real world. "We must expect that there will be some friction at times between the clergy and the laity, but this should not be surprising, inasmuch as no means have yet been found to forestall all occasions of conflict between parish priests and their bishops." The laity are to collaborate with the hierarchy, but are never to give the impression that, so to speak, the day of the priest is past.

The next speaker, Cardinal Rugambwa of Tanganyika, said the chapter should provide a more internal definition of the layman, not merely a juridical or theological one. An Indian, Bishop Lawrence Picachy of Jamshedpur, said: "We must make the laity understand that we want their collaboration. The text puts undue emphasis on the sole obligation of obedience." He asked the Council Fathers to recall the words of St. Augustine to the effect that though they are shepherds in charge of sheep, nevertheless, before the Divine Good Shepherd, they too are sheep with their people. In the name of the sixty-nine German-speaking bishops, Bishop Joseph Schröffer of Eichstätt, Germany, said that in considering the universal priesthood an excess would be better than an omission. "The danger is not that the laity will exaggerate their priestly role, but rather that they will consider themselves totally profane and not consecrated at all." Besides, the text should speak of "the hierarchy and the rest of the people of God," since the hierarchy, too, is a part of the people of God. Bishop Paternus Geise, in the name of the thirty extremely articulate bishops of Indonesia, criticized the document for not showing clearly "the Christian value of mundane activity itself. It is God's will that this world be evolved by all men, in the spirit of solidarity, so that each can live humanly." The layman's daily acts in his family, his office, and public life, consecrate the world, as it is, to God. But these actions themselves, not only their effects, are to be positively appreciated. "In speaking of the people of God," said Archbishop Lorenz

Jaeger of Paderborn, Germany, we should be careful not to use concepts that are too idealistic: "The Church is essentially holy, but in point of fact it is a pilgrim not yet at the end of his journey; it includes sinners."

Bishop Michael Klepacz of Lodz, Poland, then asked the Council to define the proper relationship between Church and State. He named two possible solutions: concordats and the system of separation. The system of concordats upholds the Church's rights, but it often renders the Church subject to the State, particularly in financial matters. The separation of Church and State, if rightly understood, can benefit the Church and the State. It gives the Church an independence that is invaluable. This matter should be treated either here or in Cardinal Suenens "Schema 17" on the Church and the modern world. He asked for the omission of the word "unfortunate," *infaustae*, with which the text describes the separation of Church and State. He noted that this question is particularly important because of the encroachment of totalitarian states in the field of human rights. Where there is separation of Church and State, he argued, the State is precluded from interference; the Church is freer and comes closer to the people. Through its independence and its ability to defend their rights, the people come to have greater respect for its moral principles. Moreover, separation is happier for the State because a free Church raises up in the State men who seek justice.

Bishop Emile De Smedt of Bruges, Belgium, in the name of more than seventy bishops, pointed out that the laity are called to share in all three of the offices proper to Christ: (a) A *sacerdotal office:* by reason of their baptism and confirmation, all their lives should be religious, offered to God especially in the eucharist. (b) A *prophetic office:* their lives should bear witness to truth and to Christ, under whatever circumstances. (c) A *kingly office:* in concrete human life, both individual and social, laymen can act effectively and well, cooperating with all men of good will in the humble service of building up Christ's kingdom, a kingdom of liberty, justice, truth, and love. The life of the layman completes the redemption of earthly reality. As the last speaker of the day, Giles Barthe of Fréjus-Toulon, France, described the pessimism common to the modern age; laymen must be heralds of hope in human life.

This, roughly, was one long day's discussion in Vatican II on the role of the layman in the Church—a far advance over non-historical orthodoxy, but not yet fully grappling with the world laymen know. The session adjourned at 12:10. The bishops filed, chatting, down out of their seats and out through the great doors of St. Peter's. They seemed, to the viewer, restrained by the police from entering the piazza, a stream of purple flowing from the great basilica and slowly dispersing down the long, gray stairs. Their buses and cars roared into life and rolled out through the barriers of the piazza, where tourists gathered. Some of the bishops smiled and blessed the people, others, tired, sought relief in cigarettes.

III

In its fourth week, the Council was heading toward the great speech of Cardinal Suenens on October 22. But it heard other solid speeches every day. The writings of Péguy, Bloy, Maritain, Mauriac, of DeLubac, Daniélou, Congar, Teilhard, and many others, seemed to be bearing fruit; there were many bishops ready to envision how the Church might find its way back into the roots of human culture, by the path of the free and mature conscience. On the other hand, Cardinals Siri, Ruffini, Bacci, and others kept insisting on the need to stress obedience to the hierarchy, the necessity for "official chan- nels," the firm grip of the clergy on all initiative or judgment. A clerical Church or a prophetic Church?—that was the underlying issue. On the one hand, the Church might appeal for its strength to the free, faithful conscience, on the other, to the trained docility of those who never step out of line. It was not freedom and authority which were in conflict, but free obedience and reflexive obedience. The latter requires constant reinforcement, constant insistence on docility. The conscience in love with the Gospels, faithful as best it can be to justice and to the light of understanding, already respects authority because it respects the source of authority. Respecting the meaning of law, it does not rely upon the threat of sanctions. What was here at stake were two separate cultural traditions about the atti- tude of men toward law.

Where law is already internalized in conscience—where people re- spect law as the defense of their own liberty; where they have a sense of social courtesy, order, and consideration—the written law needs to say very little; one can count upon the good sense of the people. Where consciences have not been developed—where people respect sanctions but have no interest in law; where each pursues his own

goals, under his own impulses, without regard for common order—
the written law must say everything possible, and attach suitable
sanctions to each provision. Where there are no sanctions, there is no
law. In such cultures as the latter, both Church and State are wont
to seem legalistic, complicated, severe. Liberty is not so much in
evidence politically or ecclesiastically, because it is quite in evidence
emotionally. The people are treated as children, to be batted up or
down, left or right (as I have heard a curial official say), according
to the rhetoric or power of those in command. Such cultures move
by impulse, and by legal sanction. Between the two, in the area of
personal responsibility, there is a vacuum.

That is why a theory about the layman arising out of such a culture is apt to oscillate between docility and license, and why it tries
to shoal itself up with rigid patterns of organization. The action of
Catholics becomes, in capital letters, Catholic Action, under the due
authority of bishops. "Lay initiative" becomes a program in a clerical campaign. Such methods are doomed to ineffectiveness in such
countries as the United States, where the best citizens are traditionally those who can be counted upon to act responsibly, according
to their commitments and the convictions of their conscience—and
to do so freely, independently. It is, in such countries, a mark of
honor to be reliable on one's own; morality, honor, conscience *mean*
that a man is reliable on his own. There is, moreover, irony in the fact
that a culture which finds its strength in the consciences of its citizens should succeed in establishing social order, social courtesy, and
social tranquillity; while a culture which makes vast attempts to legislate such goods into existence, neglecting to instruct personal consciences, seems much less stable. (On the other hand, there is much
to be said for the stimulation given the arts, and human love, in less
ordered cultures.)

The strength of the layman in the world is the maturity of his own
conscience. He is not coerced to believe in Christ, or to accept the
claims of the Church. As John Cogley pointed out to the African
bishops on October 21, apostasy and heresy were never easier than in
our day; yet the Church probably has more loyal and reflective lay
sons than ever before. If the layman remains in the Church, it is
because he loves his faith; it satisfies his scrutiny; he wishes to remain. But our age is one of transition, and many Catholics—lay and
clerical—prefer the older paternalistic ways. There are laymen who

do not wish to think for themselves, and who do not want the clergy to think, either. For nostalgic or other reasons, sometimes those of self-interest and laziness, sometimes the conviction that the Church can only thrive in a culture of the past, they do not want the Church to change. Some prefer paternalistic ways, but are not themselves notably filial. What they seem to like best about the Church is its daily irrelevance; but they want it to be present for emergencies. "Tell me what to do—I'll see if I'll do it," or "Leave me in peace, as before," express two such attitudes.

On the other hand, many others—again lay and clerical—see the chasm that separates the Church from the intellectual, cultural, social world of our time, and are becoming increasingly impatient with the defenders of non-historical orthodoxy, or with the merely cautious and prudent. They love the Church, they love the world; they do not understand how some bishops do not see the huge chasm between the two. The public forms of ecclesiastical practices and life are often ugly, offensive, or irrelevant. The exterior witness of the Church often hides or contradicts what the Church believes. Ecclesiastical language, costumes, riches, preoccupations, pomp, fear, the way doctrine is expressed, are archaic and out of touch. The Church is much more authentic than she appears to be: she appears to be phony.

Thus some in the Church try to preserve the ways of the past, historically conditioned and contingent though they be, for fear that without the support of these ways, all will be lost. Others—some with desperation, others with wise patience—try to throw threads across the chasm lying between world and Church, hoping that one day the two will be reunited. Yet neither clergy nor laymen know the limits of their relative competence in such efforts; as Cardinal Gracias pointed out, "the theologians themselves don't know." One condition of this renewal is clear enough: it must be through the free consciences of individual men. The Church must never again be identified with the world or the power of the world. The Church must be the prophetic conscience of the world, creating liberty so that the voice of justice and the clamor against injustice can always be heard. The consciences of the people are becoming mature. Not by the choice of their prince, but by the choice of their own free spirits do they accept or reject the invitation of Christ and His Church. In the world, the Church already has sufficient independence to speak with wrath, with praise, with concern, wherever the interests of liberty, justice, peace, or truth so demand; if only she has the courage.

IV

It is in this context that the debates of October 21 and 22 were carried out. The separation between "religious" values and "human" values is the radical vice of our era. Religion has come to seem like optional icing on the substantial cake of daily life. The Council Fathers tried to confront this vice. Bishop Maziers of Lyons put the point succinctly: "The layman's human life and Christian life must be one and the same." Bishop Enrique y Tarancon of Solsona, Spain, argued that laymen sanctify themselves by their life in the world, and that the traditional manuals of ascetic theology—written for monks— are nearly useless to them. The layman must be regarded "as an adult in the Church of God, and this indicates the opportuneness of a special chapter on the place of public opinion in the Church. Public opinion is the patrimony of every natural society. The Church would suffer great harm if there were no expression of public opinion in its ranks." But the method and limits of this public opinion must be assigned, he said, keeping in mind that the Church is hierarchical, not democratic.

Cardinal Meyer of Chicago solidified his reputation at the Council with another sound talk derived from contemporary Scripture studies. He thought that chapter 3, though excellent in some respects, "is neither adequate nor realistic" because it neglects the sense of sin and human weakness in the Church. He organized many texts from both Scripture and the liturgy which refer to the constant human war against the power of darkness. Men today understand very well their guilt and moral incapacity; to reach their hearts and to be truthful, a new paragraph should be inserted to describe the Church as "the home of the Father of mercies, where the sins of the prodigal are forgiven. Christ came to call, not the just, but sinners."

Tall, young, courageous Archbishop Denis Hurley, of Durban, South Africa, noted the failure of the document to distinguish between the concept of State and that of society, a distinction crucial in the question of religious liberty. The concept "society" includes all the social activities of men: domestic, educational, economic, cultural, and so forth. But the concept "State" refers strictly to political affairs, and to the machinery of government in a society. What the hierarchy is to the Church, the State is to human society. The Church, therefore, is more like human society than like the State. He then pointed out another ambiguity. At one point in the text the faithful are warned against mixing the religious with the profane, and then at another point they are warned against separating the two. We seem to be telling the laity, he said, breaking into English, "to make an omelette without breaking the eggs." To help bring the text out of this muddle, he proposed another distinction. In every human act, there is a double aspect: a moral aspect and, for lack of a better word, a technical aspect. The moral aspect of an act leads a man to act according to a good conscience, subject to the mind of the Church; in this respect, each layman acts *qua* Christian. The technical aspect of an act requires him to use his professional skill, in whatever occupation he is involved, and in this respect the Christian member of human society acts as a citizen of that society. Moreover, this aspect of his action is not subject to the authority of the Church. We need to make a strong statement, he concluded, about the Church's "vehement desire" that her sons and daughters may perform their work in the world "with freedom and without hindrance."

Earlier in the morning, Cardinal Alfredo Ottaviani, of the Holy Office, made one of his few talks in the second session of the Council. But before he even began his talk, he complained that three *periti*, unnamed, were distributing a paper asking the Fathers to give their vote in favor of the married diaconate. In the Cardinal's view, these *periti* exceeded their limits in trying to force the opinion of the Fathers. It is the duty of Council experts, he said, to assist the Fathers with their counsel and knowledge when these are required: they should speak only when asked. This protest of Cardinal Ottaviani caught most of the Fathers by surprise, for there is nothing in the rules of the Council about circulating petitions outside St. Peter's; indeed, many petitions were being circulated—on all sides of all questions, and not only in favor of a married diaconate. The Cardinal, however, next got down to the point he wanted to make. He proposed a compromise on the question of married deacons: deacons should remain celibate, and where there is a shortage of priests laymen could be ordained to the order of acolyte, which does not bind by celibacy.

A short while later, Archbishop Kozlowiecki of Rhodesia arose and to the form of the conventional greeting added the additional phrase: "*Carissimi periti!* Most beloved experts!" The Council Fathers burst into laughter and Cardinal Ottaviani himself threw back his head, enjoying the humor. The Archbishop then urged: "We are warned, in part of the text, not to extinguish the Spirit. We must take this seriously. The government exercised by bishops should not be overcentralized. We are not meant to keep a tight rein on every activity of priest and layman, but should leave to their judgment what hardly pertains to the bishops." He thought that if the special, gracious type of government proper to the Church were better understood, then most of the difficulties about obedience and submission would be eliminated.

Meanwhile, Archbishop Tchidimbo of Guinea startled many of the Council Fathers, accustomed to dozing in their seats when the Latin became too complex for them, with a strong talk about abuses in the missions. "Although political colonization in the greater part of Africa has ceased," he said, "a spiritual colonization still exists, especially by international organizations of the lay apostolate." He said these organizations often attempt to take over the responsibilities of the pastors and the people they come to help. He cited, as examples, organizations which dispense money and thus seem to believe that they are sent by God to show bishops and people how to run their own land; specialists who come to mission lands with overweening complacency; others who come with their own spiritual or theological approaches, foreign to the land in which they are working; and finally, missionary congregations and religious orders who come to spread their own programs and their own devotions. He asked the Council Fathers to remember that the first expert in a diocese is the bishop, and that he is the one responsible before God for the apostolate in his area.

Bishop Jacques Menager, of Meaux, France, confessed that the lay auditors "opened the eyes of the commission on the lay apostolate, for they all found the schema inadequate to their proper mission." They found it disappointing because it struck them as being "negative, clerical, and juridical." Bishop Ruotolo of Ugento, Italy, tried his best to come to terms with the layman in the world. One of the first things he thought of was the establishment of a new organization, a new set of colleges or "lay seminaries" where a lay elite might be trained. He also proposed a new Congregation for the Laity, with lay members, to be established in the Roman Curia to further the dialogue between laity and hierarchy. Archbishop Casimir Morcillo of Zaragoza, Spain, agreed that we needed a theological definition of the layman, not a canonical or negative one. He tried his own hand at phrasing such a definition: "The layman is one who is incorporated into Christ through baptism and enrolled among the people of God and who, not ascending to the hierarchy, lives his everyday life in a spirit of consecration to God in order to dedicate all things to God: himself, the actions and works of his fellow men, and the cosmos itself."

Had he spoken on any other day, Bishop Mark McGrath, thirty-nine, of Panama, would have received credit for one of the best speeches at the Council in the second session. As it was, his talk was overshadowed by that of Cardinal Suenens. Bishop McGrath is a leading member of the theological commission. As a professor in Santiago, Chile, for several years, he had been very active in that country's painstaking renewal in Catholic life and thought. At the first session and increasingly at the second, the bishops of Chile were in the forefront of the Latin Americans; many of the programs they had developed for their native land were now being talked about for the universal Church. As new Auxiliary Bishop of Panama, Bishop McGrath was organizing the same sort of programs in his native land. He is tall, rangy, extremely frank, as easy to talk to as another layman; there is no barrier of episcopal dignity or episcopal reserve to break through. Whatever one says will not cause scandal or raise an eyebrow.

On the 22nd, Bishop McGrath spoke in the name of more than forty bishops of Latin America. In general, he and his fellow bishops wanted to approve the schema, but they found many things "neither clear nor realistic" in it. "The description of the layman is too negative, because it describes him only in relation with the hierarchy and religious as though, like little acolytes, the laity were at the base of a clerical pyramid, subject to everyone. The treatment is unrealistic and too schematic. Our civilization does not need to be ecclesiastical, much less clerical. It is a mistake to consider the apostolate of the laity in the light of the religious apostolate in which we ourselves are involved. We must take into account the fields of human activity which claim the attention of the laity, because the Gospel cannot be preached in a void. Because this point has frequently been lost sight of, the Church is too frequently regarded as linked with the older order of things. The holiness of the people of God is to be inserted in the real world in which they live." The Bishop pointed out that in many areas of human life the layman is the superior of the cleric: the policeman on the street, the lawyer, the doctor, the artist, all have a field of competence in which they take rank over the clergyman. He also protested the exclusive preoccupation of too many in the Church with the supernatural, as though they were preaching a religion of escapism. He urged the Council to pay more attention to the world of scientific progress on the one hand, and of poverty and misery on the other—the real world, which every Christian is called to assist in bringing to perfection.

Meanwhile, the Maronite archbishop of Beirut, Ignace Ziadé, had seconded Cardinal Suenens' speech (which we will soon report) by noting that chapter 3 "suffers from an omission that is very important from the Oriental viewpoint, namely, the absence of reference to the Holy Spirit." According to Sacred Scripture and the theological tradition of the Orient, "there can be no Church without the influence of the Spirit." In the West, the theology of the Church evolved more under the influence of the relations of the Church with Christ, along juridical, legal lines. In the Orient, however, the evolution was under the influence of the relation of the Church with the Spirit; it was kept in contact with mystery. The Spirit acts upon the concrete history of the people of God through active charisms and through the sacramentality of the Church.

Cardinal Suenens had already made the word "charisms" a central word of the second session; Archbishop Ziadé simply drove it home.

11

THE CHARISMATIC CHURCH

I

CARDINAL SUENENS is a strong, direct, businesslike man. His influence at the Council seemed, for a time, second only to that of the Pope; so much so that there were those, in the early stages of the session at least, who were calling the Council "The First Council of Malines." On one occasion, when the Pope was visiting a church in Rome, Cardinal Suenens was seen taking the Pope by the arm, moving him here and there, introducing him; the Cardinal is the type of man who controls the situation in which he finds himself. His voice is emphatic and clear. His ideas are forcefully presented. He seems, par excellence, the type of the modern bishop: learned, active, capable, profound.

The Cardinal opened his discourse on the 22nd by noting that little was said in the chapter on the layman about the charisms of the faithful, with the result that the Council seemed to be treating only of a peripheral and accidental phenomenon in the life of the Church. He said that, on the contrary, it was necessary to show the vital importance of these charisms in building up the Mystical Body. The text should be clearer and more ample. Above all, he said, we must avoid letting the hierarchical structure of the Church appear as a merely administrative apparatus, without any intimate connection with those charismatic gifts of the Holy Spirit which are poured out on the whole Church. With irony, he said that the encyclical *Mystici Corporis* spoke more fully about charisms than the present document. It will be worth our while to translate more of the Cardinal's speech:

148

Those centuries of history in which the Church makes its long pilgrimage through the ages until the coming of the Lord are the time of the Holy Spirit. For it is through the Holy Spirit that the glorified Christ gathers together the people of God, purifies it, vivifies it, and leads it into truth, until the last times—notwithstanding their weaknesses and their sins. The Holy Spirit thus holds the first place (Romans 8:23), and is the pledge of the Church in this world (II Corinthians 1:22; 5:5). The Church is, therefore, called the dwelling place of God, in the Spirit (Ephesians 2:22).

But the Holy Spirit is given not only to pastors but to absolutely every Christian: "Do you not know that you are the temple of God and that the Spirit of God dwells in you?" St. Paul wrote to the Corinthians (I Corinthians 3:16). Every Christian, in baptism, the sacrament of faith, receives the Holy Spirit. All Christians are "living cells," and are built up into "the spiritual house of the Spirit, oikos pneumatikos" (Peter 2:5). The whole Church, therefore, is essentially a pneumatic reality built up not only on the foundations of the apostles, but—as Ephesians 2:20 says—also of the prophets. In the Church of the New Testament God "gave some to be apostles, some to be prophets, others to be truly evangelists, others, however, to be pastors and theologians. . . ." (Ephesians 4:11; 3:5)

The Holy Spirit manifests Himself in the Church in the multitude and the plenitude of His gifts of the spirit, which are called in Scripture pneumatika (I Corinthians 12:1; 14:1), or charismata (Romans 12:6; I Corinthians 12:4, 9, 28, 30; I Timothy 4:14; 1:6; I Peter 4:10). Certainly in the time of St. Paul even very extraordinary and wonderful charisms like the "ecstatic glossolalia" (I Corinthians 12:10, 28, 30; 14:18, 26; Acts 19:6), or the charisms of healing (I Corinthians 12:9, 28, 30; cf. I Corinthians 12:10, 12, 28 ff.) were manifested in the Church. But we ought not to think that the charisms of the spirit were exclusively or even especially to be found in these phenomena which are rather extraordinary and marvelous.

For St. Paul speaks, for example, of the charism of speaking with wisdom or with science (I Corinthians 12:8), of the charism of faith (I Corinthians 12:9), of consoling (Romans 12:8) and ministry (Romans 12:7), of the charisms of the discerning of the Spirit (I Corinthians 12:10), of the charisms of those who manage affairs and those who govern (I Corinthians 12:28), etc.

Thus to St. Paul the Church of the living Christ did not appear as some administrative organization, but as a living complex of gifts, spirits, ministry. To every Christian without exception the Spirit is given, Who to each one gives his own proper gift, his own proper charisma: "According to the special grace which is given to us, to each one differently" (Romans 12:6). "To each one, however, is given the manifestation of the spirit that is useful" (I Corinthians 12:7), i.e., "to the building up of the Church" (I Corinthians 14:12). Every Christian, whether articulate or inarticulate, has in his daily life his own charism, but as St. Paul says, so that "all things are for the building up of the Church" (I Corinthians 14:26; cf. 14:3–5). Let us listen again as the apostle affirms: "And God placed them in the Church, first apostles, secondly the prophets, thirdly the doctors . . . should all be apostles? should all be prophets? should all be doctors?" (I Corinthians 12:28) A document on the Church which would speak only of the apostles and their successors, and would not even think of the prophets and the teachers would be quite deficient in a matter of grave importance.

Charisms in the Church today: What would our Church be without the charisms of the doctors, that is to say the theologians? And what would our Church be without the charisms of the prophets, that is to say, men who speak out of the inspiration of the Spirit Who speaks within them, "in season, out of season" (II Timothy 4:2)? These men wake up the Church, which sometimes falls asleep, lest the Gospel of Christ be neglected in practice.

Not only in past times, not only in the times of St. Thomas Aquinas, or of St. Francis of Assisi, did the Church need the charisms of the theologians and prophets and the ministrations of others, but also today and especially in the ordinary daily life of our time.

Let us leave behind, then, those "clearer charisms" and come to those "simpler charisms" to which the schema on the Church alludes. Don't each of us know, each in his own diocese, laymen or women who truly, as if they were called by God, are given special charisms of the Spirit in catechetics, or in the work of preaching the Gospel, or in the field of Catholic Action, or some form of social or charitable action? Do we not, in our daily experience, know and perceive that the action of the Holy Spirit is not extinct in the Church! Certainly, charisms in the Church would be badly ordered without the ministry of pastors, but on the other hand, without charisms the ministry of the Church would be impoverished and sterile.

The office of pastors faced with charisms: A pastor, whether of local and particular churches, or of the universal Church must, with a certain instinct of the Spirit, detect, promote and augment the gifts of the Spirit within the Church. Pastors must make efforts to hear out with open heart, and again and again enter into living dialogue with laymen who, each and every one of them, is enriched with his own charismatic gifts, and most often has a greater experience in the life of today's world.

Finally, pastors must themselves emulate the better charisms (I Cor-inthians 12:31). In truth, every one of the faithful, even those in-structed by the greatest gifts, owe reverence and obedience to their pastors, but, vice versa, attention and reverence are due to the charisms and impulses of the Holy Spirit, which very often inspire lay Christians who are not in places of eminence. Thus St. Paul admonished all Christians, including pastors: "Do not extinguish the Spirit. Do not spurn your prophets. Prove everything; hold on to what is good." (I Thessalonians 5:19–21). The complex of charismatic gifts and min-istries cannot actually build up the Church or serve the Church, except in the liberty of the sons of God, which, after the example of St. Paul, every pastor ought to protect—and also promote.

Concluding: In a doctrinal order I propose that the chapter on the people of God be completed as the second chapter in the document. Then the "charismatic dimensions of the Church" should be elaborated in a whole chapter, together with the structure of ministry and service. The importance of charisms among the people of God should be more amply and much more concretely treated. Most especially, the impor-tance of prophets and theologians in the Church should be given consideration. The attitude of pastors to the charisms of the faithful should be described in a manner much more positive and constructive. The doctrine of St. Paul about the liberty in the Church of the sons of God should not fall into oblivion.

In the practical order I offer these proposals: In order that there might appear, even in the Council and in the eyes of the world, our faith in the charisms given by the Holy Spirit to every Christian: that the number and universality of the lay auditors be increased; and that women auditors be invited, since, unless I am mistaken, women make up one half of the human race. Let, finally, religious brothers and sisters, who likewise belong to the people of God, receive the Holy Spirit, and serve the Church as a part of the chosen flock of the Lord, be invited to the Council.

As Cardinal Suenens concluded his speech, his listeners were at first very moved; then they broke into the loudest applause heard up to that time in the second session. In the mind of almost everyone this was the great moment of the session. The Roman Catholic Church was once more opening itself to prophecy. It was making the distinction, beloved of Paul Tillich and the Protestant churches in general, between the priestly church and the prophetic church. Having lived since the Council of Trent on its priestly strength, almost to the neglect of its prophetic strength, the Church was now beginning to right the balance. The Protestant Reformation had torn from the bosom of the Church hundreds of thousands of ardent sons who would have been her prophets. It has taken the Church four centuries to raise up to herself again another full complement of prophets; bureaucrats are much easier to find, and much easier to control. But the Spirit blows where He will. And the Spirit is the life of the Church.

II

A Church of sinners, a Church in which the voice of the Spirit is honored—this is the realism of the Second Vatican Council. Yet the Church asks a full view from her members, lest they take one idea in isolation from many others. Freedom is a principle in the Church; as is good order. But it would be wrong to say that the problem of Catholics is to reconcile freedom and order by "striking a happy balance" or "finding the mean between extremes." Nearly every problem faced by the Council tempted the Fathers into posing such antitheses, and then compromising. To take hold of complementary ideas, however, one cannot stand midway between them, on the same level; one must climb to a new height and gain command of both extremes from above. To grasp the complementarity between freedom and order, one must appeal to a new principle: fidelity to the Spirit. It is the same Spirit Who works in laymen and in their pastors; in the Spirit there are mutual trust and harmony. It is when idols replace the Spirit, when authority prefers systematic order or when the faithful prefer their personal ideas, that conflict, disharmony, and selfishness thrive, and defensiveness replaces openness. But, of course, it is difficult to be faithful to the Spirit and never to sin against the light.

Nevertheless, it is well for the Church to put her finger on the heart of her religious system: not hierarchical structure, not untrammeled liberty, but fidelity to the Spirit. If each one in the Church listens to the Spirit, according to the requirements of his state in life, slighting none of the demands of the situations in which he finds himself, hungering to understand what can be understood, knowing how to bow to what cannot be understood, and acting as a humble servant of the light, the problem of authority and freedom is merely academic. An inferior does not fear freely to yield his obedience when he knows it is due; a superior who respects the consciences of his people does not misuse them. So long as concrete, limited decisions must be taken, an infinite range of ideas cannot be realized; proponents of some ideas will have to yield. Insofar as all concerned seek to be faithful to the Spirit, each can respect the judgments of others. In that light, each can be tolerant and brotherly. No one can boast of never having turned his back on that penetrating light, or never in offended pride having dismissed its claims.

An acute discourse on October 24 approached this problem from another direction. Pedro Cantero Cuadrado of Huelva, Spain, said that the *sensus fidei*, the "instinct of faith," has never been treated directly by the supreme teaching authority of the Church. Yet the Church regards it as the foundation of Christian life, the source of her missionary vocation, and the foundation of the lay apostolate. Although it can be confused with subjectivism and independence from Church authority, the "instinct of faith" is a gift from the Spirit, given to all members of the people of God, collectively and individually. It works as an "instinct for truth" in questions of faith and morals; it helps them avoid error, drives them to deeper understanding. Its roots lie in the inner depths of the Church, whose life springs from the Holy Spirit, and in faith, by which men live the life of God. The sense of faith is developed by the influence of the Spirit—through external preaching and internal graces—gifts dispensed as God wills, and as active in some of the faithful as in theologians. By its very nature, the Church, which is neither simply clerical nor simply democratic, is always based on the written and traditional Word of God and on the guidance of the Church's authority. The teaching office of the Church must not merely lead, approve and confirm the sense of faith, as though the faithful were only passive instruments of the teaching office; it must also promote, receive, test, and collect the fruits of the sense of faith. Thus it would be most useful if members of the hierarchy established dialogue with outstanding members of the faculties of state-controlled universities. From previous talks, the Bishop concluded, it is evident that collaboration with the layman in the formulation of doctrine is effective and necessary.

Thus the great vision of John Henry Newman entered the Council through a Spanish bishop who, perhaps, had never read him. For in his famous essay "On Consulting the Faithful in Matters of Doctrine," the great Cardinal had observed that not infrequently in the life of the Church the faith of the people has remained as a stabilizing force upon bishops who were attracted into heresy—notably at the time of the Arian heresy in the fourth century. The beliefs of the faithful, protected by the Spirit, are one more source of Catholic faith to be consulted when answering the question: "Church of Christ, what do you believe about X?" The details of such consultation have never been worked out; it is certainly not a question of juridical or political structures, of polls or votes or popular sentiment. It is a question of recognizing the power of the Spirit, who dwells in the least as in the greatest in the Church. It is a question of avoiding the feeling of superiority because of learning or hierarchical position. Were popular will to be measured against the clear voice of solemn religious authority, of course, only the weak minded would look to the majority for leadership. The charism of teaching belongs to those ordained to it; respect for the Spirit compels respect for them. But one of the sources, even if perhaps the humblest, which those ordained to teach are bound to attempt to understand—if they would be faithful to the Spirit—is the voice of their own faithful.[1]

III

On several occasions at the second session, laymen gave witness to their faith. The lay auditors met regularly at Borgo Santo Spirito, 8, to take part in discussions on the schema on the lay apostolate and on "schema 17" on the Church in the modern world. One of their number, Emilio Inglessis—and he was by no means alone in this—thought the schema on the layman "too restrictive." It gives the layman "no other function but to assist the clergy." The auditors thought their role was too passive; they wanted to speak, as well as listen.

On October 21, the African bishops asked John Cogley, formerly an editor of *The Commonweal*, to address their weekly meeting. About a hundred bishops and priests were present. Mr. Cogley told them he hoped that "however inadequately I do it, *what* I do may become a part of the normal life of the Church." He insisted on the need for dialogue *within* the Church, and he gave as an analogy for authority in the Church, not a political model, but the family. "The good father cannot be compared to a military general, a naval admiral, or a political potentate. He does not think of his children as anony-

mous names on a duty roster, or as subjects, but as fully human
beings, whose opinions matter to him, whose special needs concern
him deeply, whose views must be considered before action is taken,
whose advice he seeks sedulously. Authority," he continued, "to be
sure, remains always with the father. But authority does not exist
in Platonic isolation above and apart from those over whom it is
exercised. When it is wisely administered—I speak now as a parent—
it more often looks like cooperation in a common enterprise, the
total good of the family, than as an algebraic of command and obedience. As a result, family life, mankind's oldest experience with social
organization, remains the least onerous and the model form of
society."

For the layman, Mr. Cogley found two chief roles in the Church.
(1) The layman interprets the good things of the world for the
Church and brings them into the Church. (2) The layman testifies
within the Church about the meaning of the faith, not as it is in
theory, but as it is lived. Mr. Cogley attached great significance to
this "wisdom of the people" this "grasp of reality." He pointed out
that Catholic laymen were living the ecumenical movement with
neighbors and even relatives, long before theologians caught up with
the idea. They likewise long ago recognized the advantages of religious liberty.

In the question period after the talk, one bishop remarked that
in his diocese he had no trouble with laymen offering new suggestions,
insights, and enthusiasm; his problem was to pull his laymen out of
their apathy. Archbishop Hurley of Durban remarked that "clerical
sensitivities" are not yet prepared for the kind of frank and open
dialogue Mr. Cogley suggested. "We tend to be hurt easily," he said.
He told of a priest he knew who had encouraged such frankness in
his own parish. "He had many a sleepless night. It took him a year
to get used to it. But he's all right now." Both priest and laymen
need preparation for such dialogue: "Otherwise, the ordinary fellow
breaks under the strain."

There were also countless informal meetings of laymen, at coffee
bars and over lunches and dinners. One such took place October 11;
Martin Work, Executive Director of the National Council of Catholic
Men in Washington, James O'Gara, managing editor of *The Commonweal*, John Cogley, and another layman, met two of the lay
auditors for a long conversation in a small apartment, which bore

the name Ruffini on the bronze plate at the door, on the third floor of an old palazzo in Piazza Collegio Romano. The group met in a large sitting room, and seated themselves on soft divans and chairs. A maid dressed in a pink dress with a tiny white apron wheeled in a cart with *espresso* coffee, cigarettes, and cigars. The two auditors were eager to learn about the attitudes of laymen in the United States; the Americans tried their best to explain the position of the American Church, its coming out of the ghetto, the desire among most highly educated Catholics to enter secular organizations and associations rather than to continue in Catholic ones, and the general Anglo-Saxon suspicion of organizations. Many American Catholics insist first on the need for freedom and on ways to block abuses of clerical power, before they would wish to join organizations which might only make them "clerics in disguise." Americans begin at the other end from Europeans: not with a program, an idea, an ideology —even a Christain one—but with human society as it is. They wish to take the world as it is and respect its values. They are confident that their faith will do its work, without any special program or organization.

As the evening wore on, the maid brought in a tray of Scotch, ice cubes, and water. In a mood of relaxation, the Americans began to notice more closely the room in which they sat. One wall was lined with old books, another was hidden under heavy gray draperies. The light was soft, the furniture was old, musty, slightly damp. As these men from various regions of the world, each region with problems different from the others, sat and talked, they couldn't help reflecting on the creativity of this age in the Church's history. Here were six men, trying to think what the future of the world in which they lived would be like, knowing that the position of laymen in the world two or three generations hence, not to say centuries, would be very different from what it is at present. On one point all agreed: they wanted to leave as many doors open as possible. Not enough thought had gone into the position of the layman in the world to make it easy, as yet, to see just who the layman is or what he can do. Mr. O'Gara was especially insistent on this point. He didn't want to freeze matters by canonizing the tentative advances that have been made in the last fifty years. John Cogley, with his unassuming smile and diffident way, began to talk more and more as the evening progressed. At one point he remarked that he did not like the word, the layman's "role." He liked to think of everything the layman did as sacramental, "even," he said, looking around the room in which the men sat, "even talking in this room, carrying on this conversation here tonight, I think that it's a holy thing, a good thing."

After these meetings, and others like them, several laymen decided that they ought to make their views available to bishops and experts and others, who might be interested in them. The project was discussed on several occasions, but it was difficult to find time for a "committee meeting" to draw up such statements. As a consequence, one of their number sat down and prepared the first such document. This statement was mimeographed and a hundred copies were distributed during the week of October 18. By the following week, a second statement was ready. These statements, as Father George Tavard pointed out on his return to the States, were not very important. They had very little impact on the Council. But they were an example of laymen saying what they thought they ought to say about their experience in the Church.

IV

There is good evidence that the week of October 21 was an important one at the council: Father Ralph Wiltgen, the founder of the Divine Word News Service, organized an extraordinary number of significant conferences. Because of the greater coverage given to the press in the second session, Father Wiltgen's news service tended to be overlooked more than it had been at the first session; but he was busier than ever, scheduling conferences and interviews, and translating them. After the dismal treatment of the press at the first session, a Coordinating Center for Council Communications was set up in several basement rooms along Via del Sant' Uffizio. In those rooms in a battery of pigeonholes, so that each of the registered newsmen could have one to himself, Father Wiltgen distributed his daily news releases. In between times, the thin, active priest was on the telephone, or hurrying to submit the first written draft of a recorded interview for the approval of the man who had granted it.

On October 21, for example, Bishop John Moorman, fifty-eight, leader of the Anglican observers at the second session, told Father Wiltgen that if there is to be a final unity among Christians "There will have to be a central head of the Church, and that head will clearly have to be the Bishop of Rome." The Anglican communion as a whole "would be prepared to accept the fact of the papacy, though they would find great difficulty in recognizing the basis on which the primacy rests." Historically and exegetically "far too much has been made of the words of our Lord to St. Peter." Bishop Moorman noted that the Anglican communion allows its bishops, priests, and deacons to marry if they wish; and many do. "We believe that the advantages outweigh the disadvantages." The Bishop also thought that a permanent council of representative bishops of the whole world with the Pope "would be an improvement on the present system of a largely Italian Curia."

On October 22, Archbishop T. D. Roberts, S.J., seventy, the former Archbishop of Bombay, told a large gathering of pressmen that what he wanted to say in the Council he couldn't say in Latin, because the language simply wasn't rich enough, even for one who, like himself, had long been a professor of Latin. Besides, he said, "I know that if I give my talk to the press many more of the bishops will see it and understand it than if I give it in the *aula*." He called for an "inquisition" into the many courts of the Church. "Perhaps the most urgent of all reforms in the Church concerns the interminable delays in the marriage courts, both diocesan and Roman." He said that "a real inquiry into marriage courts might reveal, perhaps, one of the greatest causes of leakage in the Church." The Church is very careful to provide, both at Rome and in every diocese around the world, a "defender of the chain, *defensor vinculi*," but the Church should "be far more concerned with defenders of persons, defenders of human rights, than simply defenders of chains, even marriage chains." The Archbishop then recounted that in those countries most advanced in democracy, as in Scandinavia and New Zealand, the State appoints *ombudsmen*, i.e., men who have drastic powers of inquiry into any abuses of authority. Even the humblest of persons can call upon the *ombudsman* to represent them before authority. "Many of us know dioceses," he said, "where the people cry to Heaven for an *ombudsman*, even though the bishop himself is supposed to be that, by his vocation." Bishops, too, need an *ombudsman*, "to turn green the innumerable red lights that keep from the Pope not merely their persons, but even their letters."

The Church needs healthy public opinion both among the laity and the clergy to "expose and check real abuses of authority in the inquisitions that exist on the diocesan level and in Rome." The

Council Fathers "do not have to wait for reforms of the Roman Curia, but should rather take a close look at what is going on in their own dioceses."

Archbishop Roberts was one of the delightful, colorful figures at the Council. Short, active, and energetic for his age, he could always be counted on for the honest word, for the witty remark. His own past history is one of courage and tact. When he realized that the Holy See was hoping to place native Indians in the Indian sees, he took matters into his own hands by taking a leave of absence; while he was gone, Valerian Gracias was responsible for the diocese. Archbishop Roberts shipped out on a slow freighter from Bombay, and no one at Rome or in India knew where he was. In his absence of many months, Rome had a chance to name Gracias as his successor in Bombay. More recently in England, Archbishop Roberts has played a courageous role in the movement for disarmament.

On October 24, Archbishop Hurley of Durban, by using the image of the family to express the relation of bishop and layman, indicated that he had been reflecting on John Cogley's talk to the African bishops. The Archbishop thought that on the diocesan and national levels it would be relatively easy for laymen to find opportunities for making their opinions known to the hierarchy, but that the system might break down at the parish level, "a very concrete and immediate level where people have tangible, urgent, and concrete problems. . . . We of the clergy are not yet prepared mentally and emotionally to discuss problems at this level with the laity." He said he was blaming nobody, "except the whole system under which the Church has been run for decades, and perhaps centuries." The Archbishop questioned whether the paternalistic system of the past "can continue to work admirably with a laity that is becoming increasingly better educated, more critical, more vocal about the problems of the relationship of Catholic doctrine to social, economic, and domestic issues." He said that after the Council each bishop would have to think about setting up new machinery for training and reorientating his priests and seminarians.

V

At the first session, the American bishops had cut a poor figure; their poor showing continued during the first four weeks of the second. They had never spoken as a group on a given point. They seemed more than any other major group of bishops unsure of what they wanted, if they wanted anything. Apparently individualists not by conviction but by default, they simply lacked ideas on the renewal of the Church. After listening to others, each "looked into his heart." They often spoke of "they": "they'll bring that up tomorrow; they'll fight bitterly over this." The Americans seemed to be in Rome to find out what the Church was thinking, rather than to do some of the thinking for the Church; docility, not creativity, characterized them. Meanwhile, the leaders of the first wave of reform at the Council, the Germans, the Belgians, the Dutch, the French, the Africans, were somewhat subdued during the second. They had prosecuted their lines of reform; they had guaranteed a free and open Council, and led the way in the rejection of the schemata presented by non-historical orthodoxy; they had succeeded admirably in opening the doors of the Church. But by now they had been identified with certain positions, and there was a vacuum in the leadership on the floor of the Council. But the Americans prided themselves on not "lobbying" or not belonging to a "party." They boasted that a given bishop might be quite "conservative" on one point and quite "progressive" on another; which only meant that theoretical consistency was not one of the strong points of many of the bishops. Few seemed to approach problems on a deeply theological level, having worked out for themselves what Catholic faith means in the twentieth century. For years they had refused to countenance the creative intellectual work going on in France and Germany, and represented in America by such organs as *The Commonweal* and *Cross Currents*. They had made life very difficult over the last forty years for those who talked about renewal and reform. Now the bishops paid the price for their former complacency; they were not ready for the Council. They were, for the most part, intelligent, thoughtful, pious, docile, uncritical; they brought with them little of the genius or creativity of America, having long discouraged intellectual creativity in the American Church.

It was a surprise, then, when on October 23, for the first time in either session of the Council, Archbishop Lawrence Shehan, of Baltimore, arose to speak in the name of all the bishops of the United States. There had not been much organization or any discussion behind his speech. At their weekly meeting, he had simply told the American bishops what he was going to say, and asked if any would like to join him. He wished to ask that the question of Church and State not be treated at this point, because it was too important to be treated briefly and badly. He objected to the word *infaustae*, "unfortunate," used of the separation of Church and State. He went on to defend a sense of "the world" which is not pejorative but positive, the world redeemed by Christ; he deplored sermons which only condemn the world.

Then Bishop Ernest Primeau of Manchester, N.H., gave an excellent and realistic speech. The layman, he said, is conscious of his abilities and the needs of the Church; he is no longer content to remain a passive bystander or a silent sheep. He wants to be heard in the fields of his competence. He expects his pastors to have confidence in his concern for the Church. He wants some means to be established whereby he can be consulted when his talents will be of use. Laymen recognize in the Church not just a dry complex of laws, but a living body which is constantly growing and is, therefore, subject to change. "In many fields, members of the laity are much more competent than the clergy or the hierarchy. They have a genuine love for the Church and are animated with the spirit of reverence for their superiors in the Church." Unless this Council determines the respective roles of liberty among the laity, and authority among the hierarchy, there is a danger that dedicated laymen will lose interest in the mission of the Church, become discouraged and leave the Church. The obligations of the hierarchy in this respect have particular importance when dealing with intellectuals, since it is necessary to acknowledge their right to freedom of investigation and initiative. The text is too negative and too clerical. "It might be said to sum up the duty of the laity as being: believe, pray, obey, and pay." In their mission, the laity should not be regarded as mere delegates of the hierarchy; they have their own proper part in the mission of the Church. "We should put these principles into practice by giving our lay auditors an opportunity to be heard in the Council." The Council has already generated great expectations among laymen. "I am afraid that in the light of what I have said the schema will do more harm than good; for it stresses obedience when what is needed is emphasis on lay initiative, freedom, and responsibility."

The next day, attention in the Council picked up when the announcement of a speaker from Louisiana, speaking for 147 Americans, came over the loudspeaker. Bishop Robert E. Tracy, young and thoughtful, urged that the Council insert a special word for "race" in the statement on the equality of all Christians; the Romans simply had made no such distinction. The Latin word *natione* in the text was meant to cover the point, but it could be misunderstood by the people. An unequivocal statement would give support to those working in the field and, though the problem may not be international, its repercussions are; so it is not too special for the Council to attend to. His intervention was greeted with warm applause.

VI

A Spanish bishop said the text on the layman was far from adequate for the modern world; it did not reflect the minds of our contemporaries. A French bishop amassed incidents from Scripture and early Church history to show that the Church had not always been a clerical Church. But the defenses of non-historical orthodoxy are thick and high.

Cardinal Giuseppe Siri of Genoa thought that any definition of the laity should treat explicitly of their subjection to the authority of the Church. Though the notion of the people of God was acceptable to him, he did not think (against Cardinal Suenens) that a second chapter should be devoted to it. For then it might be inferred that the people of God can be or achieve something without the Church— but the Church is necessary for salvation. His third point was that the phrase "universal priesthood of the laity" is to be used only in its broadest sense. The scriptural texts which employ it are literary and should not be taken strictly. He objected to calling the priesthood of the laity "magnificent," as the text does. "It is praiseworthy to say things pleasing to the laity, but these should be more moderate." He endorsed the positions of Cardinal Ruffini. He admitted that extraordinary charisms are sometimes granted; when they are, the Church has to conduct herself prudently. "She knows that such are rare, that deceptions can easily take place, and that in the end all must abide by her judgment." Submission to Church authority must be insisted upon, "lest a church filled with illusions be erected within the Church." The *sensus fidei* of the faithful is above all else *ex auditu*—"from hearing (i.e., the hierarchy)." The value of the *Ecclesia discens* (the Church which learns), the laity, is totally dependent on the value of the *Ecclesia docens* (the Church which teaches), the hierarchy. Cardinal Siri urged that the document treat of man's fallen nature and of his daily need of redemption and regimen; and he concluded with a mysterious phrase about the need for "Christians in civil government."

The day before, Archbishop Ermenegildo Florit of Florence, Italy, had answered Cardinal Suenens on the use of the term *charism*. As usual, Archbishop Florit tried to play what he conceived to be a moderating role between non-historical orthodoxy and the other approaches to orthodoxy. (It was always a useful gauge of the pressures in the Council to observe where Archbishop Florit thought the halfway point was.) He noted that in modern usage *charism* refers only to extraordinary graces; in St. Paul's usage, however, the term refers to a variety of graces which today we simply call gifts or offices. He thought that the text of the document is correct enough according to St. Paul's usage, but that the use of *charism* might today be open to misunderstanding "This is especially true today in the face of the 'anti-conceptual' theologies which prefer an infused knowledge of theology or mystical theology to theology as an objective science and discipline." He proposed that the word *gift* be used in place of *charism*.

The last word on chapter 3, however, did not belong to non-historical orthodoxy. It came on October 24, not long after Cardinal Siri, Bishop Tracy, and several others had spoken. Archbishop George Hakim, Melkite Archbishop of Nazareth, delivered a stinging, and deserved, indictment. "In this schema and the talks on it," he said, "I have been annoyed by a triumphalism condemned in the first session and little in keeping with the teaching of Popes John XXIII and Paul VI." This is really "the Council of the twenty-first century," and it should aim to be "a genuine manifestation of the Church in the world today. . . . Consequently, we should not speak as though we are alone in the world." Anyone who lives and works in an area where members of the Church are in the minority will feel that the present schema is unsatisfactory, because it appears to pay practically no attention to the vast number of non-Christians, who constitute two-thirds of the world's population, and who in some way belong to the people of God. "This schema seems to have been conceived as a confirmation of ecclesiastical power, and not as a text which will be applicable to the greater part of the world. The strength of the Church is in the Word of God, not in self-glorification." Unless we are to be hypocrites, shouldn't we acknowledge that the Church is indeed a very tiny flock—*valde pusillus grex?* Many speakers seem to forget the existence of others; many dare to disdain married deacons, glorying over ecclesiastical celibacy in the Latin Church, and forgetting how much married Oriental priests and married ministers of other Christian communities have contributed to Christian life. "Lastly, the text is so silent on the place of women in the Church as to give the impression that they do not exist." No one can deny the immense advantages that can accrue to the Church from the dedicated services of women. If the Council gives more attention to the role of women, it will counteract the disesteem for women in certain parts of the world. The Council should exalt women's place in the apostolate of the laity and in all of the work of the Church.

At the conclusion of this speech, the standing vote of the Fathers decided that the debate on chapter 3 was at an end.

NOTES

1. It was another omen of good things that Jean Guitton made available in French a translation of Newman's famous essay, in *L'Eglise et les laïcs*, which appeared just as the second session opened. M. Guitton contributed a history of the document, a history, however, indebted to and inferior to the fuller one prepared by John Coulson in the new English edition (Geoffrey Chapman, 1961). M. Guitton also offered some of his own reflections about the role of the layman, highly rhetorical and poetic, in the best French manner.

12

HOLINESS: THE DOLDRUMS

AFTER CARDINAL SUENENS' great talk on the 22nd, and several good interventions on the 23rd, the pace of the Council seemed to slacken. Like a frigate becalmed, Ecumenical Vatican Council II seemed to lack a source of human power. After four weeks of often repetitive debate, half of the second session was almost over. Something in the parliamentary procedure was very wrong. Debate wandered freely. There was no way to ask a point of order. The famous four votes, promised on October 15 for presentation on October 17, had disappeared from sight; very little legislative work was being accomplished. There was talk, talk, talk. True enough, a great educational process was going on, and the Council was laboring at the long, slow, undramatic work of consolidating its gains of the year before. Moreover, the Council Fathers were trying to avoid the emotional outbreaks and the occasional bitterness of the first session, and thus were taking care to moderate their demands.

But there was still another factor. No one had foreseen the extent of the victory the forces of reform would win. Prepared for a long-drawn-out battle, which might, at best, end in a stand-off that would allow them the freedom they sought, they had not been prepared to find suddenly allied behind them the largest part of the Church. Thus, the reformers had overestimated the opposition (just as the opposition had at first underestimated them) and made concessions which they did not need to make, and which they now had come to rue. The reason for the Council's difficulties was that the re-

165

formers did not yet see how to regain the momentum and the sense of direction they had had earlier.

A great deal of restlessness, therefore, was mounting in the Council. The great open dispute of the year before seemed to have moved from the Council floor to unknown places behind the scenes. It was obvious that the tension in the theological commission had been rather high—in their interventions in the general assembly, the members of the commission often disagreed by wide margins on the documents they had jointly prepared. Moreover, whereas in the first session the liturgical commission had met in plenary session several times a week when their own documents were being discussed on the floor, the theological commission was being called into plenary session by its president, Cardinal Ottaviani, only once a week. True enough, its twelve subcommissions were working diligently on various matters. But it began to be obvious that the work was going slower than the time at the disposal of the Council seemed to warrant; some of the members and experts of the commission could be in Rome regularly only during the Council, not afterward.

Cardinal Ottaviani, the president of the theological commission, is an exceptionally courageous man. His views are often directly opposed to those of the majority of the Council Fathers, but, unlike some of his associates, he is not the least afraid to make his views known. Moreover, he is a very warm, pleasant, and urbane man. Personally, he is above suspicion, but professionally, as Secretary of the Holy Office and president of the theological commission, he sometimes has not scrupled to act as though he were in possession of sources of truth beyond the reach of other members of the Council.

For such reasons, no doubt, all the frustrations of the long, slow session were beginning to be directed upon the theological commission. By the end of October a considerable number of Council Fathers were saying that a document worthy of the Council simply could not be expected of that commission, under its present leadership. In theory, a conciliar commission is obliged to respect the will of the Council Fathers, on whom, after all, rests the obligation of giving official witness to the Catholic faith. The liturgical commission was daily giving proof that, with great modesty and moderation, it responded very delicately to the will of the Council. The theological commission, on the other hand, made little serious attempt to give such proof. In view of the public criticism, a public account was called for; but those who could have rendered such an account still seemed at this date to think themselves above the necessity.

But the main difficulty which hung over the Council in the fourth week of the second session was caused, not by the theological commission, but by the lack of clarity concerning the source of power in the Council as a whole. The moderators had proposed their fourfold vote, and now their move had been challenged, behind the scenes, by the council presidents and the coordinating commission. On the evening of October 23, the three groups met together, council presidents, moderators, and the coordinating commission (some of these positions overlap). After an involved discussion, from which not much satisfaction was derived, the moderators were widely reported to have suffered an 11 to 9 defeat.

When the news of this meeting was spread abroad through the various groups assembled in Rome, pessimism concerning the outcome of the Council reached a low. The report seemed to mean that the parliamentary power behind the Council was not wielded by the four moderators, but by the council of presidents. The right of the moderators to speed up and to direct the grueling hours of debate seemed to be limited. It also seemed to mean that, in this instance, the theological commission had been spared four clear mandates from the Council Fathers concerning how to revise the document on the Church on four supremely important issues. Those who distrusted the theological commission, and who were dissatisfied with the lack of clear power in the Council, were not comforted by these events.

The Council of Trent had lasted eighteen years; it began to seem that Vatican Ecumenical Council II could last twenty. Worse still, time seemed to be on the side of the Curia. The energies of the reformers seemed to have been dissipated; the great new ideas with which the second session had begun, like the Senate of Bishops proposed by Pope Paul, now seemed clouded by hesitations and parliamentary blocks. There were twenty-three hundred Council Fathers in Rome, ready to *do* something to realize these promising ideas; but they could not even vote on a reasonable suggestion made by their four moderators. Those Council Fathers who lived in Rome and thought in the Roman manner seemed safer than the Czar ever was across the vast plains before Moscow.

There was, thus, a great deal of frustration in Rome during this black week. Critics were not so much concerned that the Council was proceeding at a slow deliberate pace; nobody would have wished it to attempt to move too swiftly through matters of extreme importance for generations to come. The complaint was not at the slowness of the pace; the complaint concerned the lack of clear lines of authority within the Council. Despair was heightened by the fact that nobody knew who controlled the Council. There seemed to be too much room behind the scenes for hidden manipulations. Were the world's bishops, or were they not, responsible for what went on in the Council?

II

In the mystery of the Church, all are called to holiness, chapter 4 begins. The chapter was not a particularly exciting chapter. There was nothing penetratingly Catholic in it. It was in fact a bad chapter, a chapter based on the traditions of the Church at a weak, distorted period of its history. The text had too much to say about moral virtues and about the glory of Christian holiness, too little to say about the grace of Christ. For the heart of Christian holiness is not the effort of striving for human perfection, of trying to make oneself into a different kind of person than one is, of trying to model oneself on some ethical ideal; it is not specifically Christian to keep a notebook, like Benjamin Franklin, of one's daily faults. The secret of Christian holiness is that God has given us His own life, and that we are called to let that life grow in our intelligence and in our heart. Christian holiness, therefore, is not so much a struggle to overcome evil as a struggle to make the good placed in oneself by God thoroughly penetrate one's thoughts, emotions, and actions. The founts of Christian holiness are the life of the Holy Spirit given to the Church, given in repeated and ever deeper strength through eucharistic worship and the other sacraments. Christian holiness does not call for conformity to a code, which is pharisaism, but for creativity. It is not a system of following better rules than other people, or of following common rules better than other people. It is "a more excellent way," a way of living on a new level of life, of having more resources of life than other people, and of making these extra possibilities real.

Chapter 4 begins by affirming that Christ, our Lord, is the source of all holiness. He summons every single man, in the way of *caritas*, that peculiar form of love which is Christian love, to live the fullness of God's own life according to the possibilities of his own personality and vocation. In the second part of the text, an implicit metaphor, the pyramid, is used to show how this holiness comes down through the Church. The chapter sets up the bishop as the model of sanctity, and then affirms that also priests and those laymen who have been deputed by their bishops to carry on some apostolic activity are called to holiness. It goes on to say that this same holiness reaches even to married persons and parents, whose conjugal love is a symbol of the love of Christ for His bride, the Church. The text then concludes that, in the last analysis, all Christians are called to sanctity, and in the measure in which their own lives reflect the traits of Christ they will be witnesses of Christ in the world. It is notable that while the text uses an image for sanctity which suggests the mysterious order of holiness given to men from above, coming through the Word of God and the sacraments of which the bishops and priests are ministers, it seems to speak as if the holiness which descends through the bishops is moralistic rather than mysterious. It seems to speak as if the bishops are models of certain kinds of action, models to be imitated; whereas it should speak as if the bishops are the vessels of the divine grace which is poured out on all the people of God. The bishops are not so much to be imitated for their moral practices as to be loved and cherished for the graces that are dispensed through their hands.

Most of the rest of the text deals with persons called to the religious life, i.e., those who publicly profess to follow those three evangelical counsels so much cherished in the Catholic tradition, poverty, chastity, and obedience, in a stable form of community life approved by the Church. There are more than two million such Christians in the world, more, even, than the Congregation of Religious in Rome can account for with precision; one thousand of the Council Fathers belong to religious communities. Those who prepared this chapter on holiness deliberately avoided providing a chapter specifically dedicated to these religious, in order to emphasize that the life of the evangelical counsels is only a special means of attaining the holiness to which all the members of the Church are called. (But the Very Reverend Agostino Sepinski, Minister General of the Franciscans, charged on October 31 that the schema before the Council was not the one approved by the coordinating commission—after months of work—in 1962. The religious superiors were very distressed at the sudden substitution of a new schema in the early summer of 1963.

This surreptitious tactic was due not to the conservatives, but to the "progressives.")

The text tries to emphasize that there is only one Christian holiness, the life dominated by *caritas*. Though there are, of course, many different manifestations of this holiness, many different ways of living out this holiness. But the text does not go very far in spelling out how these manners of holiness are different, and how they complement one another; it seems a text poor in theological reflection; it merely repeats poor textbooks, or the less profound authors. It uses the misleading phrase "the state of perfection" which is traditionally used to describe the religious life; and it recalls that these states of perfection are under the authority of the Church, which approves their rules and interprets their spirit. It notes that the Pope can grant to individual orders and congregations exemption from the authority of local bishops, in order to further the common good of the universal Church by allowing these orders some measure of independence, and international scope.

The chapter insists that the vows of poverty, chastity, and obedience do not distort the human personality, provided that they are lived in the intense pursuit of *caritas*. The chapter says that the consecration of an entire lifetime, through perpetual profession of the religious vows, is on a higher plane than those professions which cover only a period of time, no matter how long; for perpetual profession symbolizes the bond of Christ with his Church. Religious have an enviable opportunity, it continues, to become more effective instruments of God, because the counsels permit greater freedom of action, and prepare those thus consecrated to understand the love of God and to live it intensely. The chapter concludes with a word of special praise for all those who live under the vows of religious life. It reminds them that they are called to the common service of love for men, each in his or her own way doing good to all. It goes on to repeat that every Christian, not merely the ones consecrated to religious life, is called, in whatever circumstances he finds himself, to show Christ to men through his life and thus to increase the holiness of the Church.

III

On Friday, the debate on chapter 4 was desultory. The text was criticized for being too abstract, remote from history, silent about the concrete lives of holy men. An Indonesian bishop said "the word 'sanctity' is used *ad nauseam*," always in a moralistic, static sense. In Scripture, he said, holiness is a gift of God, and requires of His people a continuous effort in response. Holiness is objective, descending from God; it is also a personal reply. The clarity of the text is too abstract. The description "state of perfection to be acquired" applies to all Christians, not only religious. The joy of resurrection is missing. Emphasis on faith and hope are missing. An Italian bishop said individuals are called to glorify the Father, but also to glorify the Church on earth. A Yugoslavian bishop decried the failure of the text to include the secular clergy, too, in the "state of perfection." The terminology is medieval; it defies reality; and it annoyed the bishop. "The secular clergy is left hanging in the air between the heaven of religious and the earth of ordinary Christians. The place of secular institutes adds to the present confusion."

Thus the opening discussion on holiness in the Church ended with irritation over who, in the medieval vision of the world, has the highest place in the kingdom of God.

Moreover, one of the moderators appeared to be riding roughshod over the religious superiors who tried to speak on the chapter. One superior general, of a very large order, put in his name twice, the second time (after cloture) with over fifty signatures attached, and still he was not allowed to speak. Nevertheless, others who had put in their names later than he were allowed to speak, and the second time, by Council rules, he had every right to speak. There were seventeen speakers, mostly religious, who, after cloture was invoked on the 31st, had the right to speak; and they protested being forced into silence. At a special meeting with the moderator in question—Cardinal Doepfner—they let their dissatisfaction be known in no uncertain terms. But even in presenting a rapid summary of their objections to the Council on November 7, Cardinal Doepfner did not give them the promised satisfaction. The religious superiors were extremely displeased with the newly added chapter and the hostility toward religious communities which they felt prompted it. Several became disaffected toward "the progressives," eminent members among whom, they began to feel, were seeking power for themselves, at the expense of religious. Few are the bishops who would not like to have firmer control over those religious in their diocese who are largely exempt from their authority, and directly under the authority of the Pope. In the mouths of some progressives, "collegiality" began to have a displeasing ring, as far as these religious superiors were concerned.

Holiness in the Church does not come automatically, either with baptism or with episcopal consecration. There is ambiguity in all men; both "progressives" and "conservatives" showed mixed motives and human fallibility. God, it seems, loves men not because they are are already perfect, but because they are so needy.

IV

One of the great emotional issues at the second session had meanwhile been coming to a boil. On October 1, Cardinal Raul Silva Henriquez of Chile, speaking for forty-four Latin American bishops, asked that the text on the Blessed Virgin Mary be included in the document on the Church. In Latin American nations, he said, devotion to Mary is sometimes too far removed from the proper devotional life of the Church. When doctrine on Mary is proposed as a separate theological tenet, it is difficult to relate to the whole Christian perspective on salvation. Within a week, Cardinal Arriba y Castro of Tarragona declared for sixty-six "mainly Spanish" bishops that Mary should *not* be treated in the document on the Church, "because the mystery of Mary is greater than the mystery of the Church." If included in the text on the Church, then the chapter on Mary should be the second—i.e., very important—chapter and "as profound and extensive as the matter deserves."

On October 24, it was announced that the theological commission, meeting in plenary session (at the direction of the Pope, some said), had decided to ask the Council Fathers their opinion on whether the treatment on the Blessed Virgin Mary should be included in the document on the Church or in a separate schema of its own. To make the alternative clear, the theological commission had named Cardinal Rufino Santos, the Archbishop of Manila, to argue for placing the treatment of Mary in a schema of its own: and Cardinal Franz Koenig of Vienna to explain why the treatment of Mary should be included in the document on the Church.

On October 9, the theological commission had voted, by almost a two-thirds majority, for inclusion. (On this question, as on others, the theological commission was to prove more "progressive" than the rest of the Council, numerically, though not in terms of its inner power structure.) Meanwhile, certain factions represented among the experts of the theological commission had been able to have printed on the Vatican Press a separate schema on the Blessed Virgin Mary, including high-pitched, rhetorical arguments by Father Carl Balič, O.F.M., a Yugoslav priest and consultor to the Holy Office. This document, though it was far from being an official text of the Council, was printed in the standard format of an official schema, was lettered *sub secreto* to give it the appearance of a schema, and was distributed to the Council Fathers. No complaints were voiced by those in the highest positions on the theological commission, about experts trying to sway the judgment of the bishops on a question before the Council.

The issue, though in itself it does not seem of much importance (non-Christian newsmen were baffled by the temperature of the discussion), was nevertheless of importance both emotionally and even intellectually. Two separate attitudes of mind, two different conceptions of the relation of the Church to the world, were at stake. Later, we shall have to analyze the factors that made the issue so explosive. Here, let us pause to summarize the speeches of the two cardinals delivered on October 24, and presented to the Council Fathers in printed form on October 25. (The vote was to be taken on Tuesday, October 29.)

Cardinal Santos offered eight reasons why the treatment of Mary should have a special schema of its own; the most important of his arguments were the following: The Blessed Virgin has a special dignity and a singular place in the Church. The short schema on the Church "could hardly be modified so as to include the schema on the Blessed Virgin Mary without her dignity and place in the Church thereby suffering, or without the door thereby being opened to erroneous ideas in the minds of the uninstructed." Mary plays a special role in the life of Christ, and thus within the history of the people of God; there is not enough space in the schema on the Church to express this role sufficiently. Besides, the treatment on the people of God refers only briefly to the most Holy Trinity, and if many lines are to be given to the exalted work of Mary in the history of this people, comparisons might erroneously be drawn. The difference between Mary and other Christians is not the same as the difference between the hierarchy and the laity, which is the subject of discussion in the text on the Church. Mary had a singular vocation and was full of grace from the very first moment of her existence;

although she is united in one body with all the people of God, "in some ways she is above the Church." More space is needed, because the Council has to explain the whole doctrine on the Blessed Virgin, everything which the Church holds by solemn definition, by its common teaching authority, and by the common consent of the faithful, with the approval of their pastors; for it is our duty toward our separated brethren to explain with sincerity whatever the Church believes and holds. It is difficult to find a logical place for the treatment of the Blessed Virgin among the chapters of the text on the Church as they now stand; and Mariology should not be reduced to ecclesiology.

Again, the schema on the Church is already long; the schema on Mary would have to be put into a brief appendix, as if it were something of only secondary importance. The cutting down of the schema on the Blessed Virgin would cause wonderment and might be interpreted as a lessening of the honor due her. It seems imprudent to call attention to controversies among Catholics on the status of Mariology. Then adroitly: "We have already spent more than two weeks discussing the first part of the schema on the Church . . . the schema on the Blessed Virgin Mary has its own particular difficulties, and undoubtedly numerous objections will be raised. . . .If both schemata are fused into one, this will certainly call for a new over-all discussion, and might result in a great loss of time, since we already have so many other points of doctrine on the agenda."

As Cardinal Santos left the microphone, Cardinal Koenig began his own address, which was not so successful as it might have been. He listed a series of reasons why his argument should prevail: theological, historical, pastoral, and ecumenical. The Church is the central theme of this Council, and that is where the treatment of the Blessed Virgin in this Council belongs. A separate schema would give the impression that new dogmas are being proposed, and "this is certainly not the mind of the Council." The treatment on the Church needs to be extended toward the eschatological dimension, and that on the Blessed Virgin needs to be extended to include the history of Mary's life on earth; thus the strong point of each document needs to be complemented by the strong point of the other. The Church is the people of God, and Mary is an eminent member of that people. Mary is a type of the way in which men are redeemed; thus her life should be treated in the doctrine on the Church. No one wants to obscure or lessen the dignity of the Blessed Virgin.

No one wishes to make her only one member among many, passively receiving the benefits of redemption. As the Church is the instrument of redemption in the hand of Christ, so is Mary.

The historical reasons were that all the titles of the Blessed Virgin—for example, in the famous litany of Loreto—were applied to the Church for many generations before they were applied to Mary; this is also true of the famous Chapter 12 of the Apocalypse. Again, in his opening address to the Council, Paul VI had related Mary and the Church. The Marian congress at Lourdes in 1958 had as its theme "Mary and the Church." Thus the trend of the present-day devotion of the faithful is to link Mary and the Church. The pastoral reasons: popular devotion needs to be guided and directed, lest it neglect essentials and become lost in secondary and accidental things. "This is why, not rarely, devotion to the Blessed Virgin is separated from the mystery of Christ and His Church. Thus our Mariological teaching should not stand out as something separate but as united with our teaching on the Church." The ecumenical reasons: the Orientals would more easily recognize the venerable Theotokos, the Mother of God, of their tradition; and non-Catholic Christians would have their attention drawn to the foundation of devotion to the Blessed Virgin in the testimony of Sacred Scripture and ancient tradition. He noted that the relations between Mary, the people of Israel, and the Church were today being studied by non-Catholic theologians; as were the scriptural texts (Luke 1:12; John 19:25; and Apocalypse 12) which present Mary as a figure of the Church.

The Fathers of the Council listened to both sets of arguments; they had five days to reach a decision.

V

That afternoon, Dom Christopher Butler, the abbot of Downside Abbey in England, held a press conference. He said that two tendencies in Catholic teaching on Mary were coming to a parting of the ways. Catholics are unanimous in believing that Christ's mother is that member of our race who has been most completely and radically redeemed. She is the type of all who believe; she dramatizes in her own person the meaning of the life of the Church. But on what tradition should teaching about Mary now be based? The Council Fathers had had a draft of the document on our Lady in their hands for nearly a year. Several other drafts had also been submitted to the coordinating commission. "Two such drafts are particularly interesting, because they each represent a serious attempt to go back to the biblical foundations of the Catholic belief and devotion in regard to our Lady. They thus bear witness to another aspect of the Catholic revival: the return to the Bible." These drafts are particularly appropriate for a Council charged not to forget the problems of Christian unity. Catholic belief and devotion with regard to our Lady are a serious difficulty in questions of Christian unity. "Many Protestants feel that in these matters the Catholic Church has gone far away from the purity of the original Gospels." Even sympathetic Anglicans, and the Eastern Orthodox, who are closer to Catholics than other Protestants in their attitude to the mother of God, dislike recent formal definitions of Marian doctrine, because they tend to rationalize a mystery. "There can be no question of the Catholic Church renouncing any of its dogmatic definitions about our Lady, but all Christians could meet together in meditating on what the Bible has to teach us about her and her role in the redemptive scheme." Such a treatment might help the cause of unity, whereas a further development beyond the positions already formally ratified by Popes or councils would raise further obstacles.

One of the five documents on our Lady which were being circulated in Rome had been prepared by the Abbot himself; it was receiving a great deal of support. Indeed, the opposition was alarmed. *Il Tempo* began to imply that the Abbot's text denied by omission the doctrines of the Immaculate Conception and the Assumption. At the conference, not yet foreseeing this duplicity, the Abbot concluded with the following words: "It remains to be seen what route the Council will decide to follow. Its members, it may be said, are unanimous in their desire to do honor to Christ by honoring His mother. The question is, which of the two ways now open will win the support of the majority of the Council members as best tending to realize its desire."

Indeed, what if the vote on Mary split the Council in two, or went in the direction of popular Marian devotion, apart from the biblical and patristic foundations of Catholic teaching? Because of the uncertainty of the outcome, this was the blackest week of the Council, until the session's end. The machinery of the Council had escaped from the hands of the bishops. The winds of forward motion had dropped, and storms were forming in the dark.

13

POLITICS AND THE BLESSED VIRGIN MARY

I

OVER THE WEEKEND of October 26, a vicious assault was launched in some sections of the Italian and Spanish press against the inclusion of the Blessed Virgin Mary in the schema on the Church. These assaults seemed to equate this inclusion with all that is dangerous and evil in *progressismo*. Those who launched them seemed to sense a threat to Latin spirituality, or even to the Latin political and social order. Perhaps in some ultimate sense they were not far from right. At any rate, *Il Tempo* and other right-wing groups were willing to make use of the debate on Mary for their own ends. It is impossible to understand the fierce emotion that surrounded this issue, and the later scuttling of the documents on the Jews and on religious liberty without pausing to try to find the link between Mary and the social order. Fortunately, several books which appeared on the Italian scene allow us to piece the evidence together.

Carlo Levi once wrote a beautiful book, *Christ Stopped at Eboli*, the point of whose title is that, although the name of Christ was known in this little out-of-the-way hill town, the teaching and witness of Christ had never penetrated the traditional supersition and paganism of the people; they lived, still, in the paganism of immemorial times. This theme is reinforced by the introductions which Mario Gozzini wrote to the sections of the book we have already cited, *Concilio Aperto*. Christianity introduced into history the distinction between personal conscience and the power of the State; it separated

177

the things of God from those of Caesar. But the Emperor Constantine, and especially Theodosius a century later, only reversed the pagan tradition; they made the State the instrument of religion.[1] Christianity was given a public face and public power without having to pass through the consciences of individual persons. The trappings of the Roman Empire were transferred to the Church: the Pope became the Pontifex Romanus, before whom, on the night of Christmas of the year 799, the Emperor of the West was to prostrate himself on the floor—and for a millennium afterward until the coronation of Napoleon in 1808. Thus, the culture of the northern Mediterranean world in the Dark Ages and early Middle Ages left a deep imprint on the Church's conception of herself.[2] Wars were fought in the name of the Church; the Church led the way in conquering new geographical areas. The Christian "consecration of the world" then had an altogether different meaning than it has in the minds of many who use the words today.

Since it lasted sixteen hundred years, the Constantinian vision seemed, sometimes, to give promise of being the eternal, the necessary, and the model vision, instead of only a phase in the long history of the Church. "Its typical aspect, the consecration of temporal structures, did not determine in fact, and *per se*, an effective sanctification of persons. The conversion of people under the sword of princes could not have been otherwise than superficial: it contributed certainly to softening the harshness of certain customs—and herein lay its historical necessity—but it too easily accorded the name of Christian to men who, in reality, were not yet so. On the other hand, the formal obedience of the State, the juridical privileges, the economic support, contributed, yes, to the benefit and splendor of the Church; but today we know that these were instruments unreliable (and certainly provisional) for rooting Christ in the souls of men. Princes protected the altar in the interest of their own throne; they made use of the Church, serving it only apparently; they served religion, but for motives which were exclusively political (there were certainly exceptions, but then the Church has canonized those rare princes and kings capable of placing spiritual motives ahead of their own)."[3] "The apparent security of the Constantinian situation brought with it, then, the temptation to be complacent with cornices, with ensigns; to count one's mission fulfilled when the cross was put on the façade and when the word 'God' occurred in official acts; to allow the cross and God to be compromised in facts, deeds, and projects which were Christian only in name. Two essential principles—the distinction between religious and profane authority, and the nonviolence of the missionary task—ended by being obliterated." [4]

The Middle Ages were doomed to collapse. The diminishing of ecclesiastical power in the world generated among ecclesiastics an increasing contempt for the world. No longer powerful in worldly things, churchmen began to boast about being powerful in eternal things. "The Church has all the answers. The Church lives in eternity. The power of the world is vain; its fruits are bitter. The world's progress is decline." Moreover, as the years went on, and the world changed, the polemic did not change. The world passed the Church by, but many churchmen continued to use the very arguments against the world which their forefathers had used. Some no longer knew in their own experience, from talking with the men of the world, what the men of the world now thought. "Laziness and inertia are not the only bad counselors; often, unfortunately, ignorance and lack of information are also needed, to win credence for worn-out and sterile patterns of thought, in themselves as useless as tinkling cymbals." [5]

The ignorance about the world which thrives in ecclesiastical Rome is legendary. A century ago, to his dismay, Cardinal Newman recognized that ignorance; it has not been entirely eliminated. Gozzini [6] cites two instances, originally recounted by Robert Rouquette, S.J., in *Etudes*, which are symptomatic of the general malaise. A cardinal of the Curia, knowing that Father Rouquette had many dealings with diplomats, told him that he himself knew that environment rather well. It is dominated, he said, by the man who is the greatest obstacle to faith today: Renan. "I was struck dumb with bewilderment," Father Rouquette records, "and couldn't even begin to explain to the cardinal how the most irreligious teachers of my youth considered Renan, even then, an old curiosity passed by very long before." The other instance concerned a young prelate—the unimpressive, unawakened, casual Angelo Roncalli, Nuncio in Paris —who in speaking of Teilhard de Chardin asked: why did he raise so many problems instead of contenting himself with teaching catechism and the social doctrines of the Church? "I underwent many labors to make him admit that these problems were not raised by Teilhard, but were raised by others, his contemporaries, and were such that he could not elude them."

II

The piety of non-historical orthodoxy sometimes seems more pagan than it does Christian. More exactly, it is rather the piety proper to a certain age in the life of the Church, and its accidental features which now seem so irrelevant or even blasphemous were once useful and good. Non-historical orthodoxy arose in a time when men had no hope of developing creation according to the possibilities which Providence has implanted in it; when men could think that the world always had been the same and always would be the same; when there seemed to be no remedy for the widespread poverty, disease, and ignorance of the human race. At such a time, the appeal to men that they had not here a lasting home, and that their true and real self-identity belonged rather to eternity than to the moment of history in which they lived, had to be sufficient in itself. There was no hope that the majority of men might change their lot in life, and grow up to be free, educated, and conscientious citizens of the world. It seemed that most must remain poor, ignorant, and miserable, able to base their hope only on another, better world. Universal helplessness seemed to favor a version of the doctrine of the cross, a style of de-tachment from the present world, a kind of contempt for the projects of men in history, which now seem insulting to the Creator. No doubt it was good, then, for men to leave so much in the hands of God, when there was so little in their own, and to love God so much in spite of the hardship of their life. But the technical power devel-oped by men in the world has now brought with it a new kind of moral obligation before God, a new sense of gratitude, a new kind of dependence. Men are not more secure now than they were before; far from it. But they have a religious spirit, or the prerequisites for such a spirit, that differs in all but essential respects from the religious spirit of the past. What seemed in an earlier time presumptuous is now humble; what seems irresponsible today was once the best that men could do.

Non-historical orthodoxy, however, is poorly placed to recognize the changes that are taking place in the spiritual life of men. In the earlier ages of the Church, the piety of the Christian people derived from liturgical gatherings around the eucharist and meditation on the Word of God. At a later time, it derived from the writings of the saints—some of them apocryphal and full of marvels. In the more recent times favored by non-historical orthodoxy, it has relied on the "writers of spiritual books"—largely romantic authors who reflected on the writings of the saints, the theology of the late Middle Ages, and the pietist movements of the rationalistic age. Such piety had no spirit of ecumenism, for its leaders were not oriented toward the world around them, let alone toward non-Catholic Christians in the world. It admitted of no sense of reform, for it gave up all pretense of being critical within the Church, or of being faithful to earlier Christian tradition, or of giving intense study to the Word of God; it was busy defending its own present traditions. It fell back on rhetoric which tried to awaken a fading sense of piety, which men were increasingly reluctant to imitate. The world seemed always to be getting worse; doom always lurked ahead.

There were two features in this piety, especially, which left its followers ill-equipped to understand the changes the human spirit would undergo in the twentieth century. One of these was a lack of intellectual self-criticism about its own presuppositions and origins; it did not understand accurately its own contingent role in the history of the people of God. The second was its separation from the professional world, from men who were making modern history: the scientists, the social reformers, the political theorists and practitioners, the businessmen. Christians were increasingly conscious of leading a double life: so much for Sunday piety and personal piety, the rest for the world. Non-historical orthodoxy accepted this separation placidly; what aroused its deepest fears was laicism, the desire to exclude religion altogether from public life, even from private life. Laicism—and modernism—fulfilled the deep, intrinsic need of non-historical orthodoxy for a total, determined enemy. Such an enemy could solidify non-historical orthodoxy in its favorite dogmatic positions, leaving no time for self-criticism and self-reform.

Non-historical orthodoxy is essentially masochistic. The prophecy of imminent doom is its *raison d'être*. It needs to feel attacked. It needs to profess the very items of its belief most calculated to arouse the ire of non-Catholics, in order to have assurance that the world is still at war with it. For this is how it proves to itself, rather than by critical self-examination, that it is faithful to Christ. Fundamentally, non-historical orthodoxy is a retreat from the responsibilities of living in history, and of remaining faithful to Christ under the stresses of changing circumstance. It pictures the Church as an anvil on which history rains its blows in vain; whereas the Church is also leaven in the loaf of history, a mustard seed, a growing vine.

Thus popular devotions, especially Marian devotions, loom very large in the piety of non-historical orthodoxy. Such devotions are ordinarily a refuge from the conflicts of history. They give personal, individualistic comfort. They do not awaken social consciousness, or prod the conscience of the man of affairs. The sense of sin and contrition which they stir up concerns personal sins: unkind words, gossiping, sexual misdemeanors—the items which preachers of missions and retreats concentrate upon. The man of history has little time for such devotions, such attitudes. This form of piety attempts to womanize the world, according to the spirit of an earlier century. In effect, it insists that men withdraw from the real, concrete daily work of human progress. Not by accident does non-historical orthodoxy have a stronger hold on women than on men, especially in the lower classes; these are the ones whose lives have changed least since the late Middle Ages.

Yet the simpler piety of the past was once authentic, produced many saints and still continues to inspire many people. The piety which is built around Mary, around popular novenas and devotions, around the writings of certain saints, has been and continues to be admirable. It has inspired many persons to give their lives for the sick and suffering. It has encouraged many of the wealthy to be kind, paternal, and beneficent to individuals among the poor. This piety has inspired thousands of the young people who dedicate their lives to the work of religious communities. It has produced thinkers of great erudition in the ecclesiastical world of the last four centuries. On the other hand, it must be admitted that it has achieved all these good and admirable things through a certain abstraction from the real history of our times.

In the mind of the proponents of non-historical orthodoxy, the French Revolution is the beginning of all modern evils. Nor do they sufficiently distinguish—if at all—the American Revolution from the French. They have never grasped the injustices built into the structure of the social order in which non-historical orthodoxy took its rise. The modern Popes have written encyclicals on the reconstruction of the social order, which the partisans of non-historical orthodoxy have largely ignored. Convinced that modern social and political movements injure the Christian faith, they do not approach these movements with intellectual seriousness. In their eyes, the whole world is developing in a fashion that threatens their own spiritual life and personal approach to faith. They do not see how to reconcile Christianity and the modern world. When they try to enter into the contemporary spiritual world, they lose their bearings and begin to feel terror. In order to save themselves, they find themselves opposing almost every aspect of contemporary intellectual and spiritual development.

Nor could they accept the fruits of modern theological scholarship concerning the ancient scriptural and liturgical traditions of the Church. Their own piety is based on a later period in the history of the Church, a period which was no longer liturgical or biblical. They can see in their own lives that liturgy and the Bible are not necessary. They know that they themselves love God and serve the Christian faith with all their hearts; they cannot understand how other Catholics can oppose them, without favoring the philosophers and revolutionaries of, as they think, an advancing world of unbelief. The partisans of non-historical orthodoxy, are, therefore, caught in an almost impossible emotional and intellectual position. They find themselves defending their beliefs against enemies on a thousand sides. They do not dare to admit that their critics are correct even on a single point. For, if they do make such an admission, then they know that they will have to begin re-examining their entire position; and re-examination is the one thing their position cannot sustain. For their position depends on an ignorance of the early Christian tradition, a disregard of the critical study of the foundations of their own system, and a belief that any serious consideration of the real world of our century is a concession to evolutionary theories, to the attenuation of solid doctrine, and—in a word—to modernism.

III

In the United States, the average bishop might have seemed before the Council to be very conservative, for he had grown up and been educated in a Catholic environment in which non-historical orthodoxy had been presented as the authentic and the only tradition of Catholic faith. America is a land with almost no historical or intellectual tradition; American Catholicism was established in the era of the Council of Trent, the era of the Counter-Reformation; and the American environment was aggressively Protestant. Thus, the

American experience seemed to justify non-historical orthodoxy; the antagonisms of American Protestants toward their Catholic neighbors seemed to verify the statements in the textbooks. But Americans, nevertheless, were living in a country where contemporary history was being made. As a consequence, their daily experience led them to modify the European forms of the non-historical orthodoxy they had inherited: much of the autocracy of the clergy, the lordly titles, and the interference of clerics in politics disappeared. Their common sense—that great inheritance from the Anglo-Saxon tradition—led them to a more realistic appreciation of the world in which they lived. They learned to use, rather than to despise, the world. The philosophers and politicians opposing them were less bitter than in Europe; anticlericalism was not so deep. Not so hated by the world, they could love it more, as Christ did. Their churches were not yet built; they had to occupy themselves in the world of men in order to find money and means for building them. They became skilled in economics and, in a minor way, in politics. They became engaged in the modern world. Thus, while many of the American clergy thought in terms of non-historical orthodoxy, in fact they were often living according to common sense in the real world of their times. They were not conservatives, but dualists: more realistic in practice than in theology. The Council began to show them how to unite theory and practice, according to the Gospels.

In Spain and Italy, on the other hand, social reality and the structure of the social classes still remain much more as they have been for centuries. There countries had not undergone the social revolution of our times; political groups of great power still hope to avoid this revolution. This social-political force has a deep personal stake in keeping the Church confined within the framework of non-historical orthodoxy. For this inherited style of life keeps the energy of the Church involved in private devotions to Mary and the saints. It offers the people the rhetoric of a better world in eternity, and encourages them to suffer patiently in this world. It harassed those Catholic scholars who labored at a theology of the Word of God, of the liturgy, of social action, of the return to the earlier traditions of Christianity. It tended to keep the Church, in short, in a period of history when these social-political forces were at their strongest. These forces have been, therefore, quite willing to strengthen the hand of non-historical orthodoxy when they can. In recompense, the partisans of non-historical orthodoxy can feel that they have friends in the world, men who seem to help them; who seem to support the Church, who give honor to the Church. Indeed these men often control the purse strings of the Church, or the political freedom of the Church, or law and order in the land. There is, thus, a close alliance between certain social and political elements interested in the preservation of their own vision of the Church. The vision of both groups was fashioned by the same contingent period of history, by an old social order they wish to prolong as long as possible.

IV

The roots of the great disappointments of the second session of the Vatican Council seem to lie in this alliance. To rant against the alliance is easy; the disentanglement will be gradual and painful. The government of Italy was in crisis all during the second session of the Council, as it has been for years; the solution at the end of November did not give promise of longevity. That crisis contributes to the fears of many that the Communist party will yet vote its way into power in Italy; hence the fears about proclaiming "religious liberty," which the religiously uneducated populace may interpret as freedom to vote Communist. Thus as Italian politics disrupted Vatican I, so they tend to compromise Vatican II. How a universal Church is to remain faithful to the Gospels while subject to the dislocations of Italian political and economic life is difficult to see. Many at Vatican II spoke wistfully of moving the Holy See from Rome once more, for the good of souls.

For although in Rome it seems to be accepted that "all the world" looks to Rome for edification, the reality is quite the opposite. Young seminarians leaving other lands to study in Rome are regularly warned "not to lose the faith," and to be prepared to be seriously scandalized. Ronald Knox once said: "I don't mind being on the barque of Peter, so long as I don't have to go near the machinery." But it is difficult to describe the reality without drawing accusations of sensationalism, or rousing pious incredulity: "It can't be that bad." The reality is very ugly indeed. Perhaps the best way of saying what honesty demands, yet not creating a stir, is simply to report on a book widely read in Rome during the second session, highly recommended to me, for example, by Monsignor Fenton, and sufficiently representative of the thinking of the daily *Il Tempo* and of certain Roman ecclesiastics to serve as a guide. The book was called *La Chiesa dopo Giovanni—The Church After Pope John*—and it was published by Il Borghese press in its regular monthly series. Its author, the pseudonymous Lo Svizzero, contributed, as well, a regular column in the bi-weekly *Il Borghese*. On its jacket, the book bore a flaming yellow banner which read, in black: "Communists in the Vatican under Pope John XXIII." The book is based on two beliefs: that the world is seething with confusions and trembling on the brink of moral disintegration; and that the Communists are supremely acute in taking advantage of Pope John and the Council. The author hates the free, open Council; the closed, hidden power of the Curia has long been the pillar of his social-political ambitions. Lo Svizzero calls the reign of Pope John the "winter of pessimism"; in Pope Paul he sees "the buds of hope for a new spring." [7]

The first chapter of his book creates a fantasy of a great schism building up behind the Iron Curtain, due both to the internal contradictions of the Communist system and to special religious problems. The author goes on to picture Italy as menaced by a new, clerical Communism gaining influence in the Vatican. He describes the Council as weakening the traditional Church, under the subtle pressure of Communist propaganda in the homelands of the foreign bishops, and views the complaints about the Roman Curia as a Trojan horse: "that ancient pretext, a crisis in the Roman Curia." The book has a basic contradiction. On the one hand, it wants the Church to remain faithful to "eternal principles" and "unchanging clarity," instead of attending to contemporary social realities; on the other hand, it thinks it "an error to hold that the Church has the duty only to teach the Gospels," for the Church has already been committed to the great battle (against Communism) since the end of the Second World War.[8] The role which it successfully applies is that the social-political system it defends is part of the eternal, unchanging treasure of the Church; other social-political systems are full of dangers.

No wonder, then, that the author hates and fears Pope John and the Council; they have heightened the confusions in his already threatened world, and deprived him—by attacking the Curia—of his firmest bastion of defense. Lo Svizzero makes identical complaints about Pope John and about the Council. The heritage of Pope John "proved more burdensome than was foreseen; there are many obscure points, many hesitations and uncertainties, which reveal a true religious crisis." [9] The Council, too, creates confusion: "the conciliar gathering, with its open and often violent criticisms, with its unsolved and complicated problems." [10] The one thing Lo Svizzero's system cannot sustain is criticism; the one thing that strikes fear into his heart is religious renewal, groping, and creativity.

His real enemy, therefore, is change. But he creates a fantasy of half-truths to make his fears substantial; he thinks his enemy is Communism. The Communists were the first to become alert to the new power of Catholicism in the world after the reign of Pope Pius XII; with the election of Pope John they "have developed a new form of propaganda, trying to capture the ecumenical and irenic initiatives of John XXIII in a deadly trap." [11] They skillfully awaited "the best possible moment," the Council. Their goal "is clear: to impale the Church on positions more conciliatory in the matter of practical collaboration with the 'new realities' of Marxism; to induce her to abandon her doctrinal defenses even concerning the excommunication against Marxism: to bring her to adopt 'ideological coexistence' with the Socialist world." [12]

Pope John was "full of good intentions and hopeful of the good of mankind," but his vision of a new world was "abstract, erected as if outside the present time and animated and justified only in that bursting burden of human warmth which emanated from John XXIII like a fluid." [13] Pope John was a man "living in an ideal world, and proceeding on this earth with his feet never touching the ground of reality: that 'parish priest of the world,' as he declared himself with his insight, as if to withdraw certain of his unforeseeable acts from the heavy responsibility of the pontifical office, which in fact presupposes something more than the action of the parish priest." [14] It is as though Pope John were non-historical, rather than Lo Svizzero.

To realize his vision, and to expose to criticism the firm structure of the real, curial world, Pope John needed the Council. The years of preparation for the Council had frightened Lo Svizzero. The fear was widespread; for his editor at Il Borghese, Mario Tedeschi, had even then written a book: *The Dangers of the Council*. New facts were arising "in the depths of ecclesiastical organs, which induced the Communists to intervene for their own ends. There were episodes, to say the least, most disconcerting; everything boiling up from a ferment below, especially from a foreign clergy influenced, perhaps unconsciously, by the malicious propaganda of the International Left. New ferment, we know, is the salt of wisdom and the final driving force of progress. But when a most skillful adversary sows in it the seeds of corrosive criticism, of doubt, and even of heterodoxy, then that driving force becomes a ruinous avalanche. This is all the more valid for the Catholic Church, which is a rigidly hierarchical organism, of divine origin and, therefore, not subject to internal criticism; foreign by its very nature to democratic action which, leaping up from below, conditions the orientations and the decisions of the summit." [15]

Lo Svizzero wrote that Cardinal Tardini "knew well the problems of the world" and "in particular those of the Church, having lived practically his whole life at the summit of the hierarchical ladder; he knew the ferments agitating the clergy, and the violent oscillations of certain foreign bishops, daily subjected to continuous pressure from political and religious groups certainly not suspected of sympathy for 'papism.' Truly there were many, both outside and inside the Curia, who felt that a Council should not be convoked in a period so unstable and tumultuous in the history of the world; and who feared an upheaval in the conciliar labors—as was then exactly verified." [16] For in the first session, "the frenzies of a sort of sociological modernism" rendered the Council "unsteady under the continuous clash of opposing tendencies," [17] the result of an "ever-growing Communist plot on the one hand, and, on the other, the existence of profound differences of opinion between clergy and laity, between bishops and cardinals, between Italians and foreigners in the compass of the Church." [18] "To many, it also appeared that certain currents quite near to the 'new modernism' wished to adapt the Church to the times, declaring themselves disposed to sacrifice certain doctrinal positions, a healthy slice of theology and many 'declining' political positions." [19]

Lo Svizzero was aggrieved that these forces in the Council, "if not endorsed by the highest power, were at least tolerated; indeed, these forces of agitation no longer bore the odor of heterodoxy, nor the acrid taste of rebellion; nor could their status be questioned. . . ." [20] "The plot is evident, the danger grave. If in fact there must come even from Italy the example of unnatural collaboration between Catholics and Communists, nothing more would be able to save the world from Marxist domination. Will the Church react against this colossal temptation, unique perhaps in its two-thousand-year history? Will it succeed in repelling with its ancient, adamant firmness, anchored in immutable principles, which must be diffused over the earth by divine commandment, the formidable 'come-with-me' of the Marxist world? Of that world which, to heal its own internal contradictions, today offers the olive palm to the Church that until yesterday it tried to bend to its own will? The response to these questions will condition the future of the world: from it we will know whether the humanity of the year 2000 will be Christian still or only and desolately Marxist." [21]

Lo Svizzero trusts Pope Paul VI. He believes that he will leave the Curia undisturbed. "On the path of the smiling conquests of the Christian world by Marxism, there is raised up the principal obstacle, that immovable bulwark of Catholic tradition represented by the Roman Curia." [22] To denounce the Roman Curia as intolerant and anachronistic signifies, moreover, "only that one is playing the game of those who would like to realize the 'obscene concubinage,' to unite the Catholic Church to atheistic Marxism in the name of an abstract irenicism or under the threat, indeed the blackmail, of schism. These gigantic pressures call for the abdication of a sovereignty that is divine; they pretend to correct the specific mission of the Church, which is, as all know, that of maintaining integral the deposit of faith to transmit it unaltered down the centuries to future generations." [23]

V

Lo Svizzero then makes an enlightening observation. Monsignor Tondini's tactless address, *De eligendo Pontifice*, given to the conclave of cardinals just before the election of Pope Paul VI, warning them not to elect another man like Pope John, was given, "certainly, after many and authoritative suggestions"; he was "the porta-voce of the Roman Curia." [24] Pope Paul's first radio message to the world echoed Monsignor Tondini's views of the Curia: "its diligence, its 'sense of the Church,' its prudence in action." [25] Pope Paul is a man the Curia approved as Pope, a man Lo Svizzero approves as Pope.

Thus "the Roncalli enigma" gives way to "the Montini enigma." Which way is Montini going? Such are the crushing pressures on the Pope in the Vatican that simple honesty seems impossible. As Cardinal Montini once told a friend: "Prudence is not enough; today astuteness is required." Lo Svizzero, meanwhile, was listing his own enemies: *Témoignage Chrétien, Esprit, Etudes,* in France; *Politica, Questitalia, Adesso, Il Molino,* and "numerous others" in Italy; "not to speak of the great and little press of the Anglo-Saxon and German countries, and to refrain from comment on the ironic conformism of *Civiltà Cattolica,* which once would have been engaged even to the last comma in bitterest polemics against all those who do not think as the Roman Curia thinks." [26]

Left all alone, the right wing groped toward Pope Paul for help.

NOTES

1. *Concilio Aperto* by Mario Gozzini, pp. 99–100.
2. *Ibid.,* p. 101.
3. *Ibid.,* p. 103.
4. *Ibid.*
5. *Ibid.,* p. 64.
6. *Ibid.,* footnote. The second incident is recounted more fully in "The Roncalli Enigma," translated from *Études* by *The Catholic Mind,* LXI (November, 1963), p. 38.
7. *La Chiesa dopo Giovanni* by Lo Svizzero (Rome, Il Borghese), p. 247. All the remaining references in this chapter are from this book.
8. P. 10.
9. *Ibid.*
10. P. 11.
11. *Ibid.*
12. *Ibid.*
13. P. 12.
14. Pp. 12–13.
15. Pp. 13–14.
16. P. 16.
17. *Ibid.*
18. P. 17.
19. Pp. 17–18.
20. P. 18.
21. P. 21.
22. P. 156.
23. P. 155.
24. P. 157.
25. P. 158.
26. Pp. 99–100

14

THE PRISONER OF THE VATICAN

ON MONDAY MORNING, October 28, a simple and moving ceremony was held in St. Peter's. Pope Paul VI had long before set aside that day for a special commemoration of the anniversary of Pope John's election to the papacy. In no man's living memory had a special papal Mass ever been celebrated on the anniversary of a departed Pope's election. All the Council Fathers were present, together with the press and a large number of visitors. Pope Paul entered the basilica on foot with none of the usual pomp, and began a simple, low Mass on the small temporary altar erected for the daily Mass of the Council. The Mass was a dialogue Mass, the first any one could remember that a Pope had publicly said in such a simple fashion. The Pope was so moved that he fumbled the prayers at the foot of the altar, and had to begin again. The lay auditors were privileged to receive communion from the hand of the Pope himself. (There was, however, no provision for other laymen at the Mass to receive communion, not even from auxiliary priests.[1]) When the Mass ended, the Pope went quietly to the throne erected in the usual place near the main altar, under the great twisting canopy of Bernini.

Cardinal Suenens of Belgium then ascended the steps before the throne, received the Pope's blessing, and walked with a swift, sure stride to the small platform erected for the public speakers of the Council, where he preached the sermon quoted in Chapter 2. The style and tone of his discourse was personal and warm, not at all professorial. The Council Fathers listened in attentive silence.

At the end of his discourse Cardinal Suenens received the thanks of Paul VI. Instead of allowing the Cardinal to kneel and kiss his ring, the Pope stood and embraced him with the kiss of peace. Pope Paul then descended from his place to walk to the tribune of St. Andrew's to greet the brothers of Pope John XXIII and his nephews, whom he had thoughtfully invited to attend the ceremony. He then walked again up the aisle past all the Council Fathers, humbly greeting them and receiving their greetings as fellow bishops.

It was an intensely dramatic moment. The halfway point of the session seemed an excellent time to evoke again the presence of Pope John; the Council needed him.

II

This occasion was not the only one in which Pope Paul, subtly but insistently, manifested his own mind on the questions which beset the Council Fathers. On Thursday evening October 16, he had delivered a beautiful and touching talk to the assembled non-Catholic observers. He met sixty-six of them in the intimacy of his library; glass bookcases line the brocaded walls; the front wall bears three large paintings. In these pleasant surroundings, Cardinal Bea gave the observers a warm welcoming address. Professor K. E. Skydsgaard, of the University of Copenhagen and the Lutheran World Federation, expressed the sentiments of the observers: "In receiving us here Your Holiness will certainly understand that we who are guests and observers at this Council would like, above all, to recall with affection and respect the memory of your predecessor, Pope John XXIII, who greeted us in this very place last year. . . . We shall never be able to forget him, so full was he of spontaneity and love, of wisdom and of courage."

Dr. Skydsgaard was very open. He thanked the Pope for the cordiality and frankness which had been extended to the observers, and assured him of the interest and the attention with which they had followed the deliberations of the Council, "where diverse opinions are sometimes expressed by the Council Fathers, but always in an atmosphere of objectivity and loyalty." He noted that the schema on the Church then under discussion is "today as in the past, one of the most difficult and debated of subjects. One could say in fact that the doctrine on the Church is the point at which all our divisions culminate, so that it is precisely here that they seem insurmountable, despite our sincere efforts to understand each other." Dr. Skyds-gaard then went on: "Yet in this sad and discouraging situation we have made some progress simply by reason of the fact that we jointly experience this difficulty and together bear its burden."

Dr. Skydsgaard thanked the Pope for his "sober and realistic words on Sunday, September 29," which clearly testified to the difficulty of the problem of union among Christians. "As Your Holiness said, there are grave, complicated problems to be studied and resolved, and their solution presupposes conditions which at present do not yet exist." The distinguished professor paused for a moment, then went on: "Permit me in this connnection to refer to a development which seems to me extremely important. I am thinking of the role of the biblical theology which concentrates on the study of the history of salvation in the Old as well as the New Testament. The more we progress in understanding the hidden and paradoxical history of the people of God, the more we shall begin truly to understand the Church of Jesus Christ in its mystery, in its historical existence, and in its unity. . . . Once again, allow me, Your Holiness, to express our living hope that the light of such a concrete and historical theol-ogy, that is, a theology nourished by the Bible and the teachings of the Fathers, will shine more and more in the work of this Council." Dr. Skydsgaard concluded: "We are grateful to Your Holiness, as to your predecessor, for having pointed to this twofold openness: open-ness to ecumenical dialogue in truth and love, and openness to the world in humility and service. May God bless Your Holiness in the heavy burden and responsibility of your ministry, and may He spread his spirit of repentance and truth upon all the churches of the world."

Pope Paul then took up the talk which he himself had prepared to offer in return. "To approach one another, to meet one another, to greet one another, to know one another, to speak with one another: what more simple, more natural, more human? Certainly. But here is something more again: to hear out one another; to pray for one an-other; and after so many long years of separation, after so many dolor-ous polemics, to begin to love one another: that is what renders this meeting memorable and full of promise."

The Pope was speaking in French, so he shyly looked up at his audi-ence and said: "The sincerity of our words and our sentiments urges upon us, indeed imposes upon us, this new opening of our heart in a most simple language which can, better than the solemnity of Latin, express to you something of the depth of our feelings in your regard." The Pope thanked the observers for having accepted his invitation to come to the Council. He assured them of his respect, his esteem, his desire to come to know them better in the Lord. Our attitude, he said, hides nothing, shelters no intention of disguising the difficulties of a complete and definitive union; it does not shrink from the delicateness of the discussion or the suffering of waiting. "Good faith and charity are the basis which we offer to your presence here; the esteem which we have toward your persons and toward the institutions and the Christian values which the great dialogue, of which nobody can today (given the doctrinal divergence not yet resolved) determine the duration; and confidence in our Lord Jesus Christ, to which through faith and baptism we are all united, fills our heart with a sweet and powerful hope." This reference of the Pope, not only to the individual observers, but also to the communities which they represented, was noticed by all present; it was his public recognition of the great bodies of Christians beyond the Roman Catholic fold.

The Pope then admitted that in the question of disunity, there is a temptation to let one's thoughts turn toward the past. But it is too early for such turning to the past, without opening wounds which have not yet had time to heal. "We dared in our discourse, September 29, to have recourse first of all to Christian pardon, reciprocal if possible. . . . Let us pardon one another, and ask of one another pardon. . . . The best method is not to look backward to the past, but forward toward the present, and especially toward the future. Others can and must direct their studies toward the history of the past; we prefer now to fix our attention, not on that which was but on that which must be. We turn ourselves toward a newness to be created, a dream to realize. . . . Hope is our guide; prayer our force; charity our method, in the service of the divine truth, which is our faith and our salvation. . . ."

The Pope then picked up the refrain: ". . . that divine truth which we must force ourselves without ceasing to understand more deeply, to possess better, and to live in more fully. 'To seek in order to find, to find in order to seek again': this phrase of St. Augustine, which we were pleased, Professor, to hear you cite, concerns us all. A true Christian does not know immobilism. You have opened for us on this subject insights which we could hardly neglect. These developments, which you would wish to further, of a theology 'concrete and historical, centered on the history of salvation,' we for our part subscribe to voluntarily. The suggestion appears to us totally worthy of being studied and meditated. The Catholic Church possesses institutions which might easily specialize in this type of research, and can create a new institution for this end if the circumstances permit it."

The Pope looked again at the men gathered around him in the library. "Allow us to take up again, dear friends, before leaving you, a word from your spokesman: 'We are together on a path.' As if to say: we are not yet arrived. Not more than you, dear friends, do we expect miraculous or immediate solutions. The fruit for which we hope must mature for a long time, in study and in prayer; and apparent or superficial reconciliation, which would mask difficulties instead of resolving them, would retard our march rather than aid it. For us, such vigilance as Isaias spoke of: "Watchmen, what do you say of the night? Watchmen, what do you say of the night?" (Isaias 21:11.)

Pope Paul described men standing in the dark, seeking to discern their goal, and happy when they discover in the heart of the night signs which forewarn of the dawn: "real progress in the dialogue already under way, a step forward toward the rapprochement between those who nourish themselves on the same Gospel, and feel resound to the bottom of their hearts the same joyous appeal. . . . Only one Lord, only one faith, only one Baptism, only one God and Father of all, who is above all, though all and in all." The Pope closed with the words of his namesake: "The grace of the Lord Jesus be with you, I love you all in Christ Jesus, Amen."

III

Three days later, on Sunday, October 20, when the Pope consecrated fourteen new bishops in St. Peter's, he made clear his sentiments on the sacramentality and collegiality of the Episcopate. The Pope told the new bishops that he had raised them from the order of priests to the highest rank of the hierarchy, "where there is a plenitude of powers," of which one power is for the sanctification of souls, and is received directly, and the other is for governing the Christian people, and is received virtually. He had done this, he said, by impressing on them "a sacramental mark, which is called a character, by which we are configured as closely as possible to the likeness of Christ." Pope Paul assured the new bishops that they had become successors of the apostles, able to take their place in the Council, which manifests by its very nature and its majesty, the "perpetuity of the apostolic succession. . . . This consecration by which we have inserted you among the successors of the apostles, you accept through our sacred ministry, a ministry most ample and most true even though conferred on you by the humble successor of St. Peter, to whom the promise of the Gospels in the New Testament was made: 'Upon this rock I will build my Church.' This is done to you in such a way that, almost physically, you can feel your hand taken, not indeed by us, nor, if we may so speak, by St. Peter, but by Christ himself, God most holy and omnipotent, the divine author of the Church. As if living stones, you are built upon the foundation of the house of God which is the Church." Thus the Pope put Christ clearly in the first place; the Pope is only His minister, sharing in the ordination of his brothers as successors of the first apostles. Moreover, in his quotation from the epistle of St. Peter, the Pope seemed to be emphasizing that the foundation of the Church, the rock on which it was founded, is more properly Christ than Peter: "Christ operating through our humble person, heir of the office of the prince of the apostles, to whom the keys of the kingdom were given."

IV

Again, on Sunday, October 27, Pope Paul assisted at the beatification of Dominic of the Mother of God, the Passionist priest who had been instrumental in the conversion of John Henry Newman, the famous English cardinal. In his discourse, the Pope spoke as warmly of Cardinal Newman as of Blessed Dominic, calling them at one point those "two saintly figures." He described Newman: "Newman himself, the promoter and representative of the Oxford movement, which raised so many religious questions, and excited such great spiritual energy . . . who, in full consciousness of his mission—'I have a work to do'—and guided solely by love of the truth and fidelity to Christ, traced an itinerary, the most toilsome, but also the greatest, the most meaningful, the most conclusive, that human thought ever traveled during the last century, indeed one might say during the modern era, to arrive at the fullness of wisdom and of peace. And if that phrase was true and salutary for so distinguished a representative of a great people, so high an authority of a time like ours, will it not be still true and salutary in heaven, in the heart of this beloved *Beatus* [Dominic], and here below, in the hearts of all those who celebrate his glory, and wish to imitate his example?" It would have been good for Newman to hear himself so praised in Rome, after the difficulties raised for him there and by his fellow Catholics in England during his life.

V

Not everyone in Rome shared the Pope's high regard for England. *Il Tempo* the next morning attributed to the Pope words which the Pope had not spoken, saying that he had asked, in that phrase most offensive to non-Catholics, for the "return of England to the faith." Over the whole weekend, *Il Tempo* was slandering the schema on the Blessed Virgin Mary prepared by Dom Christopher Butler, the English Benedictine, saying that his text represented a deliberate attempt to "attenuate Catholic doctrine" in order to win over the comparatively small number of non-Catholics who are offended by devotion to Mary (i.e., the Northern Protestants). In the days that followed, Dom Butler went to the offices of the editor of *Il Tempo* with his document in hand, demanding an apology. The editor laughed at him and told him that *Il Tempo* was not interested in religion but in politics, and that of course they would be glad to retract. The next day, a retraction appeared but so twisted as to make matters worse than before, linking the schema in some obscure way to anti-Communism.

VI

On October 31, Pope Paul took another step in establishing the character of his pontificate. He attended ceremonies at the Pontifical Lateran University, where he had been a student for a few months in the school year 1923–24, and where from 1930–37 he had been a professor on the faculty of canon and civil law. Thirty-five cardinals of the Roman Curia (excepting Cardinal Bea) and several others, such as Cardinals Feltin, Richaud, Spellman, and McIntyre, were present; even Bishop Carinci, once a seminarian at the Lateran in 1875 and now almost 102, was there. At the beginning of the solemn festivities, meant to mark the opening of the new school year, Monsignor Piolanti, the rector of the college, proudly announced the erection of a chair of Pauline theology under the patronage of Paul VI. Professor Cornelio Fabro gave a lecture on "St. Thomas Aquinas and Modern Philosophy," in which he surprised his audience by giving a rigid neo-Thomist interpretation to the famous address of John XXIII presented at the opening of the Council.

When Professor Fabro had finished, Pope Paul, standing in front of the huge mosaic of Christ on the wall of the auditorium, read his own talk. It was much like the one he had given to the Roman Curia on September 21. He began by recalling his "dear memories" of days he had spent in the university. He recalled his own dreams of consecrating his life to study and to university work, "which responds best to my temperament." The Pope congratulated the University of the Lateran for the way it nourished itself on the "treasures of pontifical teaching," and appreciated its blessed location "in the very shadow of St. Peter's." He congratulated it for its desire to express the pure doctrine of the Church in most faithful language, and yet language at the same time accessible to modern thought.

The irony of these remarks was not lost on some of his audience; of all the universities of Rome, the Lateran has been the most intransigent in its opposition to "neo-modernism" and the "heresies of French and German theologians." The Lateran was heavily represented on the preparatory commissions of the Council; its professors had had a large share in preparing those preliminary schemata which, one by one, the Council had had to reject because of their narrowness of view, their juridicism, and their triumphalism. Even so, the baffling Pope John had recently favored the Lateran—previously an undistinguished collection of smaller schools—with the official title of university. The new university was responsible for most of the bitter jealousy that had ended in the removal of the dean of the Biblical Institute in Rome and one of his professors, and waged constant verbal warfare in its classrooms against the other universities in Rome—and against the Council.

It was to this precise audience, then, that Pope Paul's many compliments were directed, and he concluded his remarks as he had concluded those to the Roman Curia on September 21 with a bombshell. The Pope offered his best wishes to the university that its voice "in the concert of the great, celebrated, and praiseworthy Roman institutes of high ecclasiastical culture be that of sincere recognition, fraternal collaboration, loyal emulation, mutual reverence, and amicable concord, never of jealous competition or of tedious polemic; never!—*non mai d'una gelosa concorrenza o d'una fastidiosa polemica; non mai!*" The Pope then concluded: "Thus" the university will have "a positive mission to fulfill," and "thus, it will be favored always by Our affection and sustained by Our Apostolic Benediction." The students of the Lateran got the point, and cheered and applauded with such warmth that it was only with great difficulty that the school's choir could launch into the martial alma mater *"Salve, O Roma,"* whose words were composed by Archbishop Pietro Parente, Assessor of the Holy Office.

NOTE

1. On January 2, 1963, Pope Paul remedied even this defect. In a Mass for the people of Rome before leaving for Palestine, he himself distributed communion for almost twenty minutes, and had priests in the crowd come forward to assist; the priests carried the sacrament into the crowds, distributing right and left to all who desired. The Pope's brief sermon was moving; the responses of the people to the prayers during Mass were full of enthusiasm and joy. It was a truly religious, not a courtly, celebration.

15

OCTOBER 30

ON THE BRIGHT COLD MORNING of October 29, there was tension in the air as the Council Fathers gathered for the morning session. They were met on the steps of St. Peter's by several Ukrainian bishops who were passing out petitions urging them to vote against including the schema on Mary in the schema on the Church. One of the Australian bishops, thinking, perhaps, of Cardinal Ottaviani's objections to *periti* who passed out such petitions on the diaconate, approached the desk of the Secretariat and asked whether it was permissible to pass out such petitions before a vote. He was told yes that it was perfectly legitimate to pass out petitions outside St. Peter's, but not inside. Satisfied, the Australian bishop resumed his place. He had reason later to remember this reply.

The previous night, four American experts had addressed the American bishops at their weekly meeting. Barnabas Mary Ahern, C.P., a Scripture scholar, was chairman of the panel. Father Eugene Maly, another Scripture scholar and editor of *The Bible Today*, lectured on the scriptural background of the relation of Our Lady and the Church. Father Godfrey Diekmann, O.S.B., spoke about the teaching of the early Fathers of the Church about Mary, and Father William Coyle, Redemptorist from the seminary at Oconomowoc, gave a summary of the latest conclusions of modern theologians. These talks, and the men who gave them, made such an impression on the American bishops that afterward many of the latter told the scholars that they now intended to vote for the inclusion of the treatment on Mary in the schema on the Church.[1]

Meanwhile, one of the Protestant observers said privately that if the vote was *not* for inclusion, it would be "a disaster" for the ecumenical movement. Catholic experts assured him that the vote would be overwhelming.

In the basilica, just before the vote was to be taken, Cardinal Agagianian took the microphone and stated that no vote on either side could be construed as constituting any lessening of the dignity of the Blessed Virgin Mary or any downgrading of her pre-eminent role in the Church; subsequent work on the schema on Mary would be carried out by the theological commission; an absolute majority of votes would be sufficient to decide the question. The Fathers then marked their ballots and passed them in, and the results were fed into the IBM machine. When the vote on the treatment of Mary was announced it was discovered that by the narrow margin of 40 votes, 1,114 to 1,074, the Council had decided for its inclusion in the document on the Church. Shock, pessimism, as well as relief, swept many of the Fathers. There had not been an overwhelming vote at all; the ecumenical movement had almost been torpedoed. Would the Council henceforth be split down the very center? Had there been a reversion to earlier divisions?

Meanwhile, debate had continued on chapter 4. It was criticized for being too monastic, a hodgepodge of juridical and theological elements, not centered around worship and the Bible, too moralistic, forgetful of the primacy of grace. An Italian archbishop, Vuccino, used Pope Paul's talk to the Protestant observers to urge that the text be more biblical; he pointed to Abraham, Mary, and Elizabeth as models of faith. Cardinal Ruffini criticized the text from another direction, agreeing with Cardinal Gilroy that the terms "the mystery of the Church," "the people of God," and "charisms" are unintelligible to the faithful and too much in dispute for the Council to use. He agreed with Bishop Morstabilini that the schema should emphasize the sanctity of the Church, the means of sanctification possessed by the Church, and the holiness of her members. He thought the introduction "much too inflated," the word "mystery" (which he noted was used five times in the chapter) too obscure, and, though true, inadequate. "We know much about the nature and office of the Church since it has visible elements in the social and juridical orders. We must beware of separating the Church of charity from the juridical Church." He concluded by noting that several of the scriptural texts in the document were used inaccurately.

Two different views of what it means for the Church to be "objectively holy" were becoming apparent. For one group, the holiness of the Church is institutional, "built into the structure" of the Church by its "divine constitution"; the canonization of saints shows its glory. For the other, the holiness of the Church is a mysterious gift of God, present, perhaps, *despite* the bureaucratic structure. One group emphasizes the triumphs of the Church; the other emphasizes her weakness, and marvels that God stoops to use even such a structure for His own ends.

Later that morning, without any explanation, the long-promised four votes, become in the event five votes, were passed out in printed form to each of the Council Fathers, and balloting on them was announced for the morrow. Hope was mixed with trepidation. Whatever maneuvering had taken place behind the scenes, the votes were now seeing the light of day; their re-emergence seemed timed perfectly to follow the commemoration of Pope John. The scheduling of an almost immediate vote seemed designed to obviate further propaganda warfare; it was hard not to see the hand of Pope Paul in the scheduling; the Council leadership had had a meeting with him on October 26. The minority at the Council had shot its bolt in its campaign for a special schema on Mary; they seemed surprised by the emergence of the five votes and the sudden call for a ballot. The discussion of the issues had been the longest of the Council; but now there was no time to apply pressures before the balloting. On the other hand, one wondered whether the "progressives" would not have raised a hue and cry if the minority had attempted so sudden a vote. The Fathers eagerly read the printed forms that were handed out.

II

Journalists, meanwhile, had been invited to attend the Council Mass that morning. As about twenty of them rose to join the lay auditors at communion, a young American woman, Miss Eva Fleischner, a member of the Grail and a correspondent for *Ecumenical Notes*, was the last in line on her way toward the communion rail. A male functionary motioned emphatically that she should stop. He motioned again, violently. Since the other members of the press, all men, were approaching the rail, she tried to hurry forward. The man physically restrained her; he would not let her receive communion. Elmer von Feldt of the NCWC news service saw the incident from the tribune and later protested to Council authorities. As the man had acted without any authority, only on his own impulse, apologies were tendered to Miss Fleischner. But the impulse was apparently widespread, for the next time journalists were allowed to enter St. Peter's, women were expressly excluded.[2] Meanwhile, lay-men, at least, had approached the altar rail at a mass in the solemn Mozarabic rite of Spain, at which communion had not been distributed to the people, it was said, for over two hundred years.

III

Later that afternoon, Cardinal Ruffini gave a press conference at the CCCC on the laity, "the Church's connecting link with modern society." The Cardinal's performance, especially his repertoire of sweeping gestures, was extraordinary.

The Cardinal described the confrontation of the Church and the world as that between two sets of ideologies, and two power centers, each sending out lay agents to compete for positions of power: in politics, in education, in culture, in communications, in labor, in the arts. He expressed great distress over the moral situation of the world. He spoke of the modern cinema, and said that "even in Italy" corruption had left its mark. He told of a letter which he had received from an Italian missionary in Japan, who expressed his shame that films from Italy had scandalized "even the Japanese."

The Cardinal blamed laymen for not being sufficiently active in the world; they should emulate the Communists. He immediately apologized for bringing politics into the discussion, but elaborated for a moment on the power and skill of the Communists, and the danger to the Church unless Catholics became as active as they, "especially in the universities, the universities!" This aside was just sufficient to give the correspondent from *Il Tempo* the opportunity to build his day's story around anti-Communism—a useful story, as we shall see, for a project being hatched during that week by Cardinals Siri, Ruffini, Antoniutti and Ottaviani.

Cardinal Ruffini urged the founding of a religious community to make "inspiring movies" and "television for the family." His image of lay action in the world was military. "What will officers do," he asked, "if they don't have soldiers under their orders?" What was most noticeable about his talk was its total lack of self-criticism or recognition of alternatives. His theory showed almost no debt to

Pius XI, Pius XII, or theologians who had written on the question; nor did he reflect on alternative conceptions in practice even in Italy, as under La Pira of Florence or Cardinal Lercaro of Bologna.

Cardinal Ruffini is, personally, a lovable man. Seventy-five years old, he spoke with the vigor and enthusiasm of a much younger man. He is short and stout, with a friendly face; though balding on top, he has fleecy white hair. He seemed the kind of man who would be a most affectionate uncle. He smiled often and called the newsmen his friends. For those from other cultures, of course, his violent gestures and alternating tones of voice—now imprecating, now cajoling—were astonishing. Many scoffed; many shook their heads in disbelief; many others judged him more kindly in view of his background and his age. Most, when they found out that the Cardinal had arranged to depart immediately after his talk, left early. "It was not useless for Cardinal Ruffini to leave the tribune of St. Peter's to come down into the arena to preach 'the good fight' to the press," Henri Fesquet wrote in *Le Monde*, "the journalists now know what the situation is. Undoubtedly, some would have liked to ask questions. But the Cardinal, it seems, does not like to let himself be questioned by laymen."

IV

The most important day of the Second Vatican Council dawned bright and cool. The Fathers were in the basilica early, talking, musing. Unknown to most of them, Archbishop Beckmann of Panama had just fallen on the steps of St. Peter's, seriously ill, and died almost immediately. After Mass, Cardinal Tisserant announced the death and led the Fathers in reciting the *De Profundis*.

Then the famous five points were put to a vote. The General Secretary, Archbishop Felici, reminded the Fathers that the vote did not mean approval or disapproval of a text; its purpose was to give the theological commission an indication of the mind of the Council. In that phrase lay a compromise crucial to the partisans of non-historical orthodoxy. The ballots were marked and sent to the IBM room.

While the Fathers waited for the results, there were many more talks on holiness in the Church, most expressing displeasure with the text. Cardinal Léger of Montreal begged the Council to come down to earth and deal with the world as it is: with "daily work, political affairs, cultural activities, leisure, and recreation." The Church must come to the world and the world must come to the Church. The Church, for example, would come to grapple with real life rapidly "if lay people were invited to teach on the faculties of religious science in colleges and in seminaries." He said that a return to Scripture and earlier tradition "is the heart and center of all theological renewal." Cardinal Cento of the Curia then declared that the health of the Church is measured by the number of her saints, and that "in our sin-hardened times there is a great need for reparation and for sanctity."

Cardinal Bea spoke of the schema as "not realistic enough. . . . If the Church were simply holy, there would have been no cause for the Reformation." The manner in which the document cites Scripture "is unworthy of the Council." He rapidly listed the uncited texts which "give the whole New Testament teaching on holiness." Bishop Huyghe of Arras and Archabbot Reetz of Beuron thought the schema sounded "like gnosticism," "quietism," or, again, "manicheism." "Christ founded one holy Church, not monasteries besides," the latter said, and, in arguing against the latent pharisaism in the phrase "states of perfection," quoted Nietzsche's saying that no one is as proud as a monk.

Bishop Russell of Richmond, Virginia, stated in the name of "many bishops of the U.S.A." that the text is too static and absolute. "No one except Mary can attain absolute perfection while on earth"; holiness in this life is relative and dynamic. He invoked a very recent conception: "Traditionally, sanctity is understood in three ways: those in the state of grace; those who not only avoid offending God, but strive to please God in all things; those relative few who practice heroic sanctity." He did not wish the text to seem to imply that all have an obligation to the highest sanctity, under a serious obligation.

At the American press conference later that afternoon, Father Bernard Häring gently chided Bishop Russell for his old-fashioned conception of sanctity, not directly, but by delicately insisting that sanctity was in no case a question of obligation, but rather an invitation from a person, from a God who loves us. Father Häring deplored the division of Christians according to a legalistic system in which some are bound more strictly than others; he deplored the whole legalistic—Kantian—approach to holiness.

Bishop Franič of Yugoslavia then asked that priests, religious, and especially bishops give up claim to all "immobile goods"—for example, "land holdings which they do not work with their own hands, and all buildings in which they do not live and which do not serve for apostolic purposes, and in general all material goods which bring gain according to the capitalistic system." He wanted clergy and religious "to begin to live from their own apostolic work, like St. Peter, or from their own physical work, like St. Paul, or, finally, from the spontaneous offerings of the faithful."

During the morning, the results of the voting were announced. Here, in close paraphrase, is the wording of the five questions:

Should the schema state (1) that episcopal consecration is the highest peak in the sacrament of orders; (2) that every bishop, in communion with others and the Pope, is a member of the College of Bishops; (3) that the College of Bishops in its task of evangelizing, sanctifying, and nourishing, succeeds the College of the Apostles, and that, in union with its head, the Roman Pontiff, and never without this head (whose primatial rights over all pastors and faithful remains intact), it enjoys full and supreme power over the universal Church; (4) that the aforesaid power belongs to the Episcopal College by Divine right?

These votes were the pivot on which the entire second session turned. The negative votes were: (1) 34; (2) 104; (3) 336; (4) 408. The number of those voting averaged better than 2,100. The victory of the majority was decisive.

To these was added the fifth vote, on whether it pleased the Council Fathers *"to consider the opportuneness of restoring the diaconate as a distinct and permanent rank of the sacred ministry, according to the needs of the Church in different localities."* The question of the celibacy of deacons was sidestepped. Presumably those bishops who needed married deacons in their dioceses would argue for them—and probably get them—through machinery to be set up after the Council. The affirmation was again overwhelming: 1,588 to 525.

The Council was not, then, split down the middle. Even the distribution of talks on the floor had been misleading; the majority was greater than it dreamed. The prestige of the moderators soared. They showed it immediately, by cracking down on those who spoke too

long or wandered from the point. Spirits everywhere—almost everywhere—were higher. A fresh wind was beginning to blow. Vatican II,
a proud vessel now, emerged from the storms in which she had been
locked, her final harbor in view.

V

November 1, Friday, was the Feast of All Saints and the following
Monday, November 4, was Italy's Armistice Day; both were to be
free days. After the nervous excitement of the week's great events and
the long-drawn-out five weeks of debate, the Council Fathers were
ready for nothing so much as a vacation. On the 31st, they sat list-
lessly during the morning's many talks on holiness, as bored as lay
people during a sermon. As often as they felt they could, many of the
bishops walked out to the coffee bar, where they engaged themselves
in conversation with fellow bishops, with experts, with the Protestant
observers.

The moderators, meanwhile, took a tighter grip on the Council.
Cardinal Doepfner announced that many bishops had complained
about the slowness of the pace. To preserve the right of those still
wishing to speak, and at the same time to satisfy the general desire
to close discussion and to keep moving, the moderator asked the
Fathers to confine their remarks to pertinent matter, to avoid repetition, to stay within an eight-minute time limit, and to remember
that written statements not delivered orally in the Council have
equal weight before the commissions. The bishops signified their approval with applause. When it was announced later that three of the
scheduled speakers had yielded their right to speak, there was more
applause. The moderator intervened frequently during the morning
to tell speakers they were repetitious or overstepping their time.

One such case was that of Bishop Grotti, *prelatus nullius* of Brazil
(whose first name the official press release gave as Giocondo). "What
novelties we are hearing here! Opening the Church to everybody:
pagans, separated brothers, women"—and here he meandered.
"Women were silent for more than a thousand years and now some
wish to invite them to these Council sessions, and not just to make
caffè and *cappucino* . . ." When the moderator broke in on him, he
resumed: "The Church cannot forget priests who have fallen along
the way and are kept in a hell of seclusion, from which there is no
salvation nor even hope of it. And they are our brothers. Does the

Church have a remedy for original sin but none for their sin? How many men, and what high types we are losing! I will propose concrete ideas in due time, but now I wish to ask you to open your hearts and to pray for them. Perhaps we can contrive some purgatory for them where they will be useful for themselves, for us, and for the Church. . . ." The good Father was here interrupted for a second time by the moderator, and lapsed into silence.

VI

As most of the other bishops of the world left Rome for the long weekend, the National Conference of Italian Bishops issued a mild condemnation of "Atheistic Marxism" as their celebration of Halloween. Reports insisted that the Pope and the Secretary of State had tried to prevent the statement, and then insisted on modifying it. All week long there had been "indiscretions" to the press, warning that the statement was coming. Cardinal Ruffini's brief mention of Communism in his press conference on Tuesday, which won an anti-Communist headline from *Il Tempo*, seemed in retrospect suspiciously like an attempt to build up pressure for the document. At the Italian bishops' meeting on Monday, Cardinal Siri had argued for the statement. Many of the younger Italian bishops had opposed the strong version offered them. The Communist press feared a repetition of the excommunication of Communists; the right-wing press cherished that possibility. When the document was finally released, its terms were mild; it referred in general to previous pontifical condemnations of atheistic Marxism as a system incompatible with Catholicism, but it did not mention or even describe the "opening to the left" in present Italian politics. Nor—though *Il Tempo* headlined it as if it had—did it issue further condemnations, nor rescind Pope John's distinction between an ideological system and what may become of it under the pressures of concrete history. The next day, *L'Osservatore Romano* protested the political misuse of the message by "certain elements"; *L'Avvenire d'Italia*, the Catholic daily of Cardinal Lercaro's diocese of Bologna, launched a sharp first-page attack on those papers in Rome, and, specifically, *Il Tempo*, which had tried, for "political reasons" to make the declaration against Communism seem much stronger than it was. (There was good reason to believe that most of the phrasing in the document had come from earlier pastoral letters of Cardinal Lercaro.)

What was most significant in the statement of the Italian bishops was that at last there was an organ established outside the Vatican for dealing with the socio-political problems of Italy. The National Episcopal Conference of Italy, although founded before the Second World War, had never held a meeting until the first session of the Council; and then there were only two meetings. At the second session, however, the Italians met every week at Domus Mariae—and not without differences of opinion. This newly active conference gave promise of freeing the Vatican from its long heritage of involvement in Italian politics, by offering a distinction between the policies of the Italian bishops and the policies of the universal Church. But some of the Italian bishops interpreted their action in the *other* direction, as if to say to the Pope: "The statement was a practical application of collegiality. You're not against collegiality, are you?" For it was plain that the letter had embarrassed the Pope.

VII

A turning point had been reached on October 30. The issue of collegiality was the one above all others which the Second Vatican Council had to decide. The vote on the 30th was not the ratification of a text; it was to guide the preparation of a text. But a Council of the Church does not proceed by counting heads; it proceeds by articulating the faith of those present. The expressed consensus of the Council Fathers, it seemed, could not be undone. The text to be brought back at the next session for final ratification hardly needed clearer guidance; only through the utmost foolishness, or lack of skill with a pen, could the theological commission fail to bring to a legislating vote what the Council Fathers had now decided they would approve. It seemed clear now, if it had not before, that the Roman Catholic Church has two sources of plenary and universal power, the College of Bishops, and that one among them who binds them in unity, the Pope. As Henri Fesquet wrote in *Le Monde:* "The Roman Church has ceased being, if it ever was, a pure monarchy, in order to become a collegiality."

There was great joy throughout the assembly. In vote after vote, non-historical orthodoxy had been losing its grip on the Church. Never in many centuries of urgent cries for reform had the Church universal—thanks to a missionary effort that had raised up legions of bishops from the Americas, the Far East, Near East, and Africa, to join those "from across the Alps"—been in such a good position to cleanse the institutional structures and methods of an ecclesiastical government of practices inherited from the Inquisition and the Italian Renaissance. On the evening of October 30, a nearly full moon bathed St. Peter's square in such brilliance, such serenity, as was worthy of the greatest day in Roman Catholic history since 1870.

NOTES

1. Bishop Charles R. Helmsing described in the Kansas City *Catholic Reporter* (November 8) one such favorable reaction to the talk.
2. Good sources affirm that the decision not to allow women journalists at the Council Mass came from Pope Paul. The explanation offered is that the Pope was being besieged by Sister Superiors, asking that nuns be allowed in the Council. To avoid giving them further ground for argument, the Pope sacrificed recognition of other women. American press officers knew that this decision came from the Pope, but by their silence shielded him from criticism.

16

THE INDISPENSABLE REFORM

I

OVER THE LONG WEEKEND, bishops, experts, and journalists dispersed over the Continent, from the Holy Land to Ireland, in search of respite. Some, for example, drove to Assisi and walked the lovely streets of that hilly, medieval town, climbed the parapets of the fortress on the hill, visited the church of St. Clare, said Mass at the basilica of St. Francis. They could not get entirely free of the Council. Discussion and questioning still marked their conversations.

Then, all too soon, they returned to Rome. Some drove back, like my wife and me, taking joy in Italy's tortured, hilly terrain; racing down into deep gorges and climbing the bare, denuded hills, which bands of predatory Renaissance mercenaries had once traversed on horseback.

We came into Rome at dusk, and went later to the apartment of Mr. and Mrs. Robert Kaiser, where already a group of twenty or thirty bishops, experts, and journalists had gathered for the weekly Sunday buffet supper. These suppers were a small powerhouse of energy and conversation, one of the most successful institutions in Rome. Here Father Malachy Martin, S.J., the thin, wiry Irish Scripture scholar, dashed from group to group with his rapid-fire questions and bits of information; Father Francis X. Murphy, C.Ss.R., smoked his pipe in his sly, observant way. A wide spectrum of the world's bishops appeared on alternate Sundays. Theology and speculation hovered in the conversations, simply to be picked out of the air. The consensus of the guests on the night of November 3 was that the next week would be an important and colorful one. "There should be lots of fireworks," said one auxiliary bishop from America. "It will be a crucial week," others agreed.

II

The document to be considered next by the Council was made up of five short chapters: on the relation between the bishops and the Roman Curia; on coadjutor and auxiliary bishops; on national conferences of bishops; on the proper extent of dioceses; on the establishment of parishes. Two appendices were attached to the document: a list of proposed new faculties for bishops, and a set of norms for the practices of the sacred congregations in Rome in relation to the bishops of the world. A brief introduction affirmed that the salvation of souls is the supreme law of the Church.

Bishop George Patrick Dwyer of Leeds held a press conference to explain the document. He noted that the preparatory commission which first drew up the document had among its members some of the best-known names in the Council: Cardinal Suenens, four of the Undersecretaries of the Council: Morcillo, Krol, Villot, and Nabaa; Guerry and Veuillot of France; and Carli, Gargitter, and Florit of Italy. The text it prepared had been chopped and changed by the central commission in the preparatory stages, and then by the coordinating commission once the Council was under way. Two of its chapters, Bishop Dwyer point out, are of minor importance: the one on the division of dioceses, which does not give a single general principle and is useless; the other on the division of parishes, which is insignificant. The chapter on coadjutor and auxiliary bishops has ecclesiastical but little public interest. The other two chapters, however, are "of quite considerable importance."

He noted that chapter 1 bore the title: "The Bishops and the Roman Congregations," but is intended to include the Roman tribunals and offices, like the Holy Office. "The attitude of bishops and others toward this ecclesiastical civil service ranges from placid content, to mild irritation, to considerable annoyance. In short, much like the attitude of anybody to any other civil service." In the course of time, certain matters have been reserved to Rome, and in order to deal with them a bishop needs to have special powers granted by Rome, known as "reserved faculties." The other point of debate would be how to draw bishops into regular consultation with the Pope. There has always been a certain amount of this consultation through the nuncios or apostolic delegates, or in the course of private audiences. The document proposes only that bishops should be appointed as consultors to the Roman congregations. Many bishops were suggesting more effective means. "It is not yet clear which, if any, will be adopted. It is very unlikely that nothing will be done in this regard."

The other important chapter, the Bishop continued, is the one on bishops' conferences. Strangely enough, these do not yet exist in many countries; but some are of long standing, as in England and Ireland. "So far such conferences have been informal and unofficial. They did not legislate but simply were a practical means of consultation among the bishops. . . . It is now proposed to give all these conferences an official standing in the laws of the Church and to recommend that they be set up in all countries." The Bishop went on: "The advantages are obvious; but maybe the inexperienced are expecting too much from them. The disadvantages are that if the basis is national it could foster a narrow un-Catholic spirit. The main problem is what precise authority do they have—and here we must note that, while very many bishops have 'collegiality' on their lips, they are still monarchical at heart. The whole of this question of the bishops and the Roman congregations turns on this: no bishop's authority can be entirely unlimited. We cannot have 2,500 Popes in the Church. If it is not to be limited by the Roman congregations, then it will be limited by some other means, e.g., by a majority vote in the bishops' conferences or by the local archbishop, patriarch, or other immediate superior. It is questionable if all the bishops as yet realize this."

III

The reform of the Roman Curia is the indispensable business of any council of reform for the universal Church. Crucial decisions are taken in Rome; much power is concentrated there; Rome sets the tone for the universal Church. That tone has rarely been attractive outside of Rome. But the Curia is heavy with complacency. It believes its own rhetoric of superiority. A good example of the way curial Rome retains its power was indicated in the introductions given the new schema by Cardinal Marella and Bishop Carli. The former tried to convince the Fathers that Rome has accurate knowledge of the individual dioceses of the world, from the frequent visits of bishops to Rome and from the reports from nuncios and apostolic delegates. The latter told the history of the document: how in December, 1962, *experts of the Commission residing in Rome* had added notes to the document—*no one was called to Rome for this purpose.* In February, 1963, a new subcommission *consisting of members and experts who lived near Rome* was entrusted with the revisions suggested by the coordinating commission. On March 26, Pope John ordered the document printed (before it had been seen at the plenary session of the commission to be held April 30), and, when it was set in type, *it was again amended* by members of the conciliar commission from several nations, *who were present in Rome.* Bishop Carli concluded his report with a sermon. He quoted Vatican I, and then a decree of 1791 issued by Pius VI which condemned the idea that a bishop has received from Christ all powers necessary for the proper government of his diocese without higher directives. After the vote of October 30, Bishop Carli's preachments were not well received.

Bishop Carli's talk put Cardinal Marella in a bad light. But the preceding spring Cardinal Marella, aware of his obligations, had tried three times to convince the coordinating commission that he needed to submit the text to his commission. He was three times told to send it out and "Don't worry." But when criticisms of Cardinal Marella were publicly made in the Council, the man responsible—Cardinal Doepfner—did not come to his defense. Cardinal Marella bore the criticisms silently.

After the introductions on November 5, Cardinal Liénart, in the gentle way adopted by the majority, first praised the document, and then quoted Pope Paul on the reform of the Curia, proposing a new chapter on the relations of bishops and Pope. Cardinal McIntyre of Los Angeles preached "anxiety and danger," warning against giving juridicial status to national conferences of bishops, and against placing "undue emphasis on the part of human wisdom and not enough on the supernatural." He feared "radical change in the structure of the Church." Cardinal Richaud noted the discrepencies between the document and the four votes on collegiality of October 30, and disliked the phrase "concessions" to the bishops. He wanted the Curia seriously reorganized and the schema "considerably rewritten." Then Bishop Gargitter protested that "the text as we have it now is certainly not the one drawn up by the preparatory commission; it expounds its doctrine under the one-sided light of insistence on the rights of the central organs of the Roman Curia. On the contrary, it should proceed under the light of basic theological principles on the Episcopate and it should follow a practical and juridicial order in its presentation. The text is too generic and too vague. It is completely inadequate on the necessary decentralization and internationalization of the Curia." The Curia is "in the service of the bishops and ultimately of the people of God." It is not just "that some Western nations have a privileged position in this body." He thought the bishops could cooperate in ruling the Church either (a) through a stable Commission of Bishops or (b) through a Senate of Bishops chosen from various parts of the world, which could be called to Rome by the Pope.

Bishop Jean Rupp of Monaco spoke humorously, with expansive gestures that brought laughter from the Council Fathers. "As it stands, the text of the schema is a shining model of Roman brevity." The text is "neither audacious nor virile. Where it gives solutions, it immediately gives the means for not applying them." He added: "It is regrettable that fully one-half of the members of the Council commission were not given an opportunity to express their mind on the text of the document now submitted to the Council, and that the report read in the name of the commission this morning was not drawn up conformably to the requirements of the procedural rules of the Council, that is to say, reflecting the viewpoints of the majority."

His charges were repeated by Bishop Correa of Colombia. Attacks on the document continued without interruption; it was "too juridical in tone," "out of harmony with the votes of October 30," "disorganized," "unrealistic," "out of touch with modern conditions," "a downgrading of bishops," "non-collegial," "timid," "marred by useless provisions" (e.g., "a diocese should be neither too large nor too small"). It became known later in the day that Cardinal Marella, the head of the commission, had sent a letter to the members of the commission, insisting that there is no theological ground for episcopal conferences—one of the major points of the document. The commission seemed much more non-historical than the theological commission, and the religious monarchism and juridicism of some Roman minds was clearly marked upon it

The Roman theologians who had prepared the documents came to their classrooms during these days sullen and angry. One Spanish canonist at a large Roman college—now teaching moral theology, as it happens—told his students that "the canonical profession" was under attack by the Council. "So abolish canon law! As if theologians are all they need nowadays." He liked to repeat: "The formulation of a canon, the canon itself, is a sacred cult. . . . Law is a sacred cult." He made frequent and violent attacks on the democratic principle (as he understood it), claiming that the French Revolution is "the source of all modern evils." During the same time, he interrupted a discussion on modern free love, selfishness, and the decline of the sacredness of marriage to deliver yet another aside about the Council: "Don't wonder if they vote the way they do on the Marian schema, these products of democracy and the ideals of the French Revolution!" In many colleges in Rome, seminarians were made to sit through such attacks on the collegiality of the bishops, on the new theology, and on the Council itself. Seminarians do not ordinarily revolt—at least openly—but in some houses the temperature of disgust for such professors was rising. During the second session, the Spanish professor referred to was named as a consultor to an important curial congregation.

IV

Finally, on November 6, Cardinal Ruffini came to the defense of the document. "If many observations made yesterday were followed through to their logical conclusion, the text of the schema would have to be radically revised. Nevertheless, not a few Council Fathers feel that, with some amendments, the text can be made satisfactory. The objection that the schema makes no reference to the collegiality of the bishops presumes that the matter has already been settled conclusively. This is not so."

This denial startled many of the Council Fathers; it began to dawn on them that the minority had not interpreted those votes as the majority had. It began to seem obvious, as well, that in the two weeks it took to get the votes to the floor a crippling compromise had been made: the five votes had not been made as a final approval of the text, but only as manifesting the "propensity" of the Council. The issue was to become bitterly contested; but Cardinal Ruffini had other points to make.

He agreed with Cardinal McIntyre: "The discussion of the proposed national conferences of bishops can lead into dangerous waters if these conferences are given real authority to carry out their decisions. This would open the way to undue freedom and would give rise to many dangers, because the faithful would see different aspects of the Church in different countries. It stands to reason that the Pope could hardly turn down the recommendations of these national conferences and this would, in fact and for all practical purposes, mean the disappearance of his primatial jurisdiction, which demands that he always retain the absolute right to approve or disapprove what is proposed." Did the Cardinal speak from experience? Some of the Council Fathers were wondering if the Pope were in the same dilemma when faced with the recommendations of the Curia.

Cardinals Koenig and Alfrink evaluated the conception of national episcopal conferences from several points of view—their dangers to the individual liberty of the bishops, their past fruitfulness, their stabilizing effect on the Church if curial powers are decentralized. Cardinal Alfrink denied that such conferences are a direct exercise of the collegiality of the bishops, for collegiality is universal, not regional; but he thought they would be "a sign and instrument" of collegiality. Cardinal Bea wanted the principles of Church government to be drawn from the Gospels. "According to St. Paul, the Church is a living body, having a variety of members, living and growing according to the spirit of each member, but always in close union with others." He saw no danger of schism. "In the history of the Church, and as the result of particular circumstances, many institutions grew up: the patriarchates, the erection of ecclesiastical provinces, the Roman Curia, among others. The role of authority is not to replace individual members in what they can do by themselves, but only to supply what they cannot provide for themselves." Bishops "should be able to do what they have been ordained to do." The Cardinal's words became more pointed: "Bishops from outside Rome should be brought to work with the Pope." This reform has ecumenical importance "because the traditional accusations of lust for power, ecclesistical imperialism, curialism, and centralization cannot be answered only with words. The most effective reply is in a spirit of profound reverence, for individual bishops."

Cardinal Michael Browne stated that "We do not have yet a sufficiently clear idea of just what constitutes this collegial character. Certain remarks made yesterday give rise to the suspicion that some Fathers are convinced that the bishops constitute a college in the strict juridical sense of the term, with well-defined powers. We must await the report of the theological commission for a clarification of this basic point before we can take any concrete action." There was an exchange of sour looks and an annoyed silence among many of the Council Fathers. An answer was to come from them two days later.

So the debate raged on: "The discussion is premature until the theology of the episcopate is settled," a French archbishop said. Sixty Brazilian bishops wanted the schema "completely redone." It is "too juridical" and "lacks the conciliar and ecumenical spirit." Thirteen Indian bishops said it "is out of touch with the world and out of harmony with the structure of the Church." The Pope has supreme, but not absolute, power over the Church. He is to rule with the bishops. The Roman Curia is no longer a satisfactory organ of communication between the Pope and the bishops. The conduct of the commission in not showing the document to its own members is "a scandal." (Cardinal Marella remained silent.) The bishop of Ugento, Italy, asked for more "understanding" toward the Curia. The bishop of Wheeling, West Virginia, Bishop Hodges, wanted "Roman Pontiff" distinguished from "Apostolic See" so that one might know when Pope, and when Curia, was speaking. Indeed, the Curia was restless under the mounting criticism. A Ceylonese bishop tried to get the painful discussion off the floor and into writing, to alleviate their discomfort and to prevent public scandal.

The vote was then taken on whether to accept the schema as a basis for discussion; the alternative was to await a whole new document. The Council Fathers voted 1610 to 477 to accept the present one as a start. It was the first document of a preparatory commission to be accepted without rewriting.

V

An event happened during that November week that made some observers sick at heart because of its craven, open exploitation of the Church, but that was nevertheless fundamentally ridiculous. Engraved invitations went out to the Council Fathers to attend a special showing of Otto Preminger's newest movie. Moreover, the Knights of the Order of the Holy Sepulchre, in the presence of many cardinals, bishops, and other guests in formal attire, awarded Otto Preminger the highest award of their order, traditionally bestowed on those "assisting the apostolate of the Holy Land." Cardinal Ottaviani, who has taken charge of all movies made in the Vatican, presided over the large cocktail party at the giving of the award. Mr. Preminger's new picture was *The Cardinal*; it was to have its première in Boston on December 11. But why was Mr. Preminger given the highest award of this ancient order, in the presence of so many pastors of the Church? Spokesmen of the order refused to comment to the press. Wags in Rome began calling it "The award of the Whited Sepulchre." Mr. Preminger himself took the award in stride; i.e., with a certain amount of cynicism. He was the producer of *The Moon Is Blue*.

The Cardinal, based on Henry Morton Robinson's best-selling novel, is the story of a priest, who, like Cardinal Spellman (who fought for many years to keep the film from being produced), was born in Boston, educated at the North American College in Rome, and later served with the Vatican Secretariat of State. The movie goes to Georgia for scenes of racial conflict; to Austria for scenes of Catholic solicitude for the Jews under Hitler; and into the confessional, where the priest speaks in textbook terms to his own sister, who is groping for sympathetic help out of her many troubles. The movie offers the celibate priest a flirtation with a beautiful girl, and to the audience flirtations with degradation and squalor, as well as heartbreak through motherhood and childbirth. In the words of Cardinal Cushing's advance review of the movie in *The Pilot*, the movie has "something for everyone."

The proceeds of the movie's world's première in Boston, were set aside for Cardinal Cushing's Charity Fund. A large share of the proceeds from its Roman première went to an ecclesiastical organ in Rome. It has, for the Vatican, as the engraved invitation to the Council Fathers coyly pointed out, a popular answer to the popular play of Rolf Hochhuth, *The Deputy*, which attacks Pope Pius XII's policies on behalf of the Jews under Hitler. Mr. Preminger's Roman lawyer saw to it last summer that Giorgio Montini, a Roman lawyer and the Pope's nephew, was invited to London, expenses paid, to sit in on the final cutting stages of the production.

At an open-house ceremony, seven knights in white uniforms with gold epaulettes escorted the footman who bore, on a silver tray, the red-and-white Maltese Grand Cross of the Equestrian Order of the Holy Sepulchre. The Maltese Grand Cross was then pinned on the chest of Mr. Preminger by the Marchese Mario Mocchi.

Undoubtedly, ours is the age of the layman.

VI

Patriarch Maximos IV Saïgh was later to tell a priest journalist: "Being poor, I have nothing to lose. Being eighty-five, I have no one to fear but God." On November 6, he attacked the first chapter on the Curia for its debility: to assist the Pope, it "offers only the Curia in its present structure, adding a timid suggestion that some bishops of the world will be given a share in the government of the Church. This does not answer the needs of today, nor does it reflect the collegial responsibility of all the bishops." He wanted the world's bishops, not Rome's clergy, to govern the Church with the Pope. "The very fact that the Roman cardinals are assigned to particular titular churches in Rome shows that they belong more to Rome than to the entire world." In curial government, "Those outside the Church, as well as many within, see not the universality of the Church but the particularism of one Church, which in the course of time has attained great human and temporal pre-eminence, strength, and wealth." A genuine collegial government would have in its Senate: patriarchs, cardinals taking their title from their home dioceses, and representatives of the bishops. This Senate would be superior to the Curia; in it, the Pope would have the last word. "Peoples of every tongue, mentality, and culture should feel at home in the Church. . . . The Church should impose only essentials, not accidentals. . . . The Church should allow the differences of Asia and Africa and Europe to flower. . . ." As he concluded, the Council Fathers burst into spontaneous warm and prolonged applause, the echo of which was still in their hearts as they left the basilica after the talk and the concluding prayer.

On November 7, a protégé of Cardinal Agagianian and former student of Cardinal Ruffini, His Beatitude Ignace Pierre XVI Batanian, Armenian Patriarch of Cilicia, defended the Curia: "Today the Church is living through a glorious age, thanks to the grace of God together with the Pope and his cooperators, who are the Senate of the Roman Church. . . . Every human institution has its weaknesses and we should try to correct them wisely and prudently. This does not mean publishing them and bringing them to the attention of everyone, with the risk of scandalizing or shocking certain souls. It is not right to forget all the services rendered by the Curia and to concentrate only on its weak points. We must be careful not to exaggerate and not to harm the Pope himself."

Archbishop Florit of Florence asked, in the name of fifty bishops, "mostly Italian," that a new article be inserted in the text to provide for the establishment of a central congregation of bishops which would outrank existing congregations. Such a congregation would be, in his mind, a concrete application and also a proper explanation of collegiality; for, while manifesting unity and catholicity, at the same time it would never be strictly collegial, since it depended on the Holy Father for its existence and functioning. "Yesterday in extolling collegiality, some went too far, even with the applause of the Fathers. No one can appeal to strict collegiality, since this has not yet been defined by the Council; in the strict sense that some give it, I think it undefinable. The five propositions approved in the general congregations must be taken with a grain of salt, the sign of wisdom."

Archbishop Gouyon of Rennes, France, countered that the proposed Senate of the world's bishops is "a great step forward." But he did not want this Senate "Romanized." The bishops' representatives "should not be resident in Rome" but rather should be summoned periodically, "because a prolonged residence away from their homes can cause them to lose contact with everyday situations." He wanted concrete directives inserted in the text to implement the general principle. "Otherwise there is great danger that things will not be done or will not be done properly." The bishops of Rhodesia and South Africa disliked the summoning of bishops merely to be consultors to the Curia: bishops cannot come to Rome frequently, nor prepare the material for discussion. They wanted a representative body of bishops to meet yearly with the Pope to take over the work of the Council in keeping the Church up to date. Some Latin American bishops and thirty Indonesian bishops supported them.

The great day of confrontation between the Curia and the bishops of the world was to come on November 8. But, even on the 7th, the lines were drawn. Archbishop Ziadé of Beirut attacked the theology of jurisdictional authority at its root: "It is not appointment to the Episcopate but rather actual consecration which confers the right to take part in the Ecumenical Council with deliberative vote." The power of a bishop does not depend upon a mere legal process, but rather upon sacramental consecration. It is often "the faint-hearted shepherd" who takes a case to Rome because he does not know exactly what his powers are; this faint-heartedness is one reason why the bishops lost many of their powers.

As Archbishop Ziadé was leaving the microphone, Bishop Aurelio

Del Pino Gomez, of Lerida, Spain, was already speaking. In the introduction of the chapter, he wanted it stated that the supreme law of the Church is the glory of God, not the salvation of souls. He said that he had "prayed for several days, before giving his talk," and then he rushed on: "The Roman Curia should be greatly praised for its work. Remember! what is said about the Curia is also said about the Pope. . . . Any measures intended for the Curia should be left to the paternal good judgment of Pope Paul VI, who has already made clear what his mind is on this point." He also added, consistently: "Bishops intending to serve on any central body to be organized in Rome should be chosen not by the national conferences of bishops but by the apostolic nuncios." He thought that some of the statements on the bishops implied "that they are all Popes." He thought that the idea of a senate is based on "The erroneous notion that the Pope must always act with the college," and that since Christ has said only to Peter "thou art Peter and upon this rock I will build my Church," the idea of collegiality seems devoid of all foundation. He quoted all of Scripture which pertains to the papacy, until the moderator stopped him for going overtime.

Lastly, Bishop Edoardo Mason, Vicar Apostolic of El Obedid, Sudan, who in spite of his English-looking name is an Italian, then confessed to the Fathers: "My personal experience has shown me that the Roman Curia as well as papal delegations are always a great help in difficulties and a good friend at all times." He admitted that the Curia needed *aggiornamento*, as Pope Paul had said. "We are all in need of this *aggiornamento*." The Roman Curia is the organ used by the Pope; it acts in his place and on his authority, and is especially necessary today as the Church's world-wide government. He added as a dig: "Perhaps the patriarchate also needs *aggiornamento*." Instead of asking more faculties, he told his brother bishops, "we would do well to give up some of those we now have, such as wearing a *cappa magna* with a long train and using the title 'Excellency.' A bishop can have no better title than that of 'Father and Shepherd.'"

Archbishop Eugene D'Souza had told Father Wiltgen on November 5: "The criticism will increase as the days go on. There has got to be reorganization in the Church. No one has anything to fear in giving the bishops more power. We are not children." The next day was to show how correctly he had estimated the mind of the Council.

17

THE MOST DRAMATIC DAY:
THE HOLY OFFICE

I

THE WEATHER IN EARLY NOVEMBER had been uncertain. Some days began with bright sun, only to reach mid-day with clouded skies and heavy showers, clearing later in the afternoon. Friday, November 8, the most dramatic day of the second session, was such an uncertain day. The discussion of the Roman Curia was soon to be closed without anybody having raised a voice against the practices of the Holy Office, which, in the words of one French bishop to his people, "it is permitted to call anachronistic." That morning, in fact, two eminent theologians had gone to the Council hoping to ask some of the cardinals if they would not have the courage to speak out in the name of intellectual justice. To their surprise, they found that one of the most distinguished of the Council Fathers had already come to give just such a talk.

As the first speaker of the morning concluded, old Cardinal Frings of Cologne, his sight failing so badly as to leave him almost blind, spoke calmly into the microphone. "I agree with those who think that collegiality is a fundamental principle in chapter 1. The vote of the Fathers was only indicative, but an almost unanimous consent should not be considered of no value at all. I am amazed at Cardinal Browne's remarks of yesterday which seem to indicate that the theological commission is going to give a new judgment on the matter, as though commissions had some truth properly their own which is hidden from others. The commissions are instruments of the general congregations, and their role is to execute the expressed will of the

Fathers." He went on in his calm way: "The distinction between administrative and judicial procedures in the Roman Curia should be extended to all areas, including the supreme sacred Congregation of the Holy Office. Its procedures are out of harmony with modern times, are a source of harm to the faithful, and of scandal to those outside the Church. No Roman congregation should have authority to accuse, judge, and condemn an individual who has no opportunity to defend himself. With all due reverence and gratitude for the devoted men who spend their lives in the difficult work of the Holy Office, we feel that its methods should be basically revised." At this point, as though relieved of an age-long burden, the Council Fathers burst into applause.

The Cardinal continued. "It would be advisable to diminish substantially the number of bishops working in curial offices. No one should be consecrated bishop just in order to honor him or the office he holds. If a man is consecrated bishop, then he should be bishop and nothing else. No one is ever ordained to the priesthood as a mark of honor or gratitude." Besides, many of the tasks of the Roman Curia can be performed by laymen. Consequently, efforts should be made to use "fewer bishops, fewer priests, and more laymen." As Cardinal Frings concluded, the Council Fathers again applauded. Many of the Council Fathers turned to scan the lists of coming speakers, remembering that they had seen the name of Cardinal Ottaviani on the list. He was due to speak three speakers later, and following him was Cardinal Browne—the first Council Father ever criticized by name in the Council. No one stirred from his seat.

Because of the drama taking shape on the Council floor, the talk of Cardinal Lercaro of Bologna, one of the four moderators and therefore widely presumed to be speaking for the Pope, was overlooked by the press; but he gave an excellent description of the new Senate of Bishops. "Nothing prevents the Pope from rendering more frequent or habitual the Episcopal College's exercise of its supreme (not delegated) and full power over the universal Church, at least by means of a new organ truly representing the College; as long as (1) the Pope retains final judgment on its opportuneness; (2) he remains free to act independently also, and (3) he himself protects its meaning and purpose so that it is not introduced unless it is to be the habitual way of treating major issues." This new body would not be a novelty, Cardinal Lercaro argued, but was a practical arrangement found in tradition until the sixteenth century. Already in the fourth and fifth centuries major papal decisions were made in a gathering of bishops; the Sacred Consistory met frequently at least three times a week from the thirteenth century on; and major papal decisions were never made without its consent. Trent confirmed this practice, and the Roman Curia played only a subordinate and executive role. The present Curia, he noted, resulted from a division of the Consistory by Sixtus V, for practical, not theological, reasons. The Consistory has not been the same since that time, and its failure to function properly is one of the main defects of the present Curia. "But this question so touches the Pope personally that it cannot be discussed unless he asks our mind. Therefore, (1) this matter should be dropped from the schema; (2) the Council cannot decide it by decree; (3) but it should prepare a message for the Pope; (4) and the matter should not be based on three days' discussion, but on the proper study by a special conciliar commission to be designated before the end of this session."

The next speaker was Cardinal Rugambwa, speaking in the name "of the bishops of all Africa, Madagascar, and other islands." Cardinal Rugambwa asked for the immediate creation of a central body which will be "an efficacious sign of the exercise of collegiality." In his opinion, neither the naming of episcopal consultors to the Roman congregations, nor the internationalization of the Curia would be a complete solution to the problems facing the Church. "For the good of souls, a new structuring of the central organs of the Church is needed."

Then the moment that all were anticipating had arrived. Alfredo Cardinal Ottaviani, Secretary of the Holy Office and president of the theological commission, arose and in a deeply offended tone began: "I must protest most vigorously against the condemnation of the Holy Office voiced in this Council hall. It should not be forgotten that the prefect of the Holy Office is none other than the Pope himself. The criticisms formulated proceed from lack of knowledge [*nescientia*], not to use a stronger term, of the procedures of this sacred Congregation. No one is ever accused, judged, and condemned without a thorough previous investigation carried on with the help of competent consultors and experienced specialists, selected from the Roman academies, so that the cardinals who make up the congregation can base their judgment on certain knowledge. These resolutions are then proposed to the Supreme Pontiff for approval." Having thus defended the Office he served, the Cardinal began his prepared speech, equally startling.

> Some fathers have spoken of collegiality as though it were already defined. The five points recently submitted for the approval of the Council Fathers were drawn up by the Council moderators. They should have been submitted to the theological commission for careful study, and the commission would have been able to perfect certain expressions and eliminate certain obscurities. Those who propose the collegiality of the bishops argue in a vicious circle, since they presume that the apostles existed and acted as a collegial body. From the collegial character of the apostolic college they deduce the collegial character of the body of bishops. But even learned and experienced professors of sacred Scripture will admit that this thesis has no solid foundations in the sacred books. There is no doubt that the bishops succeed the apostles. Yet, aside from the Council of Jerusalem, the apostles never acted as a college. A very competent biblical expert has confirmed to me that there exists no argument by which collegiality can be deduced from Scripture. Defending collegiality entails some limitation of at least the exercise of the universal primacy of the Roman Pontiff. The fast is that Peter alone has responsibility for the whole flock of Christ. It is not the sheep who lead Peter but it is Peter who guides the sheep. The Fathers should remember Saint Peter's admonition to bishops: "Feed the flock of God which is among you," i.e., not the universal Church. Only to Peter did Christ give the command "Feed my sheep," in other words, all the sheep.

There was faint applause—"much applause from few hands," in the words of a witness—as the courageous Cardinal resumed his place. Bishops and experts turned to one another, wondering whether the Cardinal would now have to resign, having taken refuge behind the Pope rather than shouldering responsibility himself. Would the Pope have to take sides?

Cardinal Michael Browne, also of the theological commission, then arose; but his Latin did not enable him to defend himself against the attack which had been made on him. His talk, which he delivered rather meekly, said that no objection can be raised on theological grounds against the proposal to bring bishops to Rome to assist the Pope. "But the congregations constitute the Curia and the Curia belongs to the Pope. Its cardinals, major officials, and consultors, etc., are appointed, not by the Holy See but by the Pope personally. If collegiality confers on all bishops a *right* to co-government with the Pope, then he in turn has an *obligation* to recognize this right. This would inevitably lessen the power of the Pope, who would no longer have *full* jurisdiction. This would be against the constitution *Pastor Aeternus* of Vatican I. Brothers, let us beware!"

Bishop Antoine Khoreiche, Maronite Bishop of Saïda, Lebanon, protested the phrase "without prejudice to the rights and privileges of Orientals" as a "promise which has been made repeatedly since the Council of Florence and just as repeatedly been broken." His reason for opposing this formula was that the Church is one: one in faith, sacraments, and fundamental rights for all. "There are differences in particulars; these, however, are not between the Oriental Church and the Western Church, but between particular churches, of which the Latin Church is one."

Bishop Antonio de Castro Mayer of Campos, Brazil, agreed that the notion of collegiality "has been neither sufficiently demonstrated nor as yet sufficiently studied. It is not yet proved that bishops have authority over their dioceses only through their communion with the College of Bishops. Until that proof is forthcoming, we should adhere strictly to the teaching of Vatican I. Ecumenical considerations are not sufficient motive for proposing this document. As it stands, the text needs to be corrected since the Council cannot lessen the freedom of the Pope, nor can national episcopal conferences be assured of understanding questions of universal interest." Bishop Vittorio Costantini, of Sessa Aurunca, Italy, argued: "The Curia does not claim a part in the hierarchical structure of the Church, but it is the servant of the Pope, who alone is competent to judge its efficiency and to reform it. The Curia has nothing directly in common with the College of Bishops. No one can impose an organization on the Pope." His conclusion: "Avoid criticizing the Curia. Pope Paul worked on the Curia for nearly thirty years, and knows its merits and defects."

Then Archbishop Eugene D'Souza, newly appointed to Nagpur, India, asked the world's bishops to show resolution:

> We have heard in this Sacred Synod that the question of collegiality is not yet settled, and that some of the arguments advanced against part of the schema are therefore invalid and illegitimate. There are two things I would like to say in reply.

1. Does it not seem a mockery of the Council to say that in discussion no account should be taken of the opinion expressed by 85 percent of the Council Fathers in a clear vote, especially since anyone who has listened closely to the talks given in recent weeks by our beloved and revered Pope Paul VI can sense the direction in which his own thoughts tend?

2. As a missionary, speaking in the name of ten other missionary bishops, I beg you, venerable Fathers, not to turn this into a juridical question. What concerns us above all is the good of souls, which is the decisive norm.

Pope John, whose memory will live forever, called us together for an aggiornamento of the Church. What does this mean? The Church, as a living organism, must adapt herself to the times and, as long as the essentials remain intact, should not remain changeless forever. In his unforgettable address to the Curia, our beloved Pope Paul VI said that the Curia is no exception to this law. He recalled all the many things which are to its credit, but together with him we openly raise the question of how far we should go in reforming it.

Can we expect any great gain by naming a few bishops as members or consultors of curial congregations? This would produce nothing more than a superficial difference in something which would remain basically unchanged; it would not be a thorough reform. Unless questions of this kind are clarified, unless, in accordance with the desires of the great majority here present, the power of the Curia is precisely limited, everything will be just as it was before, at least after a few years. If 2,200 bishops, gathered together from all over the world for an Ecumenical Council, sometimes find it difficult to stand up against certain pressures, what would these few bishops, scattered through the various congregations, be able to do? The last state will be worse than the first.

We know that some are afraid the increase of powers for the bishops will endanger the unity of the Church. This seems to be a false prejudice, which can be refuted in several ways.

As if decentralization were an obstacle to unity! Or, to put the issue on another level, as if a state with a federal or democratic government had no bond of unity!

And we twentieth-century bishops, are we so dangerous, after all? Have we no sense of responsibility for the Church? Are we really incapable of deciding what is good for the churches entrusted to our care? The Church is spread throughout the world, and in her spiritual, theological, and liturgical life, in her pastoral concern, she flourishes even in those lands where she lives in the diaspora. In those regions, where serious problems threaten the Church, pastors see more and more clearly that the reason why it is almost impossible to solve these problems is that laws and practical procedures have not been adapted. That, to put it bluntly, a canon law which is the same the world over becomes in their case the letter that kills.

Here we come to the heart of the problem. We cannot confuse unity with that uniformity on which the central body insists.

The Roman Curia, as a centralized power issuing uniform legislation, was certainly extremely useful, especially when kings and governments tried to dominate the bishops they used to appoint, when means of communication were also so slow that the Church had to be held together by very rigid external discipline.

At present, bishops are freely appointed almost everywhere in the world by the Supreme Pontiff without interference from civil authority. And—what is most important—means of communication are so easy that they foster unity of minds and hearts, by far the most important bond of union. Television does more to promote enthusiastic love of the Sovereign Pontiff than the acts of certain congregations. The words of Ignatius of Antioch were never so completely shown to be true: "The Roman Church presides over a universal community of love."

In all sincerity we must admit that at times this love is endangered by the present practices of the Roman Curia: when someone is punished without being heard; when general suspicion is aroused against a well-known writer without saying precisely what is objectionable in his writings and what is praiseworthy; when general regulations are issued which are not suited to local conditions; when a suggestion proposed after mature reflection by the bishops of a certain province, even of a nation, is rejected with a laconic "non expedit"—"better not"; when a petition for the dispensation from a marriage which has been celebrated but never consummated drags on for years and years without a solution.

I wish to conclude with one observation.

No one thinks the Roman Curia has to be suppressed or even seriously weakened. But it must be thoroughly reformed. This is one of the fundamental goals which have been set for the Council everywhere in the world. Let us take care, brothers, that we do not shatter these hopes.

Remember the fifth Lateran Council, which was held from 1512 to 1517. Whether it was lack of vision or lack of courage I do not know, but it failed to accomplish the reforms which men at that time hoped for. A few months later, the Church went through the worst crisis in her whole history. Brothers, let us have the courage to give an answer to the needs of our time.

There was prolonged and warm applause in the *aula*.

The morning was a long one, and non-historical orthodoxy was not without its champions. Archbishop Marcel Lefèbvre, the Superior General of the Congregation of the Most Holy Spirit, thought the chapter "well founded on Vatican I." Recent pontifical statements, he said, ask for nothing new, since the Pope qualified his address to the Curia by saying: "in conformity with the doctrine of the Church and canon law." According to canon 230, the cardinals constitute the Pope's Senate. The Archbishop appealed to the arguments of Cardinal Browne to show that "juridical collegiality cannot be proved. If it could, (a) the Church would have erred for twenty centuries by not using it, and (b) the Popes could be accused of abusing their powers." Only moral collegiality with moral bonds is justifiable. He appealed to Bishop Carli's argument that "juridical collegiality cannot be proven from Scripture, tradition, or theology."

Since all those who had wanted to speak on chapter 1 had been heard, the moderator turned the microphone over to Bishop Carli to give the introductory report for chapter 2. And then, again Cardinal Ruffini was the first to speak. The Cardinal protested against the extension of jurisdiction to coadjutor bishops in a diocese. "This is against the principle of monarchical unity praised in the schema and found in St. Paul and St. Ignatius of Antioch. Also, I would wish that no coadjutor openly have the right of succession." He did not like a reference to the Oriental Churches at the beginning of one of the articles, which "seems to make them equal to the Holy See. As I said at the beginning of the Council, this Council should make no distinction, but assert that the Pope is the head of the universal Church and leave to the new codes of canon law any individual distinctions. Divisions cannot be tolerated." He mentioned that some had been "upset" by the "*oratio aspera et molesta,* the bitter and disturbing speeches," against the Curia and the Latin Church. "The words of Patriarch Batanian were a most acceptable reparation, and I wish to thank him myself and in the name of Cardinal Siri, President of the Italian Episcopal Conference."

Cardinal Ruffini continued: It is wrong to insist on the resignation of ailing bishops. Some old men with great virtue do more good for the Church than some healthier young men. The Pope is the bishop of the universal Church and yet no one dreams of making him resign. Leo XIII died when he was ninety-three, and John XXIII was almost eighty when he became Pope. Pope John recounted once that when Leo XIII, already at an advanced age, was urging resignation on an elderly bishop, the latter looked at him calmly and said: "Holy Father, we are both old."

II

November 8 was a day the Catholic world was waiting for, and a great weight seem lifted from its shoulders. Nearly twenty of the American bishops came to hear what would be said to the press that afternoon; and at the reception given by the American bishops for the Protestant observers at the Grand Hotel that evening, the confrontation was the chief subject of conversation. A story circulated that after the session Cardinals Frings and Ottaviani, both of failing eyesight, were seen talking and laughing together like old friends.

One sequel is worth narrating. A few days after his talk, Archbishop D'Souza received a summons to the Vatican Secretariat of State. Not knowing why, he appeared as directed at the office of Monsignor Dell'Acqua. He was told that the Secretariat had received a phone call telling them that he intended to give another talk in the Council, this time against the statement of the Italian bishops about Communism in Italy. The Archbishop was speechless; the report was absolutely false, whatever its origin. Then he replied: "In the first place, if I wanted to give such a talk, not you nor the Pope himself would stop me. In the second place, I have no such intention and never had. In the third place"—and by this time the sensitive but misinformed Monsignor was noticeably embarrassed—"if you ask me my private opinion, I will tell you that I and many others were greatly distressed by the timing of that message, appearing while the bishops of the whole world are in session. Some of my simple people will not understand that the bishops of Italy are not the bishops of the universal Church." Monsignor Dell'Acqua was very polite, warm, and apologetic as the young and unintimidated Archbishop took his leave.

III

What is the Roman Curia? It is that whole ensemble of organizations grouped around the Pope, whose task is to permit him to exercise his pastoral role throughout the entire world. It derives from the conciliar commissions founded after the Church of Trent, though

the Holy Office dates from 1542. Nobody puts in question the necessity of a Curia, or the devotion of the men who give themselves to
its work. The criticisms of the Curia are not personal; they are institutional. Using Pope John's word, *aggiornamento*, and appealing to
Pope Paul's address to the Curia on September 21, the Council
Fathers could not have failed to speak up without violating courage
and loyalty. In many of their attacks, it was the Holy Office—particularly in the speech of Cardinal Frings—which was under attack.
What precisely was it that the Council Fathers were objecting to?
In the first place, it was the organizational practices of the Holy
Office, particularly its tradition of absolute secrecy, which, as one
theologian said, "are a little unusual this side of the Iron Curtain."
More than this, it was, as the words of Archbishop Garrone in his
letter to *La Semaine Catholique* of Toulouse, put it, "the condemnation, even justified, of an author who has not been permitted to
defend himself, nor to know the official reasons for his condemnation. This is a matter our century no longer understands." The attacks on the Curia then, and especially on the Holy Office, were
directed against institutional practices which do not favor truth and
liberty within the Church, and impose the special standards of non-
historical orthodoxy on authors (and Catholic publishers) around
the world, who have no chance to defend themselves.

At the American press conference on November 8, at which almost
twenty American bishops were present, Father Bernard Häring was
especially frank: "The Holy Office itself should take the initiative in
proposing reforms and bringing its procedures up to date." He said
that no one even knows the rules of procedure which govern the
Holy Office; they have been kept under secrecy for generations. Moreover, a writer is not asked about a case in which he is being judged,
or given an opportunity to state his side of the case. Generally, no
reasons are given for a warning or a condemnation. "The answer of
the Holy Office to questions on such matters is that it never gives
reasons."

The procedures of the Holy Office, he said in explanation, date
from an era when there was a great willingness to accept decisions
without explanation. The partisans of non-historical orthodoxy do
not trust openness and public fairness as the best protection of liberty and the advance of human understanding. They serve the "objective truth," which they believe they possess; no other truth has an
"objective right" to exist. Moreover, it seems impossible for the Pope

to have full knowledge of every case in which the Holy Office takes action. Father Häring cited the case of Fathers Lyonnet and Zerwick of the Biblical Institute. He could have added the case of Father Karl Rahner, S.J., against whose writings the Holy Office had issued cautions; Pope John personally expressed his confidence in Father Rahner by naming him an expert for the Second Vatican Council, and Pope Paul went out of his way in a meeting with German publishers and theologians to express his appreciation, face to face, to Father Rahner. During the second session, Pope Paul also called Father Yves Congar, another theologian long held under suspicion by the Holy Office, one of the great influences on his own theological thinking.

At the press conference, nearly everyone was called on for a statement. Bishop Ernest Primeau of Manchester, New Hampshire, cited an old Sicilian proverb: "It is necessary not only to be honest, but also to have the appearance of honesty." Auxiliary Bishop Warren L. Boudreaux of Lafayette, Louisiana, added: "I believe that the essence of the problem is the cloak of secrecy." Archbishop Joseph T. McGucken of San Francisco rose to the defense of the Holy Office; he admitted that he had been consulted at least twice by the Holy Office in connection with writings against which complaints had been made; and he admitted that these complaints, originating from laymen, had been political in inspiration. He conceded that the procedures of the Holy Office "probably could be overhauled," but in his own experience he had never seen any justification for the criticism voiced in St. Peter's. (He said privately that he thought the press panel "could show a little more loyalty," and that "his respect for Cardinal Frings had gone way down.")

Father Francis J. Connell, former dean of the School of Theology at Catholic University, stated that he personally had been consulted by the Holy Office on a charge that had been made against him. He said he gave the Holy Office officials an explanation of the matter and the case was dropped. Father Frederick McManus, professor of canon law at Catholic University, noted that the judicial procedure of canon law is highly respectful of individual liberty and is "a procedure of mercy," more humane than most civil codes; but the procedures of the Holy Office do not come under canon law. The crux of the matter—the consensus was—lay in the problem of secrecy, and in the lack of respect for the intellectual liberty of writers.

In a statement given the same day to the Divine Word News Service, Patriarch Maximos IV made a more general indictment of the Curia. "Neither the Holy Father, nor any other person in the world, whoever he might be, could adequately govern with his household an institution so vast as the universal Church, in which so many interests of Christianity throughout the world are at stake." He said that history provided sufficient examples to prove that the common good of the Church would suffer, and that catastrophes might well ensue, if the Church were ruled by the Pope, the members of his own household, and the local clergy of Rome, instead of by the Pope together with his Episcopal College, that body "constituted according to the Gospels to govern the universal Church." On this level, the objection against the Roman Curia is rather that it represents too narrow a point of view, too narrow a grasp of Roman Catholic theology and of political procedures, to justify its great power over the Catholic world.

The partisans of non-historical orthodoxy, educated by the Italian political situation, can impose their own form of life on the whole Catholic world, "as a province of the Church of Italy." The Pope cannot act without his household, and in their hands they have countless opportunities for delay, imperfect action, direct opposition, persuasion, or other means of blocking plans which the Pope himself wishes to realize. Members of the Curia constantly profess their undying loyalty to the Holy See and their great love for and absolute docility to the Pope; and all critics concede that they are faithful to their lights.

There is no doubt, for example, that men like Cardinal Ottaviani, the son of a baker from Trastevere and a long and faithful servant of the Church, are personally admirable men, and attractive personalities. Many in Rome know the good that Cardinal Ottaviani does for the orphans near the Vatican and in other pious causes. His orphans call him "Father," not "Cardinal," and show genuine love and affection for him. Moreover, Cardinal Ottaviani's friends are many and devoted; they find him the most witty, urbane, gentle, and sensitive of men. The same might be said of many other members of the Roman Curia; it is a mistake to picture them as villains, or scoundrels, or willfully dishonest pursuers of their own power. The objections that are raised against the Roman Curia, and particularly against the Holy Office, are rather that their whole conception of the Catholic faith, and of just and fair institutional practices, are conditioned by a period in Western history that is not one of its most admirable. They have a narrow, subjective vision of the Church and a special, personal view of the Church's role in history.

IV

After the attack by Cardinal Frings on November 8, the Holy Office became much more sensitive to public opinion and several of its members gave interviews to the press. The first of these interviews was given by Monsignor Henry Cosgrove, a young, handsome, capable priest from Brooklyn, New York, who serves as Cardinal Ottaviani's English secretary. The fields of competence of the Holy Office, he explained, include all matters of faith; the Pauline privilege; mixed marriage cases referred to Rome; the publication and reading of books contrary to faith; criminal cases involving apostasy, heresy, and schism; and the profanation of the eucharist. Monsignor Cosgrove made it quite clear that in criminal cases the one accused is represented by a lawyer of his own choosing and given ample opportunity to defend himself. In these cases, the secrecy of the Holy Office works to the advantage of the accused.

The Holy Office works through a pyramid of authority. First come officials called qualificators, who usually meet every Monday. The judgment of these qualificators is referred to the cardinals of the Congregation, who usually meet on Wednesday. The cardinals review the case and then make their recommendations to the Pope. Only when the Pope confirms a decision does it have effect. But, Monsignor Cosgrove noted, in matters of doctrine the author whose book is being examined is not required to be heard, though at times he may be heard. The reason for this is that, in examining a particular book, the Holy Office is not examining the thoughts or motives of the author, but only the ideas that have been expressed in the book. The first action of the Holy Office is to assign one investigator to see if the matter warrants concern. If it does, experts are assigned —two, or even as many as ten, all unknown to each other—to examine the matter and submit their findings in writing. From these experts, the matter goes to a group of consultors, averaging about twenty in number, who review the work and make a recommendation to the ten cardinals. Monsignor Cosgrove was "not in a position to answer" just how much time and study the Pope can give or does give to each case, once it comes into his hands from the cardinals.

The experts of the Holy Office are international in their background, the Monsignor said. He explained that all the work of the Holy Office is conducted under a serious obligation of secrecy, whose violation constitutes an offense from which only the Pope personally can pardon. The Monsignor declined to answer a number of questions on specific matters, because these would conflict with his own obligation of secrecy. "I like to sleep at night," he said. He added that only the Pope could change the rule of secrecy. Asked whether there was any movement afoot in the Holy Office to change this rule, he replied: "Not so far as I know." He noted that in some cases, particularly concerning the authors of books, the matter was not carried through the complete process to a final judgment by the Pope. In such cases, the individual "may merely be informed that a charge or complaint has been lodged against him, and he is asked to take note of the complaint and to correct his writing or teaching, should the complaint be warranted." He refused to surmise why there was so much irritation against the Holy Office; he said he could think of nothing in the Holy Office that needed changing. He hesitated about the matter of secrecy, but repeated that only the Pope could change that.

Monsignor Cosgrove offered his "own subjective opinion" that those working in the Holy Office are all intelligent and holy men. But he refused to answer a similar opinion as to whether they were representative of the many streams of theology in the Church. Asked about the Pope's address to the Curia on September 21, Monsignor Cosgrove said that he took the talk as applying to the Curia as a whole, rather than to the Holy Office. He said he "hadn't given any thought" to its possible bearing on the Holy Office. He said it wasn't his place to make suggestions, criticize, or to think about certain matters; he assumed that others, even the cardinals, did the same before the Pope. He told of a certain cardinal under Pius XI who once made a suggestion—and never did again.

The reporters could understand why Monsignor Cosgrove would not give answers to specific cases, but they couldn't see why even the most general, mild questions they could contrive seemed to drive him behind the wall of secrecy. It was almost impossible to converse with him. The very word "reform" seemed too strong for him—"it seems to imply" he said, "that something is bad and needs to be made good. A better word is just 'reorganization.'" One reporter asked him if "in this perfect organization which you have just described," he could think of a single matter subject to reform. Monsignor Cosgrove smiled and answered, after hesitating about the secrecy, "No." Among those present there was a great deal of nervousness and intense uneasiness about the inability to communicate. On the other hand, many admired Monsignor Cosgrove for showing himself, "in the lions' den," and thought of him as a perfect organization man. Personally, Monsignor Cosgrove seemed friendly, intelligent, and affable.

V

Several days later, Bishop Dino Romoli, sixty-three, a Dominican who had served in the Holy Office for eight years and is now the Bishop of Pescia, granted an interview to the Divine Word News Service. He distinguished between criminal cases and the condemnation of authors. In the latter matter, "it is a question of theory which considered in itself could harm the integrity of Catholic doctrine or do harm to souls. Where the orthodoxy of Catholic doctrine does not appear clear, or where orthodoxy is put in doubt, the Holy Office does not alway listen to the interested party before pronouncing its judgment." The intentions of the author are not called into question, nor are they condemned, but merely the theories the author expresses.

Asked if it might not be more human to consult with the author first before condemning his writings, Bishop Romoli said that this could readily be done in the case of an unpublished manuscript. "But once the uncertain or false doctrines have already been published," he said, "what purpose would such interrogations serve? Eventual explanations about the good intentions that an author had would not change at all the impact of his published writings on the Catholic world." The Bishop said that the Holy Office "makes a vast, accurate, and intensive investigation by consulting with highly qualified experts from various linguistic and national groups, to be incontestably objective and secure in its judgment. At times, such investigation takes several years, so great is the delicacy with which the Holy Office treats this matter."

VI

On December 1, Cardinal Ottaviani gave an interview to Georges Huber of La Croix. "It would be superfluous to inquire into the thought of the author," he said. "It is not what he thinks, but what he has written, which is the object of judgment. In effect, the damage that a book can cause to souls depends upon its content and not on what the author thinks." He repeated Monsignor Cosgrove's description of the pyramidal investigations. Cardinal Ottaviani was also proud to report "a new procedure of the Holy Office—we now avoid as much as possible issuing condemnations. We prefer to make contact with the author, using the bishop of his diocese as intermediary, so that he can withdraw the incriminating book from the market, or at least put out a new corrected edition." The Cardinal defended the secrecy of the Holy Office as necessary for the full liberty of its consultors and judges from all pressures that might be brought upon them. Besides, he thought, the secret protects the reputation of the interested persons. Asked about recommendations concerning reform in the Holy Office, he thought it would be "inopportune and hardly respectful for me to express my own opinion," since the Holy Father himself must make a decision in the matter.

Cardinal Ottaviani also granted an interview to the Italian magazine *Orizzonti* and another to *La France Catholique*. In this latter interview, reprinted in English in the *Catholic Herald* of London on December 27, Cardinal Ottaviani recognized the great power of the Holy Office. "We take these steps in secret because if we made a public announcement it would immediately damage the reputation of such a writer in the eyes of Catholics who are in good faith. When once they know a writer is under a cloud with the Holy Office, their respect for him begins to weaken, because of their loyalty to the Holy See, and their love for the faith, its purity and certainty." He said that it is "through the bishops first of all that we go for information on the author, his previous publications, and any works which he has edited. The bishop knows, then, that there are certain problems, from the point of view of the Holy Office, in a particular priest's or layman's latest book." In the Cardinal's opinion, the Holy Office does not enjoy a very good reputation in the world in general, and the Council in particular, "because people judge us on what happened in the past. They judge us from what they know of the history of the Inquisition, as it existed several centuries ago. But the modern Holy Office is quite a different matter. Its methods are all modern, with the exception of the secrecy which is often laid against us. My contention is, however, that this secrecy is necessary, both for the reputation of the priests who are brought before us, and of the writers who are, moreover, answerable to the judgment of public opinion. Their books speak out as it is, either for or against them."

Asked about the condemnation of Galileo, or of well-known French writers like Victor Hugo, Cardinal Ottaviani said: "I admit that mistakes can be made, because no human being can say that he can avoid all mistakes. I think that the condemnation of Galileo was a very regrettable mistake, but you will realize, I trust, that there were mitigating factors. Think of the state of the world at that time, or of the men who were living then. . . ." In other words, he was asked, you would not condemn Galileo today? "Certainly not. I can tell you that there was a recent session of the Holy Office during which a consultor said, 'We must be careful. We don't want to make the Galileo mistake again.' You can see, therefore, that we are thinking about this problem. Once you have made a mistake, you do your best not to make the same mistake again. This is what you call learning by experience. In any case, what human judge can say that he has never made an error? Who can say he has always made his judgments in accordance with truth and divine justice?"

Asked, "Don't you really regret that this Council has taken place, and given an opportunity for some of the speeches we have heard?" the Cardinal replied, "I think it has been useful, and, in any case, the difficulties we have had to face are nothing compared with the difficulties of earlier councils. But even these difficulties have had their use, when you consider that the propagators of the new theology had already questioned, to some degree, the primacy of the Pope." His interviewer pointed out that Cardinal Ottaviani was speaking for only a minority of the Council, and asked him, for example, about the votes of October 30.

The Cardinal answered: "You must remember that a number of statements have been made about that vote, which was not preceded by any discussion. The wording of the resolution was not even prepared by the theological commission, even though it was a matter of doctrine, and even of dogma. The whole question, therefore, was properly the affair of the commission which had the sole authority to direct such a debate. The terms proposed contain a number of phrases which are ambiguous, badly expressed, and obscure. Several of the Council Fathers complained afterward. 'Why didn't we discuss the wording?' they said. Discussion is always a good thing, you know. What would you say if you were a member of Parliament, presented with a bill, and told, two days later, vote on this bill, with out any debate? Discussion is a guarantee that there will be certainty, truth, and justice in what is finally decided."

In an earlier interview with the Divine Word News Service, Cardinal Ottaviani had called the wording of the five votes, "deficient," but he had written on the earlier draft for Father Wiltgen "erroneous." The Cardinal was quite convinced that the conception of collegiality as expressed in the five votes so minimized the primacy of the Pope as to be dangerous. Eighty percent of the Catholic bishops of the world did not share his sense of danger about that wording. It was thus harder and harder to pretend that non-historical orthodoxy best represented the Roman Catholic Church.

Perhaps it would not be improper respectfully to sharpen the objection against the Holy Office; Cardinal Ottaviani has proved himself willing to answer such objections openly. The Holy Office seems to treat books as abstract things, easily separable from the men who write them and from the climate in which they are written. The Holy Office seems to make no allowance for the fact that in modern society the condemnation of an author, or even a warning, cannot be hidden; such a matter is immediately recognized in the literary world, then in the press, and soon in the common opinion of the faithful. Thus the Holy Office is able to put a theologian, with whose ideas it is not in agreement, "under the cloud" of which Cardinal Ottaviani spoke, without ever having had a face-to-face argument with him. The Holy Office is protected by its secrecy, but the author is not.

Moreover, many of the peoples of the world have come to know in their own experience that the best interests of justice and truth are served, not by secrecy as was once believed, but by openness and public consideration of the evidence. Truth can be served under freedom and openness as well as under secrecy and sanctions; better perhaps. Isn't that the heart of the Western tradition?

VII

Cardinal Ottaviani also revealed in the *Catholic Herald* his personal view of the relationship between society and the Church. "Although the Council has been summoned for the good of the universal Church, it will also bring advantages for civilized society, for

the good of society is a natural outcome of the progress of Christian
life. As you know, we entered this session of the Council by discussing ecumenism . . . ecumenism, as the very word shows, concerns
the whole world, pagans, other religions, in China, Africa, and so
on. True ecumenism means the Church's determination to bring
Christian civilization even to those countries which have their own
civilization, but which are not yet Christian. Christian civilization
cannot fail to help these peoples to develop their resources and
advance toward progress."

The last question asked of Cardinal Ottaviani in the interview in
the *Catholic Herald* was: "Aren't you downhearted, Your Eminence,
after hearing all these criticism and attacks?" Cardinal Ottaviani
answered: "No. Criticism always produces some good, and it helps
us reflect at times. I don't deny for a moment that there are things
which need putting right, in the Holy Office, in the methods used
by the Roman Curia, in our own human nature, and in our whole
perspective, which needs to be sharper, deeper, and clearer."

One of Cardinal Ottaviani's fondest admirers, a monsignor from
the United States, loves to quote of him the line: "The lances of his
foes form a halo round his head." Without question, Cardinal Ottaviani is one of the great figures of the Second Vatican Council,
faithful to his lights, courageous, frank, an urbane and devoted man.
He is a greater man than many of his critics. But the views of the
Church and of Christian civilization which he cherishes are not the
views of all loyal and devoted sons of the Church, even though he
might wish it were so.

18

THE PROBLEMS OF
THE MANAGEMENT

TAKE THE IDEA of legitimate power and make it the moving force of an institution. Take the idea of law and make it the measure of human fidelity. The combination adds up to clarity and efficiency in organization, and it also seems to imitate the Gospels, for it emphasizes obedience. The human suffering it involves seems to be like the suffering of Christ, "obedient unto death, even the death of the cross." But it makes the Gospels juridical. What one is faithful to is human law rather than self-critical conscience. Christ himself was faithful to conscience rather than to human law; to man rather than to the Sabbath; and, at the critical points, to God's will rather than to the human religious structure—though founded by God—into which He was born. The more one reflects on Christ's fidelity to conscience—and on St. Paul's letters to the Romans and the Hebrews—the more one discovers that emphasis on lawful power and obedience to law are off center; they are not the heart of Catholic life.

In the second week of November, the Council Fathers came face to face with their own deficiencies in this regard. Too many had been taught to serve power and law. Within this context, they had, of course, managed to be substantially faithful to the Gospels. But the whole tone of the institutional life of the Church seemed off center and out of focus. Secondary things had come to be put in the first place; primary things had slid away to the pious, personal periphery—still observed, but against the official current rather than with it.

It would be a grave mistake to *oppose* the Gospels to human law, conscience to juridical authority, the primacy of love to obedience. The choice is not an either/or. Nor is it a both/and. So long as one looks at Christian life from the point of view of selfishness or self-will, then one sees a conflict of powers. Authority seems to clash with liberty. Personality runs afoul of an impersonal system. Holiness seems to involve diminution of personality, rather than greater creativity and depth. Clear, efficient organization seems to demand the sacrifice of personal conscience.

The Gospels regain their honesty and simplicity the moment we shift our point of view. Assume that the full flowering of human personality in the image of Christ depends on fidelity to one's own unrestricted, self-critical understanding. Suppose that men are so made that God lives within them, offering them light if they will be courageous enough to stand and face it. Suppose that the law of God is enkerneled in man's heart, so that it needs only man's fidelity to the light to give it warmth for its unfolding and growth. Assume that God's law is not like propositions written in catechisms, or carved on tablets of stone, but like a generator of insight and illumination in the human heart. Then we may walk with joy in the ways of the Lord. Discovering our own identity, we discover Him. He is closer to us than we to ourselves. In proportion as we halt our flights from understanding, our impulses toward darkness and self-destruction; in proportion as we are faithful to all the demands each situation places upon us—in that proportion we come to know ourselves and God. In our own inner life there are two principles: the ignorance, fears, insecurities, defensive patterns we inherit with our birth and early development; and the self-critical drive to understand our personal identity—our vocation—and to be faithful to it at all costs. It is easier to flee from understanding than to live according to it. There are not four honest men in a century, Pascal said.

The moral life and the religious life, therefore, are identical. To be faithful to understanding is to be faithful to our participation in the life of God. To be faithful to conscience is to respond to the invitation of One Who loves us and calls us to Himself.

But, because men live in society, they need to institutionalize the law. Since many must sometimes act as one, someone (a person or a legislative body) has to make concrete, limiting decisions which make actual some of the many possibilities that lie open. The effect of such limiting decisions is to cut off the freedom of some persons. That is why in a utopian society there would be very few laws. A maximum of liberty would be left to individual persons, whose insight would be so great and whose fidelity to insight so reliable that each person would be—even without institutional guidance—a principle of order in society. Liberty and order are brothers of each other, and in utopia these brothers love one another. On earth, they often quarrel.

This, in short, was the philosophical dilemma in which the Vatican Council found itself as it tried to debate the merits of proposed institutions for governing the Church. Those who thought in terms of power and law—and therefore from the point of view of individual self-will—opposed individual liberty to social authority, and the authority of the bishops to the authority of the Pope. As soon as one thinks in terms of power and law, conflicts of power and law are inevitable. The very clarity and univocity of one's conceptions bring with them inflexibility and head-on collision of interests. Those, on the other hand, who began to think in terms of sacramental grace, the mutual sharing in the mission of Christ, the communion of life and aims, had at their disposal many levels of argument, many modes of cooperation, many approaches one to another, with which to meet all the demands of the Gospels. Theirs was at once the more human and the evangelical approach. It was flexible, rich, moral, brotherly, based on each one's fidelity to the same Holy Spirit operating in divers manners throughout the whole Church. The party of power and law, on the other hand, was prisoner of conceptions too clear and unilateral to be fully human. They had to relegate to rhetoric or personal piety many of the insights and inspirations of the Gospels. Their system of law and power took first place.

These points came out with startling clarity in the debates on the document on the bishops and the government of dioceses.

II

There were four main subjects of debate in this document: a rule of mandatory retirement for bishops (probably at seventy-five); the authority to be granted auxiliary or coadjutor bishops under the "real" bishops in a diocese; the size of dioceses; the responsibility to be given national or regional conferences of bishops. The first three points are relatively minor; the last is the important one. The debate on the retirement of bishops was embarrassing; men near or over seventy-five were obviously uncomfortable, and many frantic and highly emotional pleas were heard. Yet practical matters were involved. If a bishop in poorer countries resigned, who would support him? The poverty of the Church in some countries was a revelation to many at the Council. Less touching, at first, were the fears of some that resignation would bring dishonor, or the loss of privileges and titles. Not the voice of the Gospels, but the voice of weak humanity was heard in these pleas; bishops are men.

Not a few dioceses of the world suffer from the vanities and weaknesses of men no longer able to bear burdens that they carried lightly in their youth. Should bishop or people take precedence? Compromises were offered: bishops should be *encouraged* to retire; the matter should be left to the judgment of the Pope; concrete, reliable pension funds should be established; dignities should be retained. . . . It remained for Cardinal Suenens, here as at so many points in the second session, to give the arguments their broadest, deepest affirmative expression. "When the preparatory commission first considered the problem of episcopal retirement nearly all opposed a legal age limit; but, in the end, by far the greatest number supported it." No one is a judge in his own case. On the other hand, the theology of the episcopate is not to be handled carelessly. "The bishop is the father of a family; but in a family the children gradually assume responsibility. Many repeat that the bishop is 'wed to his diocese'; yet if this is taken literally the Council hall is full of bishops divorced two or three times over." The supreme law is the salvation of souls. In this light, "a real precept with binding force is required; a pious exhortation would be next to useless."

"The accelerated rhythm of modern life demands that a bishop constantly re-examine policies and procedures." His responsibilities demand full use of mind and body. Old age creates a gap between the bishop and the world he must serve, and between himself and his clergy. In government, university, and industrial circles a retirement age is mandatory. The office of bishop is different from a purely human office, but in both cases a man's physical strength remains the same. "We have all seen the obviously sad state of dioceses ruled by aged bishops. How can we ask old priests to retire if we do not? The faithful will be scandalized if we do not act, for this is a sign of our sincerity regarding pastoral renewal." The common good of the universal Church requires that there be no mandatory retirement for the Pope; no one suggests that. A retired bishop must be decently provided for and given all that befits his state. There could be a *vacatio legis* for those now near the age limit. The Oriental Church may not need a retirement age. Extraordinary cases can always be committed to the judgment of the Pope. At the very least, the Council should decree that a bishop over seventy-five be given a coadjutor with full authority over the entire diocese.

III

The bishops of Africa took the lead in asking that auxiliary or coadjutor bishops be abolished, since their people did not understand how "after the long and tiring ceremony of consecration a new bishop doesn't yet have all the powers necessary." Again, to their people "auxiliary" means "incapable of first place"; and the auxiliary bishop was too often the Negro rather than the Eurasian. Many Africans already feel inferior in the Church. Again, the life span in Africa averages forty years; young and vigorous bishops are needed.

Other bishops wanted the number of auxiliary bishops diminished, for reasons of unity in the diocese. Cardinals Doepfner and Frings asked for a cessation of the honorary consecration of bishops for the Roman Curia. From another direction, bishops who felt insecure in their power or who had experienced dissension—not uncommon in countries where the age gap between the bishop and his auxiliary is a generation, and the theological gap is wider still—also wanted the abolition of the office of auxiliaries and coadjutors. A Spanish bishop argued that a peaceful relationship between a bishop and his co-adjutor is "practically impossible. The shadow of death hangs between them, with the bishop appearing as afraid of death, while the heir appears expectant and ready to change things according to his own will." It is "a dangerous office. . . . Since men seldom agree in all things, factions are likely to develop among supporters of the bishops, awaiting a new disposition under the heir." The office of coadjutor is "not sufficiently human, respectful, or charitable."

Other bishops argued against the unrealistic practice of giving auxiliary bishops titles to defunct sees—sometimes in the desert where the only life is that of a few nomads and their animals. A bishop of Costa Rica thought auxiliaries should receive more ample faculties, rather than have honors without powers: "They would be better to remain laborious priests rather than become lazy bishops."

On the other hand, a young auxiliary from America, Bishop Gerald V. McDevitt of Philadelphia, delighted the Council Fathers—especially the hundreds of auxiliaries among them—with a rousing, resonant talk deploring the text's *"merely* auxiliary bishops." He emphasized the importance of episcopal consecration, and wanted auxiliaries to have a presumptive right both to membership and to deliberative voice in national episcopal conferences. These requests "are based entirely on the propositions approved on October 30. I must confess that I find it difficult to understand the actions of some, even cardinals, who have worked so hard for collegiality and yet are unwilling to allow the participation of titular bishops in national conferences and the rule of dioceses." He received warm applause.

IV

On Wednesday, November 12, the moderators devised a new way of expediting the business of the Council. They proposed a vote to remand chapter 5, on the erection of parishes, to the commission for the revision of canon law, so as not to use the Council's time upon it. Their suggestion was endorsed, 2,025 to 141.

On November 13-14, in the debate on the size of dioceses, a Spanish bishop, Peralta, urged consideration of "the modern phenomenon of urban expansion and the influence that a few large cities —with their materialism—exert upon the Christian people." He asked for "suburban bishops" who, "truly residential, will share the pastoral government of large city sees. Although the government of a diocese is monarchical, it need not be absolute monarchy." He urged the use of modern efficiency experts and their surveys. A Polish bishop argued that "it takes 200,000 Catholics to support a seminary and curia; more than 500,000 make pastoral care very difficult. Although large cities cannot be divided, suburban sees can be established." Ancient dioceses, even though small, should not be suppressed, but united with other sees and share with them a common seminary and curia.

Bishop Sorrentino, of Italy, thought that the principle of dividing dioceses should be "applied without delay, although cautiously. The dioceses which are too small, as in Italy, are an obstacle to the good of souls. They cannot maintain a sufficient number of priests, nor

economic independence, nor institutions of charity and the apostolate, nor, especially, a seminary—which needs its own bishop as a
father." His phrase, "lack of economic independence," suggested to
some of his hearers that many Italian bishops depend upon Rome for
financial assistance, one more reason for their public loyalty to the
Curia. "The foundation of many of the dioceses in Italy goes back to
the year 1000. But the Church is not the 'custodian of antiquities.'
She must adapt to the many changes that have taken place since then.
. . . The criterion laid down in the Lateran Concordat was a good
one, but not acted upon. The division of dioceses should be carried
out on a general basis so as not to seem to be detrimental to any one
diocese in particular." The reference to the Lateran treaty caused
many to perk up their ears; by the Lateran Concordat, the Italian
dioceses should have been divided long ago. But the Italian government gives some support to each bishop, so that to diminish the
number of Italian sees might mean diminishing this source of
revenue.

Archbishop Urtasun of France suggested a way of combining small
dioceses to save reduplication of effort. He recounted how his own
diocese of Avignon had been created out of five ancient smaller
dioceses, to the advantage of all. He argued that the division of
dioceses "should be based on natural regions, and on cultural and
administrative affinities; experts in religious sociology should provide
accurate studies of each area." The bishop of Città Castellana, Italy,
defended small dioceses by quoting Pius XI: "Because there were
many bishops in Italy, Protestantism could not take root."

V

Meanwhile, the five votes on collegiality were still under attack by
the minority. Cardinal Doepfner, one of the four moderators, tried
on November 11 to put an end to the discussion, since the issue had
long since been closed. "The impression could have arisen in the last
few days that, while the Holy Spirit was working elsewhere, an enemy
sowed these propositions in the conciliar hall. In fact, competent
authority, the moderators, after a fifteen-day study, presented propositions which were based in word and in sense upon the text prepared
by the theological commission. Collegiality was not furtively inserted.
The voting also served as a helpful indication to the commission and
to the Fathers in discussing the present schema. These votes were not

definitive; nevertheless, what is clear should not be made obscure."

But, on November 13, Bishop Carli made another attack on the five votes. First, he had to defend his own conduct in introducing the present document. He said he had been legitimately named by a two-thirds majority, in a secret ballot, to give the introduction for the commission, that he had indicated the general lines of his report to the commission, and that no one had objected. Then, as a private Father speaking in the name of thirty others, he picked up the main point of his discourse. "Episcopal conferences cannot be based on a divine right of collegiality because (a) The votes of October 30 are of doubtful validity since they were taken without a previous *relatio* on both sides of the question, and contrary to article 30, number 2, of the *Ordo* since the Fathers were not given enough time to deliberate. (b) Even supposing a definition of collegiality, it could never be the basis for episcopal conferences because: (1) Theologically, three essential elements are lacking: the entire body of bishops, formal participation by the Pope, matters concerning the whole Church. (2) Juridically, the ordinary and immediate authority of a bishop in his own diocese would be limited by a divine right other than the Pope's. (3) Historically, the preparatory commission never thought of collegiality as the basis of conferences, and what is more, the Popes, in commending them, spoke only of pastoral reasons, and never of the divine right of collegiality." He thought that national conferences would "endanger the monarchical nature of the diocesan episcopate."

Bishop Alfred Ancel, auxiliary of Lyons, France, immediately offered an approach to collegiality very different from that of Bishop Carli. The collegial action of the bishops can take place on a territorial, as well as on a universal level, because its primary task involves a mission from Christ much more than it involves canonical jurisdiction. He insisted that legal jurisdiction *follows upon* apostolic succession, as a means follows upon an end. The exercise of collegiality has a twofold basis. On the one hand, the bishop of a diocese who cannot fulfill his mission needs to look to his brother bishops for help; on the other, bishops are obliged to help their brother bishops, not by reason of jurisdiction, but by reason of the mission which they share and which is superior to jurisdiction. "It is becoming more and more manifest that we cannot sufficiently care for our dioceses if we are left to ourselves." He asked the Fathers to reflect on the effect of "socialization," Pope John's word in *Mater et Magistra* for the interweaving complexity of contemporary life, in which no one problem can be disentangled from others. He asked them to think of national difficulties arising from large organizations and religious orders, the uneven distribution of priests, and the like. "Bishops by themselves can do little against modern difficulties. For many centuries the unanimous conviction prevailed that a bishop has no responsibility for another diocese. Help was given only out of charity. This way of thinking arose from an ignorance about collegiality, or from thinking that the mission ended where jurisdiction did. We need a true conversion of mind." Collegiality can be exercised without juridical laws, he went on, and, when necessary, such laws are to serve the needs of collegiality. He wanted the Council to put first what is first, and second what is second.

Archbishop Guerry of Cambrai reinforced his countryman's thesis by arguing that the root of collegiality is not law, nor power, but a community of faith, the *Koinonia*. The requirements of a common life of charity are prior to the need of written laws. The unity of the Council is threatened by a purely juridical conception of collegiality. Bishop Dammert of Peru added his voice on the side of collegiality as communion in life and mission. He offered a way of describing the Church as "the communion of local churches, whose union in charity, based on the eucharist, is preserved by the College of Bishops, under the primacy of the Pope." In episcopal conferences, moral unity is more important than juridical force; there is no need to make dissenters capitulate. The enactments of national conferences of bishops are not to be understood as "an exercise of authority or power, but as a bond of communion for deliberations and decisions in the service" of the people of God.

It is ironic to note that on the question of national conferences of bishops the juridical school of thought was also attacking the proposal of a juridical binding force in the conferences of bishops; their motive was to defend the monarchical authority of each bishop and of the Pope. They were against judicial force in the natural conferences, not because community comes before jurisdiction, but because clear monarchical authority comes before jurisdiction. Bishop Lorenzo Bianchi of Hong Kong played down the importance of episcopal conferences: "The monarchical structure of the Church is of divine law and conferences of bishops can cast doubt upon it. The decisions of these conferences should be consultative only, except when the vote is unanimous and approved by the Holy See."

VI

There is only so much authority to dispose of in the Church. Either Rome or groups of bishops or individual bishops will exert it. But, in listening to the bishops of the world discuss national episcopal conferences, one might have thought that a new source of power had been found in the Church, instead of a new way of arranging the power. If the power of Rome is to be decentralized, it seems reasonable that the unity of the Church is to be maintained through other centers of power in close touch with Rome. But, as Bishop Dwyer had remarked, many of the bishops are monarchical at heart. Whatever power Rome relinquished they wanted for themselves. Some of them preferred a distant centralized power in Rome, remote and unreal and therefore not always of serious concern, to a closer national center of power at home, eminently practical and compelling.

The core of the debate was twofold: the bishops of the world no longer remembered how to exercise synodal power, for they had forgotten the tradition of the ancient Church maintained in the East; and they did not trust one another. Many felt freer under Rome than under certain cardinals, or "power centers" of other bishops which might arise in their own country. Until now, national conferences of bishops had been voluntary and moral; they had done many useful things, but, still, rather resembled yearly congresses of any large national organization. They were collections of individuals, rather than true communities of action. The question was how to make them more effective—to see them in a new light, and accept them in a new spirit—without introducing a new source of uniformity and compulsion.

The conceptual difficulty lay in the legal framework in which most of the bishops spontaneously thought and expressed themselves. Thus Archbishop Garner of South Africa thought that if juridical force is taken from the chapter, "the chapter will be useless, offering nothing more than a pious exhortation. The Council should not put out such a weak schema, which merely would approve of bishops meeting to speak to one another." He thought the two cornerstones of the chapter are the juridical obligation in important matters and freedom of recourse to the Holy See in case of individual disagreement. On the other side, Bishop Franič of Yugoslavia was afraid that if more authority were given to episcopal conferences national curias would be set up which, "being near, will seem more severe than the Roman Curia."

Another difficulty in the reactivation of the co-responsibility of bishops was, of course, the monarchical conception we have so often encountered. Add to this what can only be called the solace of having, in the background, an all-knowing, all-capable father to take care of the Church, in some mystical way, and one has a potent emotional force. "National episcopal conferences," Cardinal McIntyre of Los Angeles said on November 12, "can be accepted if they are on a voluntary basis, but are to be deplored if they assume a strictly jurid-ical character." Authority given to such a body always "tends to expand." The desire to "give a national conference juridical character could be interpreted as an attack on the Curia, and thus as an in-direct attack on the infallibility of the Pope. . . . Such a cloud can be seen on the horizon." Moreover, Pope Paul "has had thirty years of experience in major curial offices, and is best qualified, with the aid of the Holy Spirit, to guide the Curia's work. No one knows better than the Pope how to provide for the needs of the Church." The Pope's natural talents are elevated by supernatural protection, which makes him the one best qualified to understand problems and find their solution. Why put strictures on him through the adoption of a juridical character for national conferences? "We should show our faith, our confidence, our reverence, and should not favor the pro-posal to give these conferences juridical character. Our faith in the Holy Spirit and our confidence in the Pope should prevail over the desire to impose juridical restrictions on the Vicar of Christ."

Cardinal Spellman of New York manifested on November 11 a similar preoccupation. "The theology we all learned in the seminary teaches us that the Pope alone has full power over the entire Church. He does not need the help of others." The Roman Curia is the execu-tive instrument of the Pope; he alone has competence to judge or reform it, and he has already indicated his own mind on the matter. The Cardinal added one last warning: "In this Council we must not determine anything that would conflict with decisions of other Popes or councils."

On November 12, the two other American cardinals took still other positions. Speaking for 120 bishops of the United States, Cardinal

Meyer of Chicago insisted on a secret ballot in the election of a president of a national conference, lest liberty be infringed or some system of automatic seniority develop. He argued that the purpose of national conferences is to further good government in individual dioceses and common collaboration; the text should avoid suggesting undue interference in the local diocese by a new form of centralization. Only a moral obligation should attach to the decisions on the national conference. In point after point, Cardinal Meyer tried to protect the liberty of individual bishops who might not wish to go along with the judgment of the majority.

Immediately after Cardinal Meyer, Cardinal Joseph Ritter of St. Louis argued that conferences with juridical power are "necessary for an effective ministry today. Only such conferences can provide the unanimity and the consequent strength" to tackle, for the good of souls, the many social and moral problems of a nation. Such national conferences would promote decentralization, for they would obviate the need for intervention from above so long as the national group could provide for its own common good. Conversely, the authoritative unity of bishops in each region would create an effective and knowledgeable bond with the Holy See, in establishing the common law of the international Church. Cardinal Ritter praised the schema for keeping juridical obligations to the bare minimum, requiring a two-thirds majority of the bishops and the approbation of the Holy See.

The American Catholic press thoroughly enjoyed this dispute among the American cardinals, for in the United States the appearances of unanimity among the hierarchy have long been scrupulously preserved. But the Americans, like others, were mesmerized by the juridical problem, and the juridical way of posing it.

Cardinal Frings, meanwhile, calmly recounted to the Fathers the achievements of the German Conference of Bishops since 1847, and then added that the conferences of the United States, Canada, and other European nations had "achieved even greater things"—none of them with juridical authority. "Of supreme importance are not the written statutes but the spirit of freedom and charity in which the bishops act."

Finally, on Friday the 14th, Cardinal Alfrink of Utrecht tried to clarify some of the confusions about these conferences. "Strictly speaking, collegiality always refers to the whole body of bishops united with the Pope." Conferences do not take their authority from that of the whole body of bishops, but from the authority which each bishop exercises in his own territory. The primary purpose of these conferences is to help individual bishops exercise their authority in their dioceses, and secondarily to reach a solution of serious national problems. The authority of these conferences comes from the supreme power in the Church, so that this power can be exercised on a more decentralized level and thus be more efficacious. Furthermore, the Council Fathers do not wish to propound a juridical definition of collegiality, but only a declaration of Catholic teaching on the power of all the bishops with the Pope: viz., that "bishops gathered with the Pope in council, or dispersed through the world but in communion with him, enjoy supreme authority in the Church."

These words, he said, are from the official report of the theological commission. They express the sense of the schema which has been in the hands of the Fathers for months, and was long debated in the Council before the five votes were taken. "The moderators should see to it that this doctrine is given to the world as soon as possible."

VII

Earlier in the week, on Tuesday, Archbishop Slipyi gave way to amusing and edifying rumination. "In the debates I see two currents: those who, like Cardinal Ruffini, dislike new things and confront them with older traditions; and those, cardinals and patriarchs, who wish to do justice to new times. No one has desired to contest the primacy of the Pope, or the merits of the Curia, not even Patriarch Maximos. Paul VI has gained the sympathy of all and the affection of all. 'Peace, then, to all!' according to the formula of the Byzantine liturgy. We are imprecise instruments in the hands of God and of the Spirit. From that come all our faults. Recent incidents remind me of an event at the Council of Trent, during the discussion on the sacraments." A French bishop, quite intelligent, spoke too long, and in a high voice which made the president, Cardinal Pole, impatient. Punning on his nationality, the Cardinal interrupted: "*Iste gallus nimis cantat*: This cock sings too long!" The Gallican Bishop replied swiftly: "May this cock awaken Peter!"

Meanwhile, several hundred bishops—reports vary, from two to six hundred—signed a petition sponsored by Cardinal Silva Henriquez, asking the Pope to intervene and establish the long-promised, much-discussed Senate of Bishops. Some twenty national conferences petitioned the Pope for a change in the personnel of the conciliar commissions, particularly in their leadership. By the end of the session, the first request remained a piece of paper on the Pope's desk but, no doubt, a project for the future. The second was to give rise to an unsatisfying compromise during the coming week. Was the Pope alert to the needs of the Council? More and more, the eyes of the Council turned toward him. Less and less did the majority find encouragement, after November had begun.

19

THE ISSUES THAT CONCERN
THE WORLD

I

ALL DURING OCTOBER, a stiff battle had been fought behind the scenes
to liberate from the theological commission the document on religious liberty which Cardinal Bea of the Secretariat for Christian
Unity had sponsored, and Pope John XXIII had favored mightily
with his encyclical *Pacem in Terris*. The theological commission,
whose competence extends to all things which touch on faith or
morals, had rightfully insisted on examining the document before
it was presented to the Council. However, as the weeks went on, the
commission did not examine it. Since those in power in the commission had long and publicly opposed the doctrine of religious liberty,
it was widely surmised that they were doing everything possible to
block discussion of the document. By early November, time was more
than pressing. The schema on ecumenism was in line for consideration, perhaps by November 15 or 18, and the document on religious
liberty was to be included in it as chapter 5.

The bishops of the United States began to grow restive. After their
informal meeting in Chicago the preceding August, they had stated
publicly that they intended to support fully the document on religious liberty. Now, quietly, they sent Cardinal Spellman to Pope
Paul. Soon the theological commission received a letter from the
Pope with explicit orders to expedite its work. By the end of the first
week of November, therefore, Cardinal Ottaviani released the document to a special subcommission, headed by Cardinal Léger of
Montreal, assisted by Bishop John J. Wright of Pittsburgh, two

Spanish bishops, and an Italian bishop. For several days, this group of five men worked at breakneck speed to prepare a report for the plenary session of the commission on November 11.

Over that single weekend, they accomplished their task. On Monday evening, the 11th, Bishop Wright invited Father John Courtney Murray, S.J., of Woodstock, Maryland, one of the great architects of modern Catholic teaching on the point, to attend the plenary session. The members of the commission sat at a large meeting table. Cardinal Santos of the Philippines and Archbishop Dearden of Detroit were the only two absent. The experts, about two dozen of them, sat in chairs around the walls of the room, speaking only when questions were directed to them. Nearly every member of the commission entered into the discussion about the report. In all, seven experts were asked to speak. At an important juncture, a question was directed to Father Murray.

For years, several of those present in the room had harassed Father Murray in his work on religious liberty, including Cardinal Ottaviani, as Secretary of the Holy Office, and Archbishop Pietro Parente, also a member of the theological commission and the Holy Office, who delivered himself that evening of an almost hysterical defense of the doctrine that error has no rights. His defense was so bad that some of his hearers were hoping he would give it at the Council, thus convincing any of the bishops who might be hesitant. Cardinal Michael Browne of the Curia and Monsignor Joseph Clifford Fenton, of Catholic University, who in past times had bitterly opposed Father Murray on this point, were also present.

Father Murray had long been prevented by the Holy Office from publishing his views on this question. His life's work was, in effect, under a cloud because of this opposition from the Holy Office and in some quarters his orthodoxy was thus rendered suspect. Moreover, after Father Murray had been invited to attend the first session of the Council as an expert, the invitation was suddenly and embarrassingly withdrawn. For the second session, Cardinal Spellman saw to it that Father Murray was accredited.

When Father Murray rose to speak before the theological commission on November 11, therefore, it was as though his whole life's work had come to a crossroads. He had only a few moments in which to speak, in Latin, and on a limited but important point. One who heard him said he spoke "clearly and very well indeed."

When the discussion was coming to an end, Bishop Wright, together with Bishop James Griffiths of New York, and many others present at the table, urged the chairman to bring the matter to an immediate vote. The chairman asked time for further study. The others insisted on a vote, arguing, with Father Murray, that the commission was charged only with giving a *nihil obstat* to the document, not with resolving its issues. When the chairman then consented to a vote, several members of the commission requested a secret ballot. As the members of the commission prepared to vote, and marked their ballots, the tension grew. Most expected that the report would pass, but not by a very large margin.

When the votes were tabulated, Bishop Wright's report stood approved by a vote of 18 to 5, with one null. Cardinal Bea's statement on religious liberty, therefore, was free for presentation to the Council.

There was much jubilation in the commission, but none greater than that in the heart of Father Murray. After years of being without the right to develop his views in the public academic forums in which they might have been criticized, stimulated, and further developed, he was having the evening of his life. Moreover, the vote of November 11 showed that freedom, discussion, and convincing reflection can win an overwhelming victory even in the theological commission. It was a great evening, not only for Father Murray, but for the Church. Yet the memory of it was to be painful by the end of the session.

II

On November 8, the coordinating commission of the Council decided to append Cardinal Bea's statement on Christians and Jews as chapter 4 in the document on ecumenism. There was world-wide jubilation—except, it must be confessed, in Arab countries and among some partisans of non-historical orthodoxy. This latter opposition was difficult to fathom. Perhaps it was opposition to change, above all, opposition toward recognition of the rights of other religious groups. It is hard to believe that racial anti-Semitism was the reason; Italy has not been much scarred by that disease. But some partisans of non-historical orthodoxy seemed to believe it doctrinally necessary to say that the Jews were guilty of the death of Christ, and doomed to suffer on that account. Whatever the motives, opposition was bitter.

On November 12, Mr. Zachariah Schuster, European director of the American Jewish Committee, gave a press conference for the Divine Word News Service. He said that Cardinal Bea's document represented "certainly one of the greatest moments in Jewish history. Jews of this generation will feel fortunate to have witnessed this historic step on the part of the Church." The document, whose imminent appearance had been rumored for several weeks, was entitled "The Attitude of Catholics Toward Non-Christians, Particularly Toward the Jews," and it made clear to Catholics that the Jews could not be called a deicide people; that Jews of today could not bear the responsibility for the crucifixion of Jesus Christ; and that the terrible events of our time exposed vicious prejudice which the Catholic people must help eradicate. Mr. Schuster commented: "It had been agreed by all those who deal with the problem of anti-Semitism that one of its causes is most likely the popular beliefs about Jews that have been transmitted from generation to generation in the Christian world." He specified the belief "that Jews are the people that bear responsibility for the crucifixion of Jesus Christ, and therefore were condemned to dispersion and persecution down through the ages." Mr. Schuster acknowledged that these beliefs had never been taught as the doctrine of the Church; but he believed that they were communicated "in Christian schools, both Catholic and Protestant, were accepted by large masses of Christian populations everywhere, and are still being taught in some catechisms used today in France, the United States, and Germany."

Mr. Schuster said that the initiative for this document came from Catholics, from the "highest authority of the Church in Rome." He specified that Pope John himself had had the idea and entrusted the project to Cardinal Bea and his Secretariat. For over three years the Vatican had solicited the views of the most competent scholars and religious leaders both Christian and Jews, and a great body of knowledge was accumulated. "One can confidently say," Mr. Schuster added, "that there was not one Jewish group, or trend, or leading Jewish thinker who has not expressed his views to the authorities in Rome, at Rome's request." He described the decree as "a total rejection of the myth of Jewish guilt for the crucifixion." He hoped that "in the course of time, no Catholic catechism or textbook used in Catholic schools and seminaries will repeat these charges." The decree speaks "with warmth and respect for Judaism, pointing out that Christianity is rooted in Judaism, and that there is a great affinity between these two great religions. . . . Never before was there such a statement and call issued by the highest authority of the Church in regard to Jews and Judaism. . . . Jews may now look forward to an new era in which Jews and Christians will begin to understand one another."

In the question period at the end, some newsmen—priests—asked doctrinal questions about relationships between Catholic and Jewish theology which Mr. Schuster felt were "premature." Then, at one point in the discussion, somebody asked Mr. Schuster about the different trends within Judaism; and Mr. Schuster answered with a brief description of the differences among Orthodox, Conservative, and Reform Jews. At the mention of the word "Orthodox," Mr. Guglielmo Rospigliosi, the correspondent for *Il Tempo*, smiled and whispered words of instruction to the young boy who kept his notes. The boy jotted several lines into his book. A few moments later, before the question period was over, the men from *Il Tempo* got up and left; they had what they wanted.

The next morning *Il Tempo* carried the following headline: "*The Russian Orthodox Oppose the Presence of Jews at the Council.*" The story opened by saying that Jewish observers would not come to the Council because certain Catholics did not want to oppose the Russian Orthodox, who objected to the presence of Jews at the Council session, and because among the Jews, on the other hand, there would be difficulties in picking out which group, Orthodox, Conservative, or Reform would represent the Jewish people. No one of the journalists present at the conference could remember anything which Mr. Schuster had said to warrant *Il Tempo*'s headline and lead sentence. The tactic was all too typical of *Il Tempo*, and did not bode well for the future of the document on the Jews.

III

On November 14 the schema on communications was the subject of an important vote. When the newsmen saw the summaries of the document that afternoon, most were seriously distressed. At the American press conference, they asked question after question about the document. The reporters from the Chicago *Sun*, the *New York Times*, the wire services, and others—Catholic and non-Catholic— gave evidence of having put much more thought into their moral responsibilities than the Council had. Without exception, they disliked the document. The reporters pressed the panel for a full explanation. Monsignor George Higgins, an expert of the Council and head of the social action department of the NCWC, said the phraseology "undoubtedly leaves the door open for censorship."

Father Bernard Häring, C.Ss.R., commented: "The direction of the document as a whole is not to emphasize the use of authority. Rather it looks for those in the communications media to use self-control. The whole effort of the Church is to emphasize the responsibility of the individual and of groups, so that recourse to negative governmental means is unnecessary. This means better information, a better formation of the conscience of individuals, and moral responsibility." But the pressmen did not think Father Häring's position was the position of the document.

After the conference, several of the Catholic journalists decided that they had to do something before the document was made law. They felt it would be irresponsible of them to allow the bishops to vote on the document without an alarm being sounded. The panel had admitted that many of the bishops had not read the document, because it came into their hands just as the new debate on ecumenism was about to get under way, and just as the long, tiring debate on the Church and Church government was being concluded.

The next morning three of the newsmen met and prepared a statement, which read as follows:

SOME COMMENTS ON THE PROPOSED DECREE

"DE INSTRUMENTIS COMMUNICATIONIS."

The proposed decree "De instrumentis communicationis socialis" hardly fits in with the tenor of a Council called to make the Church relevant to modern man. It is not an aggiornamento, but a step backward.

Where the document is not vague and banal, it reflects a hopelessly abstract view of the relationship of the Church and modern culture. It deals with a press that exists only in textbooks and is unrecognizable to us.

Item. By its moralistic emphasis and simplistic treatment of the difficult problem of art and prudence (number 5), it appears to deny the intrinsic value of a work of art and to compromise the integrity of the Christian artist.

Item. While the document speaks of the "primary" moral obligation (number 11) of those who communicate information, it never
speaks of the obligations of those who should be the sources of information which society needs (though the right to it is acknowledged in
the text). It thus fails to come to grips with the problems of all those
who are victimized by authoritarian secrecy.

Item. The flat statement in number 14 seems to imply that the
specifications of natural law and "Christian judgment" are effortlessly
provided in the Catholic press. This could be interpreted as endow-
ing the Catholic press with a teaching authority and near-infallibil-
ity that is neither proper to journalism nor helpful to the formation
of public opinion in the Church.

Item. The document appears to be setting up an intermediate
ecclesiastical authority between the individual communications worker
and his employer (number 21). This is likely to be taken as a threat
to the integrity of the media. It will seriously compromise the layman
working in the general or "secular" press.

Item. In two important passages (numbers 5 and 12), it seems to
give the state (auctoritas civilis) an authority over mass media which
is dangerous to political liberty everywhere and which in some countries like the United States is proscribed by constitutional law.

This document may seem to many a mere pastoral exhortation. But
it is proposed as a solemn decree of an ecumenical council.

No decree which the Second Vatican Council has yet discussed
could touch the lives of contemporary men so directly. And yet this
decree, as it now stands, may one day be cited as a classic example of
how the Second Vatican Ecumenical Council failed to come to grips
with the world around it.
(Signed)

> John Cogley
> Robert Kaiser
> Michael Novak

> > This statement is worthy of consideration
> > Fr. John Courtney Murray, S.J.
> > Fr. Jean Danièlou, S.J.
> > Fr. Jorge Mejia
> > Fr. Bernard Häring, C.Ss.R.

Rome, November 16, 1963.

The three signers had decided that the statement would have more effect if sharply and pointedly identified with only three authors. It seemed useful to get outstanding theologians to mark the statement as "worthy of consideration"; a shorter rather than a longer list of such signatures promised the greatest effect.

On Sunday morning, November 17, two of the journalists drove around Rome, leaving several copies of these statements at hotels and *pensioni* where numbers of American bishops were staying. They gave the statements to one of the American bishops in each household and asked him to distribute them to the others. They did the same for some English-speaking bishops of other nations. Spanish and French translations were prepared and distributed by some other bishops and theologians. In all, seven hundred copies were made available during the subsequent week.

At the same time, several of the Protestant observers were speaking to all the Council Fathers they could corner, expressing their fears about the effect of the document—they did not want the Church to hurt herself needlessly. Dr. Robert McAfee Brown, for example, prepared a private statement of his own, phrases from which later appeared in *The Commonweal* for December 27, where he wrote that though the document could be read favorably in an "extreme gesture of good will," not everyone would read it that way. Many, he was afraid, would "read it at face value and find lurking just below its surface, and sometimes right on the surface, the kind of implications with which anti-Catholics will have a field day." He then listed some of the objections and the implications which he felt would be drawn from the document:

a. *A people who use instruments of mass communications must meet the Church's standards as to what a "correct conscience" is (whether they are Catholics or not) or fear the consequences.*

b. *News can be censored if it does not edify, and art can be suppressed if it does not teach.*

c. *Novels or plays that do not at all times teach a particular and precise kind of moral rectitude are inadmissible.*

d. *The opinion of competent authorities must be sought by those who read, watch, and hear, lest they read, watch, and hear the wrong things—a notion that implies the rights of censorship, boycott, and reprisals.*

e. *The task of the Church is to protect and insulate youth from all possible contamination in the area of mass media, rather than to*

     help youth develop criteria for making their own discriminating
     judgments.
f. Reporting of news about the Church must not be critical.
g. Civil authorities must legislate widely in the field of the morals of
     mass communications.
h. Catholics should be encouraged to develop a cultural ghetto of
     Catholic press, Catholic radio, Catholic television, and so forth,
     rather than making it their primary task to raise the general level
     of all the mass communications media.
i. All that Catholics do in the field of mass communications should
     be under the strict supervision of Church authorities.

At the first session of the Council, in 1962, the Council Fathers
had spent only two days' discussion on the document. They voted
to have the document drastically shortened. It struck many of them
even then as pietistic, banal, and certainly not very relevant to the lay
world—it suffered grievously from lack of consultation with lay
journalists. On November 14, 1963, without any discussion, they
voted 1,832 to 92, to approve the new chapter 1 of the document, and
1,893 to 103 for chapter 2. In all, 368 written reservations were submitted. On November 25, the Council was asked to vote on whether
the commission's response to these reservations—a change of a word
here, a phrase there—was satisfactory; 331 fathers voted negatively.
Nevertheless, the crucial vote of accepting or rejecting the document
was taken on the same day.

Before the morning session of November 25, however, several
Council Fathers committed a tactical mistake; moreover, they were
less than honest. By now convinced that the document was a dis-
graceful and harmful one, some twenty-six bishops prepared a statement which they headlined: *Urgente!* But some of the bishops who
signed the statement had had no intention of making a public display;
one, at least, had understood that the statement, without its inflammatory title, was going privately to the Council presidency. These
bishops, from South America, Australia, Europe, Africa—not a one
from the United States—urged their brothers to vote against the
document in the final vote. The document "is hardly fitting for a
conciliar decree," their statement read; it "by no means reflects the
wishes of the people, and especially of experts who work in the field."
If the decree is promulgated, "the authority of the Council will be
called into question." Several of these bishops, with the assistance of
some priests, handed out their mimeographed statement on the
steps of St. Peter's the morning of the vote, just as the Ukrainian

bishops had on the morning of October 29. But this time, when Archbishop Felici, Secretary General of the Council, came upon the scene on the steps, he tried to take the statements from the priests who were distributing them. The priests refused to yield them up. Archbishop Felici then called upon Vatican police to assist him. Meanwhile, a German bishop who observed the action took the statements for one of the priests. When Archbishop Felici tried to take the copies from the bishop, the latter refused. Archbishop and bishop engaged in a brief physical struggle for the copies. Finally, the bishop let go. The other priests, meanwhile, surrendered their copies to the police.

Then, inside the basilica, just before the vote, Cardinal Tisserant, as chairman of the council of presidents, took the microphone. He "most vigorously" deplored the handing out of the statements against the schema outside the basilica as "an attack on the tranquillity of the Council Fathers" and as "a tactic unworthy of an ecumenical council." He said that he spoke for the council of presidents and for the moderators. At this point, Cardinal Frings, one of the council presidents, requested to speak, but was refused.

Then just before the second vote was taken, Archbishop Felici took the microphone to say that one of the Council Fathers whose name appeared on the sheet in question had sent word to Cardinal Tisserant that he had never signed the statement. (He did not announce which.) Again, a sense of scandal was created, in favor of the document. The total negative vote on November 14 had been 195. Today it climbed to 503, on a vote in which, after amendments, dissatisfaction should have decreased. To reject the document, the Council would have needed 190 more negative votes.

One of the Australian bishops who had inquired about the tactic of the Ukrainians on October 29 protested to the Secretariat that he had been assured that demonstrations outside St. Peter's were permissible. An archbishop filed a complaint of illegality because no discussion had been given the new document; he was assured his written statement would receive the "lengthy study" such a matter deserved. Moreover, two or three days later some bishops were receiving mimeographed statements against the document on religious liberty, *inside* St. Peter's. An American bishop who had been among those who received this statement took it to the front desk of the Secretariat. Not a word was said, and no public action was taken by the Secretariat.

20

UNITED FOR UNITY

ON MONDAY MORNING, November 18, Cardinal Amleto Cicognani introduced what was to become the most enthusiastically received document of the Second Vatican Council, the schema on ecumenism, or the union of all Christians. Originally there had been three documents, one prepared by the theological commission, one prepared by the commission for the Oriental Churches, and the last prepared by the Secretariat for Christian Unity. By the preceding summer, these three had been combined in one document and sent out as three chapters to all the Council Fathers. On November 8, a fourth chapter had been added, on Catholics and Jews, and now a fifth chapter, that on religious liberty, had just been appended.

Archbishop Joseph-Marie Martin of Rouen, France, introduced the first chapter, eloquently and warmly. When he praised "the most eminent and venerable Cardinal Bea," the Council Fathers interrupted with long applause.

The first chapter of this schema is called "The Principles of Catholic Ecumenism," and is four pages long. The second chapter, "The Implementation of Ecumenism," although shorter, treats of many subjects: the internal renewal of the Church; conversion of heart; mutual life according to the Gospels; Christians praying together; mutual knowledge; education and instruction; modes of expressing and explaining doctrine; social collaboration with non-Catholics.

Chapter 3, "Christians Separated from the Catholic Church," consists of almost six pages. It treats first of the Oriental Churches, specifically: the special situation of the Orientals; their spirit and history; the Catholic duty to take this history into account; the Oriental liturgical and spiritual tradition; their Church law and methods of theological research; the conditions necessary for the restoration of unity. The second part of chapter 3 is called "Christian Communities Arising After the Sixteenth Century." It treats the special situation of these communities; mutual confession of Christ; the study of Sacred Scripture; the sacrament of baptism; life in union with Christ.

The general principles of Catholic ecumenism, Archbishop Martin pointed out, assert that the unity of the Father, Son, and Holy Spirit is the heart of the mystery of unity in the Church. The Church is "gathered together in a variety of divine gifts." In the history of the "one and only Church of God, schisms have arisen, tensions have developed, and communities have broken away." The Church still recognizes as her sons those who believe in Christ and have been duly baptized in Him, and recognizes that those gifts of God which constitute the Church can be found outside her own visible borders: the life of Christ and other interior gifts, faith, hope, and charity, and some of those visible elements which manifest the unity of the Church. "The spirit of Christ does not refuse to use the separated Churches or communities as means of salvation," although "our separated brethren, whether as individuals, communities, or churches, do not enjoy that unity which Jesus Christ wished to lavish upon all those whom He regenerated into one body and revivified, together, into newness of life."

The Council "calls upon the faithful to recognize the signs of the times, which indicate that everywhere today, under the breath of the Holy Spirit, great efforts are being made in the way of prayers, word, and action to reach that fullness of unity which Christ willed." Catholics must renew the Church: "Although the Catholic Church contains the whole truth revealed by Christ and all the means of grace, yet her members do not make full use of them." It urges Catholics to welcome "a proper liberty in the various forms of spiritual life and practice, in liturgy, and in the theological presentation of truth." It asks them to "appreciate the authentic goods of Christ" found among their brothers. It asserts that whatever is truly Christian in the lives of these brothers can never be in opposition to the genuine blessings of faith. The existing divisions among Christians constitute a "tragic obstacle" to the growth of the kingdom of God. "The Council, therefore, rejoices in the ever-increasing spread of ecumenism—the movement and well-ordered activity of Christians, both in the Catholic Church and in the communities and churches of our separated brethren, to remove the obstacles which stand in the way of Christian unity." It asks Catholics to refrain from false or unjust words, judgments, or actions; it asks bishops throughout the world diligently to promote and guide ecumenical activity.

II

Shortly after the applause for Archbishop Martin's introduction had died away, debate was opened on the schema "in general." Cardinal Tappouni, the Syrian Patriarch of Antioch, introduced the complaint which was to be shared by many of the patriarchs from the Near East during the coming days: an objection to treating the Oriental Churches in the same context with the Protestant Churches of the West. "There is a basic difference in their relationships with the Catholic Church." He found it a source of wonderment that after this "amalgamation," another chapter was devoted to the Jews, and still another to religious liberty. He did not think the Jews should be discussed at all in a document dealing with Christian unity. "The secretariat largely responsible for this document was organized for the promotion of Christian unity. In some localities, this decree will be harmful to Christians who constitute a minority and may be a source of difficulty for the local hierarchy. No one denies the supernatural motivation of those who prepared the text, but the present-day political situation is such that this text is likely to engender confusion. The motives of the Council will not be understood, or they will be misinterpreted, and this will give rise to most undesirable consequences."

Cardinal Ernesto Ruffini complained that the term "ecumenism" as used in the text is "out of harmony with the authentic meaning of 'ecumenical' as applied to a council of the Church." The term had been introduced into theology by Protestant authors, he said, and the meaning they gave it was quite different from the one it had had from the beginning. "If there is to be a discussion of the Jews, who are here given what might be called honorable mention in the document, then the text should also take up those other religions whose members are often less hostile to the Church than Jews, and more open to conversion than Protestants." Moreover, he wondered why, if the doctrine is to be extended to the Jews, there should not also be mention of those "millions of baptized Christians who follow Marxism and daily contribute to the spread of atheism." He found that "the Protestant sects have little in common with the Catholic Church, aside from Sacred Scripture and baptism," and he wanted it clearly stated that the explicit permission of competent ecclesiastical authority is required in any ecumenical dialogue whatever.

Next, Cardinal Arriba y Castro of Tarragona, Spain, appealed to the principle of freedom of speech to hazard an unpopular warning. "This so-called dialogue can easily be a threat to the faith of members of the Church, especially to those who are not well-educated and thus not in a position to answer the difficulties proposed to them." The text should exhort Protestants to refrain from proselytism— which is "constantly on the increase" in Catholic countries. He wanted an ecumenical catechism to be prepared as "an effective defense of Catholic doctrine on all levels of education." He thought that dialogue is inconsistent with the special laws of the Church against the prohibition of heretical books. He wanted no one to "lose sight of the fact that the teaching authority of Christ has been conferred exclusively on the Catholic Church." He could understand prayer and sentiments of charity toward our separated brethren, as well as good example. But, in general, "the schema is unacceptable and does not seem to further the welfare of souls . . . it should be dropped and in another place the Secretariat for Christian Unity should be mentioned."

Another Spanish cardinal, José Bueno y Monreal of Seville, found the schema less unacceptable, but wanted it clear that the attitude of the Church toward the ecumenical movement "has always been one of extreme caution." The Church "has consistently refused to meet with other religions as only one among many." The beginnings of the ecumenical movement "were marked with pan-Christian tendencies and the danger of such tendencies has not been completely obviated by the present text."

Only after these dissenting voices had spoken was a favorable word heard. It fell to Cardinal Joseph Ritter of St. Louis to give the first conciliar endorsement of ecumenism, in one of the best talks of the last two weeks. The present schema, he said, explains the practical consequences of the *aggiornamento* which is the aim of the Council.

"The presentation of this text marks the end of the Counter Reformation, and obliges us to make a thorough examination of conscience." He expressed the happiness of those several Americans for whom he spoke that chapter 5 will "deal with religious liberty. Without a declaration on religious liberty, there can be no mutual discussion, and the door will be closed to any real dialogue with those outside the Church. Such a dialogue should not be based on motives of expediency. It should proceed from solid theological principles, namely, the absolute freedom of the act of faith; the inviolability of the human conscience; the incompetence of any civil government to interpret the Gospel of Christ; and the consequent independence of the Church from civil authority in the accomplishment of its mission."

He also asked that greater attention be paid to the celebration of the eucharist as a symbol of unity, and to the importance of Christian worship. He wanted a clear affirmation of the validity of the sacraments and orders of the Oriental Church. He added: "There is no valid reason for denying the use of the term 'church' to the religious groups which originated after the sixteenth century." He recognized possible dangers in the ecumenical movement: "Excessive intellectualism can make it sterile, and it can likewise degenerate into indifferentism." He recommended that a book of practical directives be published by the Council and promised, in due time, his own suggestions for such a book.

The Archbishop of Caracas said that John XXIII and Paul VI were not afraid to admit those faults of Catholics which had contributed to the divisions of Christianity. "We must confess that we were not entirely innocent; for example, at the time of the Reformation many prelates indulged in pagan ways. The rule of charity—to hate error and love the erring—was not always observed." In the name of the Japanese bishops, Cardinal Tatsuo Doi of Tokyo asked that chapter 4 on the Jews be expanded to treat of other non-Christian religions, and warned of the serious scandal which division among Christians creates in the East. "We should show that the Catholic Church has due respect and honor for religions like Buddhism and Confucianism, and make it clear that the Church, in the preaching of the Gospels, aims to satisfy the highest aspirations of nations professing these religions, whose traditions and ethical systems are providential preparations for Christ."

Stephanos I Sidarouss, the Coptic Patriarch of Alexandria, Egypt, found the schema inadequate. "Its lack of a clear presentation of the primacy of the Roman Pontiff, and its confused presentation of the notion of Christian communion, leave it open to serious criticisms, and expose us to the danger of that false irenicism against which we have been warned by recent Sovereign Pontiffs." He thought that devoting a whole chapter to the Jews is "completely out of place in a discussion of Christian unity." "Such treatment is less necessary now than it would have been at the time when the Jews were suffering great persecution. Furthermore, such a treatment could bring harm to Christianity. We have abstained from some subjects in the *aula*, for example, the relations between Church and State, lest they hurt the cause of religion in a particular nation and lest, as Cardinal Gracias said, we will have to 'face the music' as a result. We in the Near East are willing to do so if necessary, but in this case it does not seem to be called for."

Even the brave Patriarch Maximos IV Saïgh was afraid that the document would cause much trouble in the Near East. He found that the schema is "well done and can serve as a satisfactory basis for discussion." But "any discussion of the Jews is absolutely out of place in the present context. They have nothing to do with Christian unity and their presence in this text is offensive to our separated Oriental Brethren. If we are to discuss the Jews then we must likewise take up the question of Moslems, among whom we must live in a minority. This gives us a different viewpoint on the whole problem, because, as an Arab proverb has it, the man receiving blows has a different outlook from the man who only counts them." But, having done his public duty in the eyes of a local government, he closed by asking for all possible efforts "to hasten the advent of perfect unity for the glory of the Most Blessed Trinity and the welfare of the human race."

III

"A council is always behind the times," Father Gustave Weigel, S.J., one of the modest but most important figures at the session, told the American press that afternoon, "but a little ahead of what was said before it." The document "leaves dead center and begins to progress." It attempts to incorporate the progress from 1900 to 1963 into the official life of the Church; but it leaves many things undone. "Never fear: there will be much for Vatican Council III to do."

Father Gregory Baum explained why the chapter on the Jews was included in a document on the unity of Christians. First, the roots of the Church are in Israel; secondly, the division in Israel which came about through the preaching of Jesus is the prototype of all other divisions among the people of God; finally, according to St. Paul (Romans 11), Israel is a participant in the final mission of the Church and, before the end of time, there is to be unity between the Church and the Jews. The entire drift of the document on Christian unity is aimed directly toward the renewal of Christian life, but obliquely toward closer ties with the Jews. But perhaps Father Baum's reflections were "thirty years ahead of time," as one of the experts said, and "had hardly had a chance to filter down to most of the bishops." It was apparent that there would be increasing pressure on the Council floor for a separate decree concerning the Jews.

Many Spanish bishops would continue to protest the various Protestant attempts to convert Catholics in Spain, Father Weigel predicted (correctly), and many others in the Council would continue to warn against "false irenicism"—i.e., a glossing of differences, out of misplaced charity. But some who spoke thus seemed to share the view, Father Weigel thought, that truth requires rough language. The Council Fathers were not proceeding like the convert makers of the past, cherishing the "good" in non-Catholic religions which "needs completion" in the Catholic fold. The document was leading them to recognize the extent to which the Holy Spirit already operates among non-Catholics. The tone was much more positive and appreciative, much less defensive and exclusive. Doctrine had not changed, but the degree of humility had.

It was apparent to all who reflected on the course of events, as ecumenism came to be debated, that the blessings of openness and self-confidence were seizing the Catholic imagination. The initiative of Pope John and discussion in the Council had stirred many men of all faiths who were weary of religious scandal, and hungry for a religion worthy of their critical attention. Their interest was an encouraging spur to the bishops, even those who had not, themselves, given much attention to such openness in the past. Not doctrine, but encrusted stubbornness—and fear—were the sources of the great separation between men who loved God, but not each other. The example of Pope John showed how much even one man could do, and showed too that fear and stubbornness are outmoded, ready, like thick heavy skins, to be shed by all who have the courage to be faithful to themselves and open to others. Then, unencumbered, men can begin to inquire into the real and profound doctrinal differences which separate them. Truth follows on the wings of charity. No one seeks a syncretic religion; all seek fidelity to conscience, peace, and mutual love.

IV

The next morning, a few minutes before nine, the tiered seats of St. Peter's were still almost empty, but the center aisle of the basilica was alive with purple-clad bishops, and the white, black, or gray of fathers of religious communities or special traditions. At nine o'clock, bells chimed, and the Council Fathers hurried to their seats. Mass was sung in the Malankar rite of India.

The day before, it had been announced that each of the official introductions to the five chapters of the schema would be given as the chapter came before the house. Now the moderators announced a change; all the introductions would be given at once. The announcement created some optimism that the way would thus be clear for a general vote on all chapters together. This move was very important. It meant that the chapters on the Jews and on religious liberty could be brought to a vote on their general acceptability before the session closed.

Two of these introductions were especially noteworthy, that by Cardinal Bea on the chapter on the Jews and that by Bishop Émile Josef Marie De Smedt on religious liberty. Both deserve to be recorded at some length, because they were two of the most moving discourses presented during the second session.

The chapter on the Jews had not been undertaken on the initiative of Cardinal Bea's Secretariat but "by reason of the express command of the Supreme Pontiff, Pope John XXIII, of happy memory." To prevent a grievous misunderstanding, Cardinal Bea began explicitly: "There is no national or political question here. Especially is there no question of acknowledging the State of Israel on the part of the Holy See. None of these questions is treated in the schema. Nor is there any treatment of such a condition, or consideration of it in any way.

"The decree intends to recall in a solemn way those things which the Church of Christ, by the hidden design of Divine Providence, receives through the hands of the chosen people of Israel." The

Church is in some sense the continuation of the chosen people of Israel, so that Christians can be called "Israelites," not indeed "according to the flesh," but because in them are fulfilled the promises made to Abraham, the father of the people of Israel. Christian preachers may not have appreciated the bond of Christians with the chosen people of Israel, and may not have shown just gratitude. Even when Christ spoke severely of those who put Him to death, He ended by praying that they be forgiven, "for they know not what they do." God Himself through St. Paul (Romans 11), assures us that He "in no way" has rejected His chosen and beloved people. "I say then: has God cast off His people? By no means—God has not cast off His people whom He foreknew . . . for the gifts and the call of God are without repentance. . . . For I would not, brethren, have you ignorant of this mystery, lest you should be wise in your own conceits, that a partial blindness only has befallen Israel, until the full number of the gentiles should enter and thus all Israel should be saved.—For as you [the Romans, insofar as they belonged to the non-Jewish people] also at one time did not believe in God, but now have obtained mercy by reason of their unbelief, so too they have now not believed by reason of the mercy shown you, that they too may obtain mercy."

Thus the aim of the decree was to call the attention of Christians to their own tradition, rooted in Scripture. The point "is not in any way to call into doubt—as is sometimes falsely asserted—the events which are narrated in the Gospels about Christ's consciousness of His dignity and divine nature, or about the manner in which the innocent Lord was unjustly condemned." The point is rather to evoke in the minds of Christians "the gentle charity of Christ our Lord and His apostles." This is necessary precisely today because "some decades ago anti-Semitism, as it was called, was prevalent in many regions and in a particularly violent and criminal form, especially in Germany under the rule of National Socialism, which through hatred for the Jews committed frightful crimes, extirpating several millions of Jewish people. . . ." A powerful and effective propaganda had been mounted in this campaign against the Jews, and "it would have been almost impossible if some of the claims of that propaganda did not have an unfortunate effect even on faithful Catholics, the more so since the arguments advanced by that propaganda often enough bore the appearance of truth, especially when they were drawn from the New Testament and from the history of the Church."

The Cardinal insisted that it was not true that anti-Semitism drew its inspiration from Christian doctrine. But he thought it important to root out from the minds of Catholics "any ideas which perhaps remain fixed there through the influence of that propaganda." The Jews of our time can hardly be accused of the crimes committed against Christ; even the leaders of the Jews at the time were unwilling to kill the Lord "on the feastday, lest there be a tumult among the people" (Matthew 26). "We know very well that anti-Semitism also has causes of a political, national, psychological, social, and economic nature. But we affirm that the Church must most certainly imitate Christ's example of gentle charity toward the people through whom it received so many great benefits from God."

The Cardinal concluded by saying that in December of the preceding year "I set out in writing for the Supreme Pontiff, Pope John XXIII of happy memory, a discussion of this whole question . . . after a few days, the Holy Father indicated to me his full approval. The Supreme Pontiff did indeed write in this way scarcely five months before his holy death. Certainly, I am not saying that the question which we are treating was settled by these words of his; for he wanted the Council to be free, just as his successor also unquestionably wishes it. I think, however, that these words of his are dear to all the most eminent and most excellent Fathers, and that at the same time they throw light on how to follow the Lord Christ." He pointed to the example of Christ on the cross, and His prayer for forgiveness. "This is the example to be imitated by the Church, the bride of Christ. This is the road to be followed by her. This is what the schema proposed by us intends to foster and promote."

The discourse by Bishop De Smedt was a much longer one. The Bishop spoke in an eloquent and powerful manner which arrested the attention of the bishops; he was probably the best speaker at the Council. He began by setting forth four principal reasons for the document on religious liberty: the *truth* about the right to religious liberty; the *defense* of this right, against atheistic materialism, in our time; the *need* of a peaceful social life in a time when men must live together, despite varying religious convictions; and *Christian unity*, since many non-Catholics suspect the Church of a kind of Machiavellianism, which seems to demand full exercise of religion when Catholics are in a minority, and to suppress religious liberty when Catholics are in a   majority. He gave a definite meaning to religious liberty, distingishing the conception proposed by the text from other conceptions prominent in our world.

First, whenever religious liberty is defended, "it is not asserted that it is proper for man to consider the religious problem according to his own whim, without any moral obligation" (religious indifferentism); or that the human conscience "is free in the sense that it is, as it were, outside the law, absolved from any obligation toward God" (laicism); or that "falsehood is to be considered on an equal footing with truth, as though there were no objective norm of truth" (doctrinal relativism); or that "man in any way has a quasi-right to maintain a peaceful complacency in the midst of uncertainty" (dilettantistic pessimism). What therefore is the meaning of religious liberty put forth in the text? "Positively, religious liberty is the right of the human person to the free exercise of religion according to the dictates of his conscience. Negatively, it is immunity from all external force in his personal relations with God, which the conscience of man vindicates to itself. Religious liberty implies human autonomy, not from within certainly, but from without. From within, man is not free of obligations toward the religious problem. From without, his liberty is offended when obedience to the dictates of his conscience in religious matters is impeded."

The decree tries to treat the question "especially from the practical point of view." "After the manner of John XXIII," it tries "to remove the whole question from the world of abstractions which was so dear to the nineteenth century." The text tries to meet "real man in his real dealings with other men, in contemporary human and civil societies." It was with this sentence that the Bishop attempted to break the back of non-historical orthodoxy. He was asking the Council Fathers to step outside the conceptual, logical system which derived rather from Spinoza and Leibniz than from the earlier, longer tradition of the Church. He was asking the Council to consider real men, in the light of the actual history into which God had been born. He was asking them to prefer persons to abstractions; to be concerned about truth as it is understood and progressively grasped and lived in concrete society. He appealed not to indifferentism or obscurantism, but to the exercise of more care and intelligence than a logical system demands; for life is more complex than logic.

Bishop De Smedt constructed his argument in five steps, matching the five steps of the chapter he expounded. He first suggested several rules by which Catholics ought to conduct themselves toward men who do not share their faith. They ought to strive, "by prayer, penance, witness and evangelizing in the Holy Spirit," to bring their non-believing brothers to the blessings of the Gospels. Secondly, they must abstain from all direct and indirect coercion. "They must respect and esteem the right and duty of non-Catholics to follow the dictate of their own conscience, even when, after sincere and sufficient study, it errs in good faith." The reason for this respect is "found in the very nature of the act of faith." For this act is, on God's part, a gift which the Holy Spirit freely gives to whom and when He wills; and on man's part, an assent which man freely gives to God. Thirdly, Catholics are bound to love and help their non-Catholic brothers in their human needs.

The second part of the schema took a step forward, and asserted that "each and every man who follows his conscience in religious matters has a natural right to true and authentic religious liberty." The document asked that the Council "solemnly demand religious liberty for the whole human family, for all religious groups, for each human person whether his conscience be sincere and true, or sincere and false concerning faith, provided only that he sincerely follow the dictate of conscience. Therefore a general principle is laid down: *no human person can be the object of coercion or intolerance.*" The human person "can fulfill the will of God only as the divine law is perceived through the dictate of conscience. . . . From the nature of things, in forming this judgment, whereby man tries freely to conform to the absolute demands of God's rights, neither any other man nor any human institution can take the place of the free judgment of man's conscience. Therefore, the man who sincerely obeys his own conscience intends to obey God himself, although at times confusedly and unknowingly, and is to be considered worthy of esteem. When religious liberty is violated, then the very freedom of the human person is violated in its principal matter. . . ."

In part 3, the document "takes still another step forward" and says that religious liberty would be "fruitless and empty if men were not able to carry out the dictate of their conscience in external acts whether in private life, in social life, or in public life. . . ." Thus the document announced its second principle: "The right and duty to manifest externally the dictate of conscience is not unlimited but can be and at times must be tempered and regulated for the common good." For otherwise the rights of one man might conflict with the rights of another. Public authority must, in the words of *Pacem in Terris,* "coordinate social relations in such fashion that the exercise of one man's right does not threaten others in the exercise of their own right, nor hinder them in the fulfillment of their duties. Finally, the rights of all should be effectively safeguarded and, if they have been violated, completely restored." The document noted that public authority can never act except according to justice, without acting wickedly and creating a law which is, as St. Thomas Aquinas said, "not truly a law, but a kind of violence" (I–II, q.93, a.3, ad 2um).

In the most difficult part of his introduction, Bishop De Smedt tried to show how the doctrine of religious liberty had developed in the history of the Church. He singled out as the principal document the letter *Pacem in Terris* of John XXIII, and especially two points in that letter: "By the law of nature, the human person has the right to the free exercise of religion in society according to the dictates of a sincere conscience, whether that conscience be true, or captive either of error or of inadequate knowledge of truth and sacred things. Secondly, to this right corresponds the duty incumbent upon other men and the public authority to recognize and respect that right in such a way that the human person in society is kept immune from all coercion of any kind." The Bishop argued that the development of this doctrine in the Church followed the *law of continuity,* whereby the Church's doctrine and solicitude are consistent and remain unchanged. The document on religious liberty, for example, has its deepest roots in the Sacred Scriptures, which teach that man is made in the image of God.

This development follows, also, the *law of progress,* whereby the teaching of the Church responds to errors which arise, and to needs which result from the development of man and society. For example, Pope John distinguished between "false philosophical teachings and the endeavors and institutions which these ideologies give rise to or nourish. While on the one hand the ideologies are always to be condemned, on the other hand the economic, social, and civil institutions which have arisen therefrom can contain something that is good and worthy of approval." Besides, a clearer distinction can now be made between errors and the person who errs in good faith. While, on the one hand, errors must always be rejected, on the other hand the man in error "does not cease to be endowed with human nature, nor does he ever lose his dignity as a person."

"In this way, the door is opened to a correct understanding of many pontifical documents which in the nineteenth century treated of religious liberty in such words that this liberty appeared as something that had to be condemned." Bishop De Smedt quoted from the famous encyclical of Pius IX, *Quanta Cura:* "From this completely false concept of social rule [naturalism], they do not hesitate to foster that erroneous opinion which is especially injurious to the Catholic Church and the salvation of souls . . . namely, that the freedom of conscience and of cults is the proper right of each man, and this should be proclaimed and asserted in every rightly constituted society." Bishop De Smedt argued that this freedom of conscience was condemned because of the ideology of the rationalists, "who founded their conclusions upon the principle that the individual conscience is under no law, and, therefore, is subject to no divinely given norms" (*The Syllabus of Errors*, Proposition 3). Freedom of worship was condemned when it was based upon "religious indifferentism" (Proposition 15). "Finally, there is condemned that separation of the Church from the State which is based upon the rationalistic principle of the juridical omnicompetence of the State, according to which the Church is to be incorporated into the monistic organism of the State and is to be subjected to its supreme authority" (Proposition 39).

The first step in this doctrinal development had been taken by Leo XIII, when he distinguished clearly among the Church, the people of God, and the civil society. This distinction made it possible to see the autonomy which belongs to the civil order and to its juridical dispositions. With this distinction, the Church was able to begin merely to "tolerate" modern freedoms. "The reason for this caution was evident, for at that time in Europe the regimes which proclaimed the modern freedoms, religious liberty among them, consciously drew their inspiration from laicist ideology. There was a danger, therefore—and Leo XIII sensed this—that the civil and political institutions of this kind of republic, since they were of laicist orientation, would lead to such abuses that they would necessarily do violence to the dignity and true liberty of the human person." But with the rise of state totalitarianism, Pope Pius XI was called upon to develop the doctrine of religious liberty to a still more sophisticated level. There was a new danger that every kind of liberty would be destroyed. Pius XI maintained the opposition of the Church to anti-religious laicism: "Those things which Pius X condemned we also condemn; as often as there is in laicism any meaning or purpose that is harmful or contrary to God or religion, we condemn laicism, and openly declare that it must be condemned, as alien to God and religion." On the other hand, Pius XI began to distinguish between "freedom of consciences" and "freedom of conscience." He rejected the latter, as "equivocal," often signifying an absolute independence of conscience, "which is an absurdity in man who was created and redeemed by God." He accepted freedom of consciences, however: "Man as a person possesses God-given rights which must remain immune from all denial, privation, or interference on the part of society . . . the believer possesses the inalienable right to profess his faith and to practice it in a proper way. Laws which interfere with or render difficult this profession and practice are in contradiction to the natural law." These words were written in Pius XI's encyclical against the Nazis.

Pius XII, Bishop De Smedt continued, was to develop the doctrine of religious liberty further still. In enumerating "the fundamental rights of the person" in his radio message on Christmas Eve, 1942, the Pope included "the right to private and public worship of God." The year before, he had given the doctrine even greater solemnity in a radio message of June 1, 1941: "The chief duty of any public authority is to safeguard the inviolable rights that are proper to men and so to provide that each one might more easily fulfill his duties." In 1953, he wrote: "Hence the affirmation: 'Religious and moral error must always be impeded, when it is possible, because toleration of them is in itself immoral,' is not valid absolutely and unconditionally. Moreover, God has not given even to human authority such an absolute and universal command in matters of faith and morality. Such a command is unknown to the common convictions of mankind, to Christian conscience, to the sources of revelation, and to the practice of the Church."

Thus Bishop De Smedt came to see the encyclical *Pacem in Terris* as "the ripe fruit of a slow process of growth which has taken place within the Church, under the light of the Holy Spirit, throughout the whole of the last century." He noted that the present document had been studied by the central commission when Pope John, on April 11, 1963, published *Pacem in Terris*. "We believe that our text is in complete conformity with his pellucid doctrine, which was received within the Church and outside of the Church with unprecedented praise." He called attention again to the need for a historical view in the study of doctrine. "It is evident that certain quotations from the Popes, because of a difference of words, can be put in opposition to our schema. But I beseech you, venerable Fathers, not to force the text to speak outside of its historical and doctrinal context, not, in other words, to make the fish swim out of water." This was a word of advice to be applied to all formulations of doctrine—each to be studied in its historical context, not only in some eternal, abstract system.

"Let our document," he went on, "be studied as it stands. It is not a dogmatic treatise, but a pastoral decree directed to men of our time. The whole world is waiting for this decree. The voice of the Church on religious liberty is being waited for in universities, in national and international organizations, in Christian and non-Christian communities, in the papers, and in public opinion—and it is being waited for with urgent expectancy. We hope that it will be possible to complete the discussion and the approbation of this very brief, but very important, decree before the end of this second session. How fruitful our work would appear to the world if the conciliar Fathers, with the voice of Peter's successor, could announce this liberating doctrine on religious liberty!"

The bishop was profuse in thanking the theological mission for having granted the *nihil obstat* to this document; there were smiles in the *aula* as he did so. He pledged that the Secretariat would speedily study suggestions made about the schema, and would work "day and night, in order that the document might be finished before the end of the session." (Some bishops were chuckling at the contrast with the attitude of the theological commission.) From all reports, the applause that thundered through St. Peter's was by far the loudest and most enduring of the second session, surpassing even that for Archbishop Martin the day before.

Somewhere in the tribunes, John Courtney Murray may have been smiling, and perhaps recognizing "one or two" of the phrases.

21

THE BITTER END

I

ON THURSDAY MORNING, November 21, a vote was taken on the first three chapters of the schema on ecumenism. Against the rules of the Council, chapters 4 and 5 were temporarily separated from the other three. Thrice it was publicly announced to the Council Fathers that the vote on chapters 4 and 5 would be taken "on another day," "later," "within the next few days." Private assurances also were given Cardinal Bea, and to other—American—cardinals, that a vote on these last two chapters would be taken. Thus, despite some misgivings, and in the euphoria of a growing general belief in the advantages of a separate ballot, the vote was taken on the first three chapters, and only eighty-six voted against them. The ecumenical movement in the Catholic Church had been enthusiastically endorsed.

The last two chapters, however, left the public forum, not to reappear at the second session.

From this day on, spirits in the Council sank lower and lower. Many men asked: "What happened to the Council?" "What went wrong?" Esteem for Pope Paul diminished, for the root of the difficulties seemed to be his refusal to make decisions once the Council Fathers had done what they could to express their will. The Pope's "indecisiveness" seemed to mark him as siding with those who interpreted "renewal and reform" in minimal fashion. Perhaps he was only solicitous not to crush the broken reed. Perhaps he estimated that the Church had already been opened; there was no need to demand absolute victory and trample non-historical orthodoxy underfoot. But Paul's motives were unclear, and in that lack of clarity was revealed one of the great weaknesses of the present Roman Catholic system, as of all monarchical systems. Accountable to no one, the Pope was the final arbiter. By a decision here or a decision there, he could dash the hopes of one group, exalt those of another; and he could temporize with both, trying to keep his family content and united.

By the end of the first week in November, the defenders of the heartlands of non-historical orthodoxy were desperate; they needed help. They received the votes of October 30 with very bad grace. They steadily, strenuously opposed them as "deficient," "erroneous," "illegal," "ill-advised," "dangerous," "contradictory to Vatican I." The four votes on collegiality violated their monarchical conceptions. The subsequent lashing of the Curia, in the first week of November—though it was only verbal, not yet effected into law—hurt, and the warm, general applause for those who spoke against it was more than Roman pride could bear.

Why, then, push this group to the limit? They were incapable of understanding much that is important and good in Catholicism. Methodologically, they began theology from the wrong end—from their own personal conceptions of logic, objectivity, proof, and evidence. What was proof to them was irrelevant to others; what was irrelevant to them was the heart of many another's argument.

Those who still thought according to the pattern of non-historical orthodoxy found the principles on which ecumenism rests very difficult to grasp. Assume that the first principle both of intellectual work and practical action is the primacy of Peter. Let one's personal security come to be identified with this, one's faith in Peter. Then one will be able to see the consistency of non-historical orthodoxy. From Peter comes all juridical authority to act or not to act. From Peter comes the final word in all—even minor—matters of morality or faith. Without Peter, nothing.

Never was a monarchical system pushed so far. The roots of this system lay in a thoroughly non-historical and uncritical method in intellectual matters, and a thoroughly juridical method in practical matters. The life of the Gospels had been confined within the narrow skins of this double limitation, until it could endure the constriction no longer. In the Council it burst its skins, beginning a more congenial, more ample life. But the partisans of non-historical orthodoxy feared that, should their system be superseded all would be lost. They clung to the primacy as their one intellectual stay; they made it do the kind of things it was never meant to do. From being a service of all the people of God, in unity, clarity, and robustness of doctrine, they made it a principle of intellectual and juridical domination. Others loved the primacy no less than they; but others conceived of it with less indebtedness to Renaissance political and intellectual conceptions.

Four words recurred in the more than twenty-five talks by the partisans of non-historical orthodoxy cautioning against ecumenism: clarity, authority, jurisdiction, and primacy. The other Council Fathers, not previously ecumenical in outlook, had changed their perspective on what is essential to the Church; but the partisans of non-historical orthodoxy thought that *they* were defending the essentials. Like Patriarch Batanian (Cardinal Ruffini's pupil) and Cardinal Bacci, they distrusted phrases like "in charity" and "the regimen of fraternal concord," and wanted "and in authority" or "and of a teaching authority" added. Patriarch Batanian took it as a compliment when non-Catholics said to him: "You lucky Catholics! In disputes you have a supreme authority which allows you to say: 'Rome has spoken, the matter is finished!'" In his vision, the one Church of Christ "must have the essential element of every perfect society, a supreme authority." And, in his mind, dialogue is like scholastic argument: "In the dialogue, we have apodictic arguments from the New Testament and Tradition to prove this."

Some of the Irish bishops appeared rigid and scholastic even when they stood with the majority; they seemed to prefer authority to any other value, and catechetical instruction to free intellectual inquiry; and they were afraid of public competition in the presentation of their faith. Archbishop McQuaid, for example, found that in his own experience "converts want only certain Catholic doctrines as proposed by the Holy See, not nebulous formulations by private theologians"; but he did not criticize this craving for security. And Archbishop Conway wanted it clear that the ecumenical movement is to "proceed under the authority of the bishop." He expressed fear that modern means of communication affect everyone, and dangerously, unless all are well-educated in their faith—as if his people, after all these years, might not be.

Several Spanish bishops presented an ambiguous front. Archbishop Morcillo was pleased that the document was positive in tone and avoided condemnations, but he wondered whether, "since the separated brethren believe they are already in the Church of Christ, and since the Catholic Church cannot renounce its role as the foundation of truth," a true dialogue is possible. It might be possible, he concluded, if "truth is safeguarded."

Bishop Pont felt that the chapter on religious liberty, though necessary for treatment in the Council, should, because of its importance, be delayed until "the Fathers have more time to reflect on the recently proposed text." A humble and sincere asking of pardon should be the first step toward ecumenical dialogue: "If we have all sinned in many things, we all need mutual forgiveness." Then Bishop Romero thought more emphasis should be placed on the necessity of belonging to the Catholic Church for salvation. "The schema should not simply presume good faith or sincerity on the part of those outside the Church, but should declare the necessity of good faith at several places in the text. It is not that we do not think our separated brothers are sincere, but that we do not wish to attenuate by imprecise statements the necessity of belonging to the Catholic Church."

"Neither clergy nor laity in Catholic countries are accustomed to ecumenism," an Italian archbishop said, so a definition will be necessary. Like many another, he found it extremely confusing—as it is, in juridical terms—to see how non-Catholics could belong to the Church. Heretics and schismatics "are simply outside the Church's communion; it is confusing to say that they share 'a certain communion'!" Many bishops never realized that they would have to *change their perspective* to understand ecumenism; they would have to leave their fortresses and learn a non-juridical way of looking at the world. Instead they repeated, with Archbishop Nicodemo, Bishop Carli, and Cardinal Ruffini, that the document should rehearse the "full" conception of the Catholic faith: foundation on Peter, jurisdictional primacy, Vatican I. This conception seemed to represent the primary preoccupations of their own faith.

On November 20, Cardinal Bacci confessed that he was afraid that "Catholic Ecumenism" might be misunderstood as "interconfessionalism," and thought the text "ambiguous" on the primacy (it was shifting toward a notion of service and ministry). "Catholic doctrine must be declared openly, not timidly and vaguely." As the Latin expert at the Council, Cardinal Bacci complained that on October 30 he had asked permission to speak before the vote on the five propositions, and had been refused. He had since appealed this injustice to the Pope. Later in the morning, the cardinal moderator took the microphone to describe Cardinal Bacci's request. Just before the vote Cardinal Bacci had come to the moderator's bench to point out a defect in the Latin, and suggested that *ius primatiale* should be replaced by *ius primatus*. All four moderators agreed that the text was already clear, and that the matter was not worth a special intervention. Their action was confirmed by applause from the floor.

A week later, Cardinal Bacci was again at the breach: "The primacy should never slip from our mind. We seem afraid of the primacy by our timidity, vagueness, and reticence." He also defended himself against the earlier comment of the moderator, claiming that the point of Latin he made was theological and involved a dangerous ambiguity, since *primatiale* does not mean a primacy of jurisdiction, but could be accepted as meaning that the Pope is merely first among the bishops. He compared the point to a difference at the Council of Nicaea between the words *homoousios* and *homoiousios*. When Cardinal Bacci finished speaking, Cardinal Suenens said: "The moderators think there was no equivocation on this question in the minds of the Fathers." And again the Council Fathers applauded.

On the 29th, Archbishop Nicodemo was up again, arguing that "legitimate diversity" means "acceptance of Roman primacy. It is a dogmatic fact of history that, through divine Providence, Rome, which is neither Eastern nor Western but Catholic, is the principle of unity." Several of his confreres strongly disliked accusing the Church of any fault. Cardinal Ruffini insisted that "the Church is infallible and indefectible. . . . Any responsibility for separation is not to be attributed to the Roman Church but to her disobedient sons. The Church is holy and has always had many holy, faithful, and obedient children." And Bishop Constantini: the account in chapter 3 is "anti-dogmatic, because separations can never be approved; anti-historical because our thoughts are to be put in proper perspective: the Church never fails and even at times of separation had many saints; anti-pastoral because the faithful who do not investigate her wholly will be disturbed by the admission of fault on the part of the Church." The decree seems to sermonize, and to look too much to "the past and its faults."

Archbishop Mingo thought that "through devotion to Mary the Orientals have kept their patrimony, whereas Protestants have lost much because of their neglect of Mary." Abbot Kleiner of the Trappists wanted Mary mentioned more often because she is "the mother of the Church and therefore the mother of unity. . . . Some of her children know and honor her plainly, others timidly and obscurely. In my opinion, where Mary is not acknowledged, peace and unity are absent. Mary is the door to Christ—the mediatrix to the mediator. Though Mary does her unifying work in silence, her sons dare not be silent about her work." Language about Mary, of course, should be biblical, for ecumenical reasons.

But the important talks for the opposition were those by Archbishop Florit and Bishop Carli on November 21. Abstractions got in Archbishop Florit's way, and perhaps it will be worthwhile to show how. We offer our remarks respectfully, because of the importance of the issues involved; they should not be taken as careless or flippant.

Bishop Canestri of Rome was to say later: "Separated communities, as separated, do not have a role in the mystery of salvation; but some of the Church's means of salvation are preserved in them." But Archbishop Florit thought it "too optimistic" to say that "some elements" in non-Catholic churches manifest unity, because "strictly speaking, they manifest division." He did not notice that the question is: *In the concrete*, can men be saved in these churches and see signs of unity with other Christians in their own church? Those who love abstractions do not face the concrete issue. Again, Archbishop Florit thought that common prayer for unity is ambiguous, because Catholics mean one thing in their hearts and non-Catholics another. But those who pray without forcing their own conceptions on God do not have such a problem. Again, "to say that fundamental dogmas were declared by councils held in the Orient is only geographically true; theologically all honor and authority was from the decisive actions of the Popes." Not all agree. "In praising the Protestants, not all are to be praised equally, and their defects ought also to be mentioned. Perhaps the better way to unity is to arouse holy inquietude, showing them what they lack, rather than to promote tranquillity of conscience, by insisting on what they possess." But those actively engaged in dialogue are already capable of being quite frank; and few are so self-assured as to vaunt their own graces.

Archbishop Florit wanted the chapter on the Jews remanded to the theological commission for insertion in the schema on the Church, and the chapter on religious liberty saved for Schema 17. He gave an almost perfect exposition of the "love for abstractions" to which Bishop De Smedt had referred. "The central question remains:

Can there exist a natural right to diffuse a false religion in good faith?
If this right is to be founded in the dignity of the person, no. To
diffuse error is wrong, and one cannot have the natural right to be
wrong. It pertains to man's dignity to diffuse truth. Furthermore,
error in itself is against the common good, so that liberty is to be
granted in teaching error only when it does not hurt the common
good or is less harmful to the common good than a public prohibition." But the Archbishop was treating "man," "truth," "false religion," "rights" as abstractions in a logical game; their *definitions*
might have set up the contradictions his argument encountered. But
had his philosophy been based on living persons, on their vocation
in history, on complex and concrete human society, on rights as concrete and personal, not abstract, he would have had less difficulty.
A change of view is required, a new starting place; otherwise, "the
central question" will ever "remain" the same.

Bishop Carli also thought that ecumenism "is understood differently by the Church and by non-Catholics"—probably because he,
too, thought of ecumenism as a human movement with human
plans, instead of a surprising happening in our midst in which many
trust the hand of God. "All the doctrinal principles of ecumenism
should be presented in chapter 1," including: "the uniqueness of the
Roman Catholic Church through objective criteria distinguishing it
from other churches"; the axiom "outside the Church there is no
salvation"; the grave obligation for a person to join the Catholic
Church as soon as he realizes it is the true Church; a statement that
"though separated communities possess certain means of sanctification—the spoils from mother Church—it is these and not the communities as such which the Holy Spirit uses." He felt the doctrine of
the primacy was being slighted, and he did not want the *litigosa vox*
"collegiality" used because it had not yet been proved. He wanted
it stated that the apostles are the auxiliaries of Peter, "as was declared
at Vatican I."

The debate was not without humor, of course. An old Father
from Peru arose as the last speaker on November 20 to say that he
had been sent from Spain to the Peruvian missions fifty-eight years
ago and had been far away from theological schools ever since. He
wanted to know, "What is this ecumenism?" I thought, he said, that
"ecumenical" refers to the whole inhabited world. "Then we should
speak about the ecumenical God the Father, the ecumenical Christ,
ecumenical Mary, ecumenical apostles, ecumenical bishops, ecumen-

ical cardinals, and ecumenical men, who are all created by the ecumenical Father." Besides, he pointed out, to speak of Catholic
ecumenism is redundant, "like speaking of universal universalism."

More humor—and point—were provided on November 26, by
Bishop Stephen A. Leven of San Antonio, Texas, in a spirited and
much-needed talk. It was, of course, *ad hominem*, chauvinistic, and
in some ways graceless; but it was given with forethought. It should
have awakened certain bishops, but apparently few of those for
whom it was intended got the point, while some others were incensed
that it might have been aimed at them. Moreover, Bishop Leven's
talk was inserted into the schedule as "a special favor," after the
moderators had instructed the Secretariat to accept no more speeches
on chapter 1—a fact which opened the eyes of the Bishop and the
press to the way the scheduling was sometimes juggled.

Just before Bishop Leven was to speak, Bishop Campagnone—
without prompting—set the stage for him. He quoted the words of
Pope Paul on November 20: the Church has been "totally founded"
on the rock placed by Christ himself—on the Pope. "The words of
Christ were directed both in the text and context only to Peter. . . .
These words of Christ should be repeated with the same veneration
and fidelity as the form of a sacrament."

Bishop Leven arose and spoke. In immortal words, handed him
originally by Bishop Fulton J. Sheen and often reworked, the effect
was described:

> *From Texas rode young Stephen Leven,*
> *With six-shooter and cartridges seven,*
> *Who in Rome drew his gun*
> *And when he had done*
> *Sent many a bishop to heaven.*

Here is what the Bishop from Texas said:

> *Every day it becomes more clear that we need the dialogue, not only*
> *with Protestants but also among us bishops.*
>
> *For there are some Fathers who have already spoken to us fre-*
> *quently in the Council who speak as if the only text in the Holy Bible*
> *were Matthew 16:18: "Thou art Peter and upon this Rock I will build*
> *my Church." In every intervention they argue against the collegiality*
> *of the bishops. They preach to us and chastise us as if we were against*
> *Peter and his successors, or as if we desired to steal away the faith of*
> *our flocks and to promote indifferentism.*

They speak as if Our Holy Father, John XXIII, had never cited in our day the expression of St. Augustine, "They are our brothers; they will not cease to be our brothers until they cease saying Our Father." They speak as if the whole doctrine of the freedom of conscience due every man, so clearly stated in Pacem in Terris, were offensive to pious ears.

Again and again in this aula they continue to chastise us as if the prelate who feels compelled by clear evidence to acknowledge the gifts of the Holy Spirit in persons of other ecclesiastical bodies were denying the faith and giving grave scandal to the innocent.

They prefer to blame non-Catholics whom perhaps they have never seen, than to instruct the children in their parishes. Otherwise why are they so afraid the effects of ecumenism would not be good? Why aren't their people better instructed? Why aren't their people visited in their homes? Why isn't there an active and working Confraternity of Christian Doctrine in their parishes?

It seems the dangers arising from ecumenism may be exaggerated. The prelates who seek a sincere and fruitful dialogue with non-Catholics are not the ones who show disaffection and disloyalty to the Holy Father. It is not our people who miss Mass on Sunday, refuse the sacraments and vote the Communist ticket.

It is not we who make little of the well-known desire of Pope Paul VI and John XXIII, often repeated in word and example. And what of the will of God who as St. Paul says (I Timothy 2:4) wishes all men to be saved and to come to the knowledge of the truth? Jesus said (Mark 9:40): "He who is not against you is with you."

Our Catholics are good Catholics, loyal to us bishops, to Holy Mother Church and to the Holy Father. We have not lost the working class. They are the foundation and the support of the Church.

Venerable conciliar brothers, I pray you: let us put an end to the scandal of mutual recrimination. Let us proceed in an orderly way with the examination and study of this providential movement called ecumenism, so that with patience and humility we may achieve that unity for which the Lord Christ prayed at the Last Supper. Saint Paul wrote (I Corinthians 13:13) "So there abide faith, hope and charity, all three; but the greatest of these is charity."

II

In reply to the fears of the few, the bishops of the majority gently stressed several themes. In the first place, they began with history: "What a burden of history we must overcome!" (Cardinal Léger on the 19th.) "We should avoid any impression that we are imposing our concept on other Christians and condemning their concept. Furthermore, we should avoid any impression that Catholic ecumenism is a closed and perfect system. We are only at the beginning. . . ." (Cardinal Koenig). "Humility . . . and an open mind . . ." (Cardinal Rugambwa). "No sentimentality or condescension . . . no vague sentiments or benevolence . . . no unconscious retaining of non-essential elements from polemical times . . ." (Archbishop Garrone). "Ecumenism requires presenting historical facts concerning the Church as they truly are, though it be bitter. This has not always been faced honestly in the past. The Church is holy, but God has placed his gifts in vessels of clay. The early Reformers . . . wished . . . to inculcate certain fundamental truths, e.g., the apostolic rights of churches (11th century); or justification by faith in Jesus as defined at the Council of Jerusalem, personal responsibility, the importance of Scripture, the freedom of the sons of God (sixteenth century). Some Catholics, even leaders of the Church, not only minimize these truths but often sin against them" (Bishop Elchinger). "The mystery of the Church is a *communion* in faith, order, and sacramental life, and not merely a *society* of the juridical order . . . the document should stress not only the spiritual, individualistic aspect of renewal in the Church, but also the social aspect, as in liturgy, the life of the layman, and the collegiality of bishops" (Archbishop De Provenchères).

"I express the view of many bishops, especially from the United States, in urgently asking that the chapters on the Jewish people and on religious liberty, as intimately connected with both theoretical and practical ecumenism, be accepted with the others as a basis for discussion" (Cardinal Meyer, Chicago). "The renewal of the Church requires not only conversion of heart, but the renewal of human, ecclesiastical, and Latin structures in the Church. . . . The schema should speak not only of Jews, but also of Mohammedans, and of all who believe in God" (Bishop Jelmini of Switzerland). "The dialogue has as a proximate goal not individual souls, nor the upper hand in argumentation, but rather a conversation which takes place principally between communities, with a sincere effort to understand each other's faith. The ultimate purpose, visible union of all Christians, is not in our hands but in God's. . . . We of England and Wales thank God that the days of mutual recrimination are past" (Archbishop Heenan).

"The roots of ecumenism lie in the Bible and in liturgy—in Cardinal Newman and the Tractarian movement, which was deeply liturgical. . . . Dom Baudin, a liturgist, first awoke Bishop Roncalli to the importance of ecumenism. . . . The chapter on religious liberty should come first. . . . It is not an appendix or a corollary, but the fundamental principle. . . . *Unity without liberty is not religious* . . ." (Bishop Mendez, Mexico). "The faithful in Africa do not understand why Western missionaries take so much care to avoid worshiping together" (The Apostolic Prefect of Dahomey). "It is said that 'ecumenism' is a new word introduced by Protestants. But it is not a novelty in the sense of a heresy; rather it is something newly introduced by God into the history of salvation to bring about unity" (Bishop Jacq, Vietnam).

"The main cross of bishops is not the reform of the Curia or diocesan boundaries but this mass movement of workers and intellectuals away from the Church, which has come with industrialized society. We must not act as if we were still in the sixteenth century . . ." (Bishop Hoeffner). "This Council has begun to integrate certain notions from other churches into Catholicism: communion as in the Orient; saving faith, the Bible, the laity, the vernacular, as in response to the major questions of the sixteenth century. . . . Now is the time to be fully Catholic and to live by more than recent Latin tradition. . . . Unity is to be preserved in diversity" (Archbishop Ziadé, Lebanon). "Only the Catholic Church possesses the universality of the gifts Christ gave His Church. . . . The Church must embrace all that is true and good in Christianity, for this is the sign by which she can be recognized as the unique Church of Christ. . . . Catholicity can preserve unity in multiplicity, and vice versa" (Bishop Volk). "For Catholics, papal primacy and infallibility are of special importance; but perhaps in practice there are other things of more importance and usefulness with regard to our separated brothers" (Bishop Abed, Lebanon).

"Chapter 1 happily uses the term 'approach' rather than 'return' to describe the restoration of Christian unity. Formerly, converts were urged to renounce their error, adhere to our dogmas, and return to the Church, bound hand and foot, while we tranquilly awaited their return, doing nothing to change ourselves. The first condition of ecumenical work is to end our smugness and convert ourselves" (Bishop Huyghe, France). "This schema presupposes all that was said in the schema on the Church and in Vatican I concerning the primacy of the Pope. If anxieties cannot otherwise be overcome, we can state in a short preface that whatever is said in this schema . . . is to be interpreted in the light of these doctrines. . . . This schema is not a dogmatic or canonical tract. So it is not necessary to repeat over and over again, in treating ecumenism, those things which separate us from others" (Archbishop Jaeger). "The reference to Peter's triple profession of love as one of the reasons why Christ bestowed the primacy on Peter should be deleted. This event, just as Peter's triple denial of Christ, pertained to his personal life and not to his transmissible mission in the Church" (Bishop Flusin, France). "In the *aula* we have heard the accusation that the schema only indicated the foundation of the Church on the apostles, but omitted its foundation on Peter. But was Peter not an apostle? And don't they know that it was proposed in this way in order to avoid an obstacle to ecumenism? We who possess the truth have the obligation to indicate all that must be said by that truth. But we must give no reason to anyone for turning away from us because of the *way* we expound the truth" (Bishop Chang, China).

Thus most of the bishops of the world had begun to proceed from the other direction than that from which non-historical orthodoxy begins. They did not start from behind the bulwarks of a complete, perfect, juridical, logical system, which, in fact, exists only mentally. They started from the concrete history of the people of God. They did not look to a logical system of saving grace, but to the Holy Spirit, who operates in history. They are not less faithful to the Gospels or Catholic tradition, but more faithful. For the Gospels were given in history, and the Catholic tradition is historical. The growth of the doctrine of the Church has been internally consistent and progressive, but not according to an axiomatic logical system which automatically yields its implications. A fundamental defect in non-historical orthodoxy is that it employs a geometrical model for intellectual development, a model which does not allow contact with the dynamic, organic system of living things. History is not "logical" in its unfolding, and that is why non-historical orthodoxy seems so curiously remote, and yet retains such complacency. Its world is simpler and neater than the real world. The Gospels, however, develop in the real world.

Non-historical orthodoxy is both monolithic and immobile al-

though proud of its "clarity" of mind. On November 25, Cardinal
Léger of Montreal tried to show the way to a different pattern of
mind: "Many Catholics and non-Catholics," a summary of his talk
stated, "think that the Church favors an excessively monolithic unity.
In recent centuries the Church has insisted on an immoderate uniformity in doctrine, worship, and discipline, neglecting legitimate
liberty. Our separated brethren have traditions, institutions, and a
spiritual treasury which they legitimately intend to preserve. In treating unity, we should show more clearly how liberty and obedience,
unity and diversity can be harmonized. For the solution of doctrinal
questions, truth and charity must not suffer, but in the face of the
ineffable mysteries of faith intellectul humility is also needed. Catholic theological efforts often follow a methodology quite different
from the ways of thinking of the separate brethren of both East and
West. Not rarely it is said that the Catholic Church possesses the
whole of Christ's revealed truth. With proper distinctions, the statement is correct. But it hides our basic incapacity to understand perfectly the unsearchable riches of revelation. The transcendence of
God does not contradict but rather tempers the doctrine of infallibility. As Pope Paul said to the observers, 'Authentic Christianity has
no place for intellectual immobilism.' "

The word "immobilism" was the correct one, for in a non-historical
world there is only logical extension. The word "authentic" was an
even better one, for words and propositions are no substitute for the
humble, self-critical, informed habit of mind. It is the living, self-
critical mind that is the source of objectivity, and those who seek a
short cut by appeal to "objective criteria" end by falling short of
humility, perspective, and truth. The search for a short cut to certainty—without passing through the human person—leads not to
objectivity but to myth. The dichotomy between "objective" and
"subjective" is not proper to the Catholic tradition; it is a late comer.
The real is found where the "objective" and the "subjective" are one,
in the self-critical, informed, reflective person who is alive to the world
in which he lives. The starting place of fruitful religious philosophy is
in the self-critical person, motivated by the unrestricted desire to
know, that is, the hunger to see God.

III

There were many other excellent talks given in the last week of
November. Some bishops asked for a new examination of the validity

of Anglican orders; others that Catholics and Orthodox might share in the same eucharist. Many asked for more frequent worship—at least "passive"—with non-Catholics: "It is not cooperation in worship that is the scandal today," one said, "but rigorous abstention, even at funerals or weddings, ceremonies of great familial importance." Others urged less rigor—in practice, fruitless anyway—against mixed marriages; more study together; mutual confession of faults; more humility; more respect for the Holy Spirit in history; more communication with all, of all religions, who believe in God. One Father opposed the tendency "to Judaize, then to Hellenize, Latinize, and Romanize," a Catholic faith meant for all. An Italian bishop, Pangrazio, wanted the schema "less abstract," "less static"; and he thought it should show how the primary truths of revelation—Trinity, incarnation, redemption—are shared by the separated brethren, and how for many of them "Christ, actively present among them through the Holy Spirit and His grace, is their center and their bond of unity."

Other bishops referred to the meetings of the World Council of Churches, at Montreal especially, and warned their brother bishops to listen to the criticisms laid against Catholicism. A Canadian bishop told how the Anglican community of Canada had sent the Canadian bishops a telegram of good wishes and prayer; an Australian told how his neighboring Anglican bishop helped defray the expenses of his trip to Rome.

Many Spaniards, and some Latin Americans, complained bitterly of proselytism by Protestant groups from North America, who were, with money and men and sometimes calumny, they charged, cajoling simple people from their Catholic faith. Ecumenism in the twentieth and in the sixteenth centuries is different; and so ecumenism in Latin America is different from ecumenism in Europe, Cardinal Silva of Chile said, "due to many causes such as lack of clergy, an unintelligible liturgy, lack of catechetical instruction, social injustices, and the like."

The bishops from Catholic countries—Ireland not excepted—seemed gravely concerned about the low level of education among their people, which made them ill-fitted for the ecumenical movement into which modern communications thrust them. The German bishops were able from their own experience to recommend sophisticated social and economic cooperation with other religious communities. "The way to heaven is fraught with dangers," Cardinal

Frings replied to those who feared ecumenism. He also added: "Let it not be said that the Catholic Church is some superior Church to coordinate all others, but rather the Church founded by Christ on Peter, always to be reformed, moving through history toward its final glorification with Christ."

Again and again in the last week there were appeals to remember the poor, to shed riches, titles, and "everything in clerical life that smacks of wealth, ostentation, and human domination." "Christians who live the faith are the only treasure of the Church." Several theologians from the Argentine said as they were leaving Rome that the sight of the gold ceilings in Rome's churches, and of the jewels on the haloes of Renaissance madonnas, made them sad for the hungry faithful of their own lands and around the world. All during the Council, bishops, especially missionary bishops, held days of discussion and retreat on "the Church of the poor," noting that of three billion human beings, two billion belong to an army of misery. Meeting every week under Cardinal Gerlier of Lyons, the bishops of the "Church of the poor" again and again injected their preoccupation into the Council. "Our peril is not to be looked for among our enemies: we must seek it in ourselves. . . . Evil cannot touch us unless it comes from within. . . . The Christian world on the whole is a naturally rich world. It should find in its faith a powerful stimulus to deliver the non-Christian world from its miseries. . . ." They asked the Council to develop the doctrine that Christ is present in the poor, as the Middle Ages had developed the doctrine of His presence in the eucharist. They hoped, humbly, that their plea would be "intelligible to the men of our time."

IV

Meanwhile, on Thursday, November 21, in response to many requests from the bishops, Pope Paul announced that he would agree to enlarge the conciliar commissions—by five men each. Four were to be elected by the Council, one to be appointed by himself. For commissions needing more (or less) than five new members to attain a full complement of thirty, the Council would elect more (or less). Thus the Secretariat for Christian Unity, having eighteen members, would receive eight elected and four appointed by the Pope; whereas the commission for the Oriental Churches, having just had two new papal appointees, would elect three more. In all, forty-three positions were to be filled. Moreover, each commission could elect a new vice-president and vice-secretary.

The pattern of this compromise was classic. It tried to please everyone and pleased no one. It did not satisfy the purposes at which it was aimed; it left effective power in almost every commission in the hands of non-historical orthodoxy. The reformers were hoping for a major change in the commissions—say, ten new members—and new elections of the leadership of each commission. For the Council had advanced so rapidly, they felt, that the commissions elected at the first session no longer represented the mind of the Council. The schemata prepared by commissions under the present leadership had been, one after another, totally rejected or severely criticized by the majority. The will of the majority was constantly constrained and narrowed by the delays, the lack of self-criticism, the complacency and self-will of some who retained power in the commissions; the Pope himself had had to write letters to at least two of them to expedite their work. The heart of the procedural problem of the Council, therefore, remained untouched.

On the other hand, the Pope could not replace the commission heads without breaking the spirits of the men on whom the daily work of the Vatican still depends. There was no viable alternative to pacifying these few men; the facts of daily administrative power were on their side. Moreover, Pope Paul is their pastor; he had to see to their needs. The Council was hardly apt to sympathize with his delicacy at the time, however; eleven weeks in Italy had been enough to exhaust the forbearance of many with Italian bureaucracy and "saving face." Many were in the mood for a thorough housekeeping in the Church, so as to be done with it, and the problem of "saving face" seemed a minor issue in the light of the Gospels. A few, moreover, remembered how often reform movements had come into Rome in the past, and not succeeded in their purposes—in a few years, Rome returned to her normal ways. Pessimism, even cynicism, became common for the first time since the first session. The windows seemed as far open as they were going to go.

In the few days of rapid consultation and preparation of lists of candidates for the new offices, however, the effectiveness of the international "para-senate" of bishops once again emerged. This group, at one time inspired and organized by Cardinal Suenens, was composed of delegates from many of the national episcopal conferences. It had no official status, but it met once a week, and gave the bishops of the world important experience in working together. In this case, less than a week remained before the schedules of candidates were to be submitted; after much running back and forth between meetings of national conferences over the city, the para-senate was able to prepare a list of candidates which some twenty-two of these conferences supported.

In the vote of November 28, all but two of the candidates on the para-senate's "master list" were elected. Seven of the new commission members were Americans—Helmsing, Primeau, McDevitt, Comber, Lane, Babcock, and Taylor (an American who is bishop of Stockholm, Sweden); Bishop Leven narrowly missed. No other national group elected more than three. The Italians were much abashed, for only one of them won the confidence of the Council: Luigi Borromeo of Pesaro, elected to the commission for religious. The theological commission received four splendid voices: Ancel (Lyons), Butler (Downside), Heuschen (Liège), and Henriquez-Jimenez (Caracas). The election was very much to the liking of the majority —except that it was icing instead of cake. The serious imbalance between the power of the commissions and the will of the majority remained. The principle of the election of officers was, however, established; perhaps it would one day be invoked for the re-election of those in office.

V

On Friday evening, November 22, while many of the Council personnel were at their dinners, the news of the senseless assassination of President Kennedy in Dallas filtered to them by word of mouth, telephone, or accidental attention to the radio. Sickness and sadness stole swiftly into the strongest hearts; many prelates—not all Americans—cried. Many a dinner was left uneaten. This stark confrontation with the absurd, and the deep love many bore the young President, made external the frustration the Council felt in its own work. The session was never to recover its buoyancy. In our age, all men share some events; Pope John's death, and then the layman John's united men in grief. The people of Italy, like the personnel at the Council, were subdued and almost in a state of shock.

On the very day of the murder, the Council had approved with near unanimity—2,158 to 19—a great new constitution on Catholic worship, the one admirable legislative achievement of the Council. It would have allowed participation by the faithful in their mother tongue at Catholic worship. Americans in Rome sorely needed such an outlet at the late-afternoon Mass on Saturday, at Santa Susanna's, for their purposelessly taken President. Instead, they were reduced to anxious, inhibiting silence while Cardinal Spellman, inaudible, walked through a dramatically meaningless Mass. Frustration, shame, and rage built up in many Catholic hearts at the service—liturgical reform had not come soon enough. Only the use of the English ritual for a few moments at the catafalque—to which the responses of the people were lusty and full of ardor—and the Cardinal's warm and tearful personal remarks, redeemed the painful Mass.

On the floor of the Council, meanwhile, work had to proceed. Day after day went by without a sign of the promised vote on chapters 4 and 5. Without that vote, the chapters remained in limbo, introduced but not legally accepted, vulnerable to any happenstance. The American bishops did not fight hard enough for this vote; they trusted the leadership of the Council. Twice one of the moderators promised an American cardinal that "the vote will be taken." Meanwhile, the number of working days became fewer and fewer. The last of them, December 3, suddenly went for a special ceremony honoring the fourth centenary of the Council of Trent; a long Council Mass was scheduled for the remaining day, December 2. Increasingly, it became clear that the "gentlemen's agreement" was being violated. The moderators observed a glum silence—the breaking of the promise was not, apparently, their doing.

On Sunday, November 24, emergency phone calls had gone out among many of the bishops most committed to renewal and reform: "The Pope has decided to withdraw chapters 4 and 5!" Efforts were mobilized and—so two reports from separate sources insist—a clarification was won from the Pope: the questions would be delayed, not withdrawn. But why had they been withdrawn in the first place? Explanations offered were threefold: certain well-placed cardinals believe, simply, that the doctrine on religious liberty is heretical, and the chapter on the Jews inopportune; secondly, the people of certain countries are so poorly educated in their faith that religious liberty might be interpreted among them as freedom to vote Communist, or otherwise to oppose their clergy; thirdly, the political and economic situation of Italy is so dependent on Vatican policy and Vatican investments, and on the power of certain curial cardinals in handling these matters, that the threat of reforming the Curia—internationalizing it and making its financial practices public—sent a shock through the Italian national system; religious liberty would be the last straw.

The exact truth in these allegations, all of which seem credible in the light of public knowledge, cannot easily be determined. Neither the Pope nor those cardinals in question are responsible to the general Catholic public. There seems to be no way whereby the Catholic people can ask for a public investigation or receive replies to pointed questions. Public press conferences such as the leaders of nations give to earn the confidence of their people, are not yet a practice in the Church. With its motives hidden from public view, the Vatican is extremely vulnerable to scandal, whispering, and rumor. Wise men do not countenance the stories inevitably generated in Rome. But, in the vacuum of information in which they are left, they remain prudently suspicious.

Over the will of the vast majority, the chapters on the Jews and religious liberty were withheld from the legal vote of the Council. An account should have been forthcoming. If the motives were honorable, they would have been understood. If the motives could not be revealed in detail, a general "cover" could have been officially announced—not by Cardinal Bea, whose document it was, but by the authorities who deprived that document of its rightful vote.

On the last Thursday of the Council, Archbishop D'Souza, seeing the long list of speakers on chapter 3 who were, in effect, preventing a vote on chapters 4 and 5, yielded his right to speak; no others followed his example. But there was no planned filibuster. At the Council, a filibuster does not have to be organized; the discourses may touch on anything remotely related to the chapter, and among twenty-three hundred men there are always more speakers than openings. On Friday, November 29, Bishop Charles H. Helmsing of Kansas City, Missouri, after an excellent talk on the "courtesies and decencies" of ecumenical dialogue (e.g., calling churches churches), asked why a vote on chapters 4 and 5 could not be taken immediately, since the chapters had been properly introduced on the floor and a vote promised. There was widespread applause, but no authoritative comment. Those opposed to religious liberty were counting on the trust, docility, and lack of organization among the majority.

Thus the issue to win most enthusiasm in the Council—religious liberty—was left to the initiative of the Americans; and their uncritical docility was used against them by the opposition. They disappointed many other bishops of the world, who knew this was the one special project of the Americans. As they left Rome, many of the Americans were mortified and bitter. But not all; many refused to see they had been cheated. As Bishop Helmsing wrote in his diocesan *Catholic Reporter* for December 13: "My whole attitude of life has been one of, we might say, our American procedure and law, so that I think a man is innocent until he is proved guilty, and I'm not looking for a villain behind every problem when there's a difficulty." But it is not a question of "villains." It is only a question of political skill in realizing one's convictions in concrete legislation. The minority at the Council had conviction, central power, and effectiveness. They outsmarted the majority and kept the statements on the Jews and religious liberty from a vote which could easily have been taken. A vote on these two chapters "as a good basis for discussion" would have solidified their status. Without such a vote, they might have to be rewritten and go through the theological commission again.

Cardinal Bea told the Council on the last working day: "It was *only* lack of the time which prevented chapters 4 and 5 from being considered"—which was not, absolutely, true, although, given the time it took behind the scenes to win assurances for the future of these chapters, the statement was true enough. "It is good that there was full opportunity to speak on the three fundamental chapters, lest someone might say a hasty vote was taken on them and on the last two as well. These last two, which treat of matters of great importance and of considerable difficulty and newness, can be pondered without haste, so that the discussion at the next session will be serene and tranquil: 'What is delayed is not withdrawn'." Then the Cardinal added a crucial request: "Please send in, before January 31, observations on the context and the placing of these two chapters." The Secretariat was in need of strong assistance from the Council Fathers if it wished to keep these issues alive. The opposition was not going to relent.[1] Many of the Council Fathers went into the public ceremonies of December 3 and 4 quite depressed.

NOTE

1. On December 13, Cardinal Bea gave his long-scheduled address on religious liberty to the Italian jurists. The next day, *L'Osservatore Romano* reprinted a report on the talk, with excerpts, on page 2; *Il Messaggero*, the paper nearest the government, did not report the talk at all—and ignored the Italian jurists' convention until its second day.

22

THE NEW CITY

THE RESTORATION of traditional papal pomp at the commemoration of the Council of Trent on December 3 was bitterly disappointing to many at the Council. Pope Paul had heretofore avoided such pomp; at the ceremony on October 28, commemorating the election of Pope John, he had entered on foot and lifted up his arms in greeting to his brother bishops; he had not, as now, blessed them from aloft, from the *sedia gestatoria*, in full Roman and triumphalistic splendor. Cardinal Urbani of Venice delivered an extremely long sermon in Latin, linking the Council of Trent and Vatican II as "two massive pillars upholding a great arch." In tone if not in content the discourse seemed to insist on papal prerogatives, without equally clear insistence on episcopal collegiality.

Then two of the lay auditors—Jean Guitton and Vittorino Veronese—who, in a competition usually reserved for the clergy, had politely argued all week over which one of them was to have the honor, both gave brief discourses to the assembled Council, in the presence of the Pope: laymen had at last spoken in St. Peter's. But not until the last minute had it been decided whether they would speak; so both men came in formal attire, manuscripts in hand, ready for the honor. The Italian spoke simply and briefly; M. Guitton was more rhetorical.

The great event of the morning was to be the promulgation of a new decree granting the bishops a measure of freedom from curial bureaucracy. The practical effect of the document, entitled *Pastorale Munus,* was to free bishops from applying periodically to the Roman

Curia for renewal of some forty "faculties" or powers. In addition the Pope granted the bishops eight privileges or concessions. The doctrinal significance of the Pope's action, if any, was less evident.

Some Council Fathers interpreted the document as at least a small step toward affirming the view that the bishops as a body share responsibility with the Pope for governing the whole Church. Others saw the action as only a move in the direction of administrative decentralization, contributing little or nothing to the doctrine of collegiality. Missionary bishops already possessed most of the faculties extended to all bishops; the granting of faculties by the Curia had usually been routine; and many of the faculties were so minor that some bishops had been exercising them without reference to Rome. The *motu proprio* conferred no actual new powers on the bishops. It merely removed administrative restrictions, imposed by Rome in recent centuries, from the exercise of powers which bishops already have by virtue of their consecration. Two Council experts commented privately that the concessions were "trifling" and, in view of the high expectations of the Council and of the world, "an insult." Several bishops expressed displeasure at so huge a ceremony with so small a result.

Some of the faculties granted were important, including, for example, the right to dispense from the impediment of mixed religion in marriage cases, and to allow confessors to absolve from most sins and censures formerly reserved to Rome. But along with these were such faculties as one permitting clerics, lay religious, and "pious women" to wash altar linens; and one giving the right to dispense religious women from the obligation of presenting a dowry when entering the convent. Some helpful concessions were granted, allowing priests with poor eyesight or other infirmities to offer Mass; easing certain marriage problems; granting admission to seminaries to persons of illegitimate birth. *Pastoral Munus* was a small step in the right direction. In net effect, however, the faculties granted in the *motu proprio* were minor in import, of real interest only to those responsible for interpreting fine points of ecclesiastical law.

II

The concluding ceremonies on December 4 raised few spirits. Again, the ceremony was conducted in full Renaissance papal pomp, with Swiss guards, Vatican gendarmes, the papal throne in front of and higher than the center altar, and the Italian aristocracy filling their ceremonial functions. The more than two thousand Council Fathers wore white copes and mitres. It was splendid visually, but, somehow, after the penetrating language about the "Church of the poor," the need for humility and realism, the papacy as a ministry and service—somehow, the pomp struck a false note. "We've come to see that Roman Catholicism is so much better than that," a Protestant observer said afterward.

The morning lasted three hours; it was badly organized. New formal votes were taken on the liturgy and communications schemata, which were read "a part for the whole" by Archbishop Felici. The Council waited more than thirty minutes between each reading and the announcement of each vote—almost an hour and a half of enforced, formal idleness. The vote on the liturgy came back from the IBM room at 11:15: virtually unanimous approval, 2,147 to 4. Applause broke out. To promulgate the new constitution the Pope used a new formula—one which, though missed then by many at the Council, did raise their hopes when they read it: "We, along with the Council Fathers, approve . . ." The new constitution was law, to take effect after an instruction from Rome on February 16, 1964—not before, Archbishop Felici insisted ominously. Some forty minutes later, the vote on the communications decree was also brought back. There was much tension in the hall for, although the vote was supposed to be only formal and automatic, there were still many who were debating in their conscience whether they could vote for it. At last the numbers were read, gladly, by Archbishop Felici: approving 1,960; dissenting, 164. There was satisfaction for some, and, for others, (under the peculiar circumstances) pride in the 164 who still remained faithful to their consciences—as had the 4 dissenters from the liturgy document.

The Pope's closing discourse was subtly worded, open to many different kinds of interpretation. But the contrast between the opening address on September 29 and the closing address on December 4 could hardly have been more striking. Extreme caution had replaced high hopes. Even the tone of voice was strained and muted. "Can the opposition have been this strong?" many bishops of the majority were asking. "What kind of pressures have they exerted?" No one quite believed that Pope Paul had turned his back on his expressed convictions; but he was not acting like himself. His discourse did little, at the time, to buoy the spirits of the majority.

After the ceremony, one bishop told a journalist: "The conclave thought it elected John XXIII; it got another Pius IX." Many bishops —especially those displeased with the loss of the vote on religious liberty—refused to comment to the press on their views of the second session. Some outstanding theologians thought it the better part of prudence to say nothing, for what they would have to say would be too distressing.

But Patriarch Maximos IV Saïgh recalled for Father Edward Duff, S.J., of the Religious News Service, counsel Pope Paul had recently given the Oriental bishops: "You think that things are not going fast enough? Patience. One can impose reforms peremptorily. But nothing is achieved if the mentalities and the individuals are not changed. That needs time: history teaches us so." One might interpret Pope Paul's actions during the last month of the second session, therefore, as an easing of the demands he was making on "mentalities and individuals." He would do what some wanted. He would go along quietly with those with whom he did not agree. He would trust the majority to interpret his intentions generously—for the majority did not live in a world of fears, as the minority did. Meanwhile, he would show that the windows of the Church were already open, and that much could be done even at the present level of achievement. The Council was becoming too disheartening for the minority; very well, then, other methods of *aggiornamento* can be used, which seem less threatening. The Pope nourished thoughts of his own. His discourse temporized.

> . . . So many of the Council's results have not yet come to maturity, but are as grains of wheat cast into the furrows, awaiting their effective and fruitful development, which will be granted only in the future through new mysterious manifestations of the divine goodness. . . .
>
> The Church wished to grow in her consciousness and understanding of herself. See how, on the very level of her pastors and teachers, she has begun a profound meditation on that mystery from which she draws her origin and form. The meditation is not finished, but the very difficulty of concluding it reminds us of the depth and breadth of this doctrine, and stimulates each of us. . . .
>
> Let us rejoice, my brothers, for when was the Church ever so aware

of herself, so in love with Christ, so blessed, so united, so willing to imitate Him, so ready to fulfill His mission? Let us rejoice, my brothers, for we have learned to understand one another and to deal with one another, and, though we were almost strangers, through the process of union we have become friends.

The Pope then showed his grasp of the shift in point of view which had occurred at the Council. He emphasized freedom, and based authority on "love, harmony, and mutual respect" rather than on power:

And do we not, perhaps, see that if the canon law which governs the Church is developed, its growth will extend in two directions? It will accord to every person and office in the Church both greater dignity and greater power of development, and at the same time will strengthen, as it were, according to the intrinsic demands of love, of harmony, and of mutual respect, the power which unites, through hierarchical government, the whole community of the faithful. We must confess that this Council is a great achievement, a great gift of God to His Church, if our minds have been resolutely turned toward these thoughts and these proposals.

Pope Paul noted two things about the Council's work:

. . . it has been laborious and, above all, it has enjoyed freedom of expression. This twofold characteristic which marks this Council and which will set an example for the future seems to us worthy of emphasis. This is the way that the holy Church works today at the highest and most significant stage of its development.

He rejoiced at the promulgation of the constitution on the liturgy: "The first in order of intrinsic excellence and importance for the life of the Church." Many bishops had not grasped that point at the beginning of the Council. Some of the American bishops, for example, were very disappointed when so trivial a subject appeared in 1962 as the first business of the Council; they thought liturgy meant ceremony, ritual, when to bow and not to bow, and ancient lore. But the constitution of her worship is primary in the life of the Church.

For the Church is a religious society, a community at prayer. It is composed of people with a flourishing interior life and spirituality that is nourished by faith and grace.

Without worship, the Church is a power structure like other power structures; in worship, she is truest to herself—not an introverted worship, but a worship expressing itself in every aspect of her life. Worship is "a lifegiving force."

> The other fruit, not of small value, that the Council has produced is the decree on the communications media—an indication of the capacity of the Church to unite the interior and exterior life, contemplation and action, prayer and active apostolate.

Then the Pope hurried on. He seemed to refer to the votes of October 30—though few grasped this allusion at the time:

> This is not all. The Council has labored much. As you all know, it has addressed itself to many questions whose solutions are in part virtually formulated in authoritative decisions, which will be published in due time, after the work on the topics to which they belong is completed.

The party of renewal and reform had been hoping for a long Council, to work just that "change in mentalities and individuals" of which the Pope had spoken to the Oriental bishops. But now Pope Paul was saying:

> Other questions are still subject to further studies and discussions. We hope that the third session in the autumn of next year will bring them to completion.

He hoped the conciliar commissions "in whose work We place so much hope" would prepare:

> in accordance with the words of the Fathers, as expressed especially in the general congregations, proposals profoundly studied, accurately formulated, and suitably condensed and abbreviated so that the discussion, while remaining always free, may be rendered easier and more brief.

The first item of business would be the question of divine Revelation, discussed at the first session, and here the Pope hoped for:

> directives to guide the biblical, patristic, and theological studies which Catholic thought, faithful to ecclesiastical teaching and vitalized by every good modern scientific tool, will want to promote earnestly, prudently and with confidence.

"Such also," he read on,

> is the great and complex question of the episcopacy which, in both logical order and importance, is the primary concern of this Second Vatican Ecumenical Council, a council which, as we should never forget, is the natural continuation and complement of the First Vatican Council.

The Pope did not use the word "collegiality," nor did he take sides, but he did try to dispel certain fears.

> The episcopacy is not an institution independent of, or separated from, or, still less, antagonistic to the supreme pontificate of Peter, but with Peter and under him it strives for the common good and the supreme end of the Church. The coordinated hierarchy will thus be strengthened not undermined, its inner collaboration will be increased not lessened, its apostolic effectiveness enhanced not impeded, its mutual charity stirred up not stifled. We are sure that on a subject of such importance the Council will have much to say that will bring consolation and light.

He next made the only comment that won applause from the Council—applause that began toward the back and gathered momentum—as he spoke on the Blessed Virgin Mary, and her place in this Council in the schema on the Church. "After Christ her place in the Church is the most exalted, and also the one closest to us, so that we can honor her with the title *Mater Ecclesiae* to her glory and to our benefit."

The Pope, conspicuously, did not refer to ecumenism, the chapter on the Jews, or religious liberty, only of "many other" questions which the Council "was unable to treat. . . ."

> We will see to it that these questions are subjected to a thorough and deeper re-examination so as to be able to present to the next session of the Council schemata which are short and so worded that it will not be difficult to obtain a judgment of the Council on certain fundamental propositions.

Pope Paul did not much comfort the majority when he added: "It will be left to the postconciliar commissions to explain these principles more fully and to work out their practical implementation," even when he added what may have been intended as a consoling promise. For his words seemed at the time too open to a minimalist, curial interpretation. And they were merely promises, not the action that many thought should have already taken place:

> In this work, which will follow the Council, the collaboration of the episcopacy, in new ways required by the needs and the organic nature of the Church, will be very precious to Us. Naturally it will be a source of joy to Us to choose from among the bishops of the world and from the ranks of the religious orders, as was done for the preparatory commissions of the Council, distinguished and expert brethren who, along with qualified members of the Sacred College, will bring Us their counsel and help to translate into fitting and specific norms the general decisions of the Council.

The Pope was reading a prepared text, and the bishops and newsmen were following it. But where these mimeographed translations came to an end, the Pope had one more sheet to read. It broke over the assembly like a fourth-of-July rocket in the night; it seemed showy, rather than substantial. But it was to change the frame of reference for the estimation of Pope Paul's papacy. He announced that he would go to Jerusalem.

> We are so convinced that for the final happy conclusion of this Council prayers and good works are necessary, that after careful deliberation and much prayer We have decided to become a pilgrim Ourselves in the land of Jesus Our Lord. In fact, if God assists Us, We wish to go to Palestine in January to honor personally, in the holy places where Christ was born, lived, died, and ascended to heaven after His Resurrection, the first mysteries of our Faith: the Incarnation and the Redemption.

At the announcement, Cardinal Ottaviani, who was beside the Pope, listened intently; Archbishop Dante, the papal master of ceremonies, did a double-take that was either total astonishment or excellent simulation. Later on, good sources said that only three cardinals in the Vatican had known the secret—and kept it secret. The astonishment was, therefore, almost universal. The joy was marred by pessimism about what had happened to the Council; many were saying, "smoke screen." But the trip was to prove a new opening of the Church, in its own right.

That afternoon, evening, and the next morning, most of the bishops of the world left for their homes. Meanwhile, certain factions in the Curia tried to block the trip to the Holy Land—and above all the encounter with the Orthodox Patriarch Athenagoras, who, it soon developed, was announcing his delight at the possibility of meeting Paul in Jerusalem. Emissaries flew back and forth between Patriarch and Pope. To halt the meeting, a false story was "leaked" to a French newspaper that Athenagoras had denied wanting to meet the Pope. *Il Tempo* warned daily of possible assassination, Arab threats, the impossibility of guaranteeing the Pope's security. But Paul was determined to go. And, soon, attempts to halt him slackened.

III

The second session, in immediate, human terms, was a failure. Whatever may be its long-term effects or the hidden fruits of its labors, it did not live up to the expectations which it could have fulfilled. Perhaps, for example, it will not be disrespectful to note that the bishops of the world did not seem to show themselves worthy of co-government with the Pope. They did not organize themselves; they did not produce sustained leadership; they had not yet "come of age." Too many waited for "others" to act; too few showed independence and leadership; too many shunned "politics." And in a council of the Church, bishops can afford to be *a*political only at the cost of the work they are called to do. A council is a joint effort of many men; the task of unifying such an effort, and of making insights over into law, requires political skill. Good intentions are not enough, nor good speeches. When the Council Fathers do not make into law the witness of their conscience, they fail the Church.

To an observer from outside, the Council seemed to need three parliamentary reforms; it may not be disrespectful to suggest them for consideration. The first is a method for making a point of order. Any Council Father, it seems, should be able to bring a motion to the floor, alone or seconded by ten or twenty others. The Council would then be obliged to act on such a motion: to take a vote, to receive an account of the conduct of the authorities, to commission a small group to prepare a special report, etc. At present, the Council seems too inflexible and unresponsive to the freedom of the bishops on the floor. Many had questions during the second session, to which they had no way of requesting public answers.

The second need is for greater discipline over the commissions. If the commissions do not work quickly enough, or do not handle the suggestions of the Fathers sensitively enough, then the majority must have some means of directing the commissions, without being required to face the prospect of starting work all over again at a later session. At the second session, many of the Council Fathers requested the formation of new commissions, since the consensus of the Council had outrun the limits of the first session, when the commissions were elected. Pope Paul responded by allowing the election of four new members to each commission, to which he himself added another. This compromise eased the situation slightly but it did not solve the fundamental problem. Those in positions of the greatest power on the commissions—the chairmen of the commissions and the vice-chairmen—do not always represent the mind of the majority. It is just at this point that the Council has been frustrated. On the other hand, the heads of the commissions cannot be replaced without suffering personal humiliation. Moreover, some have labored long for the Gospels and, far from seeing their own efforts as a stumbling block to the good of the Church, believe their role is to save the Church from serious mistakes. It is unlikely that they would voluntarily offer their resignation, and insist on it until the Pope is forced to accept it. Nor should one ask that of anyone. It seems, therefore, that the present structure of the conciliar commissions is inevitable. A sense of political reality leads one to acquiesce in it.

The third need for reform in the Council concerns the lack of organization among the majority. It is essential that some bishops, known or unknown, young or old, begin the hard, thankless work of organizing those who agree on most issues into a political alternative to the Roman Curia. The mere sentiment of a great number of Council Fathers is not a political reality of the first importance. Structures are lacking, not good intentions. To this end, it would seem advisable for the para-senate, informally organized among the various national episcopal conferences, to be developed into a more formal and powerful unit. The delegates from each national episcopal conference should be elected with the utmost seriousness, so as to have the full confidence of their conferences. These delegates should be endowed with as much power as the national episcopal conferences can bring themselves to authorize. This body, which during the second session was already meeting once a week, could continue to meet during the third session, but its proceedings should be public. It should offer guidance and firmness to the assembly. It should organize inquiries into the procedure on the floor and behind the scenes, which are necessary to keep the work of the Council honest and swiftly moving. This para-senate would represent an initiative of the world's bishops worthy of the attention of the Pope. The Pope could then feel that he has a reliable, realistic alternative to reliance upon his own Curia. As it now stands, to whom can he turn? The majority have sent him letters and made good speeches on the floor. But can he rely on them day after day, week after week, month after month; and what sort of moral and active strength can they offer him?

The bishops of the world have not yet understood their own power, nor shown the courage and resolution to take practical political initiatives. Only realities count, in this case, structural realities. The world's bishops seem to have been asked by Providence to organize themselves into a new structure, which exposes the teachings of the Gospels in the best possible light. The para-senate is the germ of this new life. It should be a model of freedom, openness of debate, trust in one another, ruthless honesty about the Church and about the world in which we live, and wisdom in practical action. The para-senate should become the most important force at the third session of the Council.

Meanwhile, it is altogether possible that the Second Vatican Council has already gone as far as it can go in our generation. It is possible that non-historical orthodoxy has been backed up against a wall. Intellectually and morally, it has taken a serious drubbing on the floor. It would seem to be un-Christian and perhaps undignified to run it into the ground. Perhaps it is better to let the minority have a respite, and salve its pride. New energies have been released in the Church. Theologies other than non-historical orthodoxy now have the right to exist. Given this open chance, they cannot fail to embarrass their predecessor; in an open fight, non-historical orthodoxy is doomed. If the majority, therefore, has faith in its own cause, it can afford to close the Vatican Council with the openness and freedom it has achieved. Perhaps Pope Paul himself has come to understand this, and thus has showed a willingness to bring the Council to a rapid close.

Of course, this would mean that the vast educational process which the bishops of the world have been undergoing would come now to a sudden end. Instead of a graduate school of five or six years' duration, they would have had exposure to the best thinking in the

Church for but three brief sessions. Nevertheless, most of the bishops will never be the same. Perhaps it is enough that in seminaries all over the world the history of the Council has been avidly read. The theologians whose works influenced the outcome of the Council will be studied with intensity. Reform and renewal have in fact taken a grip on the Church.

After the session, Pope Paul was to show that the Council has already given the bishops of the world many powers to prosecute reform and renewal in their own dioceses, even without further legislation. The bishops of the world can give their people a worship the people can understand. The bishops of the world can go to the poor of their dioceses, to the oppressed, to those who suffer from racial and economic injustice, with a new sense of humility and service. They can speak with believers of all faiths and with nonbelievers on a common ground of good will, mutual respect, and fellowship. Pope Paul himself, in Palestine, took the Catholic Church out into the world. There is no reason why the whole Church, and Catholic theology, cannot follow him there. With the Pope, churchmen have only to pass outside the doors, begin to learn, and begin to speak. If they have the accents of Christ, men will understand. Isn't that the meaning of the joyous reception given Pope John's Council and Pope Paul's trip to Jerusalem, among all men of good will?

IV

Thus, nearly everything the Pope was to do after the session was to show that his convictions lay with the partisans of renewal and reform. He began to use Italian rather than Latin in the blessings he bestowed on the people. He held dialogue Masses in St. Peter's, and once, at least, distributed holy communion himself to the people. He went out at Christmastime to one of Rome's workers' parishes to celebrate Mass. He visited children in a hospital, and allowed L'Osservatore Romano to reprint photographs of his visit to the parish and the hospital. Paul consented to the efforts of the Secretariat for Christian Unity to arrange the visit with Patriarch Athenagoras in Jerusalem—the first encounter in five centuries between Patriarch and Pope, after nine centuries of schism. In the crowded streets—where he seemed in danger for his life—he conducted himself with skill, dignity, sweetness, and self-possession, though it must be remarked that he offended Jewish sensibilities by refusing even to use the word "Israel," by his unnecessary defense of Pius XII, and by not visiting the shrine for those who died under the Nazis—as Cardinal Tisserant did.

Pope Paul is obviously a shy man. He greets people with his head inclined slightly forward, as though it is an effort to bear their scrutiny, as though he would rather be alone, and yet, at the same time, loves to be with them as their pastor. His shyness makes him genuine; far from being a showman, he is making an effort to manifest the affection which it is not easy for him to bring to the surface.

The Pope's visit with Athenagoras proved successful, despite the efforts of some of their advisers to block it. The two men met in Jerusalem, embraced, gripped each other's hands warmly, looked into each other's eyes, and spoke words of charity, compassion and hope. The peoples of the world rejoiced, showing again how far in advance of events is the longing of the people. Two thousand pressmen followed the Pope; the world was in suspense.

On his return to Rome, the Pope found lines of people through which it took him three hours to drive, 100,000 Romans many of whom had waited four hours in the January cold to greet their bishop. The welcome was beyond all expectation. The joy and enthusiasm were spontaneous and genuine. The Pope stood alone on the back of his open car, his head slightly inclined, a sad but pleased smile on his lips, his arms raised almost continually aloft in greeting. For three hours in the cold, this slim man of sixty-six greeted his people. What must have been his joy and sense of confidence to realize that these were the people who had so dearly loved Pope John; and that it had once seemed they might not accept another for many years. And yet they were already full of joy because of the risk run by their Pope: the unheard-of flight by plane, away from Rome, to the Holy Land, to greet Moslem and Jewish heads of state, a "venerable brother" of a "sister church," under the protection of secular police.

Pope John XXIII had stirred Rome's imagination simply by driving across the city to visit the prisoners of Regina Coeli. Within less than a year, Pope Paul was shattering precedent by flying to Jerusalem; in six months he had done the seemingly impossible and come into his own. He would not go down in history as the follower of John XXIII, but as the first Pope to visit the Holy Land in nearly two thousand years.

Pope Paul was living out in action the principles of ecumenism which the Council was discussing. He was calling a schismatic Patriarch his "brother," and schismatic churches "sister churches." He spoke, even, of Eastern Orthodoxy and Roman Catholicism as "two pillars" of Christianity. He spoke of the one God and ruler of the universe, to whom both Moslems and Jews could look as well as Christians, thus bringing within the horizon of one vision the three great religious traditions of the world: Christianity, Judaism, and Islamism. Rome would never be the same. Without giving way to syncretism, still remaining faithful to herself, and merely by being open and appreciative, the Church found herself on a new path.

The perspective of the future was breathtaking. Suppose that "tomorrow" the Patriarchs of Moscow and Constantinople, the Archbishop of Canterbury, and the Pope were to sit down together and agree to unite "under Peter," with the same relationship to the Pope as the apostles had to Peter. Would Rome be willing to shed all its *Romanità* and return to an earlier simplicity of life, unity, and authority? For example, even concerning "primacy of jurisdiction," it is not "primacy" which seems to be the stumbling block, but "jurisdiction." Why should a Christian Church have to be juridical? The whole concept is a relatively late Spanish-Italian development. There are other forms of life, unity, and authority than juridical forms, of greater internal force.

On November 29, Patriarch Elias Zoghby of Egypt sketched the possibilities of development between East and West.

> Today the Catholic and Orthodox Churches believe that they are very similar despite nine centuries of division and separate evolution. Originally, there would have been no division if each Church had not followed the two temporal powers. Because no dialogue was then possible, minor points assumed major proportions. The Latin Church thought that primacy was being denied; Eastern Churches suspected an intention of domination under the pretext of the primacy. Papal primacy, always accepted in the East, was seen as an attempt to extend a local Church to the universal Church. The Orientals resisted because they had managed their own affairs by synodal rule for ten centuries without papal opposition. Perhaps Providence permitted this situation lest the Church be impoverished by the loss of the East's complementary Apostolic Traditions. Dialogue has gradually become possible, and should be accompanied by effort at decentralization in the West, as begun in this Council, and at relative centralization in

the East, so that traditional collegiality can be exercised in union with the Pope.

But meanwhile the second session had been an almost universal disappointment. Jews in America were deeply troubled by the refusal of the Council to take a vote on the chapter on the Jews. Other Americans were bitterly disappointed by the failure of the Council to speak clearly on the issue of religious liberty, which had been so eloquently presented to it. The great decisions of October 30 had been allowed to be clouded, and stood in need of reclarification. The debate about the reform of the Curia and the Holy Office had been allowed to end in words, not actions. The request signed by so many hundred bishops that the Pope name a universal Senate of Bishops still remained at the end of the Council—though it might not long remain so—a piece of paper on the Pope's desk. The request that the commissions of the Council be reorganized so as to represent more accurately the mind of the Council was met with a compromise that pleased no one. As the Council seemed stymied—or at least so "balanced" as no longer to be making much forward motion, however much hard, effective work it was doing in solidifying its gains— Pope Paul was showing how far open the windows had already been thrown. As he visited the old Jerusalem, he cast an image of the new city which Roman Catholicism had become. Perhaps it is not inappropriate to conclude our history by reflecting on the new constitution of the worship of that city.

V

At the first session of the Council, owing largely to behind-the-scenes efforts of two American bishops, one of whom was Archbishop Paul J. Hallinan of Atlanta, a member of the liturgical commission, a vote had been taken in approval of the first chapter of the schema on liturgy. That first chapter contained the general principles of the entire document. They were revolutionary principles, and by their direction and tone established the character of the entire Council.

The first chapter on the liturgy envisaged the Church as a community—a community of men who together worship God, and learn to respect and cherish each other. It stressed the importance of the conscious and active efforts of each man who assists in the worship of God, and envisaged a worship that is intelligent and suited to the conditions of the world in which men live. It recognized the diversity of that world, and the view that Catholic worship should be diverse in different parts of that world. Further, it established the principle of "practical collegiality": that regional conferences of bishops should, with the approval of the Holy See, make the decisions about the most telling form of worship for their own region. It decreed that part of Catholic worship should be conducted in the mother tongue of the faithful, and that preference always be given to those forms of worship that encourage the active and conscious participation of the people. The entire document on the liturgy, therefore, favored intelligence, common sense, and emphasis on personal consciousness. At the same time, it was far from being a moralistic or pelagian document; it insisted on the work that God does among men, through worship. In worship, He does more than they. In worship God acts in the hearts of men, illuminating them, teaching them, drawing them to Himself, pointing to the good of those around them.

Moreover, the schema established the principle of historical relevance. It pictured the people of God as inserted in history, a history which changes, in which men in one time or at one place might learn about God in one way, while those at another time or place might learn in another. It was an open document. It did not try to visualize a finished and completed form of worship which would be enforced on all men now and in the future. In insisted, instead, on reverence for the entire tradition of Christian worship, so that any new adaptations would be accepted only with seriousness, upon the recommendations of accurate scholarship, and to the benefit of real and concrete people living in given situations.

The most important principle in the document on the liturgy was that of personal consciousness. The choice of this principle, if implicit rather than explicit, was altogether reasonable and well-advised. The worship of God is not magic, superstition, or incantation. It is the conversation of conscious human persons with the Source of all conscious life, God Himself. Worship takes place in the depth of human consciousness. There is no short cut to it: worship that is unconscious is only routine, reflex, or illusion. For it is a pure conscience that pleases God; consciously, through insight and love, men share in God's life. Men do not know God directly. They can try to imagine what He is like, or to reason toward what He must be like, but their best approximations are only like so many arrows shooting in the direction of God, never quite reaching Him, falling back to earth. Worship leads, in the end, to humility, as it begins in humility. Man is not God, and it is this recognition which leads him to fall in silence on his knees. On the other hand, the more profound his silence, the more simple and purified his consciousness, the more he realizes that the gap between him and God is even greater than he thought. If at first he began with humility, he ends with wonder, silent adoration, and abandonment.

Yet, as St. John teaches us in his Gospel and in his letters, though God Himself is lost in a night men cannot penetrate, men can find their way safely to God by loving their fellow men. God is love. As long as men love, they are in communion with God, living the same life as God. The more they love their fellow men, the closer they are to God. They may not be able to penetrate the night in which God lives, but they are never without a neighbor they can see, love, and help.

In a moving address in Philadelphia in 1963, one of the experts who shared in the work of the liturgical document pointed out the way that community worship must affect community life. "We do not proclaim the death of the Lord, we trumpet the blasphemous triumph of Satan, if we eat of the Bread and drink of the Cup, and refuse to accept the Negro as our daily table guest. We are guilty of the body and blood of the Lord if we have no burning concern—if we do not share Christ's own love of the body and blood and spirit —for the equal living conditions and opportunities of our brothers in Christ." In America, the social need may lie in one direction; in another country, in another. But wherever the eucharist is consciously celebrated, it speaks of the fraternal bonds among all men. It is a lie to share in it without changing one's life.

Christian love—*caritas*—is concrete. It is not the vertigo of the infinite, a feeling in which the heart seems to dissolve, a loss of focus and perspective. Caritas does not move toward bliss, where all individual differences are eradicated, though such sentiment and sweet fancy are its most misleading imitations. Caritas is not intoxication, or infatuation. Caritas leads to the concrete, the individual, the different. It is realistic. It accepts its own limitations and those of the situation in which it finds itself. It does not dream of a better world in which it could live; it seeks the good in the limited world in which it does live.

Again, the peace which caritas brings is that of confidence, but not that of escape. No matter how terrible one's situation becomes, God is near. He tries those He loves. Having Him, a man has everything; lacking Him, nothing. Human history works out the hidden probabilities of the freedom with which God has gifted it. Whatever the catastrophes it encounters, or the barbarity into which it sinks, God draws good from evil—not, perhaps, to man's comfort. Men are not in history to be contented or comforted—whatever the Benthamite faith—but to be tried as in fire. The cross remains the pattern for every human life, and the eucharist remains the daily bread of this life. Worship and life are one.

Life itself is a part of worship—each act entered, every object handled, is sacramental, a gift from God. That anything at all should be! —this is the constant miracle at which some wonder. To step back from the flux of everyday, and to understand that everything has been given, is the first religious act. The alternative is obscurantist: not to raise questions, not to wonder. It is to turn away from too much light.

Albert Camus wrote that he stood on "the razor's edge" of the absurd, and wished to remain faithful in the "polar night." The liturgical attitude is very similar. Men do not see God. Faith is naked, comfortless, polar—the purer the faith, the less given to sentiment or reliance on creaturely assurance. *No one sees God.* In the silence which surrounds human life, believer and unbeliever stand on the same ground. In that silence, the believer says "yes," for he believes the universe to be an invitation, written in painful code, from a Person who is Insight and Love. Why does he believe this? At times he doesn't know. In his heart has been sown an instinct of affirmation, an instinct which insists that despite all horrible and concrete experiences to the contrary, insight and love are the controlling forces in this universe. The non-believer, with Ivan Karamazov, must say "no" either to creation or to God; the two seem to him incompatible.

There is no creature in the universe more beautiful than man. Yet the more a man grows, the more he comes to understand the limits of his own understanding, the limits of his own love. He cannot understand everything. When he chooses to love *this*, he in fact turns his attention from *that*. Limited and aware of his infidelities, a man is driven to reflect upon the sources of his drive to understand and his drive to love. For these drives are of such a nature that they seem, at times, to be greater than himself. When he is most faithful to understanding or to love, it seems that he is best able to pass "objective" judgment on himself. In their light, as it were, he is able to measure his own inadequacies. Thus, at the very peak of his spirit, at his noblest and most faithful, at the heart of his own self-identity, a man begins to suspect the presence of God. He begins to realize that the best he has comes not from himself but from an understanding and a love greater than he, in whose light his own stature is measured. At the height of his spirit, man turns to adoration.

Liturgy, in Guardini's phrase, is "all creation redeemed and at prayer." Prayer and life are one. God is "with all and in all." Nothing in the world is "profane" or "secular." Everything is a sign of God. Even from evil God draws good; even in sin (which is a turning from the light) lies a kernel of grace, which grows swiftly once God is found again.

These are the attitudes which the new constitution of the worship of the open Church tries to inculcate among the Catholic people. The constitution is the first fruit of the Council, and will affect millions for many generations. Were it the only fruit, the Council would have been worth all its hopes, pains, and disappointments.

III

THE BISHOPS OF
THE UNITED STATES

23

THE BISHOPS OF
THE UNITED STATES

I

THE SECOND VATICAN COUNCIL hit many of the bishops of the United States, in the words of one of them, "like another Pearl Harbor." "Many of us came," said Bishop Robert J. Dwyer of Reno, "expecting to be handed the traditional formulae, asked for our votes, and then sent home in a matter of weeks. It turned out rather differently."

At the first session of the Council, in the autumn of 1962, the Americans made a generally disappointing show. Between the first session and the second, their preparations with their theological experts were not as careful as, for example, those of the Canadians. They entered the second session rather timidly. But as it wore on through the long autumn of 1963, the bishops of the United States began to emerge more and more clearly as coming leaders of the Church. "After a disappointing start," Bishop G. Emmet Carter of Canada said, "they have begun to do brilliantly. By the third session, or the fourth, they will be the most important and vocal hierarchy in the world." What does their emergence mean for the Roman Catholic Church and for the United States?

From nearly everyone with whom one talked, the testimony was the same. A profound change had come over a large majority of the American bishops who attended that first, famous session of Ecumenical Council Vatican II, a change which was extended and deepened in 1963. "Of all the national groups," said a Negro archbishop from Ghana, "the Americans changed the most. They were humble and honest." An Indian archbishop said at the start of the second session: "The Americans have so much leadership to give. But they are afraid, afraid, afraid." "Of what?" I asked. "I don't know," he said. "But we are waiting for them to lead and they are not leading."

American bishops: a baffling group to talk about. It is not only that they are some 240 men of different builds, temperaments, and habits; it is also that over the years they have been surprisingly inarticulate. They are very difficult to type. Until midway through the second session, they seemed to lack cohesion; they resisted organization, both among themselves and even with their experts. For all their episcopal lives, each had been sovereign prince in his own proper diocese. True enough, they met once a year for two or three days in Washington, D.C., under the auspices of their national organization, the National Catholic Welfare Conference, but the NCWC had been extremely careful not to encroach on any individual bishop's liberty. Decisions were not binding on anyone who did not wish to be bound. A few bishops refused even to join.

The bishops, then, have experienced an autonomy given to few men in our time. They owed obedience to Rome—and no more obedient sons does Rome have, outside Ireland—but Rome was far away. Once every five years, each bishop had to go there for an accounting, and some of them might, at those times, be meek and in awe. But otherwise the bishop saw only subordinates. He had a great deal of business to attend to within his own diocese. With few exceptions, he scarcely had time, or made time, to keep up his reading. The bishops could hardly think of themselves as part of a community.

Under the conditions of the present Vatican Council, however, these princes in their own dioceses were crowded into cars and herded into buses like schoolboys. Among twenty-three hundred bishops, abbots, archbishops, patriarchs, and cardinals, the bishop from Diocese X or Diocese Y could for the first time in many years feel lost in a crowd. The effect was often relaxing. The man could become "human" again, talk as one among many, know that he alone would not be taken as speaking for the entire Church. The range of views in the Church is far wider than the views of any particular bishop; until they arrived at the Council, many American bishops had never experienced such theological diversity.

Here these bishops were forced out of their psychological isolation and "internationalized." Thrown among bishops from every region of the globe—in the Council hall, the coffee bars, the *pensioni*, the restaurants of Rome—they who had hitherto lived alone and made decisions alone came to recognize themselves as part of a community of fellow bishops, and began to live a different kind of life and make a different kind of decision. "If you had told me two years ago," Bishop Joseph M. Mueller of Sioux City, Iowa, told some bishop friends, "that I would be voting 'yes' for some of the things I have been voting for this session, I would have told you you were crazy."

Before the Council, the bishops of the United States were generally thought of as very "conservative." They appeared to be defensive, knowing little more than the seminary theology favored in Rome these last few generations. They seemed suspicious of any new movements which might upet present administrative order. Their vision of the Church seemed immobile, triumphalistic, and rationalistic. By the end of the second session, however, Bishop Warren L. Boudreaux of Lafayette, Louisiana, could plausibly assert that, while many of the Americans were still cautious, he could not count more than five convinced conservatives among them. A French historian estimated that Cardinal McIntyre of Los Angeles was "easily the most reactionary member of the Council." But by and large the overwhelming majorities in favor of reform—in the liturgy, collegiality, etc.—bear out the fact that most of the Americans were voting for Pope John XXIII's *aggiornamento*.

II

It would be easy, from certain points of view, to criticize the American bishops quite severely. But, within their own context, the American bishops have some right to be pleased with themselves. Many of them, of course, are too complacent; some seem to feel personally insecure and are sensitive to the slightest criticism. With most, it is difficult to carry on a frank, honest conversation. The context within which they judge themselves is that of their own episcopal dignity, the respect due the officers of the Church, a kind of "ecclesiastical realism," and a warm, individualistic personal piety. To this a few of them, like Bishop John J. Wright of Pittsburgh, add a sense of the intellectual superiority of Catholic theology—they take an eternal, Olympian view, high upon the summit beneath which worldly mortals grope in the darkness of the latest spirit of the age.

By their "ecclesiastical realism," many of the bishops are able to explain away any discrepancy between Catholic doctrine and Catholic practice, and to assume, until shown otherwise, that zeal for reform is "naïve" or "immature." They invoke the wisdom of centuries, and encourage adaptation to things as they are. Nowadays, almost all the bishops are "progressive," in some sense or other. But when they hear severe criticism on specific points they almost always become defensive. "It's a human church. One has to expect men to be men." They systematically give the benefit of the doubt to authority or to the *status quo*. It might be fair to say that the American bishops at the Council became enlightened conservatives, rather than progressives.

In comparison with other hierarchies of the world, the Americans frequently evidenced a certain feeling of superiority, and at the same time a startling modesty. They made no effort whatever to call attention to the financial and other help they give so generously to the Church in other countries, or to boast of their own efficiently run dioceses, schools, or crowded churches. In no sense did they try to push forward a program of their own, on the strength of their many advantages. On the other hand, observing the state of European parishes, many Americans could not help feeling that they had developed pastoral skills—particularly in holding the loyalty of men— to an exemplary degree.

Many American bishops were willing to admit that they showed less theological, programmatic unity than the Germans or the French, and some agreed that they had much to learn from Northern Europeans in theological sophistication. On the other hand, almost all felt that their own dioceses were better run; and their own national hierarchical organization seemed to them less dictatorial. The American cardinals neither wield, nor try to wield, quite the authority over their fellow bishops that the cardinals of many other lands do. The public unanimity of some national hierarchies at the Council seemed to the Americans suspiciously like the exercise of authority from above, rather than an accurate expression of the sentiments of all the bishops of those nations.

Finally, it began to be obvious on the floor of the Council that, when the Americans spoke, they ordinarily spoke well and to the point. Cardinals Spellman and McIntyre did not make a good impression. But Cardinals Ritter and Meyer spoke with learning and balance. Moreover, time after time in the last four weeks of the second session the talks of American bishops were greeted with the applause of the assembly. After the session, the European press— *Informations Catholiques*, the London *Observer*, the London *Tablet* —paid high tribute to the performance of the Americans.

On a more personal level, in conversation, the American bishops seemed generally kind and symathetic; only a few seemed abrupt or misanthropic. Not all, of course, would grant interviews; some are uncommonly afraid of the press, and a few afraid even of laymen. As often as we could, my wife and I visited with them at their lodgings around the city. Sometimes we drove out to the Hotel Residence Palace in Parioli, climbing up the Salita dei Parioli, just as the setting sun flared the sky behind St. Peter's and bathed the tile roofs of Rome in their evening red; sometimes to the stately Cavalieri Hilton guarding Rome like a fortress on a medieval hill; sometimes to a buff-walled *pensione* in the twisting streets of the Renaissance city; again to a convent on the crest of Monte Mario or Monte Verde; then to the huge Grand Hotel near the railway station, or the Flora on Via Veneto. We came to sympathize with each of the bishops we met, as we grasped hints of their views, aspirations, and difficulties.

Some of the bishops were quite nervous, at first. We, in turn, found them more genuine and friendly, less "administrative" or "efficient" than we had anticipated. Bishop Robert E. Tracy of Baton Rouge, Bishop William G. Connare of Greensburg, Pennsylvania, Bishop Robert Dwyer of Reno—we knew as we sat with them that they spoke honestly, and that they had a warm love for their people. Bishop Charles H. Helmsing of Kansas City wrote to his people regularly in his diocesan paper; the following statement is typical: "It is Sunday evening, Sept. 29, the feast of St. Michael. In a few minutes I will be offering Holy Mass, mindful that as I celebrate for the people of the Diocese of Kansas City-St. Joseph, the 11 o'clock Masses [there] will just be commencing. . . ."

In groups—for example, at the cocktail party they sponsored for the Protestant observers at the Grand Hotel—the American bishops look like nothing so much as a group of Rotarians or Lions, in neat black suits with a touch of red under the front of their Roman collars; clear-eyed, informal, jovial. They are more reserved than businessmen, less breezy, less buoyed up by the practiced self-assurance of executives. They seem less dignified and formal than a group of distinguished university professors. I can think of only one of them who has earned the epithet "pompous ass," and he is regarded even by his peers as aping prelates of lands other than our own. Most of the Americans seem capable, self-possessed, alert; a few seemed so shy and out of place that one wondered whether they could have made their way outside the ecclesiastical world.

We found two characteristics in many, but not all, of the bishops we met. The first is an unrealistic view of the Church. Many were unwilling to grapple with the politics of a parliamentary council. "We don't like to lobby," Bishop Robert F. Joyce of Burlington said at a press panel on November 28; he was red in the face, embarrassed, and patently honest. "Most of us, I think, feel that lobbying and subterfuge are all right in parliaments, but contrary to the spirit of a council. A certain amount of discretion has to be left to the chair. We wouldn't want to seem rebellious." One could read the letters which many of the bishops wrote home to their diocesan papers, and hardly suspect the infighting and maneuvering at the Council. But many of the American bishops in truth didn't know what was going on and, even when they began to suspect it, wanted no part of it. They seem to share the idea of many Americans that politics is "dirty," and that the hard work of realizing ideals in the concrete should somehow—at least in the Church—be pure and innocent. What is ironic is that, as good administrators in their own dioceses, they know the pressures of daily reality very well. But they still manage to retain in their thinking a theory of Christianity which separates what can be criticized and talked about from what can't: the real world from pure ideals.

No doubt this characteristic is inherited from the Irish spirituality which a majority of the bishops share. One archbishop admitted that it is a struggle for him to be honestly critical of the Church and especially of the Pope, even when he knows he should be critical. Irish politicians, so capable in the rugged infighting of the concrete, tend to leave the "ideal world" to their priests, and the clerics obligingly try to preserve it, hiding from themselves—or at least from their people—their own capacity for hard practicality. Joyce's Stephen Dedalus was torn by the opposition between real and ideal; it seems to be the peculiar affliction of the Irish soul—peculiarly transcended by John F. Kennedy, who learned his pragmatism at Harvard.

The second characteristic is related to the first. Nearly all the American bishops seem extraordinarily given to trying to put a good face on things, above all when it is a question of the Church. They seem extremely afraid of "giving scandal." Moreover, they seem in general to have been sheltered for many years from criticism "from below" and from disturbing views. In conversation, one soon learns to sense what issues one had better avoid with a given prelate. A theologian at the Council, for example, sat down with us for a drink after a two-hour session with four bishops. He sank into the chair and put his head in his hands: " 'Bishops,' I wanted to say, 'that's stupid!' But you don't say 'stupid' to a bishop."

On the other hand, the bishops do have a special problem. They are pastors not only of those well-developed and critical Catholics whose faith is not in danger when they confront the human factors in the Church, but also of those less stable ones, who in some measure or another need the Church to be as angelic as they imagine it to be. After a carefully worded statement about the possible danger of superstition in devotion to the Blessed Virgin Mary, for example, one American archbishop received a flood of angry letters, poems, and telephone calls from persons who had seen the wire-service release. They accused him of turning his back on Mary and of, somehow, being a dupe of Communism. The archbishop knew some of these letter writers personally. He was sorry the headline put over his statement was inflammatory, and perhaps sorry he had said anything. "They are my people, too," he said.

Roman Catholicism, in America as elsewhere, is often tempered to the weak reeds and the smoldering flax. The intelligent and the critical sometimes can scarcely find a place in her. The bishops at times become so habituated to dealing with the less-critical and less-demanding Catholic that they treat the inquisitive with suspicion, as if they were failing in loyalty or docility. The images of "shepherd," "sheep," and "flock" do not quite apply to human beings; but the defensive and unready pastor is liable to push them pretty far. The American professional scene is filled with countless "fallen-away Catholics" who could no longer tolerate such mediocrity.

The American bishops manifest, in short, a certain simplicity of character: they are certain of belonging to the one, true Church, and are neither critical nor restless. Whatever they might be as realtors, administrators, or local politicians, their spirituality expresses itself in pious, triumphant, loyal, and yet modest speech. Although they helped vote the new constitution on the liturgy into effect, very few of them have been formed by a liturgical spirituality. One can hear echoes of nineteenth-century spiritual books in their judgments—the categories of Sulpician seminary formation: pride versus humility, divine action versus human action, the Spirit versus the world, obedience, loyalty, fidelity to duty—colored by the easy familiarity and casualness of the American experience. Thus the American bishops, by and large, give evidence of a piety neither as severe as that of old Europe, nor as suited to the American character as it might be if seminary education were not reductively European; their piety is halfway between Europe's and America's.

Finally, those very few of them who read widely tend toward the ideals of the "well-rounded man" and that classical, rhetorical education which is associated with the common rooms of nineteenth-century English universities or with American latin schools. The books they quote, the anecdotes with which they spice their conversation, reveal what John Cogley has called a "rectory culture," which deserves a fictional chronicler. It is pleasant and refined, and is best enjoyed over a good dinner served on Irish linen and accompanied by a bottle of special wine once discovered on a long-ago excursion in Italy or France.

III

The greatest achievement of the American bishops at the Council is, ironically, one which few of them appreciate. Under the direction of Bishop Albert R. Zuroweste of Belleville, Illinois, the bishops invited a panel of eight to ten theological experts to give an hour of their time every working day to a public conference for the press. Any questions were fair, and the answers were generally direct and frank. The sessions became so lively, in fact, that the basement hall of the USO building on Via della Conciliazione, where they were held, could hardly contain the pressmen, bishops, Protestant observers, theologians of other languages, seminarians, and visitors who came to listen. That room became the center from which hundreds of millions of English-speaking peoples around the world received analyses, explanatory metaphors, and comments about the progress of the Council. As one Australian journalist said, thanking the American bishops at the final conference: "What has been said in this panel probably has done more to shape the Council than what has been done anywhere else except in St. Peter's."

In their relations with the press, however, several new aspects of the character of the American bishops came to light. For the most part, they were uncomfortable, unused to giving an account of themselves to the public, and uncertain about the value of mass communications. It was as though they were somewhat disdainful, not only of the press, but of the non-Catholic world—as if they felt sure they would be misquoted, misunderstood, or badly handled. It was difficult for the bishops to grasp that the reading public was not hostile, but wished to hear what they had to say. The uncertainty of the bishops came out in many ways, but especially in their use of sarcasm. The words "so-called," "immature," "half-baked" and the like dot their polemical prose.

Even Bishop Zuroweste, after the second session had concluded, sent a long, sarcastic letter to a certain magazine to complain of its coverage of the conclusion of the Council, and afterward released his letter to the press. The Bishop expressed a desire to speak with justice and charity, but the tone of his letter was harsh and picayune. It revealed his ignorance of that magazine's system, for he regularly blamed "your reporter," overlooking the fact that its stories are written by an editorial staff from material sent by more than one reporter in the field. More than that, Bishop Zuroweste ridiculed this hypothetical reporter.

Similarly, Archbishop John J. Krol of Philadelphia, one of the five Undersecretaries of the Council and one of the most powerful Americans in Rome, began a press conference on October 30 with several remarks about his policy of not talking to the press during the Council; he said he was present only as a favor to Bishop Zuroweste. The reporting of the Council until then seemed to him like the work of "cub reporters" on an assignment beyond their powers. He pictured the Church as an anvil on which hostile forces beat in vain. And, no doubt because of nervousness rather than ill will, he let slip several insulting remarks to the reporter from the *New York Times*.

Archbishop Krol is personally an extremely kind man; he is of imposing height, young, strong-willed, energetic. At the concluding ceremony of the second session, he was the only prelate whom Cardinal Ottaviani, standing at the Pope's right, broke ranks to greet. The Archbishop, moreover, has a deep pastoral sense, as "pastoral" was understood by spiritual writers of the last century: intensely inward-looking, individualistic, docile to authority. I linger on him because he will loom ever larger on the American Catholic scene as the years go on, and because his surprising remarks, which seemed to take the "secular" press as hostile and incompetent, are symptomatic of the state of siege under which many of the bishops grew to manhood.

Some observers at the Council were very proud of the younger group of American bishops, especially in the South and West: Archbishop Hallinan and Bishops Tracy, Reed, Buswell, and others come to mind. They looked to them for a much more open and creative future in America Catholicism. But other observers were not yet so optimistic about the new generation of bishops. These bishops seemed, of course, more widely read, more modern, more familiar with American secular traditions than the older stock of bishops from the Northeast. Some of them lived in areas where the Church was poorer and in a minority; they seemed to have had a more provocative seminary education. Several of them had been Newman Club chaplains, and publicly rejoiced in the experience of a secular campus. But they still seemed to be overawed by the older stamp of bishop. Their steps forward seemed partial, hesitant, and even defensive. They spent a great deal of energy trying to appear cautious, prudent, and not too far out of line. When they did advance a little, they tried not to call too much attention to themselves.

The overall picture of the American bishops, therefore, is that they are much closer to the wide mass of their people than to the critical, active lay journalists, scholars, and artists. In a sense, their advances during the Second Vatican Council may have made some of them more of a menace to Catholic intellectual life in America than formerly. For some now give the appearance of being progressive, but have not—and cannot be expected to have—undergone a major intellectual conversion. The spirit of many still is that of non-historical orthodoxy. A reversion to earlier ways, after a few years, is always a possibility. For in the new freedom brought about by the Council, new creative movements—and new crises—are bound to be precipitated. Cautious bishops, faced with a decision, are apt to stifle freedom.

IV

The Achilles heel of the American bishops is their uncritical loyalty. They seem to prefer loyalty to honesty. Their first impulse

in meeting criticism is to defend existing practices, or to justify established positions. They seem to be more loyal to the abstraction "The
Church" than to their own way of thinking. Their first intellectual
goal is objective alignment with what they remember of the teaching
of the Church; one rarely observes them venturing first to come to
a position of their own. As a consequence, few of the bishops give
the impression of having interiorized the mysteries of faith in the
depths of their intelligence; few seem to have achieved an intellectual
synthesis. Most appear to have trained their memories and their
reflexes deeply and personally, so that "the right answer" will be
available when they need to look for it. Their faith and their explanations of the faith are sincere. But the bishops are more like pupils
than teachers, passive recipients than active, penetrating thinkers.

On the other hand, the American bishops seem generally to be
men of common sense and good intelligence. Faced with several
alternatives in an argument, they will not necessarily act by reflex
so as to choose what they had chosen before. Most of them weighed
the arguments at the Council, and responded flexibly. "Many a
bishop," Bishop Tracy wrote to his people in Baton Rouge, "revised
the attitudes of a lifetime on certain reforms, once he saw the mood
and spirit of the Council; hence the big votes which were all but
unanimous on most points."

Many of the Americans resented being labeled as "progressive" or
"conservative," and insisted that they were "progressive" on some
points, "conservative" on others. They were not deciding issues pro-
foundly or systematically but by common sense.

For this reason, it is not certain just how deeply all the American
bishops have been affected by Pope John's renewal. Might their
docility to "the mood and spirit of the Council" change to another
mood and spirit once the Council has concluded? Some of the
stronger voices, like those of Cardinals Ritter and Meyer, Bishop
Helmsing on ecumenism, Archbishop Hallinan on liturgy, are sure
not to fail. Cardinal McIntyre is also to be admired, on the other
side, for his resistance to change; he has publicly warned that the
new constitution on the liturgy will not be implemented in his diocese
for a long time. The American Church has room for bishops who are
faithful to their own ideas, whatever the others are doing; his stalwart
indocility should work as a force for diversity and variety in American
Catholic life.

For years, many American bishops failed to come to the assistance of the forces of renewal and reform in the United States. St. John's Abbey, in Collegeville, Minnesota, the center of the liturgical movement in America, was long made to bear the burden of suspicion and harassment. Father H. A. Reinhold fought for almost thirty years against much opposition, and many another liturgist of those days remembers the long uphill fight. Readers of *Cross Currents* or *The Commonweal* are among those who will have to make the least adjustment to the era of renewal and reform; the issues fought out in the Council have long been aired in their pages. Few American bishops came to the defense of John Courtney Murray when his ideas on religious liberty were under fire. Just five years ago, those Catholics who took part in ecumenical work had to do so surreptitiously and under suspicion.

The lack of intellectual boldness and creativity among the American bishops over the past generation was no doubt responsible for their initial lack of preparation at the Council. On the other hand, the openness, modesty, and piety of the Americans made them docile once the leadership of the Church insisted on renewal and reform. Such docility is thus a two-edged sword. It teaches Americans flexibility before the "mind of the Church"; but it deprives them of leadership in helping the Church to form that mind, and it penalizes the creative forces in American Catholic intellectual life which might have made a significant contribution to that task many years ago.

V

For over a century, the American bishops have been withdrawn from the problems of the universal Church, and preoccupied with the building up of parishes and dioceses of the United States. At the time of the First Vatican Council in 1869 there were between four and five million Catholics in the United States; by the time of the Second Vatican Council there were between forty and fifty million. At Vatican I, there were some 60 bishops in the United States; for Vatican II, there are some 240. In 1869, America was still a mission country; the theological controversies of Europe were "quite remote from their daily concerns and ministry." The Second Vatican Council has marked the crossing of the threshold, as the Americans have stepped outward to confront the theological and practical issues which trouble the universal Church.

It is not the inquisitiveness or restlessness of the Americans which led them to this new awakening. Like Americans in general, they seem to have been dragged almost unwillingly into "foreign entanglements." For years they have been extraordinarily generous with men and money for churches in other lands. But they have not until recently permitted themselves to become intellectually involved in the problems of the universal Church. They have not penetrated the Catholic faith from the point of view of the American experience, and thus presented to the world a new style of Catholic life, a new cultural arrangement of faith, sensibility, intelligence, and life. The American bishops have begun to emerge as leaders of the universal Church, not so much because of their own theological energy, as because of the pre-eminence of the United States in world affairs.

The basic modern experiences of non-ideological democracy, pluralism, advanced and widespread education, the wealth and homogenization produced by technology, have been felt in the United States almost a generation before they are being felt in other lands. The phenomenon of "Americanization" is world-wide. Often in spite of themselves, non-Americans look to the United States for leadership; when the United States does not provide leadership, a vacuum is often created.

At the Second Vatican Council, the first thrust of leadership came from the Lowlands, France, and Germany; the mission bishops of Africa and Asia came to its support more forcefully than the Americans. But this first thrust was largely in the name of freedom, to assure diversity and openness in the Church. When once its goals had been achieved, that leadership faltered. How shall the bishops of the world be organized? Under what rules should a Senate of Bishops be run? What are the methods of freedom? How does one acquire the spirit of respect for law and order without long, detailed lists of laws and sanctions? The American experience has given ample testimony to the rewards of answering these questions in certain ways. But the American bishops seem unfamiliar with the theories behind these answers. They have for so long placed themselves in opposition to secular philosophy in America, and looked to Rome for their theories of law and liberty, that they are ill-prepared to speak with confidence about the American experience. Just at the point where the Council needs their wisdom, they are almost mute.

Nevertheless, at the second session the bishops began to be aware of the philosophical and theological richness latent in the American experience. When they spoke of ecumenism or of religious liberty, or of the role of the laity in the Church, they began to discover how far in advance of many other bishops of the world they were. After John Cogley, for example, spoke to the African bishops, many of the Americans, too, "discovered" him. After years in the Catholic Worker movement and at *The Commonweal*, during which many diocesan papers were subtly or openly disdainful of his efforts, Mr. Cogley found himself suddenly a symbol of American Catholic achievement.

Similarly, many of the Americans at the Council eagerly read Daniel Callahan's book, *The Mind of the Catholic Layman*. The bishop of Fort Wayne-South Bend, for example, Bishop Leo Pursley, called it "a good book, honestly and ably written, well researched and documented, absorbingly interesting." He wrote in *Our Sunday Visitor*: "Of course it is a bit depressing to be told, after upwards of forty years in the service of the Church and the people of God, that you are not quite adequate to the present needs, standards, stature and status, of the laity, but I believe sincerely that we are never too old to learn and I am ready always to listen to an enlightened and a zealous laity. For them we exist."

Bishop Pursley was not sure how many laymen Mr. Callahan spoke for, "but that question, to which there is probably no answer at all, does not invalidate what he has to say. I am disposed to take it seriously and advise our priests to do likewise. . . . Mr. Callahan will have to give us the kind of updated bishops and priests now in demand, for they must come from the laity and they will inevitably reflect the culture and piety of those from whom they spring. Meanwhile we must do the best we can not to fail our people."

This humility among the American bishops is extremely winning. It makes the too-sophisticated, somewhat condescending layman remember that the first apostles were not professors from Athens but fishermen from Galilee; it was their simplicity and humility before the Word of God given into their hands that changed the history of the world. Similarly in our own time, the demands of the future call for an increasingly close cooperation between bishops and articulate laymen, in universities, in the business world, and among the professional men of the parish. The adaptations in policy and program required for the age into which the Church is moving cannot be achieved without an ever deeper and more broadly based use of lay intelligence. Bishops who are humble enough to learn and laymen who are humble enough to moderate their own proposals to suit the good of the whole body of Catholics, as decided by their bishops, are the natural partners of the coming *aggiornamento*.

Moreover, if Catholic faith is to become alive and active as one of the major motivating forces of the coming international technical culture, the Catholic people must become ever more creative both in their penetration of their faith and in their professional effectiveness in the daily tasks of the world. Catholics must increasingly enter into the mainstream of world culture.

"To be a Catholic," Bishop Helmsing wrote in his *Catholic Reporter*, "is not only to be personally or individually good; it means to be involved in charity toward our neighbor, and it is for this reason that I rejoice in the growing involvement of our Catholic people in the Diocese of Kansas City-St. Joseph in all the problems of the community. Our eternity will depend on how we have learned to love, on how we have reached out to the poor and the needy and the afflicted, and the underprivileged everywhere, especially in our immediate environment. Involvement in the problems of our cities and communities is an absolute necessity for us all."

The bishops of the United States, of course, have much to learn about the workings of the human Church. They are sometimes much too uncritical and idealistic about the Church; they barely face the human sins of the Church. There are too few books written, too few sermons preached, about the ambiguities of all human action, the errors and omissions of the human Church, the special ecclesiastical, bureaucratic vices, the pride and blindness which are the hazard of all who believe they are doing God's work. They also have much to learn about the moral and even evangelical values of the secular world; they are much too inclined to attribute all the evils of our time to "secularism" and to overlook the fact that "secularistic" civilization is sometimes more fruitful for Christian morality and the Gospels than many aspects of Christian civilizations.

Have not, for example, the ideals of freedom, open discussion, pluralistic cooperation, the war on poverty and prejudice, education for all citizens, and other ideals of which the Second Vatican Council boasted been recovered for the world largely through the efforts of non-Christians, even non-believers? The debt of the Church to dedicated, conscientious agnostics and atheists, even when these were violently anti-Catholic, is enormous. It is surely permissible to believe that God works in history through believers and unbelievers alike, and perhaps achieves even the greatest good from what appears in another view as a threat to the faith.

The American bishops, in short, appear to be still too limited in their cultural outlook and their style of piety to contain the whole rushing force of Catholic faith and the Gospels in our time. Catholicism is exceedingly rich in new possibilities, which the Second Vatican Council has barely begun to tap. Perhaps some of the bishops have already caught glimpses of what can happen to the Church in history. Let the last words be those of Bishop Tracy of Baton Rouge, which in their own way typify the simple piety, the muted critical sense, and yet the tentative openness of the American bishops.

"As the long slants of sunlight fall into the north transept, you just wonder what the Fathers of Vatican I would think of the debates of Vatican II. And when you consider that some of the questions, such as reform of the Liturgy, Ecumenism, and the debate on Divine Revelation, would not even have been thought of as far back as fifteen years ago, you can imagine how the same questions would be taken were the Fathers of Vatican I able to come back and hear them!

"But from council to council, through 2000 years, God takes care of His Church in ways that men can never fathom or understand. And it is consoling to know that, in spite of the little human qualities that are bound to appear in any human gathering, the hand of the Lord is still at work, operating in His Church forever and for the good of souls."

IV

THE OPEN CHURCH

24

THE OPEN CHURCH

THERE IS A TEMPTATION, in interpreting the intellectual struggle at the Second Vatican Council, to describe the conflict as one between essentialists and existentialists, or between a notional and a pastoral theology.[1] To yield to this temptation is a serious mistake, for it makes the partisans of non-historical orthodoxy appear to be defending the heart and center of the Church, while the majority of the Council Fathers, less careful about authentic Catholic doctrine, busy themselves around the periphery of doctrine, in order to become more relevant to the world. This mistake is tragic, for the reality of the intellectual situation is quite different.

The reason it has been difficult for thinkers everywhere to analyze the struggle at the Council is a reason common to the Western intellectual world of our time: the critical problem, raised in modern philosophy by Hume and Kant, has not been solved. The relationship between abstract conceptions and concrete particulars has often been imagined as a gap which must be bridged; the theories which propose to bridge the gap usually prefer one side. Shall one be an essentialist or an existentialist? What for one man seems "objective" and "certain" to another man seems exactly what is "subjective" and "uncertain." Anglo-American philosophy often opposes the necessary truths of logic to the immediate deliverances of experience—almost the same dichotomy which plagues non-historical orthodoxy among Roman Catholics. In France and Germany, existentialists and phenomenologists have attacked logicians, rationalist philosophers, scholastics, and scientists. The curious feature in all these intellectual struggles is that each side is always convinced that it is more realistic than the others, and that its starting place is the very one that is indubitable.

In trying to chart the path for the development of the open Church of the future, Catholic philosophers and theologians need to undercut this problem as best they can. One way is to focus attention on two facts of cognitional experience. The first of these is the human drive to understand. The second is the act of insight. These are the important cognitional facts in religious experience, and in the development of religious faith in history. The words "drive to understand" and "insight" may of course sound too rationalistic for many readers, especially those who incline toward existentialist or personalist vocabularies. On the other hand, they may seem too non-conceptual, too intuitional, for those who incline to what Bertrand Russell calls the "hardheaded" philosophies. But most men would be loath to deny that they are trying to understand; few like to admit that they are without insight. No one boasts of systematic obscurantism; no one is proud of never having had an insight. It is the *experiences* of the drive to understand and of the achievement of insight that must be emphasized; most men, have shared such experiences. Readers who do not like the words "drive to understand" and "insight" may systematically substitute words of their own. In loving another person, for example, it is not enough to have benevolent feelings toward him. One must love him realistically, as he is; and this requires diligence and insight, lest one be "loving" a figment of one's own imagination.

The drive to understand is crucial to the religious impulse, for if men systematically ceased to reflect, they would cease to pray. Those, in fact, who satisfy their drive to understand *within* the circle of human life, do cease to pray.

Provided one makes an effort to confine one's aspirations and one's wonder, "naturalism" offers a satisfying way of life. But naturalism is an abstraction. Its credibility depends on the blocking of a human impulse in one's own intelligence. No one, of course, denies that many factors can contribute to the easy blocking of that impulse. Like any other human impulse, it is experienced by some people more than by others; some people are religiously tone-deaf. Others can busy themselves about so many things that the religious impulse, like the sexual impulse, can be channeled into pedestrian activity. The religious impulse is natural, common, ordinary. Men who are religious add nothing "extra" to their life; they simply allow liberty to a basic impulse, and attempt to become learned in all that it has to teach them. They try to understand themselves and their destiny. They try to be objective and realistic about themselves.

It is important to trace the root of the religious impulse to the drive to understand, for otherwise religion is left without any defense against magic, superstition, and the illusions of the dark. One need not be conceptualistic and propositional in one's religious life, although conceptions and propositions are aids to clear thinking. Human vocabulary does not suffice to express one's own self-identity or that of God. Nevertheless, men are required, under the penalty of turning away from clarity, to push conceptualization as far as it will go. Moreover, in selecting the exact point at which to halt, in adoration, men will always differ. Some are offended by the poor efforts of reason in matters concerned with God or with reason's own source; these deep matters lead them to silence rather than to speech. For at the core of the self is one's own drive to understand. This drive is superior to any particular effort to fulfill one of its demands; it cannot be exhausted in words. Moreover, no words derived from the ordinary commerce of human life suffice to describe God. Neither the source of one's own intelligence nor the Source of all intelligence can be adequately spoken of in words.

Emphasis on the drive to understand is important to religion for another reason. It is this drive which leads religious men constantly to purify their own reflections, lest they establish an idol in the place of the Living God. It is also this drive which leads them to reflect upon their own conduct, so that they might understand it in the light of their belief in God. The sacrifice which pleases God, one is told—both in Scripture and in one's own intelligence—is a pure conscience. A pure conscience is one which in thought, word, and action is faithful to the relentless drive to understand. One cannot act well without insight into all the claims of a particular situation. It is, furthermore, because conscience is related to the drive to understand that it is flexible, realistic, and not trapped in inherited patterns. Human conscience is not the Freudian superego. As religion, so also personal freedom is rooted in the drive to understand, and to live according to one's understanding. Both the religious community as a whole and the individual person develop and mature according as they are faithful to the claims of understanding; or, negatively, according as they are not fixed in counter-rational patterns. Meanwhile, because their development takes place according to the demands of a developing self-understanding, their progress is self-consistent.

Implicitly, Pope Paul VI was appealing to the drive to understand in both his opening and his closing addresses at the second session. The Church, he said, is trying to reach "a new consciousness of herself." With the experience of yet another century behind her, she is trying to discover again who and what she is. The changes recognized by such reflection may prove to be as great as those between a boy of sixteen and a man of forty-five; and there are many things from earlier times she may now regret. But self-identity will remain. To change in history does not mean to be adrift in a kind of historical relativism, in one age one thing, in another something else; it does mean to be different in each age, yet always oneself. Faithfulness to the drive to understand allows both such flexibility and such fidelity to oneself.

Secondly, the act of insight is important to religion, not only because it is the fruit sought by the drive to understand, but also because it is living, free, and personal. Insight is the mediating act between vital concrete situations and already formalized conceptions. Every act of intelligence is suffused with insight: the selection of the relevant data, the correct posing of the problem to be understood, the choice of the method for solving it, the emergence of the solution into consciousness, the choice of words to express it, the ability to relate it to other solutions or a conceptual system, the ingenuity to verify it, the knack of communicating it to others, etc. As air to breathing, insight is so necessary to intelligence that it is commonly overlooked. Moreover, once we fasten our attention upon the act of insight—the sudden or long-awaited "light" which emerges in consciousness and prompts us to say: "I have it!" or "Now I get it!"—we have a way of resolving problems of method which are resistant to solution if we fasten, instead, on conceptions, propositions, images, or the like. The act of insight is more basic than any of these other elements. Insight is operative in all of them. In science, in logic, in existential situations, in poetry, in love, in the strategy of games or war or preparing a meal, insight is fundamental.

A Christian theology based on attention to insight does not in the least neglect received formulations; but it is not imprisoned by them. A supposed opposition between essentialist and existentialist (or between "Greek" and "Hebrew" mind) is false to an authentic understanding of Christian theology. The moving force in all the many

Christian theologies is the drive to understand, which culminates in insight. In one culture, one set of data is especially favored, or one way of conceiving of theology is favored; correspondingly, a certain characteristic set of insights and modes of expression emerge in that culture. In another culture, or in another school of thought, another set of insights emerges. How is communication to be established from one culture, or one school, to another? This is one important problem for the open Church of the future.

The characteristic of the closed Church of the last several generations has not been attention to insight; it has been admiration for certain *conceptions*, which have emerged in one culture and indeed in one school of thought. Even there, instead of fixing attention on the *insights* generated by this school of thought, the masters of that school have concentrated on the formulae, the words, the conceptions. Verbal skill has come to be more appreciated than insight. The isolation of this school has thus been twofold. One wall has separated it from appreciation of the insights of other cultures and other schools of thought. A second wall has separated it, so to speak, from its own insights, by focusing attention, instead, on its fixed notions and its system of such notions. How many students of this school early in their careers gave up the effort to understand and, docilely, began to learn the skills of using the proper words correctly? How many preachers have not dared to give sermons unless they heed the accepted words, because they were not sure of the insights which those words were trying to express, and so could not with confidence find other words for them when the traditional ones failed to communicate? When Pope John called for a pastoral Council, surely it was this failure of the traditional words which had arrested his attention. But the root of the trouble did not lie in the inaccessibility to the modern mind of dated, technical conceptions. The root of the trouble lay in the admiration for conceptions rather than for insights. To prefer conceptions to insights is to prefer second things to first, the product to its source, the letter to its living spirit.

On the other hand, as soon as one puts first things first, and prefers living insight to verbal conceptions, no matter how perfect these latter are in themselves, one has the freedom of two worlds. One need not despise conceptions; on the contrary, one has every reason to admire the technical conceptual achievements of other men and other ages. One wishes "to climb upon their shoulders." One rejoices at not having to do all their work over again. But meanwhile, cherishing insight, one can seek in the concrete, present world whatever insights can be found. Even systematically, and making all relevant methodological adjustments and necessary distinctions—and these are many [2]—one can move from culture to culture, school of thought to school of thought, mode of expression to mode of expression, and learn fairly and accurately from each. A transcultural philosophy is surely possible; to create such a philosophy is one of the major tasks of the future. Wherever one man fails in this effort, he has in the drive to understand and in the resources of his already acquired insights the means to criticize his efforts, revise his methods, and begin again more adequately. And where one man fails, others can benefit by his efforts and advance the labors he could not accomplish.

The fundamental intellectual problem of the Church is that it is universal in intent, but so far historically has been limited to development in only a few of the possible and promising directions of religious thought. By its vocation, Catholic thought must be as diverse and extensive as human thought; nothing human is foreign to it. By its development until the present, Catholic thought is too confined within the conceptual achievements of only a part of the human race. Moreover, in the system of non-historical orthodoxy, Catholic thought has been identified, not with an unrestricted drive to understand and with living insights, but with certain finite, fixed conceptions. Non-historical orthodoxy is not defending the "essence" of Catholic thought or Catholic doctrine, but one way of conceiving of that thought or doctrine. Non-historical orthodoxy is no more at the heart of the matter than other Catholic theologies. It has only had the power to impose its particular conceptions upon Roman Catholicism for a relatively short period of Catholic history. The primary achievement of the Second Vatican Council was to displace non-historical orthodoxy from its position of exclusive power, and to moderate its pretensions by making other theologies and ways of insight effectively present at the heart of the Church.

Non-historical orthodoxy has given good service to the Church. Those who criticize it must recognize that, in admirable ways and in others not admirable, it has brought the Church intact through the collapse of the Middle Ages, and leaves her hardy and eager at the threshold of the new era on which the world is now embarking. The closed Church has functioned as a cocoon. Now it is time for a new form of life, not discontinuous with the old, but more beautiful. On the other hand, there are certain scars which the closed orthodoxy of the past has left upon the children of the Church, whose healing as they move into a new age will need time and attention. We must consider a few of them.

II

There are four chief weaknesses which many in the Church have contracted from too long an association with non-historical orthodoxy. These are: an uncritical use of abstractions; the loss of honesty and candor; an undue admiration for uniformity, with a lack of esteem for diversity; and a blindness to the spiritual values promoted in the secular world. All these weaknesses are related. Love for abstractions discourages personal insight and authenticity. Lack of personal insight favors safe generalizations rather than honesty in specifics. Tepid devotion to honesty leads then to stress on public conformity rather than on individual differences. The remoteness of ecclesiastical abstractions from actual life does not favor a just appreciation for the characteristic values of secular civilization.

An addiction to abstractions generates a world of concepts which often can not be fully verified in the world. Those who are the victims of these abstractions never come to understand the world in which they live. Their prejudices and "warning systems" do not allow them to be at peace in the real world, and they live out their lives as in a dream. The awakening to the real world, meanwhile, if it ever does occur, comes with the force of a great and liberating conversion. Many in the Church seem to need this conversion to the world, if they hope to live in it and redeem it.

Catholics often seem to speak in abstractions which have no referents, or referents so different from what their language seems to say that outsiders must believe that they are speaking in riddles. Once one learns the habit of translation, it is easy to understand the jargon; but the need for such a habit brings upon Catholics the accusation of "doublethink." Three examples of such abstractions come to mind: that the Church is sinless, essentially never changes, possesses the whole truth.

"The Church," Catholics will say, is sinless and indefectible; but they will admit that ecclesiastics and laymen are sinners, and that even the just "sin seven times daily." What, then, is this "Church" that is sinless? It exists nowhere but in the abstracting mind. *Under a certain aspect*, namely, the life of God which it shares, the Church is sinless. But the Church is concrete. The Church in which God lives is Pope Paul, the seventy-nine living cardinals, the bishop of Diocese X, the crotchety monsignor at Our Lady of Good Hope, the curate at Sacred Heart, the weary sisters of the parish convent, the mother of too many children and the mother of too few, the corrupt politician at the communion rail, the divorced man who hasn't been to church for twenty-seven years, the girl whom everybody thinks is an angel but who, terrified, has fled into an illict love from which she can't escape. The Church in which God lives is not a platonic abstraction. The Church is part of history and it is composed of concrete, particular, living men vivified by the Spirit. The Church, like Christ, is incarnate. This is what makes faith beautiful: it is real, not mythical.

Again, granted that many members of the Church have already reached the term of their personal pilgrimage, and are united, as all hope to be, with the Lord; still, not even their presence with God justifies us in speaking of the Church as an abstraction. Even in their case, the Church is real and concrete: it is this and that person from such a town at such a time, from such a city and such an age in history, who under so many personal pressures, and having manifested such and such a fidelity, has forged his present identity before the Lord. This is the Church: real people, from real times, and real places, either already with the Lord face to face; or here on earth with the hidden Lord they do not see; or yet to be born. The Church is concrete, real, and individual. It lives in tangled history and in the presence of its Lord; here on earth and with God.

The second manifestation of the vice of abstractions which corrupts the Catholic mind is the phrase "in essentials the Church never changes." It is difficult to find an "essential" that has not "changed" in the Church. It took many generations for collegiality to be forgotten, the primacy of Rome to develop (imagine saying *infallibilitas* or *Pontifex* to St. Peter), the institution of the diaconate to atrophy, the canon of Scripture to be decided, the sacraments to be distinguished from one another and formalized, the meaning of belief after belief to be conceptualized. In such matters, the language of "essences" according to a logical model is misleading; everything in the Church is life and growth. The Church has grown organically and with consistency, but rather by the rules of organic self-identity than by the rules of implications unfolding from "essential" definitions.

The more one studies the history of doctrine, the more one sees how uneven, rolling, spiraling the development of the self-consciousness of the Church has been. On the other hand, as Newman shows, the internal consistency, seen under the light of organic transformation rather than under that of static "essences," has been little short of startling. It is a curiosity of history that Catholics are insistent on the language of essences when they make the point that the Church "never changes," since the point of view of "essences" does so little justice to the reality of the Church. It is curious that there should be such an impassioned devotion to the superficial appearances of changelessness, and such a lack of devotion to the deep organic development which is the Church's greatest glory. An acorn is different from an oak, and a man of sixty from a boy of sixteen; it is the glory of acorn and boy to have changed rather than to have been changeless. Moreover, even in an Aristotelian language of "essences," change is the law of life; living things do not at once realize their own "form" but are only on their way to doing so. Knowledge of their "form" is derived from knowledge of the "final cause" toward which they are developing, rather than from an initial changelessness. Individual men are not yet rational animals, but are only striving to become so.

"Essence" and "substantially the same" are comforting words in a world of flux. They have the appearance of logical solidity and clarity; but they are false to history. The conscious possession of historical identity is not like the possession of a logical essence which has never changed; history and logic are separate orders. While embracing the concrete, different, particular moment, the Catholic spirit retains its sense of identity—but not by memorizing an essential definition of itself. The Catholic spirit is adaptable to nearly all cultures, places, times; changeability, not changelessness, has surely been the chief characteristic of its long life. It remains itself not by "accidental changes" around a core of "unchanging essence," nor by "clothing itself" in the external garments of varying cultures. Nothing so static! The Church truly belongs to Italy, to Ireland, to Africa, to India—to whatever culture it is inserted in—but not by superficial "adaptations." The Church *becomes* Italian, Irish, African, Indian. It retains its identity as Catholic by a certain almost inarticulate self-consciousness. But this sense of identity is not like a firmly held definition of its essence any more than an old man remembers his identity as the boy of many years ago by means of a definition of himself. The sense of identity is not a logical concept but a psychological one. The Church knows her "essential" sameness not by way of the essences of logic, but by way of the as yet little-understood laws of conscious life.

Far from doing justice to the reality of the Church, then, logical models are seriously misleading. The doctrines of the Church are not changeless like the necessary laws of logic. They are changeless like the laws of conscious life. They undergo many changes—like boys becoming men—while retaining their identity. An inarticulate self-consciousness remains, from which through reflection the Church tries to elicit a language to express her present understanding of herself. Her doctrines deserve praise for the degree to which they are deepened or broadened through reflection and love, as much as for their changelessness. *Semper eadem* is ambiguous as praise of the Church. If the image in mind is logic or geometry, it is not praise but insult. If the image is of organic growth, the praise may be graciously accepted. What else should a living principle in history be but self-identical and always changing? When a living thing ceases to change, it ceases developing toward its own full identity.

A third manifestation of the vice of abstractions is the sentence "The Catholic Church possesses the whole truth." It was perfectly evident at the Council that bishops and cardinals disagreed with one another, even on important points. Who, then, in the Church, *in the concrete*, possesses the whole truth? What Catholic possesses the whole truth? As soon as we take up the language of concrete persons, the pretentiousness of the claim is embarrassing. Once recognized as a roundabout use of language, "the Church possesses the whole truth" no longer appears to mean anything offensive. It is only a misleading way of saying that the Holy Spirit, the Spirit of Truth, vivifies the Church as it struggles in history, and gives it enough light to answer to its needs.

In short, the abstract concept of a perfect Church, full of truth, never changing, may give comfort to those who need creatures of the imagination to comfort them; it does not exist in the concrete world of history. In the concrete world, God lives and acts in the Church through limited and stiff-necked men, with His unchanging graciousness. God is perfect, full of truth, never changing, but the band of His servants is not.

The only cure for the disease of thinking in abstractions is to pull oneself down to earth each time an abstraction comes to mind. "To what individuals am I referring?" "In the concrete, what am I thinking of?" To point to concrete individuals for each generalization gives solidity to one's thought. And thus generalizations which pretend to cover all the ground can at certain points be made to touch the ground, and misleading myths can be dispelled.

III

The third session of the Council is to take up the problems of the Church in the modern world and—as briefly introduced in the last few minutes of the second session—the document on the lay apostolate. Laymen will hope that the discussion is concrete and historical. For in talking about the laymen, one must be doubly careful to exorcise abstractions from one's mind. The world of the layman does not lend itself easily to abstractions. There are laymen in America whose lives are totally different from those of laymen in Africa or even in Italy. Moreover, there are laymen of this or that profession, of this or that personal wealth, of this or that talent, of this or that spiritual perception, of this or that personal religious history. There are laymen who love the Church, and those who despise it. There are laymen who are disgusted with their clergy, and laymen who admire them devotedly. When one is speaking of the Catholic layman, one is speaking of hundreds of millions of individuals of particular places, times, stages of development and background. If one does not speak concretely, one says little of value or interest to the layman.

It would have the worst possible effect, one might imagine, if the Council were to attempt to begin the discussion of the layman by beginning with a *definition*, or with certain *abstract categories:* "(1) the official lay apostolate, (2) Catholic associations, (3) the layman in the secular world," for example. For then, in fact, one would be beginning at an imagined "heart of the matter" and deducing downward, with less and less conviction, until one finally touched the ground where most laymen were living. Laymen in the secular world would seem to be those farthest from the heart of the faith. Such an approach would seem to them very abstract, misleading, and irrelevant. It would have begun "from the wrong end," with definitions and notions. The layman *in fact* lives in the world. It is there that discussion of him should start.

To speak about the layman, it would be useful to learn the layman's habitual mode of thinking: beginning with individuals, particulars, the concrete. It is necessary to reflect upon the different levels of education in the various regions of the world, and the different stages of economic, political, and social development of the different areas. It might be well to reflect upon the different concepts of authority found in different parts of the world, and on the special roles of religion, the clergy, and individual laymen in the traditional social life of the various nations. It might be well to begin close to the layman, in a world he recognizes, and only slowly and tentatively come to some reflective, theological judgments about his vocation. This would seem to be the way to begin at "the right end," in the actual world. Only then will the layman feel that his role in the Church is being treated honestly.

For, at present, the greatest difficulty of the layman in the Church is the dishonesty in which he is constantly forced to live. Definitions and notions are constantly preventing him from being honest. This dishonesty begins in school or in catechism classes, where he memorizes definitions that he does not wholly accept, since often he does not understand them. But correct answers win good marks; and if he asks the teacher unsettling questions he is labeled rebellious or impertinent. The same system of falsehoods characterizes most of his experiences in the confessional. He says what he is expected to say, and he often arouses impatience when he trys to do otherwise. Again, the sermons he hears are often irrelevant and unreflective, and sometimes lack even simple piety; moreover, they are occasionally so inaccurate in their theology as to be hardly Catholic. But even here he cannot correct the priest or raise questions; he must tolerate an untruthful situation. Finally, on those rare occasions when the educated layman does converse with a priest—for most parishes in the United States, at least, resemble service stations, which one visits briefly every Sunday for the "efficient administration" of the sacraments— he notices immediately the warning signals as to what he cannot say. Clerical life, its language, and its views of the world have drifted so far from the daily reality of life that honest communication is often impossible.

Moreover, most clergymen, even with the best will in the world, are not prepared for the argument, criticism, requests, and difficulties building up ever more powerfully in the breasts of many laymen. The presence of the Church in the world is sometimes so absurd in the light of ordinary common sense that one despairs of ever getting the clergy—who alone can change it—to see the absurdity. Day after day in life in the world, one encounters fallen-away Catholics, non-Catholics affronted by the external life of the Church, and laymen increasingly disturbed by the half-truths and misleading characteristics of ordinary Catholic life. Only gradually, even to "open" priests (whose numbers are increasing), does one confide even a part of one's reflections; much less does one put them in a book for public perusal. Even as it is, one encounters priests and bishops shocked by criticisms of the mildest sort; honesty is much inhibited in their presence.

Let us take some examples. Criticize Catholic life, the clergy, or events at the Council, and one hears: "This sort of thing can't do our side any good. How can a man who calls himself a Catholic write things like that?" Again, the Pope is treated—even by most bishops—as something more than a man, more even than Christ's humble vicar; it would be virtually impossible for a Catholic writer to criticize him respectfully, directly, and frankly, as he might criticize the president of his own country, without causing the most acute discomfort to many clerics and other laymen. Can we really believe it healthy to preserve the Pope from open criticism? Can we really believe it to be good for the Church to treat him like a god or a monarch rather than a man? On the contrary, it is difficult to believe that much harm is not done, to the Pope, to the Church, and to the honesty of each of us, by lack of open criticism. For such criticism would be a constant spur toward the best possible fulfillment of his ministry. Criticism is not idle or in vain; it is the daily bread of normal men, and a great help to them.

Let us move resolutely to other matters. The Church is still burdened with anthropomorphisms which today cause scandal. What can an indulgence of "thirty days" mean? What are we to think of the pamphlets still being printed about the privileges of those who wear the scapular and receive communion on the first Saturday of every month, that Our Lady will free them from purgatory "on the Saturday" next after their death? Are not our people, in the United States at least, sufficiently sophisticated to be systematically corrected on such matters? There are countless such bits of inaccuracy perpetuated in the parochial schools; any parent can supply dozens of examples from the lessons still being learned by his children. A realistic Catholic education, lively and self-critical, can hardly be expected from schools which do not wage relentless war on careless belief, anthropomorphism, historical falsehoods, and all other sins against honesty. A Catholic education to be worthy of the name is an education in ruthless moral and intellectual honesty. Otherwise, it is unfaithful to the very roots of religion, in the drive to understand;

and it is a radical lie. No wonder a bad Catholic education has such an enduring effect on children made to suffer it.

Again, how can one accept nuns, priests, and bishops as human beings relevant to our century when their very clothing indicates plainly that they do not belong in spirit to our century, or that they need to be safely distinguished from people of our century?

On a more intellectual level, let us say at once that non-historical orthodoxy—which has prevailed in our schools and our pulpits—has long seemed to many (although they could not say so), what the Council revealed it to be. Let us say, moreover, that the wave of relief which swept the Catholic world as the first session of the Council unfolded, and as the honest, critical reports about its proceedings appeared in print, was because honesty had at last returned to the Church. It was going to become possible to speak. Where only one school of thought had been heard, now many could be heard. Now one could disagree, challenge, demand evidence for assertions. Without forever fighting an abstract, impersonal system, one could now grab hold of one's own conscience, and try to understand one's personal vocation, commitments, and beliefs. One could be faithful to the drive to understand, without justifying every public move before those who are faithful to a system of propositions.

Moreover, it seems conceivable that within a generation the air will be so cleared that one will be able to speak one's honest mind about marriage, sex, and childbearing. For there is almost no honesty upon these questions at the moment, nor is much possible yet, given the formation and sensitivities of many.

It is difficult to think of a single belief, practice, or aspect of the Church in which educated laymen have not long had more comments to make than they have yet been asked to make, or dare to take the initiative to make. As the Church grows more accustomed to mutual honesty, these comments will undoubtedly emerge from private conversations into public hearing. It is one of the ironies of our time that, while the clergy are concerned to protect the faith of the ordinary people from too much truth at once, educated laymen seem to be protecting the clergy from still more truth. It is an exciting but precarious time for everyone.

IV

In the open Church, recovery from the disease of abstractions and return to the principle of honest speech are the first two orders of business. A third is related to them: respect for diversity. The issue confronting the Church is no longer that of freedom versus authority; today it is clear that a man is bound to follow his own conscience, and in following his conscience to accept the just claims of authority. Both liberty and authority are respected; the theoretical disequilibrium of preceding generations has been evened out by the passage of time. The new version of the perennial problem, however, is how to reconcile diversity and unity. To what extent can a man be his own kind of Catholic? The problem is not that of minimizing Catholic doctrine, but rather that of penetrating it and assimilating it in countless individual ways.

The problem has always existed, but we have not always noticed it. Catholics already live in great diversity. Italian sexual mores differ noticeably from those of Ireland. French *liberté* is quite different from American freedom; so are clergy-lay relations. English law is different from Spanish law; and the ordinary moral conscience in each land differs accordingly. Catholics in Los Angeles have a different style of faith from Catholics in Chicago; and these differ from those of Boston. Catholics sometimes differ more from other Catholics, in their idea of God, fidelity, and grace, than one group of Protestants differs from another. Sometimes a Catholic and a Protestant can be closer to each other in actual religious belief than either is to his own co-religionists.

For faith takes root in persons, in personal ways, rather than in sects, systems, or abstract propositions. The diversity of spirits mirrors the infinity of God. Creed, system, and community cannot mask the fact that each person has his own perception, sensitivity, and experience, and that the same words spoken by different men can have almost opposite meanings. It is a common experience of laymen in the pews to recognize that the God spoken of by Father X is not the God of Father Y, and that the image of Christ given by Father Z is almost the reverse of that of Father Q. No doubt many Catholics have the experience of listening to another Catholic speak about his faith, and saying to himself: "That's not my faith at all!"

Catholics have not noticed this diversity among themselves because their preference for abstractions leads all to repeat the same words, without reflecting on the fact that each penetrates the meaning differently. Non-historical orthodoxy pictures Catholic doctrine as propositional; one has to "believe" certain formulae. But in an older tradition of the Church, in the days of primitive catechesis continuing even until the age of St. Augustine, doctrine was treated more as a life to be lived than as lessons to be learned. Doctrine was not a series of formulae whose interrelationships one must master logically; it was a series of insights to be acquired. Moreover, only a constant conversion of life prepared one to integrate these insights into one's flesh, so to speak: one's sensitivities and perceptions. It did not suffice to repeat the words; anyone could do that. Again, anyone who knew the language could "understand" the words grammatically and logically. But to understand a doctrine intellectually, personally, religiously, one had to know how it changed the quality of one's life. Until a doctrine affected one's imagination, desires, daily judgments, it had not been grasped; its words were merely on one's lips.

It was accepted, in those days, that individual Catholics differed in the quality of their faith and the actual state of their beliefs. In our day, an impersonal, notional system has replaced personal belief as the primary fact in the consciousness of Catholics. Ask a Catholic what his faith is, and he replies with the words of the catechism. Ask him what he *believes*, and he won't tell you unless he trusts you. He may even be afraid to admit his beliefs to himself, lest they reveal him as a "heretic." Many Catholics repress their doubts and questions. Such repression misses the whole point of growth and penetration into Catholic life.

When it becomes possible for more Catholics to feel responsible for the depth and solidity of their own faith, then the diversity of the Catholic people, which has always been operative, will be publicly apparent. For individuals then will not be afraid to speak of insights peculiar to themselves, or of personal objections to points they have never understood. Diversity will return to the Church when honesty returns. In a living Church, moreover, diversity is at least as admirable and breathtaking an ideal as uniformity. Nor does diversity destroy unity. All Catholics are united in fidelity to the drive to understand. All love the same Christ, receive the same baptism and the same eucharist, respect the same ministers of the Word. Within this community of faith and order, each Catholic, in his perception and his fidelity, is and should be different from every other.

V

The fourth order of business for the open Church is secularization. For the Church at present is ecclesiastical, clerical, special, precious;

it has little in common with the world. If it wishes to sanctify present history, it will have to be secularized in its mode of speech, habits of thought, ways of acting. This does not mean it should cease to judge the world or cease to retain its independence of spirit: quite the contrary. The secular world needs and desires prophetic, honest guidance; it despises pretense, sycophancy, or infidelity to self. Moreover, if the secular world now despises the Church—and among educated people, as among countless ordinary people, it does—it is because the Church does *not* seem to speak with an independent voice. Too often, the voice of the Church sounds like the voice of the world— the world of the eighteenth or nineteenth century. What is this *Romanità*, what are these rationalistic Latin propositions, if not echoes of the secular world of two centuries ago? Only it is now many generations since the world itself abandoned that style. The changelessness of the Church does not appear to be due to fidelity to Christ; it seems rather like a delayed imitation of the world, as if the Church only becomes secularized fifty years or so behind the times.

The backwardness of the Church until Pope John and the Council was tragic, because the Gospels make excellent sense to many in the world in which we live. Many men believe in God in their hearts, even though they are loath to articulate their faith, because they so despise the organized religions they observe. Even to the man of good will the Catholic Church is not attractive; its outer appearance provides many unnecessary hurdles. If, for a moment, one imagines oneself not a Catholic, it is very difficult to see how one could ever find one's way into the faith. Imagine looking around: building fund campaigns; Masses on television; billboards about the family that prays together; a public obsession with sexual morality, which sounds manichean rather than Christian; a legalistic morality; the lack of creativity; the public lack of candor; the defensiveness; the bored faces of ministers at the altar; the listlessness of the people; the misleadingly expressed doctrines; the censoring of books. How would one ever believe that this religion was that of the Christ of the Gospels? The reality of Catholicism is so much deeper and richer than these appearances, but the gap between appearances and reality is huge. It sometimes seems that Catholics want to keep people of good will at a distance. It sometimes seems that Catholics need to be despised. It sometimes seems that if Catholics sat down and *planned* to mislead the world they could not do it more successfully than they do at present.

While God taught His chosen people directly, He instructed the pagan world by signs written into the natural world of history. So also in our day, many of the deepest revelations about God (at least, what He is *not*) and about men have been discovered by non-believers, who reflect on man's history, rather than by religious men. The freedom of speech at the Second Vatican Council, its independence from heads of state, the inspiration of many of its finest speeches came from ideas generated in the secular world, or in any case from outside the small pale of Catholicism. The inspiration and evangelical ideas of the ecumenical movement grew up, under the Holy Spirit, outside the Catholic Church, and for many years met strong resistance from the Catholic Church. The role of laymen in the Church has become important largely because of universal education, an ideal championed not by Catholics but by "freethinkers." Thus, in many ways, the Second Vatican Council revealed the Church's indebtedness to modern secular society. As the Church entered the tissue and marrow of Constantinian, medieval, Renaissance, and other cultural systems, so she must study and make her own the forms of secular, pluralistic society.

In the open society of our century—the society founded on the concrete rights of persons, rather than on abstract ideas—the Church can live under conditions highly favorable to her inner necessities. No previous form of life was so well adapted to manifesting the message of the Gospels: the freedom of the act of faith, the free community of believers, the service of believers to their neighbors. In the open society, the privileges and postures of princes and lords seem a trifle ridiculous. Political pressure as an instrument of the Gospels is doubly condemned: by the Gospels and by political tradition. The generosity of the free body of believers proves more fruitful for the material needs of the Church than State support. The competition of ideas in the universities and in the mass media sends the faithful ever deeper into an examination of their faith.

Moreover, the open society has much to gain from an open Church. The open society needs sources of independent moral insight, and prophetic witness to religious reality. There is already too much conformity, standardization, and spiritual mediocrity in the open society. It does not need a dependent, fawning, religious organization, but a religious community which knows its own mind and speaks it. It will admire the independent, prophetic voice, if that voice is relevant and offers reasons; if it offers insight rather than trying to enforce its own conceptions. Without relevance, insight and reasons, such a voice is only another voice in the winds—and a hateful one, if it uses force to support its arbitrariness. But, if it offers insight and evidence, that voice will be respected even by those who remain, personally, unconvinced. The open society is, at its best and in principle, a community of reasonable discourse. It has its own rules and style of presentation, and these rules and this style of argument are not those of medieval or Renaissance cultures. When these rules and styles are learned, they will not be found to inhibit, but rather to enhance, the message of the Gospels.

According to these rules, one speaks most effectively in a low key, presenting considerations which may persuade, rather than ultimatums which attempt psychological coercion. One speaks from personal authenticity, with convictions already interiorized, rather than as the spokesman of a system from which one draws a salary. One speaks from beliefs one has chosen critically, into which one has insight and for which one has reasons, not from beliefs which one has accepted without recognizing alternatives. Freely accepted belief, fully assimilated belief compels attention. The fanaticism and arbitrariness of "the true believer" are not in the least esteemed.

Both the open society and the open Church draw their force from the same source: the unrestricted drive to understand, and the quest for insight. Insight has two moments: one, the moment of intuition; the other, the moment of reflective judgment as to whether the intuition meets the claims of the facts. Thus, discourse both in the open society and in the open Church has two moments: one, the moment of trying to bring others to see as one oneself sees; the other, the moment of presenting the evidence to support one's own vision. Without the first moment, argument is obscure and blind. Without the second, it is groundless. Communication among men requires both moments.

That is why an open Church has an important role to play in an open society. It brings into such a society a new source of insight: the Word of God and a long intellectual tradition. It also brings into such a society persons living interiorly according to the deepest laws of the human spirit: fidelity to understanding, humble charity, affirmation. The lives of such persons are, moreover, the best evidence for religious claims. Besides, the devotion of religious men to the drive to understand pushes the members of an open society ever further in their own quest for understanding. Suppose there is a God? Suppose my hunger to understand and my drive for love are, in fact, the clearest signs of His presence in the world? To the open society, the open Church brings a new range of vision, a new depth of understanding. It raises the mind and heart beyond the daily pragmatic task of building up the earthly city, which is man's vocation in history: "Increase, multiply, and possess the earth." It raises mind and heart, not for escape, but for renewed commitment. Catholic faith is committed to this world, not to a platonic other world; though it does not try to make itself believe that understanding and love end with death.

But perhaps we are already looking too far into the future. Neither the open societies of our day nor the open Church are yet faithful to themselves, nor to the drive to understand. Both still have their predilected stopping places, prejudices, and points beyond which their courage fails them. It is in pursuit of the drive to understand that both open society and open Church find their separate identity and their complementarity. In the tangles and complexities of the concrete history of the race, of course, it is rarely wholly clear what the next step in the line of fidelity to the drive to understand should be. But that is the risk, burden and joy of being human—to labor faithfully in the night, with or without consolation. The Second Vatican Council has furthered the vision of an open Church in an open society, as a new achievement of men in their pilgrimage through history.

Men who before were pusillanimous are doing great deeds and dreaming great visions. Old patterns are dissolving. In such a time, the Spirit's activity is almost tangible. Those who are faithful to understanding see possibilities hidden for centuries, and act on them. The jesters of the fountains smile and say, "This, too, shall pass," but meanwhile an age of creativity has begun.

NOTES

1. For various attempts to explain the intellectual struggle in the Churches cf. E. Schillebeeckx, O.P., "Misunderstandings at the Council"; Gérard Philips, "Two Tendencies in Contemporary Theology"; Peter Fransen, S.J., "Three Ways of Dogmatic Thought"; Joaquin Salaverri, S.J., "Methods in Dogmatic Theology"—all digested in *Theology Digest*, XI, 3 (Autumn, 1963). Fransen's article appears in full in *Cross Currents*, XIII, 2 (Spring, 1963), and Schillebeeckx's in *Life of the Spirit*, 18 (1963). *See also* Gustave Weigel, S.J., "How Is the Council Going?" *America* (December 7, 1963).
2. These problems are spelled out in great detail in Bernard Lonergan's *Insight: A Study of Human Understanding* (Longmans, Green, 1957; 2nd edition, 1958).

INDEX